MARSHALL GOLDSMITH is corporate America's pre-eminent executive coach. Goldsmith is one of a select few consultants who have been asked to work with more than eighty CEOs in the world's top corporations. He has helped implement leadership development processes that have impacted more than one million people. His Ph.D is from UCLA and he is on the faculty of the executive education programs at Dartmouth College's Tuck School of Business. The American Management Association recently named Marshall one of fifty great thinkers and business leaders who have impacted the field of management, and *Business Week* listed him as one of the influential practitioners in the history of leadership development. In 2006, Alliant International University renamed their schools of business and organizational psychology the Marshall Goldsmith School of Management.

MARK REITER has collaborated on thirteen previous books. He is also a literary agent in Bronxville, New York.

Marshall Goldsmith has been praised as:

- a "great thinker and leader ... [in] the field of management" by the American Management Association;

- a "top executive educator" by *The Wall Street Journal*;

- a "great communicator" by *O, The Oprah Magazine*;

- one of the "five most-respected executive coaches" by *Forbes*;

- an "influential practiti_____:lopment" by *BusinessWeek*; and

- one of "the most credi_____business" by *The Economist*.

What business leaders and learning professionals have to say about working with Marshall Goldsmith:

"I love Marshall Goldsmith for lots of reasons: his generous soul, his capacity to bring out the best in people, his zen-like ability to create an evocative community—the mark of a great teacher, and his way of getting people, just about everybody, to laugh their way into deep and penetrating insights. He is the very model of a professional—reliable, trustworthy, always 'on'—and always has your interest at heart."

—WARREN BENNIS, Distinguished Professor of Business,
University of Southern California, and bestselling author

"We were a very successful team who took our performance to the next level. With Marshall's help we identified our two areas and went to work. We used everyone's help and support, exceeded our improvement expectations, and had fun! A team's dedication to continuous improvement combined with Marshall's proven improvement process ROCKS!"

—ALAN MULALLY, CEO, Ford Motor Company, former president and
CEO, Boeing Commercial Airlines

"Helping high achievers recognize their sharp edges, become self-aware, and increase their personal effectiveness is at the heart of leadership development. Marshall brings to this task a deep commitment to excellence, sensitivity, candor, and results. Many years of patient practice have made him the best 'diamond cutter' in the business—he can take a rough diamond and polish it rapidly to reveal its brilliance. He is one of a kind."

—C. K. PRAHALAD, bestselling author and Paul and Ruth McCracken
Distinguished University Professor of Corporate Strategy and International
Business, University of Michigan

"Marshall Goldsmith has helped me become a more effective leader, as judged by the people who are most important at Getty Images—our employees. Marshall has helped me and my executive team members to be much better positive role models for living our Leadership Principles."

—JONATHAN KLEIN, CEO, Getty Images

"Marshall is a great coach and teacher. He has done a lot to help both me and our high-potential leaders. His approach is practical, useful, helpful, and fun!"

—J. P. GARNIER, CEO, GlaxoSmithKline

"Marshall's valuable insights on leadership development and the related responsibilities of coaching and mentoring are critical to our general officers and their spouses. These are turbulent times, and the tools and techniques that Marshall shared with them are therefore vitally important as they return to their various commands and leadership responsibilities."

—GENERAL ERIC K. SHINSEKI, former Chief of Staff, U.S. Army

"Perhaps the greatest teacher of leadership on the planet. I have personally watched him help thousands of executives in three companies improve their leadership in measurable ways. As a result, their performance improved, their relationships improved, and they lived happier lives."

—JIM MOORE, served as the chief learning officer of BellSouth, Nortel, and Sun Microsystems

"There is simply no better coach for your most important leaders than Marshall Goldsmith. He excels on the only metric that matters—he achieves positive, measurable change."

—MARC EFFRON, chief learning officer, Avon, and co-author of *Leading the Way* and *Human Resources in the 20th Century*

"Marshall helped GE human resources professionals customize his coaching process for use with our high-potential leaders. Our internal HR coaches have achieved outstanding results with hundreds of our leaders. Marshall's model has been a real win for us!"

—LINDA SHARKEY, vice president, Organizational Development and Staffing, GE Capital Solutions

"Marshall Goldsmith easily ranks among the very best teachers and coaches of executives anywhere—bar none. His years of experience and his proven methods have helped hundreds of leaders achieve positive, lasting behavioral change."

—JOHN ALEXANDER, president, Center for Creative Leadership

"Marshall helped us determine that the role of a leader is about inspiring others. He showed us how to inspire others and build lasting relationships. He challenged our team and they loved working with him."

—CASS WHEELER, CEO, American Heart Association

"For over a decade I have worked with Marshall in corporations and seen him teach at Dartmouth. In my opinion, Marshall is the best at what he does, bar none. He has that rare combination that makes a great teacher—thought leadership, classroom management, and presence. He is a tremendous asset to Tuck School at Dartmouth."

—VIJAY GOVINDARAJAN, professor and director,
   Center for Global Leadership, Tuck School, Dartmouth

"With great energy and excellent content, Marshall engaged, excited, and even enthralled his audience of several hundred participants at the Wharton Leadership Conference. Marshall was a star!"

—DR. MICHAEL USEEM, William and Jacalyn Egan Professor of
   Management and director of the Center for Leadership and Change
   Management, Wharton Business School, University of Pennsylvania

"I consider Marshall to be the number one thought leader and coach in the field of leadership and executive development today. I sincerely appreciate his honest, straightforward, positive, and purposeful approach to executive coaching—it is second to none."

—LOUIS CARTER, president and CEO, Best Practice Institute,
   a global leader in creating and sustaining communities of practice

"As the CEO of the Girl Scouts, I was working to help a great organization be 'the best that we could be.' The first person Marshall volunteered to work with was me—this sent an important message. I was exuberant about the experience, I improved, and we moved this process across the organization. Twenty-four years later, I am chairman of the Leader to Leader Institute—and we are still working together to serve leaders."

—FRANCES HESSELBEIN, winner of the Presidential Medal of Freedom

"Marshall is a dynamo. He helps highly successful people get better and better and better. His advice helps me enormously at work, but it makes an even bigger impact at home. My wife and kids stand up and applaud Marshall for helping me become a better husband and dad. What could be better than that?"

—MARK TERCEK, managing director, Goldman Sachs & Co.

"At McKesson, we are on a mission—together with our customers—to fundamentally change the cost and quality of how health care is delivered. To fully realize the potential that lies in this transformation, our leaders must be able to demonstrate values-based leadership practices to maximize employee engagement each and every day. Marshall's teachings remind us of how personal growth and change are a never-ending journey."

—JOHN HAMMERGREN, CEO, McKesson

"A great coach teaches you how to improve yourself. Marshall is a great coach! He has a unique ability to help you determine what you can improve and what will have the greatest impact on the people you lead and love."

—BRIAN WALKER, CEO, Herman Miller

"Marshall is the coach's coach. No one is more of a listener, who learns from us (his students), from what we say or do not say. Taking from what he has heard, he molds for all of us a program to make us and our people better for having been in his presence."

—ALAN HASSENFELD, chairman, Hasbro

"Marshall Goldsmith has a simple, yet powerful approach for helping leaders excel. Its power lies not only in its simplicity, but in his unique ability to deliver practical insights that leaders can act upon. I seldom leave a session with Marshall without feeling a bit wiser than before."

—JON KATZENBACH, founder, Katzenbach Partners,
    former director, McKinsey and Company, and author
    of many books, including *The Wisdom of Teams*

"Marshall is the rock star of coaching. His adoration is well deserved. He cares about the people he works with. He focuses on their issues. He connects great people with other great people so that they can continue to learn. He is honest, helpful, bold, and sensitive. He focuses on what can be, not what has been, and creates a future unbound by the past."

—DAVID ULRICH, leading HR consultant
    and author of many books, including *Why the Bottom Line Isn't*

"Marshall has a unique gift and a rare skill—the gift to get beneath the surface issues to identify the core developmental needs that must be resolved for someone to be successful, and the skill to make the person aware of them in a no-nonsense manner that, somehow, stimulates change rather than creating denial and resistance."

— STEVE KERR, CLO, Goldman Sachs & Co., former CLO, GE, and president, Academy of Management

"In his charming, rascal-like manner, Marshall is able to address uncomfortable issues in a non-threatening way. As a result, not only does the leader get better—the whole team gets better!"

— GEORGE BORST, CEO, Toyota Financial Services

"Marshall has helped me personally to improve as a leader and has provided the tools and dynamics to turn a well-functioning management team into a high-performance team where all the members have improved individually and considerably added to team performance."

— DAVID PYOTT, CEO, Allergan

"While Cessna focused on continuous improvement of business results, Marshall helped me focus on leadership team continuous improvement. The impact is amazing. His practical no-nonsense approach is making a positive impact both professionally and personally on all of us. I have never had so much fun working on such a tough topic. Thank you, Marshall!"

— JACK PELTON, CEO, Cessna

"Marshall Goldsmith is the world's greatest coach because he has extraordinary life skills, the ability to connect deeply with others while remaining objective, and a passion for sharing everything he knows. He focuses—and helps others to focus—on what matters most in life, and brings unforgettable insights and excitement to every encounter."

— SALLY HELGESEN, global expert on developing women leaders and author of *The Female Advantage* and *The Web of Inclusion*

What Got You Here Won't Get You There

How Successful People Become
EVEN MORE SUCCESSFUL!

Marshall Goldsmith

with Mark Reiter

PROFILE BOOKS

First published in Great Britain in 2008 by
Profile Books Ltd
3a Exmouth House
Pine Street
Exmouth Market
London EC1R 0JH

First published in the United States of America in 2007 by Hyperion

1 3 5 7 9 10 8 6 4 2

Book design by Gretchen Achilles

Printed and bound in Great Britain by CPI Bookmarque, Croydon, CR0 4TD

ISBN 978 1 84668 137 0

To all successful leaders
who want to
"take it to the next level"
and get even better

"Happy are they that can hear their detractions and put them to mending."

—WILLIAM SHAKESPEARE,
Much Ado About Nothing

Contents

SECTION FOUR

Pulling Out the Stops

Acknowledgments

This book is a collaborative effort that has been built upon the contributions of many great people:

My mentors and teachers: Peter Drucker and Richard Beckhard, who will never cease being my heroes; Paul Hersey, who gave me the opportunity to be an executive educator; Frances Hesselbein, my permanent role model; Bob Tannenbaum, John Ying, and Fred Case, who were great teachers and made sure that I graduated.

My collaborator and agent: Mark Reiter, who has helped me "find my voice" and communicate in print the way that I communicate in person.

My publisher: Will Schwalbe, Ellen Archer, Bob Miller, Zareen Jaffery, and all of the folks at Hyperion who have supported our book.

My family: Lyda, Kelly, and Bryan, whom I love and who love me (in spite of my annoying habits); they keep everything in perspective and make it all fun.

Alliant International University: President Geoff Cox and his staff, who have had the faith required to name a college after me, the Marshall Goldsmith School of Management; and their faculty and students; working with them has been a joy.

My professional partners over the past thirty years: from Keilty, Goldsmith and Company, to A4SL, and now Marshall Goldsmith Partners, who have helped me spread the word; Linkage, IMS, the Conference Board, the AMA, HR.com, ChartHouse, Talent Management, and Targeted Learning, who have helped me to reach over a million leaders; Sarah McArthur, John Wheaton, and Andrew Thorn, who provided specific contributions to this book (they know where, what, and why).

My writing friends: John Byrne at *BusinessWeek*, who has always encouraged me to express myself; Larissa MacFarquhar at *The New Yorker*, who wrote a wonderful profile about my work; Gardiner Morse at the *Harvard Business Review*, Bob Lenzner at *Forbes*, Ken Shelton at *Leadership Excellence*, and, closest to home, Michael Kinsman at the *San Diego Union*

Tribune. All have written stories about me that were both fun and fair. Mark Vamos at *Fast Company* as well as Wiley, Amacom, FT, and Davies Black, who have published my work in the past and who have given me permission to build upon that work in this book.

And, most importantly, my clients, who are already unbelievably successful, yet strive to get even better. They have taught me far more than I have ever taught them.

Despite the help of all of the people named above, I am sure these pages contain at least a few errant statements. For these I ask your forgiveness and take full responsibility. To paraphrase another hero of mine, Buddha: *Please just use what works for you and let go of the rest.*

What Got You Here
Won't Get You There

The Trouble with Success

In which we learn how our previous success often
prevents us from achieving more success

The Trouble with Success

CHAPTER 1

You Are Here

YOU KNOW THOSE MAPS in shopping malls that say, "You Are Here"? They exist to orient you in unfamiliar territory, to tell you where you are, where you want to go, and how to get there.

A few people never need these maps. They're blessed with an internal compass that orients them automatically. They always make the correct turn and end up where they intended via the most economical route.

Some people actually go through life with this unerring sense of direction. It guides them not only in shopping malls but in their school years, careers, marriages, and friendships. When we meet people like this, we say they're grounded. They know who they are and where they're going. We feel secure around them. We feel that any surprises will only be pleasant surprises. They are our role models and heroes.

We all know people like this. For some of us, it's our moms or dads—people who served as moral anchors in our stormy childhoods. For others it's a spouse (the proverbial "better half"). For others (like me) it's a college professor who was the first person to puncture our pretensions (more on that later). It could be a mentor at work, a coach in high school, a hero from the history books such as Lincoln or Churchill, a religious leader such as Buddha, Mohammed, or Jesus. It could even be a celebrity. (I know one man who solves every dilemma by asking himself, "What would Paul Newman do?")

What all of these role models have in common is an exquisite sense of who they are, which translates into perfect pitch about how they come across to others.

A few people never seem to need any help in getting to where they want to go. They have a built-in GPS mechanism.

These people do not need my help.

The people I meet during the course of my working day as an executive coach are great people who may have lost their internal "You Are Here" map. For example:

Case 1. Carlos is the CEO of a successful food company. He is brilliant, hard-working, and an expert in his field. He started out on the factory floor and rose through sales and marketing to the top spot. There is nothing in his business that he hasn't seen firsthand. Like many creative people, he is also hyperactive, with the metabolism and attention span of a hummingbird. He loves to buzz around his company's facilities, dropping in on employees to see what they're working on and shoot the breeze. Carlos loves people and he loves to talk. All in all, Carlos presents a very charming package, except when his mouth runs ahead of his brain.

One month ago his design team presented him with their ideas for the packaging of a new line of snacks. Carlos was delighted with the designs. He only had one suggestion.

"What do you think about changing the color to baby blue?" he said. "Blue says expensive and upmarket."

Today the designers are back with the finished packaging. Carlos is pleased with the results. But he muses aloud, "I think it might be better in red."

The design team in unison roll their eyes. They are confused. A month ago their CEO said he preferred blue. They've busted their humps to deliver a finished product to his liking, and now he's changed his mind. They leave the meeting dispirited and less than enthralled with Carlos.

Carlos is a very confident CEO. But he has a bad habit of verbalizing any and every internal monologue in his head. And he doesn't fully appreciate that this habit becomes a make-or-break issue as people ascend the chain of command. A lowly clerk expressing an opinion doesn't get people's notice at a company. But when the CEO expresses that opinion, everyone jumps to attention. The higher up you go, the more your suggestions become orders.

Carlos thinks he's merely tossing an idea against the wall to see if it sticks. His employees think he's giving them a direct command.

Carlos thinks he's running a democracy, with everyone allowed to voice their opinion. His employees think it's a monarchy, with Carlos as king.

Carlos thinks he's giving people the benefit of his years of experience. His employees see it as micromanaging and excessive meddling.

Carlos has no idea how he's coming across to his employees.
He is guilty of Habit #2: Adding too much value.

Case 2. *Sharon is the editor of a major magazine. She is highly moti-vated, energetic, articulate, and loaded with charisma. For someone who has spent much of her adult life working with words and pictures, she has devel-oped impressive people skills. She can coax delinquent writers into meeting their deadlines. She can inspire her staff to stay at their desks late into the night when she decides to tear up the next issue at the last minute. She believes she can persuade anyone if she really puts her mind to it. Her publisher often invites her on sales calls to advertisers because of her charm and her ability to sell the magazine.*

Sharon is particularly proud of her ability to spot and nurture young edi-torial talent. The proof is in the bright energetic editorial team she has assem-bled. Editors at competitive magazines call them the Sharonistas, because of their almost militant allegiance to Sharon. They've been working with her for years. Their loyalty is unwavering. And Sharon returns their affection with equally fierce loyalty. That loyalty may seem excessive, especially if you work for Sharon but don't quite qualify as a Sharonista.

In today's editorial meeting, where future assignments are meted out to the staff, Sharon offered up an observation that might make a good cover story. One of the Sharonistas immediately seconded the idea, saying it was "brilliant." Sharon assigned the story to her. And so the meeting proceeded, with Sharon handing out plum assignments to her staff favorites—all of whom returned the favor by fawning over Sharon and agreeing with every-thing she said.

If you happened to be one of Sharon's favored staffers, the lovefest at the editorial meeting would be the highlight of your month. On the other hand, if you were not one of Sharon's favored staffers or happened to disagree with her, the sycophancy level in the room would have been transparent and sickening. After a few months of this treatment, you would have been emailing your ré-sumé to other magazines.

None of this was apparent to Sharon, who was otherwise extremely shrewd about people and their motives. She believed she was being an effective leader. She was developing people who shared her vision for the magazine. She was building a solid team that could operate seamlessly.

Sharon thought she was encouraging the staff to grow and eventually emulate her success. The staffers outside her inner circle thought she was encouraging sucking up.

Sharon is guilty of Habit #14: Playing favorites.

Case 3. *Martin is a financial consultant for a prominent New York City firm. He manages money for high-net-worth individuals. The minimum starting account is $5 million. Martin is very good at what he does. He takes home a seven-figure salary. That's a lot less than most of his clients make in a year. But Martin doesn't envy or resent his clients. He lives and breathes investments. And he loves providing a valued service for his well-heeled clients, many of them CEOs, some of them self-made entrepreneurs, some of them entertainment stars, and the rest of them beneficiaries of inherited wealth. Martin enjoys rubbing shoulders with his clients. He likes talking to them on the phone and giving them the benefit of his expertise over lunch or dinner—almost as much as he likes beating the market by four points each year. Martin is not a manager of other people. He operates as a lone wolf at his firm. His only obligation is to his clients and seeing that they're happy with the state of their portfolios from year to year.*

Today is one of the biggest days of Martin's life. He's been invited to manage a portion of the investment portfolio of one of America's most admired business titans. People with enormous net worth often do that, parceling out their millions to several money managers as a protective hedge. Martin has a chance to join an elite group in the titan's stable. If he's successful, there's no telling how many more clients will spring from this relationship.

He's calling on the titan in his office perched high atop Rockefeller Center. Martin knows that this will be his only chance to make a good impression on the titan. He has one hour to gain his confidence and trust—and the millions in his account.

Martin has done this many times. He has a veteran's poise and confidence when he sells himself to a prospect—and he also has a superlative track record of market-beating returns. So it's a little surprising that he doesn't rise to the occasion in his meeting with the titan.

Immediately upon entering the titan's office, when the titan says, "Tell me a little about yourself," Martin starts selling his expertise. He tries to dazzle the titan with a rundown of his more prescient trades, explaining in great detail his investment rationale and how he ended up miles ahead of the competition. He talks about some of his more prominent clients. He outlines some ideas he has for the titan's portfolio and where he sees various markets heading in the near and long terms.

Martin is on such a roll that he doesn't notice that the scheduled hour has gone by in a flash. That's when the titan stands up and thanks Martin for taking the time to see him. Martin's a little surprised by the abrupt ending to the meeting. He never got the chance to ask the titan about his goals, his attitude to risk, and what he was looking for in a portfolio manager. But as he rewinds the meeting in his mind, Martin is satisfied that he presented a strong case for himself, hitting all the high notes in his pitch.

The next day Martin receives a handwritten note from the titan thanking him again but informing him that he will be going in another direction. Martin has lost the account and he has no idea why.

Martin thought he was winning over the titan with overwhelming evidence of his financial acumen.

The titan was thinking, "What an egotistical jackass. When's he going to ask what's on <u>my</u> mind? I'm never letting this fellow near my money."

Martin is guilty of Habit #20: An excessive need to be "me."

It's not that these people don't know who they are or where they're going or what they want to achieve. Nor is it that they don't have an adequate sense of self-worth. In fact, they tend to be very successful (and their self-esteem can often be excessive). What's wrong is that they have no idea how their behavior is coming across to the people who matter—their bosses, colleagues, subordinates, customers, and clients. (And that's not just true at work; the same goes for their home life.)

They think they have all the answers, but others see it as arrogance.

They think they're contributing to a situation with helpful comments, but others see it as butting in.

They think they're delegating effectively, but others see it as shirking responsibilities.

They think they're holding their tongue, but others see it as unresponsiveness.

They think they're letting people think for themselves, but others see it as ignoring them.

Over time these "minor" workplace foibles begin to chip away at the goodwill we've all accumulated in life and that other people normally extend to colleagues and friends. That's when the minor irritation blows up into a major crisis.

Why does this happen? More often than not, it's because people's inner compass of correct behavior has gone out of whack—and they become clueless about their position among their coworkers.

In an article that ran in *The New Yorker*, film director Harold Ramis commented on the reasons behind the fading career of Chevy Chase, one of the stars of Ramis's *Caddyshack*. Ramis said, "Do you know the concept of proprioception, of how you know where you are and where you're oriented? Chevy lost his sense of proprioception, lost touch with what he was projecting to people. It's strange because you couldn't write Chevy as a character in a novel, because his whole attitude is just superiority: 'I'm Chevy Chase and you're not.'"

Well, I work as an executive coach with successful people who have a slightly dented sense of proprioception. They look at the map of their life and career. It tells them, "You Are Here." But they don't accept it. They may resist the truth. They may think (like Chevy Chase's famous line), "I'm successful and you're not." Which is their license to think, "Why change if it's working?"

I wish I had the power to snap my fingers and make these people immediately see the need to change. I wish I could beam them into *Groundhog Day* (another Ramis film and one of my all-time favorites because it's about how people can change for the better), and make them relive the same day—perhaps their worst day—over and over again until they mend their ways. I wish I had the temperament to shake them by the shoulders and make them face reality. I wish I could turn their flaws into life-threatening diseases—because it would compel them to change, on pain of death.

But I can't and I don't. Instead, I show these people what their colleagues at work *really* think of them. It's called feedback. It's the only tool I need to show people, "You Are Here." And in this book, I will show you how to wield that weapon on yourself and others.

It doesn't take much to get people reoriented—out of the maze and back on the right path. The problems we'll be looking at in this book are not life-threatening diseases (although ignored for too long they can destroy a career). They're not deep-seated neuroses that require years of therapy or tons of medication to erase. More often than not, they are simple behavioral tics—bad habits that we repeat dozens of times a day in the workplace— which can be cured by (a) pointing them out, (b) showing the havoc they cause among the people surrounding us, and (c) demonstrating that with a slight behavioral tweak we can achieve a much more appealing effect.

It's a little like a stage actor who keeps stepping on a pivotal line in a comedy, thus ruining any chance of securing a big laugh from the audience. It's the director's job to notice this and alter the actor's delivery so that the line elicits the essential roar of laughter from the audience. No laugh, no play. If the actor can't adjust his delivery successfully, the producer will find someone who can.

Well, think of me as a caring director who helps you deliver your lines for maximum effect.

A journalist once told me that the most important thing he's learned in his career is this: "Put a comma in the wrong place and the whole sentence is screwed up." You may have an admirable skill set for a journalist. You can investigate the facts like the CSI team. You can interview people as if you've known them all your life. You can empathize with victims and excoriate the bad guys. You can spin words together beautifully on deadline and create rich meaningful metaphors that leave readers gasping with admiration. And yet, if you put a comma in the wrong place, that tiny sin of commission can wipe out the rest of your contributions.

Think of me as a friendly grammarian who can shield you from bad punctuation.

A chef at one of my favorite restaurants in San Diego told me that his signature dish succeeds or fails on one secret ingredient (which, like Coca-Cola's heavily guarded recipe, he refuses to reveal). Leave it out and the patrons' plates come back to the kitchen only half eaten. Sprinkle it in the proper amount and the plates come back clean.

Think of me as the honest diner who sends back the meal untouched to let you know that something is missing.

Actors stepping on a line. Writers misusing commas. Chefs leaving out a key ingredient. That's what we're talking about here in the workplace: People who do one annoying thing repeatedly on the job—and don't realize that this small flaw may sabotage their otherwise golden career. And, worse, they do not realize that (a) it's happening and (b) they can fix it.

This book is your map—a map that can turn the maze of wrong turns in the workplace into a straight line to the top.

In the arc of what can be a long successful career, you will always be in transit from "here" to "there."

Here can be a great place. If you're successful, here is exactly the kind of place you want to be. Here is a place where you can be the CEO of a thriving company. Here is a place where you can be the editor of one of America's top magazines. Here is a place where you can be an in-demand financial manager.

But here is also a place where you can be a success in spite of some gaps in your behavior or personal makeup.

That's why you want to go "there." There can be a better place. There is a place where you can be a CEO who is viewed as a great leader because he doesn't get in the way of his people. There is a place where you can be a great editor who builds a strong team and treats all of her direct reports with respect. There is a place where you can be a financial pro who listens well and delivers the message that he cares more about his clients' goals than his own needs.

You don't have to be a CEO or leading editor or financial wizard to benefit from this book. Look at your own personal map. Trace the distance between your vision of here and there.

You are here.

You can get there.

But you have to understand that what got you here won't get you there.

Let the journey begin.

CHAPTER 2

Enough About You

LET'S TALK ABOUT ME. Who am I to tell you how to change?

My career as an executive coach began with a phone call from the CEO of a Fortune 100 company. I had just given a leadership clinic to the CEO's human resources department. That's what I was doing back then in the late 1980s: Advising HR departments about identifying future leaders in their companies and creating programs to form them into better leaders. The CEO attended the session and must have heard something that struck a nerve. That's why he was using his very valuable time to call me. Something was on his mind.

"Marshall, I've got this guy running a big division who delivers his numbers and more every quarter," said the CEO. "He's a young, smart, dedicated, ethical, motivated, hard-working, entrepreneurial, creative, charismatic, arrogant, stubborn, know-it-all jerk.

"Trouble is, we're a company built on team values, and no one thinks he's a team player. I'm giving him a year to change, or he's out. But you know something, it would be worth a fortune to us if we could turn this guy around."

My ears perked up at the word "fortune." Up until then I had been teaching large groups of leaders how to change behavior—their own and that of their peers and direct reports. I had never worked one-on-one with an executive before, and certainly not with someone who was one click away from the CEO's chair at a multi-billion-dollar company. I didn't know this fellow, but from the CEO's terse description I had a good picture in my mind. He was a success junkie, the kind of guy who had triumphed at each successive rung of the achievement ladder. He liked to win whether it was at work, at touch football, in a poker game, or in an argument with a stranger. He could charm a customer, turn everyone around to his position in a meeting, and get his bosses to want to help him advance through the organization. He had "high potential" stamped on his forehead since the day he entered the company. He was also financially independent—rich enough that he didn't *have* to work, he *wanted* to.

All of these ingredients—the talent, charm, and brains, the unbroken track record of success, the screw-you money in the bank that let him think he could flip off the world—made this fellow a potent mix of stubbornness and pride and defensiveness. How could I help someone like this change, someone whose entire life—from his paycheck to his title to the hundreds of direct reports who did his daily bidding—was an affirmation that he was doing everything right? More important, even if I had an inkling how to do it, why would I want to beat my head against this particular wall?

I was intrigued by the challenge—and the word "fortune." I had coached plenty of mid-level managers in groups before. These were people on the verge of success, but not quite there yet. Could my methods work on a more elite flight of executive material? Could I take someone who was demonstrably successful and make him or her more successful? It would be an interesting test.

I told the CEO, "I might be able to help."

The CEO sighed, "I doubt it."

"Tell you what," I said. "I'll work with him for a year. If he gets better, pay me. If not, it's all free."

The next day I caught a return flight to New York City to meet the CEO and his division chief.

That was twenty years ago. Since then I've personally worked with more than one hundred executives of similar status, brainpower, wealth, and achievement, who have at least one incredible career-damaging interpersonal challenge.

That's what I do now. I have a Ph.D. in organizational behavior from UCLA and 29 years of experience measuring and analyzing behavior in organizations. Now I apply it one-on-one with very successful people who want to be more successful. My job is not to make them smarter or richer. My job is to help them—to identify a personal habit that's annoying their coworkers and to help them eliminate it—so that they retain their value to the organization. My job is to make them see that the skills and habits that have taken them this far might not be the right skills and habits to take them further.

What got them here won't get them there.

But I don't work only with the super-successful. That's a critical part of my business, but I spend most of my time teaching people who reside somewhere below the absolute top rungs of the organizational ladder. They need help too. There is no correlation between an individual's standing in the corporate pyramid and what his coworkers think of his interpersonal skills. Middle managers are no less immune than CEOs to being perceived as arrogant, inattentive, rude, and unfoundedly omniscient. My target audience is the huge cohort of people who are successful in their own minds but want to be even more successful.

I train people to behave effectively in the workplace—by enrolling them in a simple but brutal regimen.

First, I solicit "360-degree feedback" from their colleagues—as many as I can talk to up, down, and sideways in the chain of command, often including family members—for a comprehensive assessment of their strengths and weaknesses.

Then I confront them with what everybody really thinks about them. Assuming that they accept this information, agree that they have room to improve, and commit to changing that behavior, then I show them how to do it.

I help them *apologize* to everyone affected by their flawed behavior (because it's the only way to erase the negative baggage associated with our prior actions) and ask the same people for help in getting better.

I help them *advertise* their efforts to get better because you have to tell people that you're trying to change; they won't notice it on their own.

Then I help them *follow up* religiously every month or so with their colleagues because it's the only honest way to find out how you're doing and it also reminds people that you're still trying.

As an integral part of this follow-up process, I teach people to *listen without prejudice* to what their colleagues, family members, and friends are saying—that is, listen without interrupting or arguing.

I also show them that the only proper response to whatever they hear is *gratitude*. That is, I teach them how to say "Thank you" without ruining the gesture or embellishing it. I am a huge apostle for thanking.

Finally, I teach them the miracle of *feedforward*, which is my "special sauce" methodology for eliciting advice from people on what they can do to get better in the future.

It's often humbling for these overachievers, but after 12 to 18 months they get better—not only in their own minds but, more important, in the opinions of their coworkers.

As I say, it's a simple process but how I got here could fill a book—this book. And I hasten to add that it is a book that can help a lot more people than just the super-successful among us. That would be like writing a golf instructional just for PGA Tour players. An interesting exercise, perhaps, but useful to only .000001 percent of the golf playing universe. It's not worth the effort.

I don't use a golf analogy lightly. I live next to a golf course, where I can observe golfers, and I am convinced that in the context of helping successful people get better, nothing is more relevant than golf instruction. Golfers suffer all the symptoms of successful people, perhaps even more acutely.

For one thing, they're delusional about their success. They claim (and even believe) they're doing better than they really are. If they break 90 one time out of a hundred rounds, that exceptional round will quickly become their "usual game."

Golfers are also delusional about how they achieved success. That's why they award themselves second shots (called mulligans) when the first ones go in the wrong direction, move the ball from an awkward lie, conveniently neglect to count the occasional errant stroke, and otherwise fiddle with the rules and scorecard, all in an effort to buff up their handicaps and take credit for a better game than they actually possess.

Golfers, like business people, also tend to be delusional about their weaknesses, which they deny. This explains why they spend much of their time practicing what they're already good at and little time on areas of their game that need work.

How are these traits any different than bosses who claim more credit for a success than they're entitled to, who stretch the truth to gain an advantage, and who think they're strong in areas where others know they are weak?

Golfers, like the leaders I coach, have one singularly noble quality: No matter how good they are, whether they sport a 30 handicap or play to scratch, *they all want to get better.* That's why they're always practicing, scheduling lessons, trying out new equipment, fiddling with their swing, and poring over instructional advice in magazines and books.

That's the spirit underlying this book. It's aimed at anyone *who wants to get better*—at work, at home, or any other venue.

If I can help you consider the possibility that, despite your demonstrable success and laudable self-esteem, you might not be as good as you think you are; that all of us have corners in our behavioral makeup that are messy; and that these messy corners can be pinpointed and tidied up, then I can leave the world—and your world—a slightly better place than I found it.

Okay. Enough about me. Let's get back to you.

CHAPTER 3

The Success Delusion, or Why We Resist Change

UNUM, THE INSURANCE COMPANY, ran an ad some years ago showing a powerful grizzly bear in the middle of a roaring stream, with his neck extended to the limit, jaws wide open, teeth flaring. The bear was about to clamp on to an unsuspecting airborne salmon jumping upstream. The headline read: YOU PROBABLY FEEL LIKE THE *BEAR*. WE'D LIKE TO SUGGEST YOU'RE THE SALMON.

The ad was designed to sell disability insurance, but it struck me as a powerful statement about how all of us in the workplace delude ourselves about our achievements, our status, and our contributions. We

- Overestimate our contribution to a project

- Take credit, partial or complete, for successes that truly belong to others

- Have an elevated opinion of our professional skills and our standing among our peers

- Conveniently ignore the costly failures and time-consuming dead-ends we have created

- Exaggerate our projects' impact on net profits because we discount the real and hidden costs built into them (the costs are someone else's problems; the success is ours)

All of these delusions are a direct result of success, not failure. That's because we get positive reinforcement from our past successes, and, in a mental leap that's easy to justify, we think that our past success is predictive of great things in our future.

This is not necessarily a bad thing. This wacky delusional belief in our godlike omniscience instills us with confidence, however unearned it may be. It erases doubt. It blinds us to the risks and challenges in our work. If we had a complete grip on reality, seeing every situation for exactly what it is, we wouldn't get out of bed in the morning. After all, the most realistic people in our society are the chronically depressed.

But our delusions become a serious liability when we need to change. We sit there with the same godlike feelings, and when someone tries to make us change our ways we regard them with unadulterated bafflement.

It's an interesting three-part response.

First, we think the other party is confused. They're misinformed and don't know what they're talking about. They have us mixed up with someone who truly does need to change, but we are not that person.

Second, as it dawns on us that maybe the other party is not confused—maybe their information about our perceived shortcomings is accurate—we go into denial mode. The criticism does not apply to us, or else we wouldn't be so successful.

Finally, when all else fails, we attack the other party. We discredit the messenger. "Why is a smart guy like me," we think, "listening to a loser like you?"

Those are just the initial surface responses—the denial mechanisms. Couple them with the very positive interpretations that successful people assign to (a) their past performance, (b) their ability to influence their success (rather than just being lucky), (c) their optimistic belief that their success will continue in the future, and (d) their sense of control over their own destiny (as opposed to being controlled by external forces), and you have a volatile cocktail of resistance to change.

Four key beliefs help us become successful. Each can make it tough for us to change. And that's the paradox of success: These beliefs that carried us *here* may be holding us back in our quest to go *there*. Let's look more closely at each of these beliefs that can prevent us from changing our "proven" ways.

Belief 1: I Have Succeeded

Successful people believe in their *skills and talent.*

Successful people have one idea coursing silently through their veins and brains all day. It's a mantra that goes like this: "I have succeeded. I have succeeded. I have succeeded." It's their way of telling themselves that they have the skills and talent to win and keep winning. Whether or not they actually voice it inside their heads, this is what successful people are telling themselves.

You may not believe it applies to you. You may think this is egos run amok. But look at yourself. How do you have the confidence to wake up in the morning and charge into work, filled with optimism and desire and the eagerness to compete? It's not because you're reminding yourself of all the screw-ups you created and failures you've endured in recent days. On the contrary, it's because you edit out the failures and choose instead to run the highlight reel of your successes. If you're like most people I know, you're constantly focusing on the positive, calling up images of performances where you were the star, where you dazzled everyone and came out on top. It might be those five minutes in a meeting where you had the floor and nailed the argument you wanted to make. (Who wouldn't run that highlight in their head as if it were the Sports Center Play of the Day?) It might be your skillfully crafted memo that the boss praised and routed to everyone in the company. (Who wouldn't want to re-read that memo in a spare moment?) Whatever the evidence, if it has a happy ending that makes us look good, we'll replay it for ourselves and retell it to anyone who'll listen.

You'll see this confident mindset in your successful friends, simply by the stories you hear them repeat. Are they recountings of their blunders? Or are they tales of triumphs? If they're successful friends, it's the latter.

When it comes to the thoughts we hold inside our heads, we are not self-deprecating. We are self-aggrandizing. And that's a good thing. Without it, we might not get up in the morning.

I once got into a conversation about this with a major league baseball player. Every hitter has certain pitchers whom he historically hits better than others. He told me, "When I face a pitcher whom I've hit well in the past, I always go up to the plate thinking I 'own' this guy. That gives me confidence."

That's not surprising. To successful people, past is always prologue—and the past is always rose-colored. But he took that thinking one step further.

"What about pitchers whom you don't hit well?" I asked. "How do you deal with a pitcher who 'owns' you?"

"Same thing," he said. "I go up to the plate thinking I can hit this guy. I've done it before against pitchers a lot better than he is."

In other words, not only did he lean on his past success to maintain his successful attitude, but he relied on it even when his past performance was *not* so rosy—i.e., when the evidence contradicted his self-confidence. Successful people never drink from a glass that's half empty.

They do the same even when it's a team effort. No matter how much they respect their teammates, when the team achieves great results, they tend to believe that *their contribution* was more significant than facts suggest.

I once polled three business partners to estimate the percentage that each of them contributed to their partnership's profits. Since I knew the senior partner in this particular enterprise, I knew the true numbers. And yet the three partners' combined estimate came to over 150 percent! Each man thought he was contributing more than half of the firm's profits.

This is not merely true of the people I work with, it's true in any workplace. If you asked your colleagues to estimate their percentage contribution to your enterprise, the total will always exceed 100 percent. There's nothing wrong with this. You want to surround yourself with confident people. (If your total ever comes to less than 100 percent, I suggest you find new colleagues.)

This "I have succeeded" belief, positive as it is most times, only becomes an obstacle when behavioral change is needed.

Successful people consistently compare themselves favorably to their peers. If you ask successful professionals to rate themselves against their peers (as I have done with more than 50,000 people in my training programs), 80 to 85 percent of them will rate themselves in the top 20 percent of their peer group—and 70 percent will rate themselves in the top 10 percent. This number goes even higher among professionals with higher perceived social status, such as physicians, pilots, and investment bankers, 90 percent of whom place themselves in the top 10 percent.

Doctors may be the most delusional. I once told a group of MDs that my extensive research proved that exactly half of all MDs graduated in the bottom half of their medical school class. Two doctors in the room insisted this was impossible!

Imagine trying to tell people like this that they're doing something wrong and need to change.

Belief 2: I Can Succeed

This is another way of saying, "I am *confident* that I can succeed."

Successful people believe that they have the capability within themselves to make desirable things happen. It's not quite like a carnival magic act where the mentalist moves objects on a table with his mind or bends steel. But it's close. Successful people literally believe that through sheer force of personality or talent or brainpower, they can steer a situation in their direction.

It's the reason why some people raise their hand and say, "Put me in, coach" when the boss asks for volunteers to solve a problem—and others cower in the corner, praying they won't be noticed.

This is the classic definition of self-efficacy, and it may be the most central belief driving individual success. People who believe they can succeed see opportunities where others see threats. They're not afraid of uncertainty or ambiguity. They embrace it. They want to take greater risks and achieve greater returns. Given the choice, they will always bet on themselves.

Successful people tend to have a high "internal locus of control." In other words, they do not feel like victims of fate. They see success for themselves and others as largely a function of people's motivation and ability—not luck, random chance, or external factors.

They carry this belief even when luck does play a critical role. Several years ago six of my partners wanted to get involved in a very large deal. Since I was a senior partner, they needed my approval. I was against it, telling them it was idiotic. I finally agreed, but kicking and screaming. Seven years later the return on my "idiotic" investment was the biggest lump sum check I'd ever received—seven digits to the left of the decimal point. There's no other way to describe it except dumb luck. But some of my more successful friends didn't see it this way. They insisted that my good fortune had little to do with luck and was really a payoff for years of hard work. This is the classic response from successful people. We tend to believe that success is "earned" through an individual's motivation and ability (even when it is not).

Of course, this belief makes about as much sense as inheriting money and thinking you're a self-made man. If you're born on third base, you shouldn't think you hit a triple. Successful people, however, believe there is always a link between what they have done and how far they have come—even when no link exists. It's delusional, but it is also empowering.

This belief is certainly better than the alternative. Take the example of people who buy state lottery tickets. It is a statistical fact that state-run lotteries are "regressive taxes" on people who are not the highest income earners. Serious lottery players tend to believe that any success is a function of luck, external factors, or random chance. (This is the opposite belief of most successful people, and why you rarely see millionaires scratching tickets.) These serious scratchers see the lottery as a manifestation of the randomness of success. They feel that they might get lucky and win millions of dollars if they buy enough lottery tickets. Studies show that people with these beliefs tend not to be high achievers or high wage earners.

To make matters worse, many people who win high payouts in the lottery often do a poor job of investing their winnings. The same beliefs that led them to buy hundreds of lottery tickets are reinforced when they win the lottery. That is, they make irrational investment decisions, hoping again that luck—rather than their skill and intelligence—will make them richer. That's why they plunge into questionable schemes. They don't have the base belief that they can succeed on their own, so they rely on luck.

Successful people trade in this lottery mentality for an unshakable belief in themselves. And that presents another obstacle for helping them change their behavior. One of the greatest mistakes of successful people is the assumption, "I am successful. I behave this way. Therefore, I must be successful *because* I behave this way!" The challenge is to make them see that sometimes they are successful *in spite of* this behavior.

Belief 3: I Will Succeed

This is another way of saying, "I have the *motivation* to succeed."

If "I have succeeded" refers to the *past*, and "I can succeed" to the *present*, then "I will succeed" refers to the *future*. Successful people have an unflappable optimism. They not only believe that they can manufacture success, they believe it's practically their due.

As a result, successful people tend to pursue opportunities with an enthusiasm that others may find mystifying. If they set a goal and publicly announce it, they tend to do "whatever it takes" to achieve the goal. That's a good thing. But it can easily mutate into excessive optimism. It explains why successful people tend to be extremely busy and face the danger of overcommitment.

It can be difficult for an ambitious person, with an "I will succeed" attitude, to say "no" to desirable opportunities. The huge majority of executives that I work with feel as busy (or busier) today than they have ever felt in their lives. I have never heard one of my clients say, "I don't have enough on my plate." And this busy-ness is not because they have so many problems to deal with. When I surveyed executives about why they felt overcommitted, none of them said they were trying to "save a sinking ship." They were overcommitted because they were "drowning in a sea of opportunity."

Perhaps this has happened to you. You do something wonderful at work. Suddenly, lots of people want to rub up against you and associate themselves with your success. They think, quite logically, that since you pulled off a miracle once, you can pull it off again for them. So, opportunities are thrust at you at a pace that you have never seen before. You are not experienced or disciplined enough to say no to some of them. If you're not careful, you'll be overwhelmed in due course—and that which made you rise will bring about your fall.

In my volunteer work, my favorite European client was the executive director of one of the world's leading human services organizations. His mission was to help the world's most vulnerable people. Unfortunately (for all of us), his business was booming. When people came to him for help, he didn't have the heart or the inclination to say no. Everything was driven by this belief that "we will succeed." As a result, he promised even more than the most dedicated staff could deliver.

The danger with this, of course, is that, unchecked, this "we will succeed" attitude leads to staff burnout, high turnover, and a weaker team than the one you started with. His biggest challenge as a leader was avoiding overcommitment.

This "I will succeed" belief can sabotage our chances for success when it's time for us to change behavior. I make no apology for the fact that I'm obsessed about following up with my clients to see if they actually get better by using my methods. Almost every participant who attends my leadership development programs *intends to* apply what he or she has learned back on the job. Most do, and get better! And, as our research (to be discussed later) shows, many do absolutely nothing; they may as well have spent the time watching sitcoms instead of attending my training program.

When the "do-nothings" are asked, "Why didn't you implement the behavioral change that you said you would?" by far the most common response is, "I meant to, but I just didn't have time to get to it." In other words, they were overcommitted. It's not that they didn't want to change, or didn't agree with the value of changing. They just ran out of hours in the day. They thought that they would "get to it later"—and "later" never arrived. Overcommitment can be as serious an obstacle to change as believing that you don't need fixing or that your flaws are part of the reason you're successful.

Belief 4: I Choose to Succeed

Successful people believe that they are doing what they choose to do, because they choose to do it. They have a high need for self-determination. The more successful a person is, the more likely this is to be true. When we do what we *choose* to do, we are *committed*. When we do what we *have* to do, we are *compliant*.

You see the difference in any job, even where money is not related to performance. When I attended high school back in Kentucky, even a skeptical wise-cracking jokester like me could see that some teachers had a calling for the profession and some teachers did it to make a living—and the best teachers were the former. They were committed to us rather than being controlled by external forces (such as a paycheck).

Successful people have a unique distaste for feeling controlled or manipulated. I see this in my work every day. Even when I've gotten the greatest advance build-up as someone who can help people change for the better—in other words, I'm effective at helping—I still meet resistance. I have now made peace with the fact that I cannot *make* people change. I can only help them get better at what they *choose* to change.

The basketball coach Rick Pitino wrote a book called *Success Is a Choice*. I agree. "I choose to succeed" correlates perfectly with achievement in virtually any field. People don't stumble on success; they choose it.

Unfortunately, getting people who think "I have chosen to succeed" to say "and I choose to change" is not an easy transition. It means turning that muscular commitment on its head. Easy to say, hard to do. The more we believe that our behavior is a result of our own choices and commitments, the less likely we are to want to change our behavior.

There's a reason for this, and it's one of the best-researched principles in psychology. It's called *cognitive dissonance*. It refers to the disconnect between what we believe in our minds and what we experience or see in reality. The underlying theory is simple. The more we are committed to believing that something is true, the less likely we are to believe that its opposite is true, even in the face of clear evidence that shows we are wrong. For example, if you believe your colleague Bill is a jerk, you will filter Bill's actions through that belief. No matter what Bill does, you'll see it through a prism that confirms he's a jerk. Even the times when he's not a jerk, you'll interpret it as the exception to the rule that Bill's a jerk. It may take years of saintly behavior for Bill to overcome your perception. That's cognitive dissonance applied to others. It can be a disruptive and unfair force in the workplace.

Yet cognitive dissonance actually works in favor of successful people when they apply it to themselves. The more we are committed to believing that something is true, the less likely we are to believe that its opposite is true, even in the face of evidence that shows we may have chosen the wrong path. It's the reason successful people don't buckle and waver when times get tough. Their commitment to their goals and beliefs allows them to view reality through rose-tinted glasses. That's a good thing in many situations. Their personal commitment encourages people to "stay the course" and to not give up when the going gets tough.

Of course, this same steadfastness can work against successful people when they should change course.

How Our Success Makes Us Superstitious

These four success beliefs—that we have the skills, the confidence, the motivation, and the free choice to succeed—make us superstitious.

"Who, me?" you say. "No way. I don't believe in that stuff. I'm successful because I earned it."

That may be true for "childish" superstitions such as bad luck ensuing from walking under a ladder, or breaking a mirror, or letting a black cat cross our path. Most of us scorn superstitions as silly beliefs of the primitive and uneducated. Deep down inside, we assure ourselves that we're above these silly notions.

Not so fast. To a degree, we're all superstitious. In many cases, the higher we climb the organizational totem pole, the more superstitious we become.

Psychologically speaking, superstitious behavior comes from the mistaken belief that a specific activity that is followed by positive reinforcement is actually the cause of that positive reinforcement. The activity may be functional or not—that is, it may affect someone or something else, or it may be self-contained and pointless—but if something good happens after we do it, then we make a connection and seek to repeat the activity. Psychologist B. F. Skinner was one of the first to highlight this inanity by showing how hungry pigeons would repeat their twitches because doing so was randomly followed by small pellets of grain. After twitching in a certain way and then immediately getting fed, the pigeons learned to repeat the twitches. They mistakenly believed that twitching led to food. Twitch, they hoped, and you get fed. Twitch again, and you eat more.

Sounds silly, doesn't it? We would never behave this way. We assure ourselves that we are more highly evolved than Skinner's pigeons. But from my experience, hungry business people repeat certain behavior all the time, day in and day out, when they believe large pellets of money and recognition will come their way because of it.

Superstition is merely the confusion of correlation and causality. Any human, like any animal, tends to repeat behavior that is followed by positive reinforcement. The more we achieve, the more reinforcement we get.

One of the greatest mistakes of successful people is the assumption, "I behave this way, and I achieve results. Therefore, I must be achieving results because I behave this way."

This belief is sometimes true, but not across the board. That's where superstition kicks in. It creates the core fallacy necessitating this book, the reason that "what got us here won't get us there." I'm talking about the difference between success that happens *because of* our behavior and the success that comes *in spite of* our behavior.

Almost everyone I meet is successful *because of* doing a lot of things right, and almost everyone I meet is successful *in spite of* some behavior that defies common sense.

One of my greatest challenges is helping leaders see the difference, see that they are confusing "because of " and "in spite of " behaviors, and avoid this "superstition trap."

This was my biggest hurdle when I worked with an executive I'll call Harry. He was a brilliant, dedicated executive who consistently made his numbers. He wasn't just smart. Harry saw things no one else at the company could see. Everybody high and low conceded this. His creative ideas led to groundbreaking new processes and procedures, for which everyone credited him profusely. There was no doubt that Harry had been instrumental in turning around his organization. Plus, Harry had other positives going for him. He sincerely cared about the company, employees, and shareholders. He had a great wife, two kids enrolled in top colleges, a beautiful home in a great neighborhood. The works. Life was very good for Harry.

The flaw in this perfect picture—and there's always a flaw when superstition comes into play—was that Harry was a poor listener. Even though his direct reports and coworkers respected him, they felt that he didn't listen to them. Even when you factor in that they were somewhat intimidated by his quick mind and creativity, and thus more willing to accept that Harry *didn't have to listen to them all the time,* Harry was still a world-class aggressive non-listener, not just a distracted genius who sometimes didn't pay attention. His colleagues consistently felt that if Harry had made up his mind on a subject, it was useless to express another opinion. This was confirmed up and down the company by feedback I conducted. And it was confirmed at home too, where his wife and kids felt that Harry often did not hear a word they said. If Harry's dog could speak, I suspect he would have barked out the same conclusion.

I suggested to Harry that he was probably successful because of his talent, hard work, and some good luck. I also said that he was probably successful in spite of being an appalling listener.

Harry acknowledged that other people thought he should become a better listener, but he wasn't sure that he should change. He had convinced himself that his poor listening actually was a great source of his success. Like many high achievers, he wanted to defend his superstitious beliefs. He pointed out that some people present awful ideas and that he hated cluttering his fertile brain with bad ideas. Bad ideas were like brain pollution. He needed to filter them out, and he wouldn't pretend to hear out bad ideas simply because it made other people feel better. "I don't suffer fools gladly," he said, with a little more pride than patience.

This was defensive reaction number one. It always happens with people caught in the superstition trap. They cling to the notion that their success is causally linked to specific behavior, good or bad, responsible or risky, legitimate or inappropriate. They refuse to accept that not all good things flow to them because of the less-than-good things they do. Sometimes there's no causal connection at all.

It was my job to make Harry see his flawed logic.

When I asked if he really believed that his coworkers and family members were fools, he shamefacedly conceded that his comment may have been over the top. These were people he respected, people he needed to get things done, people on whose backs his entire success rested.

"Upon further reflection," he said, "perhaps sometimes I am the fool."

That was a big step for Harry—both *conceding* the legitimacy of other people's feelings and *recognizing* that "perhaps sometimes" he was acting like a fool.

But then Harry went into defensive reaction number two: fear of overcorrection. He was concerned that he might start listening too much and that doing so would diminish his creative impulses. He would become too unwilling to share his opinions and eventually dry up creatively. I pointed out that the danger that a 55-year-old man who had been a bad listener for his entire life would overcorrect and suddenly become excessively interested in other people's opinions was extremely remote. I assured him that he could remove this concern from his things-to-worry-about list. We were fixing one bad behavior, not manufacturing a religious conversion. Ultimately Harry decided it was more productive to hear people out than waste time justifying his own dysfunctional behavior.

Harry's case isn't an isolated event. Virtually all of us are superstitious, attaching too much value to bad behavior that we confusedly associate with our success.

I've worked with people who insist their cruel comments to colleagues are absolutely necessary because their pithy memorable zingers are where their great ideas begin. (I ask them if they've ever met a nice person as creative as they are? Hmmm . . . it gets them thinking.)

I've worked with salespeople who think their pushy, belligerent sales tactics with customers are the reason they close more deals than their peers. (If that were true, I point out, how do your nicer colleagues sell anything at all? Could it be that you're selling a great product or making more sales calls?)

I've worked with executives who insist their remoteness, their inscrutable silences, their non-accessibility to their direct reports is a controlled, calculated tactic to get people to think for themselves. (Fostering initiative among the troops is a leader's job, I point out, but are you doing this intentionally for a legitimate purpose? Or are you justifying it after the fact because that is who you are and you refuse to change? Couldn't your people think *better* for themselves if you were steering them in the right direction and showed them how you think? Is it possible that they're thinking for themselves in spite of the fact that you ignore them?)

Now let's turn the spotlight on you, because few of us are immune to superstition. Pick a quirky or unattractive behavior that you habitually do, something that you know is annoying to friends or family or coworkers. Now ask yourself: Do you continue to do it because you think it is somehow associated with the good things that have happened to you? Examine it more closely. Does this behavior help you achieve results? Or is it one of those irrational superstitious beliefs that have been controlling your life for years? The former is "because of" behavior, the latter "in spite of."

Getting out of this superstition trap requires vigilance. You must constantly ask yourself, Is this behavior a legitimate reason for my success, or am I kidding myself?

If you tote up your "because of" and "in spite of" activities, you might be shocked at how superstitious you really are.

We All Obey Natural Law

Barry Diller, the chairman of IAC/Interactive Corp., was at Harvard Business School explaining the rationale behind the mosaic of interactive commerce companies he had assembled at IAC, such as Ticketmaster, Hotels.com., Match.com, and LendingTree.com. One of the students pointed out that these various businesses seemed to be operating independently, not in a coordinated synergistic fashion.

Diller erupted in mock anger. "Don't ever use that word synergy. It's a hideous word," he said. "The only thing that works is natural law. Given enough time, natural relationships will develop between our businesses."

I agree. What applies to disparate parts of a giant company also applies to disparate people in an organization. You can't force people to work together. You can't mandate synergy. You can't manufacture harmony, whether it's between two people or two divisions. You also can't order people to change their thinking or behavior. The only law that applies is natural law.

The only natural law I've witnessed in three decades of observing successful people's efforts to become more successful is this: *People will do something—including changing their behavior—only if it can be demonstrated that doing so is in their own best interests as defined by their own values.*

I'm not being cynical here, or implying that the only motive in life is selfishness. Plenty of people perform selfless acts of goodness *of their own volition* every day with no obvious tit-for-tat payback to themselves.

What I am saying, though, is that when you take self-volition out of the equation and forces beyond your control are involved, natural law applies. In order for me to get you to do what I want, I have to prove that doing so will benefit you in some way, immediately or somewhere down the road. This is natural law. Every choice, big or small, is a risk-reward decision where your bottom-line thinking is, "What's in it for me?"

None of us has to apologize for this. It's the way of the world.

It's the force that gets squabbling rivals to begin cooperating. If you drill down deep enough, you'll find that they're not doing it out of altruism or newfound saintliness. It's the only way each of them can get what they want. You see this all the time in politics when bitter rivals from across the aisle agree to support the same legislation because different parts of the bill will benefit their different constituencies.

It's the force at work when people swallow their pride and admit they were wrong. Hard as it is for many folks to do, they'll do it if it's the only way to put the trouble behind them—and move on.

It's the reason people will turn down a better-paying job because they sense the new situation will not make them happier. They're asking what's in it for them, and concluding that they'd rather be happier than richer.

For my purposes, thank heaven for natural law! Without it, getting successful people to mend their ways would be impossible.

As I mentioned, successful people have very few reasons to change their behavior—and lots of reasons to stick with the status quo, to dance with what brung 'em.

Their success has showered them with positive reinforcement, so they feel it's smart to continue doing what they've always done.

Their past behavior confirms that the future is equally bright. (I did it this way before. Look how far it's gotten me.)

Then there's the arrogance, the feeling that "I can do anything" which develops and bulges like a well-exercised muscle in successful people, especially after an impressive string of successes.

Then there's the protective shell that successful people develop over time which whispers to them, "You are right. Everyone else is wrong."

These are heady defense mechanisms to overcome.

For some people, telling them that everyone hates the way they act doesn't make a dent; they don't care what others think. They assume that everyone else is confused.

For others, warning that their behavior is ruining their chances for promotion fails to scare them; they assume they can snap their fingers and get a better job elsewhere. (Forget whether it's true; they believe it!)

Persuading people to change by invoking an endgame that doesn't matter to them is very hard work. I was once asked to work with a software wizard. He was the technical guts of the company—virtually indispensable. The CEO wanted him to be more of a team player—to mix more with others in the hope that maybe he could spread some of his "genius" around to the rest of the company.

Only problem—which was evident after five minutes with him—was that this man was basically antisocial. His ideal world was a room, a desk, a computer screen, and (oh yes) a state-of-the-art sound system providing round-the-clock background music (opera, as I recall). He didn't want to play well with the other children. He wanted to be left alone.

I suppose we could have threatened to take his toys away if he didn't change. But what would that have accomplished? He wouldn't be better or happier, and the company would have "lost" its most valuable asset. Changing him wasn't worth it, which is what I recommended to the CEO.

"Your plan is nice in theory. But what you are asking is not connected to what he values," I said. "Let him be. He's happy. He's not going anywhere. Why scare him away by turning him into someone that is just not him?"

This fellow was the exception—an aberration.

Most people's resistance to change can be overcome by invoking natural law. Everyone, even the biggest ego in the room, has a hot button that can be pushed—and that button is self-interest. All we have to do is find it. It's not the same thing in all people.

If there's any art to what I do (and believe me, there isn't much), maybe it happens here—at the decisive moment when I discover someone's hot button.

Fortunately, successful people make it easy to find the button. If you press people to identify the motives behind their self-interest it usually boils down to four items: money, power, status, and popularity. These are the standard payoffs for success. It's why we will claw and scratch for a raise (money), for a promotion (power), for a bigger title and office (status). It's why so many of us have a burning need to be liked by everyone (popularity).

The hot button is different for each person. And it changes over time, but it's still guided by self-interest. My personal coaching clients have money, power, and status—and most are popular. Having achieved these goals, they turn to higher-level goals, such as "leaving a legacy" or "being an inspiring role model" or "creating a great company." If you look for the hot button of self-interest, it's there.

One of my more notable successes occurred with a sales executive named John, who was consumed by his rivalry with another executive at the firm. The two men had been dueling for years (although it's not clear whether the "other guy" shared this obsession). No matter what John did—playing golf at a company retreat or posting quarterly profits—he didn't "win" unless the other guy finished behind him.

The CEO had called me in because John was a top candidate for the COO spot. Some of his rough edges needed to be smoothed out. John's issue, said the feedback, was an obsessive need to win (surprise!), which manifested itself in a constant one-upsmanship with his direct reports. He always corrected their ideas or improved them by insisting that his suggestions were better.

Getting John to change required a subtle appreciation of what motivated him. Making more money didn't stir the guy; he had enough. Power and status didn't appeal to him either; he was already higher in the organization than he had ever dreamed. Popularity wasn't an issue; with his salesman's touch for getting people to like him, he was already popular. What made him commit to change was the abhorrent thought that failing to do so meant ceding ground to his arch rival. Not the noblest of motives, but I don't pass judgment on why people change. I only care that they do.

Another time when I worked with an executive who was notoriously nasty and sarcastic, he agreed to change because he could see that his two sons were imitating his behavior at home. He didn't want his legacy to be two sarcastic jerks. (More on him in Chapter 6.)

Take a look around you at work. Why are you there? What keeps you coming back day after day? Is it any of the big four—money, power, status, popularity—or is it something deeper and more subtle that has developed over time? If you know what matters to you, it's easier to commit to change. If you can't identify what matters to you, you won't know when it's being threatened. And in my experience, people only change their ways when what they truly value is threatened.

It's in our nature. It's the law.

The Twenty Habits That Hold You Back from the Top

In which we identify the most annoying interpersonal issues in the workplace and help you figure out which ones apply to you

CHAPTER 4

The Twenty Habits

Knowing What to Stop

As a 10-year board member of the Peter Drucker Foundation, I had many opportunities to listen to this great man. Among the myriad wise things I have heard Peter Drucker say, the wisest was, "We spend a lot of time teaching leaders what to do. We don't spend enough time teaching leaders what to stop. Half the leaders I have met don't need to learn what to do. They need to learn what to stop."

How true. Think about your organization. When was the last retreat or training session you attended that was titled, *Stupid Things Our Top People Do That We Need to Stop Doing Now*? When was the last time your CEO delivered an internal talk, designed to motivate employees, that focused on his negative traits and his efforts to stop this destructive behavior? Can you even imagine your CEO (or immediate supervisor) admitting a personal failing in public and outlining his efforts to stop doing it?

Probably not.

There are good reasons for this, largely allied to the positive tone and fast-forward momentum organizations try to maintain. Everything in an organization is designed to demonstrate a commitment to positive action—and couched in terms of doing something. We will start paying attention to our customers (rather than stop talking about ourselves). We must begin to listen more attentively (rather than stop playing with our BlackBerries while others are talking).

Likewise, the recognition and reward systems in most organizations are totally geared to acknowledge the *doing* of *something*. We get credit for doing something good. We rarely get credit for ceasing to do something bad. Yet they are flip sides of the same coin.

Think of the times you've seen colleagues go on a sales call and return with a huge order. If they're like the salespeople I know, they'll come back to the office brandishing the lucrative sales order and regaling anyone who'll listen with a blow-by-blow account of how they turned the prospect around. They will recount their triumph for months. But turn it around. What if during the sales call these salespeople added up the numbers and realized that they were about to close a deal that actually costs the company money with every unit sold? What if they decided on the spot to stop negotiating and say no to the sale? Do they rush back to the office and boast about the bad deal they've just avoided? Hardly—because avoiding mistakes is one of those unseen, unheralded achievements that are not allowed to take up our time and thought. And yet . . . many times avoiding a bad deal can affect the bottom line more significantly than scoring a big sale.

Think of Gerald Levin when he was the much-admired chairman of Time Warner in the 1990s. Levin was hailed as a visionary CEO, the man who foresaw the future of cable TV and helped invent HBO, transforming Time Warner from just a combo of magazines, movies, and music into a broadcasting powerhouse.

But then in 2000 Levin made a mistake. He merged the venerable Time Warner with the upstart online service AOL. It was the biggest corporate merger in U.S. history at the time—promising to create a company that would dominate for decades. Of course, it didn't work out that way. The merger nearly destroyed Time Warner. The stock lost 80 percent of its value. Thousands of employees lost the bulk of their retirement savings. As for Levin, he lost his job, a big chunk of his net worth, and all of his reputation. He went from being chairman of Time Warner to being the architect of the worst corporate merger in U.S. history.

Now, imagine if Levin at any point in the negotiation with AOL had applied the brakes and walked away from the deal? Chances are, we'd

never know about it. Levin would not hold a press conference to announce, "We are not merging!" He'd keep it to himself, as just one more
example of a bad decision avoided. And yet . . . if he had done this—if he
had simply *stopped* what he was doing—his reputation and net worth
might have remained intact.

That's the funny thing about stopping some behavior. It gets no attention, but it can be as crucial as everything else we do *combined*.

For some reason, we are less likely to poison our thinking this way in
normal everyday life. When it comes to stopping behavior or avoiding
bad decisions outside the workplace, we congratulate ourselves all the
time.

A few years ago my wife and I decided not to invest in a real estate
venture. Too risky, we thought. Fortunately for us (though not for
some of our friends), it went bust. Not a month goes by when Lyda and
I, sitting around the kitchen table paying our bills, don't say to each
other, "Thank God we didn't plunk our money into that scheme." We're
quiet for a moment, think sadly of our friends' losses, and then resume
paying our bills. This is our way of honoring the bad decision we
avoided.

Likewise with stopping a bad habit in our personal life. If we successfully stop smoking, we regard it as a big achievement—and congratulate
ourselves all the time for it. Others do too (as well they should when you
consider that the average smoker tries to quit nine times).

But we lose this common sense in the can-do environment of an
organization—where there is no system for honoring the avoidance of a
bad decision or the cessation of bad behavior. Our performance reviews
are solely based on what we've done, what numbers we've delivered, what
increases we have posted against last year's results. Even the seemingly minor personal goals are couched in terms of actions we've initiated, not behavior we have stopped. We get credit for being punctual, not for stopping
our lateness.

We can change this. All that's required is a slight tweak in our mindset, in how we look at our behavior.

Get out your notepad. Instead of your usual "To Do" list, start your
"To Stop" list. By the end of this book, your list may grow.

Shifting into Neutral

We have to stop couching all our behavior in terms of positive or negative. Not all behavior is good or bad. Some of it is simply *neutral*. Neither good nor bad.

For example, let's say you're not regarded as a nice person. You want to change that perception. You decide, "I need to be nicer."

What do you do?

For many people, that's a daunting assignment, requiring a long list of positive actions. You have to start complimenting people, saying "please" and "thank you," listening to people more patiently, treating them with verbal respect, etc., etc., etc. In effect, you have to convert all of the negative things you do at work into positive actions. That's asking a lot of most people, requiring a complete personality makeover that is closer to religious conversion than on-the-job improvement. In my experience very few if any people can institute that many positive changes in their interpersonal actions all at once. They can handle one at a time. But a half dozen or more changes? I don't think so.

Fortunately, there's a simpler way to achieve the goal of "being nicer." All you have to do is "stop being a jerk." It doesn't require much. You don't have to think of new ways to be nicer to people. You don't have to design daily tasks to make over your personality. You don't have to remember to say nice things and hand out compliments and tell the little white lies that lubricate the gears of the workplace. All you have to do is . . . nothing.

When someone offers a less-than-brilliant idea in a meeting, don't criticize it. Say nothing.

When someone challenges one of your decisions, don't argue with them or make excuses. Quietly consider it and say nothing.

When someone makes a helpful suggestion, don't remind them that you already knew that. Thank them and say nothing.

This is not a semantic game. The beauty of knowing what to stop—of achieving this state of inspired neutrality—is that *it is so easy to do*.

Given the choice between becoming a nicer person and ceasing to be a jerk, which do you think is easier to do? The former requires a concerted series of positive acts of commission. The latter is nothing more than an act of omission.

Think of it in terms of a box. Being a nicer person requires you to fill up the box with all the small positive acts you perform every day to establish the new you. It takes a long time to fill up the box, and even longer for people to pay attention and notice that your box is full.

On the other hand, ceasing to be a jerk does not require learning new behavior. You don't have to fill up the box with all your positive achievements; you simply have to leave it empty of any negatives.

Keep that in mind as you go through the list of interpersonal issues in this section and determine if any apply to you. Correcting the behavior, you'll discover, does not require polished skills, elaborate training, arduous practice, or supernatural creativity. All that's required is the faint imagination to stop doing what you've done in the past—in effect, to do nothing at all.

What's Wrong with Us?

Before we can talk about fixing faulty behavior, we must identify the most common faults.

I hasten to add that these are a very specific breed of flaws.

They are not flaws of *skill*. I can't fix that. If this were a baseball team and I was a coach, I'm not the guy to teach you how to hit a hanging curve ball. That's the hitting instructor's job. I'm the coach who teaches you how to get along with your teammates—how to play nice rather than how to play baseball.

Nor are they flaws in *intelligence*. It's too late for me to make you smarter. If that's the issue, the causative events probably occurred somewhere between birth and the time you left college. I wasn't around. And I couldn't have helped anyway.

Nor are they flaws of unchangeable *personality*. We're not attempting psychiatry here, and we can't deliver vital pharmacological medication via a book. Consult an M.D.

What we're dealing with here are challenges in interpersonal behavior, often leadership behavior. They are the egregious everyday annoyances that make your workplace substantially more noxious than it needs to be. They don't happen in a vacuum. They are transactional flaws performed by one person against others. They are:

1. **Winning too much:** The need to win at all costs and in all situations—when it matters, when it doesn't, and when it's totally beside the point.

2. **Adding too much value:** The overwhelming desire to add our two cents to every discussion.

3. **Passing judgment:** The need to rate others and impose our standards on them.

4. **Making destructive comments:** The needless sarcasms and cutting remarks that we think make us sound sharp and witty.

5. **Starting with "No," "But," or "However":** The overuse of these negative qualifiers which secretly say to everyone, "I'm right. You're wrong."

6. **Telling the world how smart we are:** The need to show people we're smarter than they think we are.

7. **Speaking when angry:** Using emotional volatility as a management tool.

8. **Negativity, or "Let me explain why that won't work":** The need to share our negative thoughts even when we weren't asked.

9. **Withholding information:** The refusal to share information in order to maintain an advantage over others.

10. **Failing to give proper recognition:** The inability to praise and reward.

11. **Claiming credit that we don't deserve:** The most annoying way to overestimate our contribution to any success.

12. **Making excuses:** The need to reposition our annoying behavior as a permanent fixture so people excuse us for it.

13. **Clinging to the past:** The need to deflect blame away from ourselves and onto events and people from our past; a subset of blaming everyone else.

14. **Playing favorites:** Failing to see that we are treating someone unfairly.

15. **Refusing to express regret:** The inability to take responsibility for our actions, admit we're wrong, or recognize how our actions affect others.

16. **Not listening:** The most passive-aggressive form of disrespect for colleagues.

17. **Failing to express gratitude:** The most basic form of bad manners.

18. **Punishing the messenger:** The misguided need to attack the innocent who are usually only trying to help us.

19. **Passing the buck:** The need to blame everyone but ourselves.

20. **An excessive need to be "me":** Exalting our faults as virtues simply because they're who we are.

Perhaps Machiavelli could paint these flaws as virtues and demonstrate how they function as clever counterintuitive tactics for getting a leg up on our rivals. But in the course of examining each of these irritants, I will demonstrate that correcting them is the best way to enlist people as our allies—which in the long run is a much more promising success strategy than defending behavior that alienates people.

Admittedly, this is a scary pantheon of bad behavior, and when they're collected in one place they sound more like a chamber of horrors. Who would want to work in an environment where colleagues are guilty of these sins? And yet we do every day. The good news is that these failings rarely show up in bunches. You may know one person guilty of one or two of them. You may know another with one or two different issues. But it's hard to find successful people who embody too many of these failings. That's good—because it simplifies our task of achieving long-term positive change.

There's more good news. These faults are simple to correct. The fix is in the skill set of every human being. For example, the cure for not thanking enough is remembering to say, "Thank you." (How tough is that?) For not apologizing, it's learning to say, "I'm sorry. I'll do better in the future." For punishing the messenger, it's imagining how we'd like to be treated under similar circumstances. For not listening, it's keeping your mouth shut and ears open. And so on. Although this stuff is simple, it's not easy (there's a difference). You already know what to do. It's as basic as tying your shoelaces or riding a bike, or any other skill that lasts a lifetime. We just lose sight of the many daily opportunities to employ them, and thus get rusty.

Check yourself against the list. It's unlikely (I pray) that you're guilty of all of these annoying habits. It's not even likely that you can claim six to eight of them as your own. And of those six to eight, it's also unlikely that *all of them* are sufficiently significant problems that we have to worry about. Some are going to be more serious issues than others. If only one out of twenty people says that you have an anger management issue, let it go. On the other hand, if sixteen out of twenty say it, let's get to work.

Whittle the list down to the one or two vital issues, and you'll know where to start.

In that sense, my job is to show you how to do it. It's little more than teaching people to use their positive skills rather than expose their negative flaws. What could be simpler than that?

The Higher You Go, the More Your Problems Are Behavioral

There's a reason I devote so much energy to identifying interpersonal challenges in successful people. It's because the higher you go, the more your problems are behavioral.

At the higher levels of organizational life, all the leading players are technically skilled. They're all smart. They're all up to date on the technical aspects of their job. You don't get to be, say, your company's chief financial officer without knowing how to count, how to read a balance sheet, and how to handle money prudently.

That's why behavioral issues become so important at the upper rungs of the corporate ladder. All other things being equal, your people skills (or lack of them) become more pronounced the higher up you go. In fact, even when all other things are *not* equal, your people skills often make the difference in how high you go.

Who would you rather have as a CFO? A moderately good accountant who is great with people outside the firm and skilled at managing very smart people? Or a brilliant accountant who's inept with outsiders and alienates all the smart people under him?

Not a tough choice, really. The candidate with superb people skills will win out every time, in large part because he will be able to hire people smarter than he is about money and he will be able to lead them. There's no guarantee the brilliant accountant can do that in the future.

Think about how we perceive other successful people. We rarely associate their success with technical skill or even brainpower. Maybe we say, "They're smart," but that's not the sole factor we attribute to their success. We believe they're smart and something else. At some point we give them the benefit of the doubt on skill issues. For example, we assume our doctor knows medicine, so we judge him on "bedside manner" issues—how he tolerates our questions, how he delivers bad news, even how he apologizes for keeping us cooling our heels too long in his waiting room. None of this is taught in medical school.

We apply these behavioral criteria to almost any successful person—whether it's a CEO or a plumbing contractor.

We all have certain attributes that help us land our first job. These are the kind of achievements that go on our résumé. But as we become more successful, those attributes recede into the background—and more subtle attributes come to the fore.

Jack Welch has a Ph.D. in chemical engineering, but I doubt if any problems he encountered in his last 30 years at General Electric were in any way related to his skill at chemical titration or formulating plastics. When he was vying for the CEO job, the issues holding him back were strictly behavioral—his brashness, his blunt language, his unwillingness to suffer fools. He did not pick up these issues back at the University of Illinois chemical engineering labs. General Electric's board of directors didn't worry about his ability to generate profits. They wanted to know if he could behave as a CEO.

When people ask me if the leaders I coach can really change their behavior, my answer is this: As we advance in our careers, behavioral changes are often the only significant changes we *can* make.

Two Caveats

First Caveat: In this book, as we go through the pantheon of personal flaws that none of us is immune to, I don't want readers to think that the people I work with are bad people. To the contrary, they're not. They are outstanding people, invariably in the top two percent of their organization. But they may be held back by a personal failing or two that they either (a) do not recognize, (b) have not been told about, or (c) are aware of but refuse to change.

Keep this in mind, because at times it will seem like I spend my days working in corporate purgatories populated exclusively by psychopaths, misfits, and jerks. Look around you at work. My clients are no different from the most outstanding people in your organization. Actually, they are no different from you except perhaps in one sense: Unlike many people, they accept their flaws and have made a commitment to getting better. That's a significant difference.

Second Caveat: In the course of going through the following list of common flaws, you may recognize yourself. "That's me," you'll say to yourself. "I do that all the time. I had no idea I was coming across that way."

The chances that you'll get a little nudge of self-recognition here are fairly high.

The chances that you'll admit it's a *problem* are less high.

The chances that you'll take corrective action to mend your ways are even slimmer.

But even if you were that extraordinarily enlightened open-minded individual who could cop to all this, I'd still say we're getting ahead of ourselves. You're not ready to change yet.

For one thing, I'm a little skeptical of self-diagnosis. Just as people tend to overestimate their strengths, they also tend to overrate their weaknesses. They think they're really bad at something at which they're only mediocre or *slightly* poor—an F when they're really a C minus. In other words, they see cancer where a professional would see a muscle pull. So let's hold off on self-diagnosis for a moment.

More important, even if the diagnosis were correct—say, you are a chronic interrupter—you cannot be sure that it's a serious problem to other people. It might be a personality tic to your colleagues, a foible they tolerate. But if it doesn't bother them or affect their opinions of you or isn't holding you back at work, you can ease up on yourself—at least on this issue.

We'll get to picking the right thing to fix soon enough in Chapter 6. But first, let's be clear about what the interpersonal challenges really are.

Habit #1 Winning too much

Winning too much is easily the most common behavioral problem that I observe in successful people. There's a fine line between being competitive and overcompetitive, between winning when it counts and when no one's counting—and successful people cross that line with alarming frequency.

Let's be clear: I'm not disparaging competitiveness. I'm pointing out that it's a problem when we deploy it at the service of objectives that simply are not worth the effort.

Winning too much is the #1 challenge because it underlies nearly every other behavioral problem.

If we argue too much, it's because we want our view to prevail over everyone else (i.e., it's all about winning).

If we're guilty of putting down other people, it's our stealthy way of positioning them beneath us (again, winning).

If we ignore people, again it's about winning—by making them fade away.

If we withhold information, it's to give ourselves an edge over others.

If we play favorites, it's to win over allies and give "our side" an advantage. And so on. So many things we do to annoy people stem from needlessly trying to be the alpha male (or female) in any situation—i.e., the winner.

Our obsession with winning rears its noisome head across the spectrum of human endeavor, not just among senior executives. When the issue is important, we want to win. When the issue is trivial, not worth our time and energy, we want to win. Even when the issue is clearly to our disadvantage, we want to win.

If you've achieved any modicum of success, you're guilty of this every day. When you're in a meeting at work, you want your position to prevail. When you're arguing with your significant other, you'll pull out all the stops to come out on top (whatever that means!) Even when you're in the checkout line at the supermarket, you're scouting the other lines to see which is moving faster.

I was at a backyard party once watching a one-on-one basketball game between a father and his 9-year-old son. The father had a two-foot height advantage over the son, plus 120 pounds, and 30 years of experience. He was also the dad, trying to have a good time and maybe impart some court smarts to the young spawn of his loins. The game started off merrily and nonchalantly—with the dad giving the young kid gimmes and do-overs to keep him enthused. But about ten minutes into this alleged fun, the father's "gotta win" genes kicked in, and he started playing as if the score mattered. He guarded his son closely, engaged in trash talk, and actually took pleasure in beating him 11 baskets to 2. That's how pervasive this urge to win is. Even when it's beyond trivial—when it actually can scar someone we love—we still want to win.

It's easy to disapprove of this father's behavior from a distance. We assure ourselves that we would never behave so insensitively.

Is that so?

Let's say that you want to go to dinner at restaurant X. Your spouse, partner, or friend wants to go to restaurant Y. You have a heated debate about the choice. You point out the bad reviews Y has received. But you grudgingly yield and end up going to restaurant Y. The experience confirms your misgivings. Your reservation is lost and you have to wait 30 minutes. The service is slow, the drinks weak, and the food tastes like ripe garbage. You have two options during this painful experience. Option A: Critique the restaurant and smugly point out to your partner how wrong he or she was and how this debacle could have been avoided if only *you* had been listened to. Option B: Shut up and eat the food. Mentally write it off and enjoy the evening.

I have polled my clients on these two options for years. The results are consistent: 75 percent of clients say they would critique the restaurant. What do they all agree that they *should* do? Shut up and have a good time. If we do a "cost-benefit analysis" we generally conclude that our relationship with our partner is far more important than winning a trivial argument about where to eat. And yet . . . the urge to win trumps our common sense. We do the wrong thing even when we know what we should do.

It gets worse.

A few years ago, I offered my coaching services free to one of the U.S. Army's top generals. He asked, "Who would be your ideal client?"

I told him, "Your generals are busy people, with even less free time than I have, so let's make it count. I'd like to work with someone who is a smart, dedicated, hard-working, driven-to-achieve, patriotic, wants-to-do-what's-right, technically gifted, hard to replace, brilliant, competent, arrogant, stubborn, opinionated know-it-all. Do you think you could find me one?"

"Find you one?" he laughed. "We have a target-rich environment."

So, I had the opportunity to train many Army generals that first year.

In one group training session with the generals, their wives attended too. It was fun to watch how the generals handled the dinner quiz. About 25 percent of the generals said they would do the right thing—i.e., they'd shut up and enjoy dinner. That's when their wives stood up, gave their husbands a non-approved salute, and ripped into them. The wives said that their husbands would do no such thing. That's how strong the urge to win is. Even with a material witness in the room (i.e., their spouse) who they know will dispute them, many generals still tried to give the answer that made them appear in the most attractive light.

If the need to win is the dominant gene in our success DNA—the overwhelming reason we're successful—then winning too much is a perverse genetic mutation that can limit our success.

What I'm going to suggest repeatedly in this book is the heretical notion that we can become more successful if we appreciate this "flaw" and work to suppress it in our interpersonal relations.

Habit #2 Adding too much value

The two men at dinner were clearly on the same wavelength. One of them was Jon Katzenbach, the ex-McKinsey director who now heads his own elite consulting boutique. The other fellow was Niko Canner, his brilliant protégé and partner. They were plotting out a new venture. But something about their conversation was slightly off. Every time Niko floated an idea, Katzenbach interrupted him. "That's a great idea," he would say, "but it would work better if you . . ." and then he would trail off into a story about how it worked for him several years earlier in another context. When Jon finished, Niko would pick up where he left off only to be interrupted within seconds by Jon again. This went on back and forth like a long rally at Wimbledon.

As the third party at the table, I watched and listened. As an executive coach, I'm used to monitoring people's dialogues, listening with forensic intensity for clues that reveal why these otherwise accomplished people annoy their bosses, peers, and subordinates.

Ordinarily I keep quiet in these situations. But Jon was a friend exhibiting classic destructive smart-person behavior. I said, "Jon, will you please be quiet and let Niko talk. Stop trying to add value to the discussion."

What Jon Katzenbach was displaying in full flower was a variation on the need to win—the need to add value. It's common among leaders used to running the show. They still retain remnants of the top-down management style where their job was to tell everyone what to do. These leaders are smart enough to realize that the world has changed, that most of their subordinates know more in specific areas than they ever will. But old habits die hard. It is extremely difficult for successful people to listen to other people tell them something that they already know without communicating somehow that (a) "we already knew that" and (b) "we know a better way."

That's the problem with adding too much value. Imagine you're the CEO. I come to you with an idea that you think is very good. Rather than just pat me on the back and say, "Great idea!" your inclination (because you have to add value) is to say, "Good idea, but it'd be better if you tried it this way."

The problem is, you may have improved the content of my idea by 5 percent, but you've reduced my commitment to executing it by 50 percent, because you've taken away my ownership of the idea. *My* idea is now *your* idea—and I walk out of your office less enthused about it than when I walked in. That's the fallacy of added value. Whatever we gain in the form of a better idea is lost many times over in our employees' diminished commitment to the concept.

Katzenbach and I had a laugh over this dinner incident later on. As one of the world's leading authorities on team building, Jon should have known better. But that's how pernicious the need to win can be. Even when we know better, we fall into its clutches.

Don't get me wrong. I'm not saying that bosses have to zip their lips to keep their staff's spirits from sagging. But the higher up you go in the organization, the more you need to make other people winners and not make it about winning yourself.

For bosses this means closely monitoring how you hand out encouragement. If you find yourself saying, "Great idea," and then dropping the other shoe with a tempering "but" or "however," try cutting your response off at "idea." Even better, before you speak, take a breath and ask yourself if what you're about to say is worth it. One of my clients, who's now the CEO of a major pharmaceutical, said that once he got into the habit of taking a breath before he talked, he realized that at least half of what he was going to say wasn't worth saying. Even though he believed he could add value, he realized he had more to gain by not winning.

As for employees who have to bear the brunt of their boss's need to add value, be confident about your expertise, and, short of being insubordinate, stick to your position.

Years ago a chocolate maker I know in San Francisco agreed to make a sampler box of twelve chocolates for the late designer Bill Blass. They designed a dozen different chocolates for Blass's approval, which he insisted upon since the chocolates would bear his name. But sensing that he would resent not having a choice, they seeded the selection with a dozen other types which they regarded as clearly inferior. To the chocolatier's horror, when Blass entered the room for the tasting, he liked all the inferior chocolates. The chocolatiers hadn't expected Blass to be so firm in his opinion. But Blass was a man of great taste, used to getting his way, and he knew what he liked. He needed to add value to the process. After Blass left the room, the chocolate makers looked at each other, all thinking the same thing: *What are we going to do? He picked all the wrong ones.*

Finally, the head of the company, which was a family business that had thrived for seven generations, said, "We know chocolate. He doesn't. Let's make the ones we like and he'll never know the difference."

Sweet.

Habit #3 Passing judgment

There's a cute scene between Jack Nicholson and Diane Keaton in the movie *Something's Gotta Give*. Keaton plays a successful fiftyish divorced playwright, while Nicholson is a sixtyish tycoon with a lothario reputation who happens to be dating her daughter. Nicholson is forced to spend a few nights at Keaton's lavish weekend home, recovering from a mild cardiac episode. He and Keaton start off loathing each other but cool off sufficiently to have a flirtatious discussion late one evening in Keaton's kitchen while she prepares a midnight snack.

Keaton says, "I can't imagine what you think of me."

Nicholson asks, "Do you ever miss being married?"

"Sometimes," she says. "Yeah, at night. But not that much anymore."

The subject shifts momentarily to what they want to eat, but Keaton, in a not-so-subtle attempt to elicit feedback, brings the conversation back on point.

"Did one of us just say something interesting?" she muses.

"You said you can't imagine what I think of you."

"You don't have to answer that," she says.

"Okay," he says agreeably.

"But if you have an opinion I'd be curious," says Keaton.

"Will you tell me first why you only miss being married at night?" says Nicholson.

"Well, the phone doesn't ring that much at night. The whole alone thing happens at night. Sleeping by myself took some getting used to. But I got the hang of it. You gotta sleep in the middle of the bed. It's absolutely not healthy to have a side when no one has the other side," she says.

Encouraged by her explanation, Nicholson says, "Now I'm convinced that what I think of you is right. You're a tower of strength."

"Ugh!" says Keaton.

"Try not to rate my answer," says Nicholson.

I know it's only a romantic comedy, but the scene rings true. Even in the most gentle, intimate moments, when people are offering us their most acute (and helpful) snapshots of ourselves, we can't help passing judgment. We can't help ranking what they tell us—lining it up as more pleasing or insightful than what we expected them to say, or what we think ourselves, or what we have heard from others on the same subject.

There's nothing wrong with offering an opinion in the normal give and take of business discussions. You want people to agree or disagree freely.

But it's not appropriate to pass judgment when we specifically ask people to voice their opinions about us. In those moments when other people have passed judgment on advice they have solicited from me, my first thought is, "Who died and made you the Critic in Chief?"

This is true even if you ask a question and agree with the answer. Consciously or not, the other person will register your agreement. And he or she will remember it with great specificity when you *don't* agree the next time. The contrast is telling. The person thinks, "What was wrong with what I said? Why did I bother?"

It's no different than a CEO in a meeting asking for suggestions about a problem and telling one subordinate, "That's a great idea." Then telling another subordinate, "That's a good idea." And saying nothing at all to a third subordinate's suggestion. The first individual is probably pleased and encouraged to have the CEO's approval. The second individual is slightly less pleased. The third individual is neither encouraged nor pleased. But you can be sure of two things. First, everyone in the room has made a note of the CEO's rankings. Second, no matter how well-intentioned the CEO's comments are, the net result is that grading people's answers—rather than just accepting them without comment—makes people hesitant and defensive.

People don't like to be critiqued, however obliquely. That's why passing judgment is one of the more insidious ways we push people away and hold ourselves back from greater success. The only sure thing that comes out of passing judgment on people's efforts to help is that they won't help us again.

How do we stop passing judgment, especially when people are honestly trying to help us?

One of the awkward situations in my line of work is clients being concerned about whether I approve or disapprove of their behavior—and by extension how I feel about the change they're trying to make.

I try to disabuse them of this thinking immediately.

I tell them that in any campaign for effecting long-term positive change, we have a choice. We can view the campaign in an approving light, a disapproving light, or with complete neutrality. Mission Positive. Mission Negative. Or Mission Neutral.

I assure them that I am mission neutral. I don't deal in approval or disapproval. I don't judge. It's not my job to weigh in on whether you're a good person or bad because you've decided to change A rather than B.

It's the same as a medical doctor dealing with patients. If you walk into the examining room with a broken leg, the doctor doesn't pass judgment on how you broke your leg. He doesn't care if you broke your leg committing a crime or kicking the dog or tripping down the stairs or getting hit by a car. He only cares about fixing your leg.

You need to extend that same attitude—the doctor's mission-neutral purpose—to dealing with people trying to help you. And here I am not referring only to the people who are trying to help you change. You are not allowed to judge any helpful comment offered by a colleague or friend or family member. No matter what you privately think of the suggestion, you must keep your thoughts to yourself, hear the person out, and say, "Thank you."

Try this: For one week treat every idea that comes your way from another person with complete neutrality. Think of yourself as a human Switzerland. Don't take sides. Don't express an opinion. Don't judge the comment. If you find yourself constitutionally incapable of just saying "Thank you," make it an innocuous, "Thanks, I hadn't considered that." Or, "Thanks. You've given me something to think about."

After one week, I guarantee you will have significantly reduced the number of pointless arguments you engage in at work or at home. If you continue this for several weeks, at least three good things will happen.

First, you won't have to think about this sort of neutral response; it will become automatic—as easy as saying, "God bless you" when someone sneezes.

Second, you will have dramatically reduced the hours you devote to contentious interfacing. When you don't judge an idea, no one can argue with you.

Third, people will gradually begin to see you as a much more agreeable person, even when you are not in fact agreeing with them. Do this consistently and people will eventually brand you as a welcoming person, someone whose door they can knock on when they have an idea, someone with whom they can spitball casual ideas and not end up spitting at each other.

If you can't self-monitor your judgmental responses, "hire" a friend to call you out and bill you hard cash every time you make a judgmental comment. It could be your spouse at home, your assistant, or a buddy at work. If you're docked $10 for each incident of gratuitous judgment, you'll soon feel the same pain you've been inflicting on others—and stop.

Habit #4 Making destructive comments

Destructive comments are the cutting sarcastic remarks we spew out daily, with or without intention, that serve no other purpose than to put people down, hurt them, or assert ourselves as their superiors. They are different from comments that add too much value—because they add nothing but pain.

They run the gamut from a thoughtless jab in a meeting ("That wasn't very bright") to gratuitous comments about how someone looks ("Nice tie"—with a smirk) to elaborately planned critiques of people's past performances that everyone but you has forgotten. ("Do you remember the time you . . .")

Press people to list the destructive comments they have made in the last 24 hours and they will quite often come up blank. We make destructive comments without thinking—and therefore without noticing or remembering. But the objects of our scorn remember. Press them and they will accurately replay every biting comment we've made at their expense. That's a statistical fact. The feedback I've collected says that "avoids destructive comments" is one of the two items with the lowest correlation between how we see ourselves and how others see us. In other words, we don't think we make destructive comments, but the people who know us disagree.

One of my clients told me that for his fortieth birthday, his colleagues and friends held a "roast" where the evening's theme required everyone to recite one biting remark that he had made over the years at their expense. An interesting gambit: They were making fun of the birthday boy by revisiting the times he had made fun of them. It was a raucous, hilarious evening.

"Here's the thing," said my client. "Of the dozens of nasty funny comments I heard that night, I didn't remember saying one of them. That's how thoughtless they were. Also, my friends didn't hate me for it. They may be called 'destructive' comments but in my group they didn't do any destruction. People considered it a part of who I am, and it wasn't a problem."

He was right; it wasn't. That's the other interesting thing about destructive comments. We think it's common but statistically it's only a problem in 15 percent of my clients. That doesn't mean the other 85 percent of the world is not guilty of making destructive comments. We all make them every day. It indicates that only 15 percent of us do it to the point where it *is* a problem with our colleagues.

What you need to find out is whether that 15 percent includes you.

That's when the real problem begins—because once the comment leaves your lips, the damage is done and it's very hard to undo. You can't take it back. No matter how fervently you apologize—and even if the apology is accepted—the comment lingers in the memory.

One of my clients was having a casual downtime conversation with his assistant about eye color (of all things!).

"What color are your eyes?" he asked, squinting to peer at her eyes.

"They're blue. Can't you see that they're blue?" she said.

"Well, they're not really blue," he said.

"Yes they are," she insisted. "They're a sparkling blue."

"Let's put it this way," he snorted. "If your eyes were diamonds, they'd be selling at Zales, not Harry Winston."

She was visibly crushed by this cruel, gratuitous jab.

The aftermath of this episode is instructive. Within moments of uttering these words, my client erased them from his memory. But his assistant didn't. Even though the comment came at her expense, she replayed the exchange to all her friends—as proof that her boss was a jerk. She replayed it to me when I interviewed her for feedback about her boss. She was making the point that, although she loved working for her boss, he habitually made destructive comments, which she didn't love.

How do we stop making destructive comments? That was my problem several years ago. I was running a small consultancy with a dozen employees. As a feedback professional, I naturally experimented on myself. I had my staff do a full 360 degree evaluation of my behavior. The feedback said I was in the 8th percentile on "avoids destructive comments"— meaning that 92 percent of the people in the world are better at it than I was. I had failed a test that I wrote!

My specific challenge (and I'm not proud of this) was *not* that I made nasty comments to people directly. I would do it when they weren't in the room. This was a problem for me as a manager. In an environment where everyone's preaching the value of teamwork and reaching out in the organization, what happens to the quality of teamwork and cooperation when we stab our coworkers in the back in front of other people? It does not go up. And I wanted the business to succeed.

So I talked to my staff. I said, "I feel good about much of my feedback. Here's one thing I want to do better: Quit making destructive comments. If you ever hear me make another destructive comment about another person, I'll pay you $10 each time you bring it to my attention. I'm going to break this habit."

Then I launched into an emotional pep talk, encouraging them to be honest and diligent about "helping" me. Turns out it wasn't necessary. In fact, they would trick me into making nasty comments because they wanted the $10. They'd mention names of people guaranteed to bring up some bile—and I took the bait each time. They mentioned a colleague named Max and I said, "Can you believe he has a Ph.D? He has no idea what he's talking about." Ten bucks. A customer called and I remarked,

"He's too cheap to pay." Ten bucks. By noon, I was down $50. I locked myself in my office and refused to speak to anyone for the rest of the day. Of course, hiding helps you avoid the issue; it doesn't help you fix it. But the financial pain got me thinking in the right direction. The next day my nasty comments cost me $30. The third day, $10. This policy was in force in our office for several weeks. And it cost me money. But eventually I brought my score up to the 96th percentile. I don't make destructive comments anymore—at least not so it's a problem.

My experience proves a simple point: Spend a few thousand dollars and you will get better!

Destructive comments are an easy habit to fall into, especially among people who habitually rely on candor as an effective management tool. Trouble is, candor can easily become a weapon. People permit themselves to issue destructive comments under the excuse that they are true. The fact that a destructive comment is true is irrelevant. The question is not, "Is it true?" but rather, "Is it worth it?"

What you need to see is that we all spend a great deal of time filtering our truth-telling during the course of each day. I'm not only referring to the little white lies (e.g., complimenting someone's haircut rather than saying it looks ridiculous) that we employ to smooth out each day's routine social exchanges. We instinctively avoid destructive comments when it's a survival issue. We know the difference between honesty and full disclosure. We may think our boss is a complete ass, but we are under no moral or ethical obligation to express that—to the boss's face or to anyone else for that matter.

You need to extend this survival instinct not only up the organization but across and down as well.

Warren Buffett advised that before you take any morally questionable action, you should ask yourself if you would want your mother to read about it in the newspaper.

You can apply a similar test to help you avoid destructive comments. Before speaking, ask yourself:

1. Will this comment help our customers?

2. Will this comment help our company?

3. Will this comment help the person I'm talking to?

4. Will this comment help the person I'm talking about?

If the answer is no, the correct strategy does not require a Ph.D. to implement. Don't say it.

Habit #5 Starting with "No," "But," or "However"

A few years ago the CEO of a manufacturing company hired me to coach his COO. The COO was talented, but stubborn and opinionated.

The first time I met with the COO to go through his direct reports' feedback, his reaction was, "But Marshall, I don't do that."

"That one is free," I said. "Next time I hear 'no,' 'but,' or 'however' it's going to cost you $20."

"But," he replied, "that's not . . ."

"That's $20!"

"No, I don't . . ." he refuted.

"That's $40!"

"No, no, no," he protested.

"That's 60, 80, 100 dollars," I said.

Within an hour, he was down $420. It took another two hours before he finally understood and said, "Thank you."

A year later I knew the COO was getting better when a woman at the company gave a presentation to top management about how few women were in the company's upper ranks (always an explosive issue that makes men jumpy and defensive). After listening to her fundamental argument, the CEO said, "You're making some very interesting points, but . . ."

The COO stood up and cut his boss off. "Excuse me. I think the correct response is, 'Thank you.'"

The CEO glared at him, then smiled and said, "You're right. Thank you." He turned back to the woman and asked her to continue.

When you start a sentence with "no," "but," "however," or any variation thereof, no matter how friendly your tone or how many cute mollifying phrases you throw in to acknowledge the other person's feelings, the message to the other person is *You are wrong*. It's not, "I have a different opinion." It's not, "Perhaps you are misinformed." It's not, "I disagree with you." It's bluntly and unequivocally, "What you're saying is wrong, and what I'm saying is right." Nothing productive can happen after that. The general response from the other person (unless he or she is a saint willing to turn the other cheek) is to dispute your position and fight back. From there, the conversation dissolves into a pointless war. You're no longer communicating. You're both trying to win.

There aren't too many cheap, surefire, simple, guaranteed 100 percent accurate peeks into the competitive makeup of our colleagues and friends. But the following drill fits the bill. For one week monitor your coworkers' use of "no," "but," and "however": Keep a scorecard of how many times each individual uses these three words to start a sentence.

At the very least, you'll be shocked at how commonly used these words are.

If you drill a little deeper, patterns will emerge. You'll see how people inflict these words on others to gain or consolidate power. You'll also see how intensely people resent it, consciously or not, and how it stifles rather than opens up discussion.

I monitor my clients' use of "no," "but," and "however" instinctively now, the same way an orchestra conductor hears musicians playing sharp or flat. Without even thinking, I keep count of their usage. It's such an important indicator that I do it on autopilot. If the numbers pile up in an initial meeting with a client, I'll often interrupt him or her to say, "We've been talking for 40 minutes. Do you realize in that time you have started 17 responses with either no, but, or however?"

The client is *never* aware of it. That's the moment a serious talk about changing behavior begins.

If this is your interpersonal challenge, you can do this for yourself just as easily as I do it for my clients.

Stop trying to defend your position and start monitoring how many times you begin remarks with "no," "but," or "however." Pay extra-close attention to those moments when you use these words in sentences whose ostensible purpose is *agreement* with what the other party is saying. For example, "That's true, however . . ." (Meaning: You don't think it's true at all.) Or the particularly common opener, "Yes, but . . ." (Meaning: Prepare to be contradicted.)

As in almost any one of these exercises to stop annoying behavior, in addition to self-monitoring, it's easy to monetize the solution. Do what I did with the manufacturing COO. Ask a friend or colleague to charge you money every time you say "no," "but," or "however."

Once you appreciate how guilty you have been, maybe then you'll begin to change your "winning" ways. (Irony intended.)

That said, it's still a challenge.

A few years ago I taught a class at a telecom headquarters. One of the men in my class mocked me when I mentioned this problem we have with "no," "but," and "however." He thought it was easy not to use the words. He was so sure of himself that he offered $100 for each time he used them. I made a point of sitting with him during the lunch break. I asked him where he was from, and he replied Singapore.

"Singapore?" I said. "That's a great city."

"Yeah," he replied, "it's great but . . ."

He caught himself and reached into his pocket for cash, saying, "I just lost $100, didn't I?"

That's how pervasive the urge to be right can be. "No," "but," and "however" creep into our conversations even when the discussion is trivial, even when we should be hyperaware of our word choices, even when it costs us $100.

Habit #6 Telling the world how smart we are

This is another variation on our need to win. We need to win people's admiration. We need to let them know that we are at least their intellectual equal if not their superior. We need to be the smartest person in the room. It usually backfires.

Many of us do this covertly and unwittingly all day long.

We do it whenever we agree with someone offering us some practical advice, whenever we nod our heads impatiently while people are talking, whenever our body language suggests that we are not hearing something we haven't heard before. (Are those your drumming fingers I hear?)

We do this more overtly when we tell someone, "I already knew that."

(Alternative phrasings run the gamut from the gently chiding, "I think someone told me that," to the sarcastic, "I didn't need to hear that," to the downright arrogant, "I'm five steps ahead of you.") The problem here is not that we're merely boasting about how much we know. We're insulting the other person.

What we are really saying is, "You really didn't need to waste my time with that information. You think it's an insight that I haven't heard before. But I agree with you and totally understand what you are saying. You mistake me, the ever so wise and lovely me, for someone who needs to hear what you are saying right now. I am not that person. You are confused. You have no idea how smart I am."

Imagine if someone actually said all that to your face. You'd think they were a jackass. But that's what people hear (and think) when you say, "I already knew that." You're better off hearing them out and saying nothing at all.

The paradox is that this need to demonstrate how smart we are rarely hits its intended target.

A friend was interviewing for a research assistant's job with a psychology professor. The professor was writing a book on genius and creativity. During the course of the interview, the subject turned to great geniuses—specifically Mozart. The professor boasted that he had read everything he could find about Mozart. This is typical of academics; they are exceedingly proud of their intellects and never pass up a chance to tell the world how smart they are. But this professor went a step further. To prove his depth of knowledge he challenged my friend to ask him any question about Mozart.

My friend demurred, a little surprised at the strange turn the job interview had taken. But at the same time, his brain was working overtime. Classical music and opera, as luck would have it, were his great passion. He, in fact, knew more than most people about Mozart.

"Go ahead," said the professor, "don't be shy. I can handle it."

My friend begged off again, although by now he was running potential questions through his mind. Where was Mozart born? When did he die? What was his sister's name? (All too easy.)

"Indulge me," the professor insisted. "Unless of course you don't know enough to ask a question."

That rhetorical slap in the face clinched it for my friend.

"Okay," he said, "name thirteen Mozart operas."

To a self-proclaimed Mozart fanatic, identifying thirteen operas (Mozart composed at least 20 of them) should have been a snap—like asking a presidential historian to name all the vice presidents. Alas, the professor could only name nine.

An awkward moment in the interview, thought my friend, feeling both sheepish and triumphant. There *was* a smart person in the room, but he wasn't the one boasting about it.

To the professor's credit, he didn't hold it against my friend. He offered him the job on the spot.

To my friend's credit, he declined.

Being smart turns people on. Announcing how smart you are turns them off.

So, how do you tone down the need to tell the world how smart you are?

The first step is recognizing our behavior. Have you ever done this? Your assistant dashes into your office with a document that needs your immediate attention. What your assistant doesn't know is that you've already been alerted to the situation a few minutes earlier by another colleague. What do you do? Do you accept the document and thank your assistant, omitting the fact that you already are up to speed on the matter? Or do you find some way to make your assistant aware that you are privy to the information?

In my experience, this seemingly insignificant moment is a litmus test for our excessive need to tell people how smart we are.

If you can let the moment pass with a simple "Thank you," you're doing fine.

If you're like most people, though, you won't let it go so easily. You'll find a way to communicate that you are a step ahead of your assistant. The manner in which you do this may vary from a simple, "I already knew that," to a dismissive, "Why are you bothering me with this?" But either way, the damage is done.

The implication is that your assistant has just wasted your time, that your assistant has confused you with someone who is *not up to speed* on all things vital and urgent, that your assistant has no clue how smart you really are.

Stopping this behavior is not hard—a three-step drill in which you (a) pause before opening your mouth to ask yourself, "Is anything I say worth it?" (b) conclude that it isn't, and (c) say, "Thank you."

If you can stop yourself in this minor moment with someone who works closely with you and presumably knows you well—in other words, when nothing is at stake and you don't have to flex your muscles—you have the skill to stop telling the world how smart you are. After all, if you can resist the urge in a really comfortable moment when you are in a dominant position, you will certainly hesitate in other situations when you are not so dominant and comfortable. Think about it. If your CEO walked into your office brandishing the same document, would you tell him or her in the same contemptuous tone that you "already knew that"?

Habit #7 Speaking when angry

Anger has its value as a management tool, I guess. It wakes up sleepy employees. It raises everyone's metabolism. It delivers the clear message that you give a damn—which employees need to hear on occasion. But at what price?

Emotional volatility is not the most reliable leadership tool. When you get angry, you are usually out of control. It's hard to lead people when you've lost control. You may think you have a handle on your temper, that you can use your spontaneous rages to manipulate and motivate people. But it's very hard to predict how people will react to anger. They will shut down as often as they will perk up.

Whenever I hear managers justify anger as a management tool, I wonder about all those other leaders who do not need anger to make their subordinates toe the line. Without anger to strike fear in the troops, how do these steady composed leaders ever get anything accomplished?

But the worst thing about anger is how it stifles our ability to change. Once you get a reputation for emotional volatility, you are branded for life. Pretty soon that is all people know about you. For example, basketball coach Bob Knight won three NCAA titles at Indiana University and is only one of two coaches in college history with 800 or more victories. By any measure, he's one of the greatest coaches of all time. But he also has a well-documented history of arguing with referees and tossing chairs across the court. That reputation overwhelms Knight's record. When people think of Bob Knight, their first thought is his volcanic temper, not his won-lost record.

It's the same in the workplace. We save a special place in our minds for our chronically angry colleagues. No matter what else they do, we brand them as easily combustible. When we talk about them, the first words out of people's mouths are, "I hear he has a temper."

That hothead image is tough to live down. Given the fact that our efforts to change are judged not by us but by the people around us, you may need years of calm, collected behavior to shake such a reputation.

How do you stop getting angry?

I don't have a definitive answer. Anger management is not the subject of this book, and even if it were, I doubt if I could shut down your rages at life's injustices and follies. But I can make you appreciate that (a) you're probably not angry at the proverbial "other guy" and (b) there's a simple way to lose your reputation for getting angry.

On the first point, when I have to deal with anger in my line of work, it's invariably one-on-one rage—the anger that one human being induces in another. It's my job to show clients that anger is rarely someone else's fault. It's a flaw that's solely our own.

A Buddhist legend tells of a young farmer who was covered with sweat as he paddled his boat up the river. He was going upstream to deliver his produce to the village. He was in a hurry. It was a hot day and he wanted to make his delivery and get home before dark. As he looked ahead, he spied another vessel, heading rapidly downstream toward his boat. This vessel seemed to be making every effort to hit him. He rowed furiously to get out of the way, but it didn't seem to help.

He yelled at the other vessel, "Change direction, you idiot! You are going to hit me. The river is wide. Be careful!" His screaming was to no avail. The other vessel hit his boat with a sickening thud. He was enraged as he stood up and cried out to the other vessel, "You moron! How could you manage to hit my boat in the middle of this wide river? What is wrong with you?"

As he looked at the other vessel, he realized that there was no one in the other boat. He was screaming at an empty vessel that had broken free of its moorings and was going downstream with the current.

The lesson is simple. *There is never anyone in the other boat.* When we are angry, we are screaming at an empty vessel.

All of us have people in our lives who drive us crazy, whom we hate with a passion. We may have spent countless hours reliving the moments when this person was unfair, unappreciative, or inconsiderate to us. Even remembering this person bumps up our blood pressure.

It's obvious that the best course of action for dealing with people like this is to not let them make us angry. Getting angry doesn't improve the situation and life's too short to waste on feeling bad. A sage would say that the person making us so angry cannot help who he is. Getting mad at him for being who he is makes as much sense as getting mad at our desk for being a desk. If we had his parents, his genes, and his background, we would be him. That's easier said than done, but it comes closer to the real issue: More often than not, we might as well be him because we are really angry at ourselves.

As to the second point, I can help you lose your reputation as a person who gets angry with one simple piece of advice. It is this: *If you keep your mouth shut, no one can ever know how you really feel.*

That's asking a lot, I know. You have to suppress your natural inclination and bite your tongue. But once you appreciate the payoff of saying nothing—that if you're silent, you cannot make an ass out of yourself or make an enemy out of someone else—then you might have a chance of getting better.

I learned this after spending a week at a retreat at a small monastery in Plum Village, France, a few years ago. Our guide was the Vietnamese Buddhist monk, Thich Nhat Hanh. Each day Thich Nhat Hanh encouraged us to meditate on a variety of topics. One day the topic was anger. He asked us to think of a time in our lives when we had become angry and lost control. Then he asked us to analyze who was responsible for our unattractive behavior.

I thought of my daughter Kelly when she was in her teens. She came home wearing a large brightly colored article of jewelry called a navel ring. These are common among the younger set, along with tattoos in hard-to-reach places of the human anatomy. There is no use having a navel ring if people can't see it! So Kelly had also acquired a heroically skimpy outfit designed to highlight the navel ring (and nearly everything else about her abdomen).

A navel ring on a daughter is one of those moments that truly tests a father's tolerance and love. But for me it was a little more complicated, I guess. I reacted with something less than enthusiasm. In fact, I devolved into a raving, ranting caricature of an angry father.

As I meditated on this event in the quiet confines of the monastery, I wondered, "What was I thinking about?" I realized that my first thought was that someone would see my daughter and think, "What a cheap-looking, trashy kid! Who are her parents?"

My second thought was worse. What if one of my friends saw her and thought, "I can't believe Marshall allows his kid to parade around town like that."

Who was I concerned about in this case? Kelly or me? Was the bigger problem her navel ring or my ego?

If I had to do it over again, I would still suggest she lose the navel ring. (One week of enlightenment in France is good, but not *that* good!) However, I would stop reacting with anger and making a fool out of myself. I may be raging like a lunatic inside. But if I stop speaking when angry, no one has to know about it.

The next time you start to speak out of anger, look in the mirror. In every case, you'll find that the root of your rage is not "out there" but "in here."

Habit #8 Negativity, or "Let me explain why that won't work."

We all know negative people—or what my wife calls "negatrons"—in the workplace. They're the people who are constitutionally incapable of saying something positive or complimentary to any of your suggestions. Negativity is their default response. You could walk into their office with the cure for cancer and the first words out of their mouth would be, "Let me explain why that won't work."

That, in my experience, is the telltale phrase of negativity. I cite it as a major annoyance because it's emblematic of our need to share our negative thoughts even when they haven't been solicited.

"Let me explain why that won't work" is not quite the same as adding too much value—because no value is being added.

It's not like overusing "no," "but," and "however," because we're not hiding our negativity under the mask of agreement.

Nor is it the same as passing judgment on someone else's ideas—because we're not rating or comparing anything. We're not saying it's good, better, or best.

It's clearly not the same as making destructive comments—because it's not overtly nasty.

"Let me explain why that won't work" is unique because it is pure unadulterated negativity under the guise of being helpful.

We employ it (or its variations such as "The only problem with that is . . .") to establish that our expertise or authority is superior to someone else's. It doesn't mean that what we say is correct or useful. It's simply a way of inserting ourselves into a situation as chief arbiter or senior critic. The only problem with that (to coin a phrase) is how little we like or respect our critics. They're annoying. And over time, we treat them as if they're carrying avian flu. We avoid them. We stop working with them. We refuse to help them.

I used to know a woman named Terri who ran a lecture bureau in New York City. Two or three times a year she would book me to speak to a corporate group. I'd talk about leadership and helping people change. At the end of each speech, invariably one or two people in the audience would come up to me, hand me their cards, and invite me to speak to their group in the near future. Apparently, I was delivering a message that they thought other people would want to hear.

I could have handled the details of the speaking appearance myself, I suppose, but because the invitation occurred on a date that Terri had set up for me, I felt obliged to turn it over to her. I thought it was only right that she negotiate for me and earn her commission. I'd call her up immediately after the appearance.

She'd ask how the event turned out. Was the host pleased? That sort of thing.

I'd say, "Great. In fact, a couple of people want me to speak to their groups."

Then I'd read the contact information off their business cards so she could follow up with them.

Without fail, Terri's first response was always some variation on "Let me explain why that won't work."

The company had a history of paying low fees, so they couldn't afford me. (Message: I was too expensive.)

The company's employees were yokels who didn't need to hear my message or were too ignorant to "get it." (Message: I was too sophisticated.)

The company would abuse my time; they'd want me to stay all day, including dinner, costing me an extra travel day. (Message: I'd be overworked.)

When Terri responded this way, I'd hold the receiver out and stare at it, dumbfounded. Here I was throwing easy money at her, and she was coming up with bogus reasons to shoot me down. Perhaps she thought she was protecting me from a potentially "bad deal." But in trying to prove to me that she knew more about her business than I did, she only proved that she didn't understand me at all. I don't overcharge clients. My message is simple, not complicated. And I'm not afraid of work; if clients want me to stick around all day, I take it as a compliment, not an abuse of my time.

It made me wonder if I really wanted Terri "presenting" me to the world.

Eventually I realized that I could have been forwarding Terri an invitation for me to host the Academy Awards and she would have found a way to put a negative spin on the opportunity. I stopped working with her.

If negativity is your flaw, my first impulse would be to have you monitor your statements the moment someone offers you a helpful suggestion. If you've read this far, you know that I firmly believe that paying attention to *what we say* is a great indicator of what we're doing to turn people off. If you catch yourself frequently saying, "Let me tell you why that won't work," you know what needs fixing.

But in this case, the more revealing clue would be to take a personal inventory of how your colleagues deal with you.

How often do they come to you with helpful suggestions—without you having to ask?

How often do they knock on your door and sit down to shoot the breeze or give you a heads-up about a development that may affect you?

How does the floor traffic around your desk compare with other colleagues? Are you a popular item, or are you beginning to gather dust on the shelf? If you get even the vaguest sense that there is an imaginary "Do Not Enter" sign outside your office, you've just become a little smarter about what you must change.

When the issue is negativity, I prefer this form of observational feedback to mere monitoring of speech patterns. Checking what you say doesn't automatically tell you what other people think of you. You may be overly negative, but your colleagues may be capable of living with it. But seeing how people relate to you provides proof that *your flaw is serious,* that it matters to people, that it's a problem.

Habit #9 Withholding information

In the age of knowledge workers, the cliché that information is power is truer than ever—which makes withholding information even more extreme and irritating.

Intentionally withholding information is the opposite of adding value. We are deleting value. Yet it has the same purpose: To gain power. It's the same old need to win, only more devious. And it appears in more forms than merely playing our cards close to our vest. You see it in people who exaggerate the virtue of keeping a secret; they use it as an excuse to leave you out of the information flow. You see it in people who answer every question with a question; they believe revealing *anything* puts them at a disadvantage. You see it in its passive-aggressive incarnation in people who don't return your phone calls or answer your e-mails or only give partial answers to your queries.

If you don't understand why it annoys people, reflect on how you felt about the following events:

- A meeting you weren't told about

- A memo or e-mail you weren't copied on

- A moment when you were the last person to learn something

The problem with not sharing information—for whatever reason—is that it rarely achieves the desired effect. You may think you're gaining an edge and consolidating power, but you're actually breeding mistrust. In order to have power, you need to inspire loyalty rather than fear and suspicion. Withholding information is nothing more than a misplaced need to win.

What I'm describing here is not just the willful poison-sowing refusal to share information, the way people behave when they want to divide and conquer. I'm not sure I have the skill or patience to alter that Machiavellian behavior.

What I'd prefer to focus on are all the unintentional or accidental ways we withhold information.

We do this when we're too busy to get back to someone with valuable information.

We do this when we forget to include someone in our discussions or meetings.

We do this when we delegate a task to our subordinates but don't take the time to show them exactly how we want the task done.

One of my neighbors asked his teenaged son to wash his Lexus SUV. The son pulled out the water hose, filled a bucket with soapy water, and went to work with a sponge. Problem was, the sponge was one of those two-sided designs, one side scratchy, the other soft. By the time the father came out to inspect the results, the son had scrubbed away a good deal of the Lexus's shiny enamel finish. The Lexus's once-gleaming surface looked like an ice skating rink after a hockey game. The father was enraged. His Lexus was ruined. How could his son be so stupid?

"Don't you know how to do something as simple as washing a car?" he asked between snorts of rage.

But as my neighbor thought about it (and as he saw that his son was embarrassed and upset), he said something wise. "Son, I'm not mad at you. I'm mad at myself—because I should have told you how to do this job properly. I never taught you how to wash a car, and that's my fault."

Whatever tension hovered over that scene in the family driveway at that moment instantly disappeared when my neighbor realized that he had left some vital information out of his son's basic education. The son felt relieved. The father was no longer upset, either at his son or at the sorry condition of his Lexus. It's now a running family joke whenever someone sees a sponge.

More often than not, we don't withhold information out of malice. We do it because we're clueless. That's a good thing. Willful maliciousness is not a "flaw" that we can fix here. But cluelessness is easy to change.

I was advising a friend who was having trouble with his assistant. They weren't meshing as a team, he told me. But he didn't know why or how to fix the problem. All he had to go on was a vague feeling that "our timing is off."

Before I talked to his assistant, I asked him, "What would your assistant say is your biggest flaw as a boss?"

"That I don't communicate enough with her," he answered. "I don't share information. I leave her out of the loop."

"Anything else?" I inquired.

"No, that's it," he said. "Isn't that enough?"

"Do you think she's right?" I asked.

"Yes."

Interesting, I thought. You don't hear too many bosses taking all the blame for some interpersonal dysfunction.

Then I asked his assistant why they didn't mesh. She agreed. Her boss didn't share information well.

Because he was a friend, and I was helping him pro bono, I did something I don't normally do. I pretended to be a consumer researcher who tracks how people use a company's product all day. In this case, I tagged along with him from the moment he walked into work and observed his behavior with his assistant until he left work.

What I saw explained everything. He arrived at the office about fifteen minutes before his assistant. The first thing he did was check his e-mails. Then his cell phone rang and he answered it. During this conversation, his assistant arrived at her desk. She poked her head in to say good morning. He waved while still talking. When he ended the call, he turned to his computer screen and jotted down some notes and answered a few e-mails. His assistant popped in to say that one of his accounts was on the line. Did he want to take that call? He did. Three other calls came in during this twenty-minute conversation. When he hung up, he returned those calls—all the while scanning his computer for incoming e-mails. This pattern continued all morning.

By noon I had seen enough.

"Is this what it's like around here every day?" I asked.

"Pretty much," he said.

My friend, indeed, was guilty of keeping his assistant in the dark. But he wasn't doing so maliciously or, for that matter, intentionally. His work life was like a haphazard fire drill. He was so distracted, so disorganized, so busy responding to calls and putting out fires that he never had time to sit down with his assistant for a daily debriefing.

If he had, I suspect it would have solved their information sharing issue.

I also suspect that's a big reason why so many of us withhold information. It's not that we want to keep people in the dark. It's simply that we're too busy. We mean well. We have good intentions. But we fail to get around to it. As a result we become bad at sharing information—whether it comes in the form of a news bulletin, or a heads-up, or instruction that teaches people how to do something that we don't have time to do ourselves. Over time it begins to look as if we are *withholding* information.

Being bad at sharing information doesn't mean we are willfully withholding it. The two are not exactly the same thing. But the net result is the same in the eyes of the people around us.

How do you stop withholding information?

Simple answer: Start sharing it.

That's what my friend did. He made sharing information a higher priority in his busy day. He scheduled time to debrief his assistant on what he was up to. And he made that time inviolate. It couldn't be cancelled or postponed or interrupted by a phone call.

If this is your issue, I advise the same solution. In doing so, you will not only improve your communication, but you'll be proving that you care about your coworkers—demonstrating that what they think matters to you. It's not often that we get such an obvious two-for-the-price-of-one solution to our interpersonal challenges. But making the subtle shift from withholding to sharing information is one of them.

Habit #10 Failing to give proper recognition

This is a sibling of withholding information. In withholding your recognition of another person's contribution to a team's success, you are not only sowing injustice and treating people unfairly but you are depriving people of the emotional payoff that comes with success. They cannot revel in the success or accept congratulations—because you have choked off that option. Instead they feel forgotten, ignored, pushed to the side. And they resent you for it. If you really want to tick people off, don't recognize their contributions.

In depriving people of recognition, you are depriving them of closure. And we all need closure in any interpersonal transaction. Closure comes in many forms—from the emotional complexity of paying our last respects to loved ones before they die to something as pro forma as saying, "You're welcome" when someone else says, "Thank you." Either way, we expect closure.

Recognition is all about closure. It's the beautiful ribbon wrapped around the jewel box that contains the precious gift of success you and your team have created. When you fail to provide that recognition, you are cheapening the gift. You have the success but none of the afterglow.

This happens at work and at home.

In training programs, when I ask participants, "How many of you think you need to do a better job of recognizing others for their great work?" without fail eight out of ten people raise their hands.

When I ask them why they fail at recognition, the answers say more about the people responding than the people who aren't being recognized. "*I* just got too busy." "*I* just expected everyone to do great work." "*I* never realized how important it was to them." "*I* was never recognized for my great work—why should they be?"

Note the aggressive use of the first person singular pronoun. It's a hallmark of successful people; they become great *achievers* because of their intense focus on themselves. *Their* career, *their* performance, *their* progress, *their* needs. But there's a difference between being an achiever and a leader. Successful people become great *leaders* when they learn to shift the focus from themselves to others.

One of my clients taught me a wonderful technique for improving in the area of providing recognition.

1. He first made a list of all of the important groups of people in his life (friends, family, direct reports, customers, etc.).

2. He then wrote down the names of every important person in each group.

3. Twice a week, on Wednesday morning and Friday afternoon, he would review the list of names and ask himself, "Did someone on this page do something that I should recognize?"

4. If the answer was "yes" he gave them some very quick recognition, either by phone, e-mail, voice mail, or a note. If the answer was "no" he did nothing. He didn't want to be a phony.

Within one year this executive's reputation for providing positive recognition improved from poor to excellent. He was amazed at how little time this took.

Of all the interpersonal slights we make in our professional or private lives, not providing recognition may be the one that endures most deeply in the minds of the slighted. Except for . . .

Habit #11 Claiming credit that we don't deserve

Claiming credit is adding insult to the injury that comes with overlooked recognition. We're not only depriving people of the credit they deserve, but we are hogging it for ourselves. It's two crimes in one.

Imagine those moments in your life—whether as a schoolkid or an adult in the workplace—when you did something wonderful and waited for the praise and congratulations. And waited. And waited. It happens all the time. The world isn't always paying attention when we excel. People have their own agendas to pursue. If it happens when we're kids, we sulk and whimper about being overlooked. "It's not fair!" we whine. But as we mature, we learn to handle the neglect. "It's the way of the world," we tell ourselves. It doesn't alter the fact that we did something special—even if we're the only ones to know it. We move on to something else.

But even the most highly evolved human being would have a tough time grinning and bearing when neglect turns to larceny. That's what it is when someone claims credit that they do not deserve: theft. It's as if they're stealing our ideas, our performances, our self-esteem, our life. We didn't like it when it happened to us as children (and the stakes generally involved little more than our teachers' approval). But we actively hate it when it happens to us as adults (in part because the stakes in terms of our careers and financial rewards are so much greater). When someone you work with steals the credit for a success that you created, they're committing the most rage-inducing interpersonal "crime" in the workplace. (This is the interpersonal flaw that generates more negative emotion than any other in my feedback interviews.) And it creates a bitterness that's hard to forget. You can forgive someone for not recognizing your stellar performance. You can't forgive that person for recognizing it and brazenly claiming it as his or her own. If it's happened to you, you know how hard it is to shed that bitter taste.

Now turn the tables. Imagine you're the perpetrator rather than the victim.

If you look closely, you'll see that claiming credit that we don't deserve is another sibling of the need to win. You wouldn't claim someone else's résumé or college degree as your own. That's because those achievements are well-documented. Your claim can be challenged. But when it comes to determining exactly who came up with the winning phrase in a meeting or who held together an important client relationship during a rocky phase, the evidence gets fuzzy. It's hard to say who deserves the credit. So, given the choice between grasping the credit for ourselves or leaving it for someone else to claim, we fall into the success traps described in Chapter 3—I can succeed, I will succeed, I have succeeded, I choose to succeed—and give ourselves the benefit of the doubt. We claim more credit than we have earned, and slowly begin to believe it. In the meantime, the victims of our injustice are seething. If you know how you feel as a victim, you should know how people feel about you for doing the same. It's not a pretty picture, is it?

There's no telling what a group can achieve when no one cares who gets the credit. We know this in our bones. We know it because we remember how good we felt about our colleagues when they accorded us the credit we deserved.

So why don't we reciprocate when someone else deserves the credit?

I don't have the answer for that. Even if we can legitimately blame our parents or our upbringing or some petty slight in high school for our credit hogging, that doesn't begin to solve the problem. It's focusing on the past (which we cannot change) rather than arming ourselves with concrete actionable ideas for the future.

The best way to stop being a credit hog is to do the opposite. Share the wealth. Here's a simple drill that will transform you from a credit miser to a credit philanthropist.

For one day (or longer if you can handle it) make a mental note of every time you privately congratulate yourself on an achievement, large or small. Then write it down. If you're like me, you'll find that you pat yourself on the back more often than you think during a normal day—for everything from coming up with a big idea for a client to showing up on time for a meeting to dashing off a clever note to a colleague.

"Hmm," we think as we survey our beautiful handiwork. "We did good."

There's nothing wrong with these private thoughts. This pleasure that we take in our own performance is what keeps us merrily motivated as we chug our way through a long, arduous day. I wouldn't be surprised if one day yielded two dozen episodes of self-congratulation for each of us.

Once you've assembled the list, take apart each episode and ask yourself if it's *in any way possible* that someone else might deserve the credit for "your" achievement.

If you showed up on time for a meeting across town, is it because you are heroically punctual and thoughtful? Or was it because your assistant hounded you that morning about the meeting and actually chased you off a phone call and made sure you were out the door to get across town in sufficient time?

If you came up with a good idea in a meeting, did it spring unbidden from your fertile imagination? Or was it inspired by an insightful comment from someone else in the room?

As you go through your list, consider this make-or-break question: If any of the other people involved in your episodes were looking at the situation, would they accord you as much credit as you are claiming for yourself? Or would they hand it out to someone else, perhaps even themselves?

It's possible as you review your list that you conclude you deserve *all* the credit. But I doubt even the most self-involved among us would see things this myopically. We have a strong bias to remember events in a light most favorable to us. This drill exposes that bias and makes us consider the possibility that someone else's perspective is closer to the truth.

Habit #12 Making excuses

When Bill Clinton published his best-selling memoir in 2004, he knew he would have to deal with the Monica Lewinsky scandal during his second term. He did so by *explaining* it as a personal failure, a yielding to private demons. "Once people reach the age of accountability, no matter what people do to them," he said, "that is not an excuse for any mistakes they make. On the other hand, one does seek to understand why he or she makes the mistakes they make. I was involved in two great struggles at the same time: a great public struggle over the future of America with the Republican Congress and a private struggle with my old demons. I won the public one and lost the private one. I don't think it's much more complicated than that. That's not an excuse. But it is an explanation, and that's the best I can do."

Bill Clinton understood the distinction—and not just because his behavior was inexcusable. There simply is no excuse for making excuses.

When you hear yourself saying, "I'm sorry I'm late but the traffic was murder," stop talking at the word "sorry." Blaming the traffic is a lame excuse—and doesn't excuse the fact that you kept people waiting. You should have started earlier. What's the worst that could happen? You arrive ahead of schedule and have to wait a few minutes in the lobby? Are you really worried about having to say, "I'm sorry I'm early but I left too soon and the traffic was nowhere near as bad as I anticipated."

If the world worked *that* way, there would be no excuses.

I like to divide excuses into two categories: blunt and subtle.

The blunt "dog ate my homework" excuse sounds like this: "I'm sorry I missed our lunch date. My assistant had it marked down for the wrong day on my calendar."

Message: See, it's not that I forgot the lunch date. It's not that I don't regard you as important, so important that lunch with you is the unchangeable, nonnegotiable highlight of my day. It's simply that my assistant is inept. Blame my assistant, not me.

The problem with this type of excuse is that we rarely get away with it—and it's hardly an effective leadership strategy. After reviewing thousands of 360-degree feedback summaries, I have a feel for what direct reports respect and don't respect in their leaders. I have never seen feedback that said, "I think you are a great leader because I love the quality of your excuses." Or, "I thought you were messing up, but you turned me around when you made those excuses."

The more subtle excuses appear when we attribute our failings to some inherited DNA that is permanently lodged within us. We talk about ourselves as if we have permanent genetic flaws that can never be altered.

You've surely heard these excuses. Maybe you've used them to describe yourself:

"I'm impatient."

"I always put things off to the last minute."

"I've always had a quick temper."

"I am horrendous at time management. I've been told for years by my coworkers and spouse that I waste time on pointless projects and discussions. I guess that's just the way I am."

It's amazing how often I hear otherwise brilliant, successful people make willfully self-deprecating comments about themselves. It's a subtle art because, in effect, they are stereotyping themselves—as impatient, or hot-tempered, or disorganized—and using that stereotype to excuse otherwise inexcusable behavior.

Our personal stereotyping may have its origins in stories that have been repeated for years—often from as far back as childhood. These stories may have no basis in fact. But they imprint themselves in our brains, and establish low expectations that become self-fulfilling prophecies. We behave as if we wanted to prove that our negative expectations were correct.

I'm a good example of this. Growing up in Valley Station, Kentucky, I might naturally have become involved in cars, tools, and mechanical things. My dad owned a two-pump gas station. Many of my friends liked to work on cars and race them on Saturday nights at the drag strip.

As a child, however, I gained a different set of expectations from my mother. Almost from birth, she told me, "Marshall, you are extremely smart. In fact, you are the smartest little boy in Valley Station." She told me that I wasn't just going to go to college—I could go to graduate school!

She also said, "Marshall, you have no mechanical skills, and you will never have any mechanical skills for the rest of your life." (I think this was her way of making sure I wouldn't pump gas and change tires at the service station.)

It's interesting how my mother's imprinting and expectations affected my development. I was never encouraged to work on cars or be around tools. (As a teenager in the 1960s, I thought a universal joint was something that hippies smoked.) Not only did my parents assume that I had no mechanical skills, my friends knew it, too. When I was 18 years old, I took the U.S. Army's Mechanical Aptitude Test and scored in the bottom second percentile of the entire nation. So, it was true.

Six years later, however, I was at UCLA, working on my Ph.D. One of my professors asked me to write down things I did well and things I couldn't do. On the positive side I jotted down "research" and "writing" and "analysis" and "speaking" (which was a not-so-subtle way of writing "I am smart"). On the negative side, I wrote, "I have no mechanical skills. I will never have any mechanical skills."

The professor asked me how I knew I had no mechanical skills. I explained my life history and told him about my dismal showing on the Army test.

"How are your mathematical skills?" he asked.

I proudly replied that I had scored a perfect 800 on the SAT Math 1 achievement test.

He then asked, "Why is it that you can solve complex mathematical problems, but you can't solve simple mechanical problems?"

Then he asked, "How is your eye-hand coordination?"

I said that I was good at pinball and had helped pay my college expenses by shooting pool, so I guessed that it was fine.

He asked, "Why is it that you can shoot pool but you can't hammer nails?"

That's when I realized that I did not suffer from a genetic defect. I was just living out the expectations that I had chosen to believe. At that point, I was old enough to know better. It was no longer just my family and friends reinforcing my belief that I was mechanically hopeless. And it wasn't the Army test, either. I was the one who kept telling myself, "You can't do this!" I realized that as long as I kept saying that, it was going to be true.

The next time you hear yourself saying, "I'm just no good at . . . ," ask yourself, "Why not?"

This doesn't just refer to our aptitudes at mathematics or mechanics. It also applies to our behavior. We excuse our tardiness because we've been running late all our lives—and our parents and friends let us get away with it. The same with any of the other annoying habits we've been describing. Passing judgment, making destructive comments, refusing to share information? These are not genetic flaws! We weren't born that way, no matter what we've been brought up to believe.

Likewise the next time you hear one of your coworkers try to worm their way out of accepting responsibility by saying, "I'm just no good at . . . ," ask them, "Why not?"

If we can stop excusing ourselves, we can get better at almost anything we choose.

Habit #13 Clinging to the past

There is a school of thought among psychologists and behavioral consultants that we can understand a lot about our errant behavior by delving into our past, particularly our family dynamics. This is the school that believes, "When it's hysterical, it's historical."

If you're a perfectionist or constant-approval seeker, it's because your parents never said you were good enough. If you operate above the rules and feel you can do no wrong, it's because your parents doted on you and inflated your importance. If you freeze around authority figures, it's because you had a controlling mother. And so on.

That school is on permanent recess here.

I don't have much patience with "therapy" that clings to the past—because going backwards is not about creating change. It's about understanding.

One of my earliest clients used to spend hours telling me, "Marshall, you don't understand. Let me explain why I have these issues. Let me explain my mother and father." It was one long unendurable whine. Finally, I reached into my pocket for a coin and said, "Here's a quarter. Call someone who cares."

Don't get me wrong. There's nothing wrong with understanding. Understanding the past is perfectly admissible if your issue is *accepting the past*. But if your issue is *changing the future*, understanding will not take you there. My experience tells me that the only effective approach is looking people in the eye and saying, "If you want to change, do this."

But even with the blunt talk, clients who cling to the past—who want to *understand* why they are the way they are—remain my toughest assignments. It takes me a long time to convince them that they can't do anything about the past. They can't change it, or rewrite it, or make excuses for it. All they can do is accept it and move on.

But for some reason, many people enjoy living in the past, especially if going back there lets them blame someone else for anything that's gone wrong in their lives. That's when clinging to the past becomes an interpersonal problem. We use the past as a weapon against others.

We also cling to the past as a way of contrasting it with the present— usually to highlight something positive about ourselves at the expense of someone else.

Do you ever find yourself beginning a long self-serving story with the phrase, "When I was your age . . ."?

What's really going on here?

When we make excuses, we are blaming someone or something beyond our control as the reason for our failure. Anyone but ourselves. But sometimes we blame other people not as an excuse for our failure, but as a subtle way of highlighting our successes. It's no more attractive than making excuses, but we usually require a really smart person whom we love to point it out to us.

I learned this from my daughter, Kelly.

She was seven years old. We were living in a nice house in San Diego (still my home). One day, annoyed over a professional setback, I came home and took out my annoyance on Kelly. I trotted out the sorriest, most pathetic speech any parent can give a child, the one that begins, "When I was your age . . ." Inevitably, it's a self-pitying lecture that points out how difficult and miserable the parent's childhood was in comparison with the childhood the parent is now providing for his or her children.

I started yammering about growing up in Kentucky in a gas station and how we didn't have money and how hard I had to work to become the first person from my family to graduate from college. Contrasting this, of course, with all the wonderful things Kelly had.

She patiently listened to my diatribe, instinctively letting me vent. When I was finished, she said, "Daddy, it's not my fault you make money."

That stopped me in my tracks. I realized, "She's right." How could I expect her to know what it's like to be poor—when I was damn sure she never would be? I chose to work hard and make money. She didn't. In effect, I was bragging about how hard I had it and how clever I was to have triumphed over such great adversity—and masking that boasting by dumping my frustrations on her. Fortunately, she called me on it.

Stop blaming others for the choices you made—and that goes with double emphasis for the choices that turned out well.

Habit #14 Playing favorites

I have reviewed custom-designed leadership profiles at more than 100 major corporations. It's my job to rewrite them. These documents typically feature boilerplate language that describes the leadership behavior each company desires. Such chestnuts include "communicates a clear vision," "helps people to develop to their maximum potential," "strives to see the value of differing opinions," and "avoids playing favorites."

Not one profile has ever included the desired behavior that read "effectively sucks up to management." Although given the dedication to fawning and sucking up in most corporations—and how often such behavior is rewarded—it probably should. While almost every company says it wants people to "challenge the system" and to "be empowered to express your opinion" and "say what you really think," there sure are a lot of performers who are stuck on sucking up.

Not only do companies say they abhor such comically servile behavior, but so do individual leaders. Almost all the leaders I have met say that they would never encourage such a thing in their organizations. I have no doubt that they are sincere. Most of us are easily irritated, if not disgusted, by derriere kissers. Which raises a question: If leaders say they discourage sucking up, why does it dominate the workplace? Keep in mind that these leaders are generally very shrewd judges of character. They spend their lives sizing up people, taking in first impressions and recalibrating them against later impressions. And yet, they still fall for the super-skilled suck-up. They still play favorites.

The simple answer is: We can't see in ourselves what we can see so clearly in others.

Perhaps you are thinking now, "It's amazing how leaders send out subtle signals that encourage subordinates to mute their criticisms and exaggerate their praise of the powers that be. And it is surprising how they cannot see it in themselves. Of course, this doesn't apply to me."

Maybe you're right. But how can you be so sure you're not in denial?

I use an irrefutable test with my clients to show how we all unknowingly encourage sucking up. I ask a group of leaders, "How many of you own a dog that you love?" Big smiles cross the executives' faces as they wave their hands in the air. They beam as they tell me the names of their always-faithful hounds. Then we have a contest. I ask them, "At home, who gets most of your unabashed affection? Is it (a) your husband, wife or partner; (b) your kids; or (c) your dog?" More than 80 percent of the time, the winner is the dog.

I then ask the executives if they love their dogs more than their family members. The answer is always a predictable but resounding no. My follow-up: "So why does the dog get most of your attention?"

Their replies all sound the same: "The dog is always happy to see me." "The dog never talks back." "The dog gives me unconditional love, no matter what I do." In other words, the dog is a suck-up.

I can't say that I am any better. I love my dog, Beau. I travel at least 180 days a year, and Beau goes bonkers when I return home from a trip. I pull into the driveway, and my first inclination is to open the front door, go straight to Beau, and exclaim, "Daddy's home!" Invariably, Beau jumps up and down, and I hug him and pat him and make a huge fuss over him. One day my daughter, Kelly, was home from college. She watched my typical love fest with Beau. She then looked at me, held her hands in the air like little paws, and barked, "Woof woof."

Point taken.

If we aren't careful, we can wind up treating people at work like dogs: Rewarding those who heap unthinking, unconditional admiration upon us. What behavior do we get in return? A virulent case of the suck-ups.

The net result is manifestly obvious. You're encouraging behavior that serves you, but not necessarily the best interests of the company. If everyone is fawning over the boss, who's getting work done? Worse, it tilts the field against the honest, principled employees who won't play along. This is a double hit of bad news. You're not only playing favorites but favoring the wrong people!

Leaders can stop encouraging this behavior by first admitting that we all have a tendency to favor those who favor us, even if we don't mean to.

We should then rank our direct reports in three categories.

First, how much do they like me? (I know you can't be sure. What matters is how much *you think* they like you. Effective suckups are good actors. That's what fawning is: acting.)

Second, what is their contribution to the company and its customers? (In other words, are they A players, B, C, or worse?)

Third, how much positive personal recognition do I give them?

What we're looking for is whether the correlation is stronger between one and three, or two and three. If we're honest with ourselves, our recognition of people may be linked to how much they seem to like us rather than how well they perform. That's the definition of playing favorites.

And the fault is all ours. We're encouraging the kind of behavior that we despise in others. Without meaning to, we are basking in hollow praise, which makes us hollow leaders.

This quick self-analysis won't solve the problem. But it does identify it—which is where change begins.

Habit #15 Refusing to express regret

Expressing regret, or apologizing, is a cleansing ritual, like confession in church. You say, "I'm sorry"—and you feel better.

That's the theory at least. But like many things that are fine in theory, it's hard for many of us to do.

Perhaps we think apologizing means we have lost a contest (and successful people have a practically irrational need to win at everything).

Perhaps we find it painful to admit we were wrong (we rarely have to apologize for being right).

Perhaps we find it humiliating to seek forgiveness (which suggests subservience).

Perhaps we feel that apologizing forces us to cede power or control (actually the opposite is true).

Whatever the reasons, refusing to apologize causes as much ill will in the workplace (and at home) as any other interpersonal flaw. Just think how bitter you have felt when a friend failed to apologize for hurting you or letting you down. And how long that bitterness festered.

If you look back at the tattered relationships in your life, I suspect many of them began to fray at the precise moment when one of you couldn't summon the emotional intelligence to say, "I'm sorry."

People who can't apologize at work may as well be wearing a t-shirt that says, "I don't care about you."

The irony, of course, is that all the fears that lead us to resist apologizing—the fear of losing, admitting we're wrong, ceding control—are actually erased by an apology. When you say, "I'm sorry," you turn people into your allies, even your partners.

I picked up on this paradox when I began studying Buddhism in graduate school. As a Buddhist I believe that we reap what we sow. If you smile at people, they will smile back. If you ignore them, they will resent you. If you put your fate in their hands—i.e., cede power to them—they will reward you.

But I didn't "get it" until I was 28 years old and found myself in New York City, dining alone at Le Perigord, a tony French restaurant on Manhattan's East Side. I had never been to a restaurant like this, where the flower arrangements required separate tables, the cutlery had the heft of an ax, and the waiters were dressed in black tie and sported impenetrable French accents. I confessed to the waiter that I was intimidated by the surroundings, that I only had one hundred dollars, tip included, to spend on the meal, and that I couldn't read the menu, which was hand-written in French.

"Would you please bring me the best one-hundred-dollar meal you have," I asked.

I am convinced that the meal I was served that night—not only the extra courses, the cheese tray, and the constant refills of my wine glass, but also the ridiculously solicitous service—was worth at least 50% more than my hundred-dollar budget. I admitted I was a rube, and the staff responded by treating me like the Sun King.

This experience instilled in me the conviction that if you put all your cards in someone else's hands that person will treat you better than if you kept the cards to yourself. I'm sure this is what Benjamin Franklin believed when he said, "To gain a friend, let him do you a favor."

You see this principle at work in the first step I help every successful person take in order to become more successful. I teach them to *apologize*—face to face—to every coworker who has agreed to help them get better.

Apologizing is one of the most powerful and resonant gestures in the human arsenal—almost as powerful as a declaration of love. It's "I love you" flipped on its head. If love means, "I care about you and I'm happy about it," then an apology means, "I hurt you and I'm sorry about it." Either way, it's seductive and irresistible; it irrevocably changes the relationship between two people. It compels them to move forward into something new and, perhaps, wonderful together.

The best thing about apologizing, I tell my clients, is that it forces everyone to let go of the past. In effect, you are saying, "I can't change the past. All I can say is I'm sorry for what I did wrong. I'm sorry it hurt you. There's no excuse for it and I will try to do better in the future. I would like you to give me any ideas about how I can improve."

That statement—an admission of guilt, an apology, and a plea for help—is tough for even the most cold-hearted among us to resist. And when you employ it on coworkers it can have an alchemical effect on how they feel about you and themselves.

My client Beth was the highest-ranking woman at a Fortune 100 company. Her bosses loved her. So did her direct reports. By contrast she was loathed by some of her peers. When I surveyed her coworkers I learned that she had a particularly toxic relationship with a hard-boiled division chief named Harvey. Beth was a smart, know-it-all young hotshot brought in by the CEO to stir things up. Harvey, however, saw her as arrogant and felt she didn't respect the company's history and traditions. The two of them were in a perpetual turf war, and it brought out the worst side of her personality: Her mean, vindictive streak. We agreed that this is the behavior she would change.

The first thing I had Beth do was apologize—to Harvey. I could see her bristle at the suggestion. I told her, "If you can't do this, you can't get better. And by the way, I'm outta here. I can't help you." The thought of yielding to Harvey was so distasteful to her that I actually scripted out the apology. I didn't want any misgivings or hesitations to creep in and pollute the apology (which would destroy the effect). To Beth's credit she followed the script.

She said, "You know, Harvey, I've got a lot of feedback here and the first thing I want to say is that I'm positive about a lot of it. The next thing I want to say is that there are some things at which I want to be better. I've been disrespectful to you, the company, and the traditions in the company. Please accept my apologies. There is no excuse for this behavior and . . ."

Harvey cut her off before she could finish her apology. She looked at him with alarm, poised for another fight, until she noticed that he had tears in his eyes. The first thing he said was, "You know, Beth, it's not just you. It's me. I have not been a gentleman in the way I've treated you. I know that this was hard for you to tell me these things and they are not all your problems. This is my problem, too. We can get better together."

That's the magic in this process. When you declare your dependence on others, they usually agree to help. And during the course of making you a better person, they inevitably try to become better people themselves. This is how individuals change, how teams improve, how divisions grow, and how companies become world-beaters.

Now that you know *why* apologizing works, we'll deal with the mechanics of actually doing it more thoroughly in Chapter 7.

Habit #16 Not listening

This is certainly one of the most common complaints I hear in my professional life. People will tolerate all sorts of rudeness, but the inability to pay attention holds a special place in their hearts—perhaps because it's something all of us should be able to do with ease. After all, what's it take to keep our ears open, our eyes looking at whoever's talking, and our mouths shut?

When you fail at listening you're sending out an armada of negative messages. You're saying:

- I don't care about you.

- I don't understand you.

- You're wrong.

- You're stupid.

- You're wasting my time.

- All of the above.

It's a wonder people ever talk to you again.

The interesting thing about not listening is that, for the most part, it's a silent, invisible activity. People rarely notice you doing it. You can be not listening because you're bored, or distracted, or busy composing what you want to say—and no one will know it.

The only time people actually see that you're not listening to them is when you're displaying extreme impatience. You want them to hurry up and get to the point. People notice that. And they rarely think better of you for it. You may as well be shouting, "Next!" at them.

That's what happened when I worked with a group of executives who comprised the top management team of one of the world's most respected research and development organizations. Their problem: Retaining young talent. Their flaw: During presentations everyone in senior management had developed the annoying habit of looking at their watches, motioning for junior scientists to move it along, and repeating over and over, "Next slide. Next slide." This annoying habit explained the problem.

Have you ever tried to make a presentation while a manager grunted at you and kept telling you to move it along? Well, that's how the junior scientists at this company felt.

Senior management's challenge: listening patiently while junior scientists made presentations.

It's easy to see why the bosses were so impatient. They were all brilliant. They all sported advanced degrees from MIT and Harvard. As a result, they found it hard to sit still while those below them on the pecking order talked because (a) they often felt they already knew what they were about to hear and (b) their minds worked so fast that they could comprehend any message by filling in the blanks themselves. When I told this story to the head of another pharmaceutical company, he ruefully admitted, "I was worse. Instead of, 'Next slide!' I said, 'Last slide. Last slide.'"

The executives learned that they had to change—because the world had changed. In the old days, the junior scientists at a major corporation might not have had a better option for employment. It was a choice between one big company and another.

As the executives slowly learned, as they watched talent walk out the door, times change. Today these junior scientists have the option of working in small start-ups or venturing out on their own. They're not hostages to a bunch of old men in white shirts. They can wear blue jeans to work. They can have beer blasts on Fridays. In many cases, they can get very rich at a very young age.

The reality for leaders of the past and leaders in the future is that *in the past very bright people would put up with disrespectful behavior, but in the future they will leave!*

When you find yourself mentally or literally drumming your fingers while someone else is talking, stop the drumming. Stop demonstrating impatience when listening to someone. Stop saying (or thinking) "Next!" It's not only rude and annoying, but it's sure to inspire your employees to find their next boss.

Habit #17 Failing to express gratitude

Dale Carnegie liked to say that the two sweetest words in the English language were a person's first and last name. He maintained that using them liberally in conversation was the surest way to connect with a person and disarm them. After all, who doesn't like to hear their name on other people's lips?

I'm not sure Dale was right. To me, the two sweetest words in the language are "Thank you." They're not only disarming and pleasant to the ear, but they help us avoid so many problems. Like apologizing, thanking is a magical super-gesture of interpersonal relations. It's what you say when you have nothing nice to say—and it will never annoy the person hearing it.

There's really no art to saying, "Thank you." You shape your mouth in the appropriate manner, flex your vocal cords, and let the two monosyllabic words float past your lips and out upon the grateful appreciative ears of anyone within shouting distance.

Yet people still have a tough time executing this rudimentary maneuver. Whether they're receiving a helpful suggestion or unwanted advice or a nice compliment, they get confused about how to respond. They have too many options. They can dispute the comment, question it, fine-tune it, clarify it, criticize it, amplify it. They'll do practically everything but the right thing: Say "Thank you."

Has this ever happened to you? You're at a party. It doesn't matter if you're a man or woman. You see a female neighbor wearing a stunning dress. You tell her, "You look great, Barbara. That's a gorgeous dress."

Instead of saying thank you, she turns into a flustered schoolgirl. "Oh, this old thing?" she says. "It's just some rag I found in the closet."

You tune out. She's going on and on about the dress, but you're looking at her in puzzlement. You've just handed her a sweet compliment, and she's arguing with you! In effect, she's saying, "You are confused if you think this is a beautiful dress. It is nothing compared to the other really beautiful dresses in my closet. If you were smarter, you would know that this pathetic old rag is hardly conclusive evidence of my exquisite sartorial taste."

Of course, she doesn't mean it that harshly. But that's the chilling effect of not saying thank you. You create a problem where none should exist.

I try to teach people that, if they don't know what to say, their default response to any suggestion should be, "Thank you."

I was watching golfer Mark O'Meara playing in the Skins Game with his buddy Tiger Woods. The Skins Game is a made-for-TV event where the golfers wear microphones, so you can hear everything they say. Golf is a game of etiquette. Golfers say "nice shot" throughout the round. Every time someone would say "nice shot" to O'Meara, he'd respond, "Thank you. I appreciate that." He never wavered. He must have said it fifty times during the match.

That's not hard to understand. O'Meara was getting positive feedback from his playing partners. What else is there to say? But even if he were getting negative feedback—"Tough shot, Mark!"—I'd recommend the same response. "Thank you. I'll try to do better next time."

I'm not sure how many people would do that. It means letting go of our overwhelming need to win, to be right, to add value, to come out on top.

What's needed is a slight tweak in our mindset for accepting other people's comments. My friend Chris Cappy, an expert in executive learning, has a saying that put this into perspective for me. No matter what someone tells him, he accepts it by reminding himself, "I won't learn less." What that means is when somebody makes a suggestion or gives you ideas, you're either going to *learn more* or *learn nothing*. But you're not going to *learn less*. Hearing people out does not make you dumber. So, thank them for trying to help.

If you examine the alternative, you'll see that almost any response to a suggestion other than "thank you" has the potential to stir up trouble. Intentionally or not, you appear as if you are attacking the person talking to you.

The troublemaking phrase I always look out for is, "I'm confused"— because it is so subtle and dishonest. Have you ever had this happen to you? You make a sincere suggestion to your boss: "Boss, have you ever considered . . . ?" The boss looks at you and says, "I'm confused by what you're telling me."

The boss doesn't mean he's confused. He's saying *you're confused*— which is another way of saying, "You're wrong."

What the boss should say is, "Thank you. I had never considered that." It's almost irrelevant whether the boss gives the idea any further thought. The critical issue is that saying "thank you" keeps people talking to you. Failing to say "thank you" shuts them down.

We all know this instinctively. From our earliest years we're taught that "please" and "thank you" are the basics of etiquette. That's why it's mystifying when so many people fail to appreciate the power of thanking. A bigger mystery to me is why we delay expressing gratitude. We believe we have to wait for the perfect moment—as if only a grand theatrical thank you will do the job properly. The trouble is, we rarely know when that perfect moment comes. This belief makes no sense.

I was talking with one of my clients about the lost art of expressing gratitude.

He claimed it was one of his strong points.

As proof, he told me a story about his wife. He had always wanted his own private-office-cum-library at home. He talked about it for years, but never had the time or energy to do all the work required for a major home renovation. But his wife did.

She found an architect to design the addition, hired a contractor, arranged the home improvement loan with the bank, shuttled the plans through the local building board's tortuous approval process, and then oversaw the entire project as workers tore down walls, laid down a foundation, and built the new addition.

"Why are you telling me this?" I asked.

"Because the room is almost done and I haven't thanked her yet. I'm planning to do so with a big gift for her when it's finished."

"Why don't you thank her now?" I asked.

"Because I want to wait. It'll be more impressive when the job is done."

"That may be true," I said. "But do you think she'll resent it if you thank her now and thank her again with a bigger gesture when the job is completed? Do you think she'll resent you for thanking her *twice*?"

Gratitude is a skill that we can never display too often. And yet for some reason, we are cheap and chary with gratitude—as if it were rare Bordeaux wine that we can serve only on special occasions. Gratitude is not a limited resource, nor is it costly. It is as abundant as air. We breathe it in but forget to exhale.

Of all the behavioral challenges we are covering here, this one should be the easiest to conquer. Pick something to be grateful for. Find the "guilty" party. Tell him or her, "Thank you." Do it now.

Everything else you need to know about expressing gratitude can be found in Chapter 10.

Habit #18 Punishing the messenger

Punishing the messenger is like taking the worst elements of *not giving recognition* and *hogging the credit* and *passing the buck* and *making destructive comments* and *not thanking or listening*—and then adding *anger* to the mix.

It manifests itself in big and little ways.

It's not merely the unjust retaliatory action we take against a whistle-blower or the angry tirade we heap upon an employee who tells us something we don't enjoy hearing.

It's also the small responses we make throughout the day whenever we are inconvenienced or disappointed. Until someone points it out to us, we're not aware how we punish the messenger all day long.

It's the momentary snort of disgust you exhale when your assistant reports that the boss is too busy to see you. It's not your assistant's fault that the boss is avoiding you. But that's not how your assistant interprets your disgust.

It's the expletive you neglect to delete in a meeting when a subordinate announces that a deal fell apart. If you had calmly asked, "What went wrong?" no damage would be done. The subordinate would explain what happened and everyone in the room would be wiser for it. However, that little flash of temper evident in your expletive sends a different signal. It says if you want to tick off the boss, surprise him with bad news.

It's not just bad news, however. It's all the times that people give us a helpful warning about something—a red light up ahead when we're driving, the fact our socks don't match as we head out the door in the morning, whatever—and we bite their heads off or argue with them for trying to help us.

If your goal is to stop people from giving you input—of all kinds—perfect your reputation for shooting the messenger.

On the other hand, if your goal is to stop this bad habit, all you need to say is, "Thank you."

For example, I'm on the road nearly every week of the year, but I'm religious about being home for weekends. As a result, I'm almost always in a car on Sunday afternoon or Monday morning heading to the airport. I do this so frequently that I've become very adept at putting off my departure for the airport until the last possible minute. Not surprisingly, I am usually in a mad rush to get there. On one particular drive to the airport, my wife, Lyda, was sitting in the front seat. My two children, Kelly and Bryan, were sitting in the back seat. As usual, I was late, driving too fast, and not paying attention. Lyda (who is, to make things worse, a licensed clinical psychologist with a Ph.D.) said, "Look out! There's a red light up ahead!"

Being a trained behavioral science professional, a person who teaches *others* the value of encouraging input, I naturally screamed at her. "I know there's a red light! Don't you think I can see? I can drive as well as you can!"

When we arrived at the airport, Lyda, for some peculiar reason, abandoned her usual farewell ministrations. She neglected to kiss me goodbye or, for that matter, say anything at all. She walked around the car, slid behind the wheel, and drove off.

Hmmm, I thought, I wonder if she's mad at me?

During the six-hour flight to New York, I did a cost-benefit analysis. I asked myself, "What was the cost of her saying, 'There is a red light up ahead'?" Zero. "What was the potential benefit? What could have been saved?" Many benefits came to mind, including—my life, her life, the lives of our children, and the lives of other innocent people.

When someone gives us something that has a huge potential benefit and costs absolutely nothing, there's only one adequate response: "Thank you!"

I landed in New York feeling guilt and shame. I called Lyda and told her my cost-benefit story. I said, "The next time that you help me with my driving, I am just going to say, 'Thank you.'"

"Sure you will!" she said (sarcasm free of charge).

"Just watch. I am going to do better!"

A few months passed, and I had long forgotten this incident. Again, I was racing to the airport, not paying attention, when Lyda said, "Look out for the red light!" My face turned crimson. I started breathing hard. I grimaced and then yelled, "Thank you!"

I am a long way from perfect. But I am getting better!

The next time someone offers you advice or "helps you" with something as important as your driving, don't punish the messenger. Don't say a word. Stop whatever you're thinking of saying—unless it's "Thank you!"

Habit #19 Passing the buck

Passing the buck is one of those terrifying hybrid flaws. Take a healthy dose of *needing to win* and *making excuses.* Mix it with *refusing to apologize* and *failing to give proper recognition.* Sprinkle in a faint hint of *punish the messenger* and *getting angry.* And what you end up with is passing the buck. Blaming others for our mistakes.

This is the behavioral flaw by which we judge our leaders—as important a negative attribute as positive qualities such as brainpower, courage, and resourcefulness. A leader who cannot shoulder the blame is not someone we will follow blindly into battle. We instinctively question that individual's character, dependability, and loyalty to us. And so we hold back on our loyalty to him or her.

Unlike most of the other flaws listed here, which are subtle and masked by clever rhetoric, passing the buck is one of those obviously unattractive personal habits—as obvious as belching in public. When we pass the buck, everyone notices—and no one is impressed. When was the last time someone said to you, "We think you're a great leader because we love your ingenuity at avoiding responsibility." Or, "It seemed like you were making a lot of silly mistakes, but you changed my mind when you passed the buck and demonstrated that someone else was to blame."

Passing the buck is the dark flip side of claiming credit that others deserve. Instead of depriving others of their rightful glory for a success, we wrongfully saddle them with the shame of our failure.

What's strange about passing the buck is that unlike the other flaws listed here, which we're rarely aware of, we don't need other people to point out that we're passing the buck. We're well aware of it. We know we must shoulder the blame for a failure, but we can't bring ourselves to do it. So we find a scapegoat.

In other words, we know we're guilty of an interpersonal "crime" but we do it anyway.

This was the challenge when I worked one-on-one with a media executive named Sam. Sam was a rising star at his company, but the CEO who hired me said there was something lacking in the man's leadership skills. My job was to find out why people didn't like following Sam's lead.

It didn't take me long to figure out what and why after I canvassed his colleagues. Sam had impeccable taste in spotting talent. He had exquisite social skills, which helped in dealing with high-maintenance producers and writers. He had a golden touch when it came to giving the green light to one project over another. It seemed that he could do no wrong. And he liked to promote that aura of infallibility. His invincible self-image, in fact, explained his meteoric rise to a senior position at the company. He was clearly a winner, someone who would go far.

But that sense of infallibility was also Sam's Achilles heel. A person who thinks he can do no wrong usually can't admit that he's wrong. The feedback on Sam said that he was always missing in action when one of his projects ran into trouble or an idea flopped. As good as he was at picking winners, he was a genius at pinning the blame on someone else when the occasional loser materialized.

This was his form of passing the buck. Needless to say, it didn't endear him to his staff or impress them with his leadership skills.

When I sat down with him to go over the feedback, he said, "I don't need to hear the results. I know what you've learned. People say I'm not good at accepting responsibility."

"That's right," I said. "People think you pass the buck. As a result, you're losing their respect. You'll never get to the top of this or any other company with that behavior. How come you know this about yourself and still do it?"

Sam was silent. Even now, with the feedback on the table, Sam had a tough time admitting he was wrong. But there were only him and me in the room. There was no one else to scapegoat.

I looked around his office, which was dotted with baseball memorabilia, and decided to ease him into the discussion with a baseball analogy.

"No one is perfect," I said, stating the obvious. "None of us is right all the time. In baseball, of the more than million major league games played, fewer than 30 have been perfect games. No hits, no walks, no batters reaching first base. Even the greatest hitters in their best years, such as Ty Cobb or Ted Williams, made an out at the plate 60 percent of the time. What makes you think you have to be better than Ted Williams?"

"I guess I need to be perfect," said Sam. "So I dump any imperfection on someone else."

We spent the next hour discussing the paradox that Sam's sense of infallibility made him look even more fallible to his colleagues. Sam thought he was preserving his reputation for making good decisions, everyone else thought he was passing the buck. It was such an unattractive quality that it cancelled out all of Sam's positives.

The irony, of course, is that infallibility is a myth. No one expects us to be right all the time. But when we're wrong, they certainly expect us to own up to it. In that sense, being wrong is an opportunity—an opportunity to show what kind of person and leader we are. Consumers judge a service business not so much when it does things right (consumers expect that) but rather by how the business behaves in correcting a foul-up. It's the same in the workplace. How well you own up to your mistakes makes a bigger impression than how you revel in your successes.

Once Sam could see that passing the buck was jeopardizing his career, the process of change could begin. It wasn't a difficult process, but it took time. Sam had to apologize to all his coworkers for his behavior in the past. He promised to do better in the future. He asked his coworkers to help him change and give him ideas that would make him a better leader. He asked them to point out any incident where he was deflecting responsibility. He thanked them for doing so, even when he wasn't sure they were right. And he had to do all this consistently. Any backsliding and all of Sam's efforts to change would be undone. Over time, as Sam doggedly pursued this strategy, his reputation for passing the buck began to vanish. Eighteen months later when I conducted my last review of his colleagues, Sam's scores on accepting responsibility were close to perfect.

If passing the buck is your challenge, you're probably already aware that you're doing it. My goal here is to make you see that you're not fooling anyone—except perhaps yourself—and that no matter how much you think you're saving your hide, you're actually killing it.

Habit #20 An excessive need to be "me"

Each of us has a pile of behavior which we define as "me." It's the chronic behavior, both positive and negative, that we think of as our inalterable essence.

If we're the type of person who's chronically poor at returning phone calls—whether it's because we're overcommitted, or we're simply rude, or we believe that if people *really* need to talk to us they'll call again until they get through—we mentally give ourselves a pass every time we fail to get back to callers. "Hey, that's me. Deal with it." To change would be going against the deepest, truest part of our being. It would be inauthentic.

If we are incorrigible procrastinators who habitually ruin other people's timetables, we do so because we're being true to "me."

If we always express our opinion, no matter how hurtful or noncontributory it may be, we are exercising our right to be "me."

You can see how, over time, it would be easy for each of us to cross the line and begin to make a virtue of our flaws—simply because the flaws constitute what we think of as "me." This misguided loyalty to our true natures—this excessive need to be me—is one of the toughest obstacles to making positive long-term change in our behavior. It doesn't need to be.

Some years ago I worked with a top executive whose chief documented roadblock was that he wasn't very good at giving positive recognition to his staff.

As I went over his scores with him, I said, "This is quite remarkable. You have some of the highest scores I've ever seen in seven key areas, and then there's this one area—giving positive recognition—which *nobody* thinks you're good at."

"What do you want me to do? Go around praising people who don't deserve it?" he asked. "I don't want to look like a phony."

"Is that your excuse? You don't want to look like a phony?" I asked.

"Yes, that's what I'm saying."

We went back and forth on this for a while as he desperately defended why he scored so miserably on giving positive recognition. He had high standards and people didn't always meet them. He didn't like to hand out praise indiscriminately because it cheapened the value of praise when it was legitimately earned. He thought singling out people could weaken the team. On and on this went in a dazzling display of sophistry and rationalization.

I finally stopped him and said, "No matter what you say, I don't believe you have a problem with handing out praise. Nor is it that you think doing so means you're a phony. The real problem is your self-limiting definition of who you are. You define phony as anything that isn't . . . *me*! When you hand out praise, you're thinking, 'This isn't me.'"

So I started to work with him to answer the question, "Why isn't this you?"

His scores proved that he had many qualities that defined him very positively—and he accepted them. My job in helping him change was to make him see that he could add one more definition of himself—that he could see himself as a boss who is good at giving recognition.

I asked him, "Why can't this be you, too? Is doing so immoral, illegal, or unethical?"

"No."

"Will it make people feel better?"

"Yes."

"Will they perform better as a result of this positive recognition?"

"Probably."

"Will that help your career?"

"Probably."

"So why don't you start doing it?"

"Because," he laughed, "it wouldn't be me."

That was the moment when change became possible—when he realized that this stern allegiance to his definition of himself was pointless vanity. If he could shed his "excessive need to be me," he wouldn't see himself as a phony. He could stop thinking about *himself* and start behaving in a way that benefited *others.*

Sure enough, when he let go of this devotion to "me," all his other rationalizations fell by the wayside. He began to see that his direct reports were actually talented hard-working people who did indeed deserve his periodic praise. He began to see that congratulating people, patting them on the back, singling out their contributions warmly in a meeting, writing "Good job!" on a report—even when the performance wasn't 100% perfect—didn't damage his reputation as a demanding boss. The payoff in terms of improved morale and performance was enormous. Within a year, his scores for giving positive recognition were on a par with his other scores—all because he had lost his excessive need to be "me."

The irony of all this wasn't lost on him either. The less he focused on himself and the more he considered what his staff were feeling, the more it benefited him. His reputation as a manager soared. His career did too.

It's an interesting equation: Less me. More them. Equals success.

Keep this in mind when you find yourself resisting change because you're clinging to a false—or pointless—notion of "me." It's not about you. It's about what other people think of you.

CHAPTER 5

The Twenty-First Habit: Goal Obsession

THERE'S A REASON I have given goal obsession a special stand-alone place in this section on our interpersonal challenge. By itself, goal obsession is not a flaw. Unlike adding value or punishing the messenger or any of the other twenty annoying habits, goal obsession is not transactional; it's not something you do to another person. But it is often the root cause of the annoying behavior. Goal obsession turns us into someone we shouldn't be.

Goal obsession is one of those paradoxical traits we accept as a driver of our success. It's the force that motivates us to finish the job in the face of any obstacle—and finish it perfectly.

A valuable attribute much of the time. It's hard to criticize people for wanting to do things 100 percent right (especially when you consider the sloppy alternative). But taken too far, it can become a blatant cause of failure.

In its broadest form, goal obsession is the force at play when we get so wrapped up in achieving our goal that we do it at the expense of a larger mission.

It comes from misunderstanding *what we want in our lives*. We think we'd be truly happy (or at least happier) if only we made more money, or lost thirty pounds, or got the corner office. So, we pursue those goals relentlessly. What we don't appreciate until much later is that in obsessing about making money, we might be neglecting the loved ones—i.e., our family—for whom we are presumably securing that money; in obsessing about our weight with extreme diets we might actually end up doing more harm than good to our bodies; in pursuing the corner office we might trample upon the colleagues at work whose support and loyalty we will need later on to *stay in* that corner office or move even higher. We start out with a road map heading in one direction but end up in the wrong town.

It also comes from misunderstanding *what others want us to do*. The boss says we have to show ten percent revenue growth for the year, so when it appears we will miss that target, goal obsession forces us to adopt questionable, less than honest methods of hitting the target. In other words, the honorable pursuit of a difficult goal set by someone else transforms us into cheaters. If you examine it more closely, we're not really obsessed with hitting the ten percent growth; our true goal is pleasing our boss. The only problem is that we either don't see this or we refuse to admit it to ourselves. Is it any wonder our values get mixed up? Goal obsession has warped our sense of what is right or wrong.

As a result, in our dogged pursuit of our goals we forget our manners. We're nice to people if they can help us hit our goal. We push them out of the way if they're not useful to us. Without meaning to, we can become self-absorbed schemers.

Consider a marketing executive named Candace with whom I worked. By all accounts, Candace was the poster child for "having it all." She was 38 years old, with a happy marriage and two healthy perky children at home. She was so energetic and capable that the company gave her two personal assistants. Her staff admired her for her creativity and poise—and for the breakthrough results she produced. She delivered the numbers—and then some. Her office was littered with "Marketing Executive of the Year" plaques and tributes from the industry trade magazines. Her CEO considered her his eventual successor.

So, what's wrong with this picture? Candace had a problem retaining her talented staff. A lot of them asked to be transferred to other parts of the company or simply left. My job was to figure out why people didn't want to stick around working for such an obvious star.

When I talked to Candace's colleagues, no one was willing to fault her powerful ambition. They praised her for the fact that she set very clear goals for herself. She wanted to be a "superstar" in her field—and she was well on the way to achieving that goal. But that goal obsession had worn away some of the warmth in Candace's otherwise sunny, optimistic personality. She was becoming hard and cold to her subordinates. As one staffer told me, "You could chill a six-pack of beer next to her heart."

When I dug a little deeper, the universal complaint about Candace was that she always had to be front and center in every success. She hogged the spotlight. It wasn't that Candace withheld praise or recognition. If one of her staff came up with a great marketing campaign, Candace would shower him or her with praise. But she would always take center stage when she reported the success to her superiors.

That was her flaw. Goal obsession had turned Candace into someone who claimed credit for everything, even when she didn't deserve it.

If I could make her see that her goal of being a star—as opposed to being an effective leader—was misguided, then everything else would fall into place. She wouldn't be so desperate to purloin credit from her peers and staff. She could learn to accept that *their* triumphs said something positive about her as a leader.

As I say, this is why I've given goal obsession its own special corner. It's not a flaw. It's a creator of flaws. It's the force that distorts our otherwise exemplary talents and good intentions, turning them into something we no longer admire.

It's one thing to pursue your dreams—but not if that pursuit turns a dream into a nightmare.

Take the movie *The Bridge on the River Kwai* and the lead character, Colonel Nicholson, which won Alec Guinness the Best Actor Academy Award. In it, Guinness plays a prisoner of war in Burma who is compelled to lead his fellow prisoners in building a bridge for their Japanese captors. Nicholson is an officer of high integrity, dedicated to excellence, a great leader of men—and thus well trained to complete any mission he is given. So he doesn't just build a bridge, he builds a beautiful bridge. At film's end, he finds himself in the painful position of defending the bridge from attack by fellow officers who want to destroy it to prevent Japanese trains from using it. There's a chilling moment of realization, right before he detonates the bridge, when he utters the famous line, "What have I done?" He was so focused on his goal—build the bridge—that he forgot the larger mission was winning the war. That's goal obsession. Our quest for a successful outcome may end up doing more harm than good to our organizations, our families, and ourselves.

The canyons of Wall Street are littered with the victims of goal obsession. I asked one hard-driving deal maker, "Mike, why do you work all of the time?" He replied, "Why do you think? Do you think I love this place? I am working so hard because I want to make a lot of money!"

I continued my inquiry, "Do you really need this much money?"

"I do now," Mike grimaced. "I just got divorced for the third time. With three alimony checks each month, I am almost broke."

"Why do you keep getting divorced?" I asked.

The answer came out as a sad sigh. "All three wives kept complaining that I worked all of the time. They have no idea how hard it is to make this much money!"

This sort of classic goal obsession would be laughable if the irony—or more accurately the failure to appreciate the irony—weren't so painful.

One of the most ironic examples of goal obsession was the "Good Samaritan" research done by Darley and Batson at Princeton in 1973. In this widely-referenced study, one group of theology students was told that they were to go across campus to deliver a sermon on the topic of the Good Samaritan. As part of the research, some of these students were told that they were late and needed to hurry up. They believed people would be waiting for them to arrive. Along their route across campus to the chapel, Darley and Batson had hired an actor to play the role of a "victim" who was coughing and suffering. Ninety percent of the late students in Princeton Theology Seminary ignored the needs of a suffering person in their haste to get across campus. As the study reports, "Indeed, on several occasions, a seminary student going to give his talk on the parable of the Good Samaritan literally stepped over the victim as he hurried on his way!"

My guess is that few, if any, of these seminary students were "bad people." Like Colonel Nicholson, they probably were ethical, well-meaning people who deeply believed in the value of helping others. But goal obsession clouded their judgment.

What happened to Candace, Colonel Nicholson, Mike, and the seminary students?

They were chasing the spotlight. They were under pressure! They were in a hurry! They had deadlines! They were going to do something that they thought was important! Other people were depending upon them!

These are the classic conditions that can lead to goal obsession. Great follow through. Terrific discipline. Awesome goal obsession. Short-sighted goal.

A recipe for disaster.

Candace was climbing to the top, but stomping on her supporters to get there. Colonel Nicholson was building a bridge, but not winning a war. Mike was making money, but losing a wife. The seminary students were on time for a sermon, but not practicing what they preached.

The solution is simple, but not easy. You have to step back, take a breath, and look. And survey the conditions that are making you obsessed with the wrong goals.

Ask yourself: When are you under time pressure? Or in a hurry? Or doing something that you have been told is important? Or have people depending upon you?

Probable answer: All the time. These are the classic conditions of the goal obsessed. We confront them every minute of every day. They do not go away. This makes it all the more important to reflect upon our work, match it up against the life we want to live, and consider, "What am I doing?" and, "Why am I doing this?"

Ask yourself, "Am I achieving a task—and forgetting my organization's mission?"

Are you making money to support your family—and forgetting the family that you are trying to support?

Are you on time to deliver a sermon to your staff—and forgetting to practice what you're preaching?

After all this effort and display of professional prowess, you don't want to find yourself at a dead end, asking, "What have I done?"

How We Can Change for the Better

In which we learn a seven-step method for changing our interpersonal relationships and making these changes permanent

TAKE A BREATH.

Did I scare you in the previous section? Did I paint a picture of a workplace so dense with fractured personalities that you're wondering if you should go back to work tomorrow?

It's not that bad.

If you step back and look at most of these interpersonal flaws, they revolve around two familiar factors: information and emotion.

The journalist/novelist Tom Wolfe has a theory he calls *information compulsion*. He says that people have an overwhelming need to tell you something that you don't know, even when it's not in their best interest. Journalists would have a hard time surviving without information compulsion. People wouldn't call them with tips on a good story, or agree to be interviewed, or spill secrets about their company, or hand out delicious quotes.

The same compulsion blossoms into full flower in our daily lives. It's the reason we like to dazzle our friends at dinner parties with the esoterica we know (even when we suspect we may be overstaying our welcome), or why coworkers like to gossip around the water cooler (even when they know that their chatter may get back to the people they're prattling about), or why friends tell us in excessive detail about their health or their love lives (even though they close their ears when the tables are turned). It's the reason "that's too much information" has entered everyday speech. We all have an overwhelming need to display and share what we know. And we do it excessively.

Study the twenty annoying habits and you'll see that at least half of them are rooted in information compulsion. When we add value, or pass judgment, or make destructive comments, or announce that we "already knew that," or explain "why that won't work" we are compulsively sharing information. We're telling people something they don't know. We're convinced that we're making people smarter or inspiring them to do better, when we're more likely to achieve the opposite effect. Likewise, when we fail to give recognition, or claim credit we don't deserve, or refuse to apologize, or don't express our gratitude, we are withholding information.

Sharing or withholding. They're two sides of the same tarnished coin.

The other habits are rooted in a different kind of compulsion, one that's centered on emotion. When we get angry, or play favorites, or punish the messenger, we are succumbing to emotion—and displaying it for all the world to see.

Information and emotion. We either share them or withhold them.

There's nothing wrong with that. The world would be a more dangerous and less interesting place if we didn't understand how to either share information or withhold it. It's good to share information that helps people. Likewise, it's good to withhold it when it harms people (that's why many secrets *should* be kept). The same goes for emotion. Worth sharing sometimes. Other times, not worth it at all.

At the risk of complicating this with too much information, I would add another dimension here. When dealing with information or emotion, we have to consider if what we're sharing is *appropriate*.

Appropriate information is anything that unequivocally helps the other person. But it veers into inappropriate when we go too far or risk hurting someone. Discussing a rival company's good fortune can be positive if it gets your people working harder, but it's usually inappropriate information when it soils other people's reputations. Instruction is usually appropriate, to a point. It's the difference between someone giving you simple directions to their house and telling you every wrong turn you can make along the way. The latter is inappropriate. At some point, with too many details and red flags, you will get lost, confused, or wary of making the trip at all.

The same with emotion. Love is often an appropriate emotion. Anger is not appropriate. But even saying "I love you" can be inappropriate if we employ it too often or at awkward moments. And conversely, anger can be a useful tool if we parse it out in small doses at opportune moments.

When sharing information or emotion, we have to ask *is this appropriate* and *how much should I convey?*

I realize these are broad generalizations involving delicate subject matter. But they will give some context to understand these challenges. We are not lancing deep-rooted psychological "tumors" here. We're asking blunt questions about basic behavior.

Is it appropriate?

How much should I convey?

You can do a lot worse than pause and pose these questions as guidelines for anything you do or say as you follow the instructions in this section's seven chapters. From feedback to feedforward, I will show you how to identify your specific flaws, how to determine if they matter, and how to change your annoying behavior so that you are not only better for it but also so that your colleagues notice the change (very important).

CHAPTER 6

Feedback

A Brief History of Feedback

Feedback has always been with us, ever since the first man knelt down at a pool of water to get a drink and saw his face reflected in the water's surface. Formal up-the-ladder feedback designed to help managers didn't appear until the middle of the previous century—with the first suggestion box. The feedback that matters to me is a more recent development of the last 30 years. It's commonly called 360-degree feedback, because it is solicited from everybody at all levels of the organization. Until something better comes along, confidential 360-degree feedback is the best way for successful people to identify what they need to improve in their relationships at work.

Successful people only have two problems dealing with negative feedback. However, they are big problems: (a) they don't want to hear it from us and (b) we don't want to give it to them.

It's not hard to see why people don't want to hear negative feedback. Successful people are incredibly delusional about their achievements. Over 95 percent of the members in most successful groups believe that they perform in the top half of their group. While this is statistically ridiculous, it is psychologically real. Giving people negative feedback means "proving" they are wrong. *Proving* to successful people that they are wrong works just about as well as *making* them change. Not gonna happen.

Feedback generally doesn't break through to successful people even when we adopt the eminently sane guideline of *depersonalizing* the feedback. That is, talk about the *task*, not the *person*. This is easy in theory.

But successful people's identities are often so closely connected to what they do that it's naive to assume they will not take it personally when receiving negative feedback about the most important activity in their lives.

Basically, we accept feedback that is consistent with our self-image and reject feedback that is inconsistent.

It's also easy to see why we don't want to give feedback. In big organizations, successful people have power over us—over our paycheck, our advancement, our job security. The more successful these people are, the more power they have. Combine that power with the fairly predictable "kill the messenger" response to negative feedback and you can see why emperors will continue to rule without clothes. (Spot quiz: When was the last time your efforts to prove the boss wrong worked as a career-enhancing maneuver?)

I have other issues with traditional face-to-face negative feedback—and almost all of them boil down to the fact that it focuses on the past (a failed past at that), not a positive future. We can't change the past. We can change the future. Negative feedback exists to prove us wrong (or at least many of us take it that way). Feedback can be employed by others to reinforce our feelings of failure, or at least remind us of them—and our reaction is rarely positive. (Spot quiz: When your spouse or partner reminds you of all your shortcomings, how well do you accept this trip down memory lane?)

More than anything, negative feedback shuts us down. We close ranks, turn into our shell, and shut the world out. Change does not happen in this environment.

But enough about what's wrong with feedback. I'm not trying to prove that negative feedback creates dysfunction. Feedback is very useful for telling us "where we are." Without feedback, I couldn't work with my clients. I wouldn't know what everyone thinks my client needs to change. Likewise, without feedback, we wouldn't have results. We couldn't keep score. We wouldn't know if we were getting better or worse. Just as salespeople need feedback on what's selling and leaders need feedback on how they are perceived by their subordinates, we all need feedback to see where we are, where we need to go, and to measure our progress.

We need honest, helpful feedback. It's just hard to find. But I have a foolproof method for securing it.

The Four Commitments

When I work with a coaching client, I always get confidential feedback from many of my client's coworkers at the beginning of the process. The fewest I have ever interviewed is eight and the most is thirty-one. My average is about fifteen. The number of interviewees depends upon the company's size and the executive's job. Before I begin these interviews, I involve my client in determining who should be interviewed. Each interview lasts about an hour and focuses on the basics: What is my client doing right, what does my client need to change, and how my (already successful) client can get even better!

Today, all of my personal coaching clients are either CEOs or executives who have the potential to be CEOs in major corporations. If my client is the CEO, I get his or her opinion on who should be interviewed. If my client is not the CEO, the CEO must also approve my list of interviewees. (I don't want the CEO to feel that I left out important people.) One reason so many people deny the validity of feedback is that they believe that the feedback was delivered by the "wrong people." Since my clients pick their raters, it is hard for them to deny the validity of the feedback.

I have been asked if my clients ever just "pick their friends" and ignore valuable feedback from people who may be critical. In theory I see how this could happen, but I've never had this experience.

As part of my interview process, I enlist each of my client's coworkers to help me out. I want them to assist, not sabotage the change process. I let the coworker know how my process works by saying, "I'm going to be working with my client for the next year or so. I don't get paid if he doesn't get better. 'Better' is not defined by me. It's not defined by my client. 'Better' is defined by you and the other coworkers who will be involved in this process."

The raters usually respond well to that. People like hearing that they are the customer and they have the power to determine if I get paid. After all, if change happens, the raters taste victory with a dramatically improved boss and work environment.

I then present these coworkers with four requests. I call them The Four Commitments. I need them to commit to:

1. Let go of the past.

2. Tell the truth.

3. Be supportive and helpful—not cynical or negative.

4. Pick something to improve yourself—so everyone is focused more on "improving" than "judging."

Almost every coworker agrees to my four requests. In a couple of cases, coworkers have just said "no." They felt that they could not "let go" of the past and help my client try to get better. In these cases they had psychologically "written off" my client. Since all of the interviews are confidential, I don't tell this to my client. I only request that the coworkers not participate in the final feedback report. If we aren't going to try to help our colleagues, why should we be allowed to judge them?

As you contemplate changing your behavior yourself—without my hands-on assistance—you will need to do the same with your colleagues. Here's how you can get the people you know to commit to helping you.

First commitment: Can they let go of the past? Whatever real or imagined sins you have committed against people in the past, they are long past correction. You can't do anything to erase them. So, you need to ask people to let go of the past. This is simple, but it is not easy. Most of us have never forgiven our mothers and fathers for not being the perfect parents. We cannot forgive our children for not being the ideal kids. We don't forgive our spouse for not being the perfect partner. Quite often, we can't forgive ourselves for not being the perfect us. But you have to get this first commitment. Without it, you can't shift people's minds away from critic toward helper. As a friend wisely noted, "Forgiveness means letting go of the hope for a better past!"

Second commitment: Will they swear to tell the truth? You don't want to work your butt off for a year, trying to get better based on what people have told you that you were doing wrong—and then find out that they *didn't really mean it*. That they were jiving you, that they were only saying what they thought you wanted to hear. That's a waste of time. I'm not naive. I know people can be dishonest. But if you solicit—no, demand—honesty from people, you can proceed with the confidence that you're going in the right direction—and that you won't get a rude surprise at the end.

Third commitment: Will they be supportive, without being a cynic, critic, or judge? This is asking a lot of people, especially if they are in a subordinate position to you. People are just as likely to suspect or resent their superiors at work as respect and admire them. So you have to remove any and all of their judgmental impulses from the equation. Do that and people are much more inclined to be helpful. At some point, they realize that if you get better, they have won something too. They get a kinder, gentler, better boss.

Fourth commitment: Will they pick one thing they can improve in themselves? This is the subtlest commitment, but it only sounds like you're asking a lot from your colleagues. What you're actually doing is creating parity, even a bond, between you and the other person. Imagine if you walked into work one day and announced that you were going on a diet. Most people would respond to that announcement with a massive yawn. But what if you announced your plans and also asked a colleague to help you—for example, to help you monitor your eating habits and stay on track? Since most people like to help their friends, you'd probably get a much more involved and sincere response to your objective. Finally, what if you add the compelling reciprocal twist of saying, "Now, what would you like to change in yourself? I'd like to return the favor and help you"? If you do that, you won't have any problem enlisting support. Suddenly, both you and the other person have become equals: fellow humans engaged in the same struggle to improve.

Imagine if you were in a marriage in which both you and your spouse were unhappy being, say, 25 pounds overweight. What if one of you decided to go on a diet and shed those excess pounds? Wouldn't your chances of succeeding increase if you could enlist your spouse to join you on the diet? Suddenly, you'd both be involved in planning the day's meals, you'd both be goading each other to maintain the discipline. You'd both be checking the scale to see how you're hitting your targets. That's certainly a lot better than sticking with your regimen at the dinner table while your other half continues eating the foods that packed on the excess weight in the first place. The two of you are going in opposite directions. That's an unpromising formula for getting where you want to go; one of you will be miserable, more likely both.

This fourth commitment is the final piece in making the process a two-way exchange.

And it is crucial if you want people to stick with you through the 12- to 18-month process. I learned this early on with my clients. When I had to figure out who to talk to for initial feedback, it seemed like common sense to me that the client should pick the people rating his performance. After all, these colleagues were the people telling me what this fellow needed to change. Wouldn't they be in the best position to tell me if and when he was getting better? So I had to draft them into the process and get *them* to play on my terms too. I told each coworker about my client's plan to change and I asked him or her to commit to help him. I was being scientifically rigorous and practical. I wanted the folks filling out the *first* report card to fill out *all* the report cards. It would make the results more valid and credible. However, it took me a little trial and error to appreciate the massive side benefits of getting other people involved— especially the part where they committed to changing something too. It enriched the entire experience. The client not only changed for the better because he was getting support from his coworkers, but the coworkers changed too because of what they learned by supporting him. This is a rich and subtle dynamic, proving that *change is not a one-way street. It involves two parties: the person who's changing and the people who notice it.*

As you begin your personal self-reclamation project, don't slough off this fourth commitment. Put equal emphasis on changing yourself *and* the people who will determine whether any change has occurred. You and the people helping you are both equal parts of a delicate equation. You can't ignore the "other guy" in any interpersonal transaction and think you're accomplishing something "interpersonal" or engaged in a "transaction."

Then, and only then, are you ready to solicit feedback about yourself.

Finding a bunch of people to tell us the truth about ourselves is not hard. You just have to know where to look.

I didn't go through this listing of the four commitments to impress you with the rigor of my methodology. It's the criteria you should be applying once you've decided on the people you want to provide feedback.

First on your list should probably be your best friend. We all have a best friend at work—someone with whom we don't compete, who has no agenda when it comes to our success, who has our interests at heart. By definition, this person fills the four commitments:

If he's our best friend, he surely isn't bitter about something in our mutual past, so he won't keep bringing up the past or hold it against us.

He's comfortable with leveling with us. He has no reason to lie. He'll consider telling us the raw unvarnished truth a badge of honor.

He's there to support us.

And he'll be willing to play along and get into the change process with us.

That would be my first choice. But it doesn't have to be yours.

Make a list of the last dozen or so people with whom you've had professional contact. They could be colleagues, subordinates, customers, clients, even long-term competitors. As long as they're people who can make legitimate observations about your behavior, they're eligible. Then run the four commitments against each name. If any of them qualify on all four commitments, they're as good a place to start getting feedback as any.

Treat it as if you're conducting voir dire to assemble a trial jury—because that in effect is what's going on here.

Remember, this process (especially at the beginning) is not supposed to be difficult. Getting feedback is the easy part. Dealing with it is hard.

Stop Asking for Feedback and Then Expressing Your Opinion

Years ago I was riding an elevator with a famous trial lawyer who was well into his 80s at the time (but still practicing law). The elevator doors opened and a man smoking a cigarette got on. (This was in the early 1980s, before smoking was universally banned.) The lawyer panicked. He was allergic to smoke and he vainly tried to jump off the small cramped elevator so he wouldn't have to breathe the smoke. Too late. The doors closed.

"Are you okay?" the smoker asked the lawyer.

"You know, you're not supposed to smoke on elevators," he told the man. "It's against the law."

The man said, "What are you, a lawyer?" He was in no mood to apologize or put out the cigarette. He was clearly prepared to argue with the lawyer, to defend his right to smoke.

"I don't believe this," said the lawyer. "You're acting as if I'm wrong—that you're the victim because I happen to be in the elevator while you're breaking the law."

It was one of those small but outrageous moments that remind you how defensive people can be, whether they are right or wrong—especially if they're wrong.

I think about that elevator ride every time someone asks me for my advice and then after I give it, they render a less-than-glowing verdict about the quality of my advice. "I can't believe it," I say, with the lawyer's words ringing in my ears. "You asked me for my opinion and now you're arguing with me."

It's no different than our behavior when we argue with someone who's giving us advice, offering feedback, or otherwise trying to help us. And we do that every time we ask for feedback and unthinkingly respond by expressing our opinion. When we ask a friend, "What do you think I should do in this situation?" we are setting up the expectation that we want an answer—and that we will give the answer full consideration and quite possibly use it. We are not announcing that we're initiating an argument.

But that's exactly what we're doing when we ask for feedback from someone and then immediately express our opinion. This is certainly true when our opinion is negative ("I'm not sure about that. . . ."). Whatever we say, however softly we couch it, our opinion will sound defensive. It will resemble a rationalization, a denial, a negation, or an objection.

Stop doing that. Treat every piece of advice as a gift or a compliment and simply say, "Thank you." No one expects you to act on every piece of advice. If you learn to listen—and act on the advice that makes sense—the people around you may be thrilled.

Feedback Moments: How to Get Good Feedback on Your Own

I realize few of you have the resources to hire a professional to do the "fieldwork" of getting great feedback.

When I work with executives I spend my first hours on the job conducting a 360-degree feedback review. I don't want to drape the process in complexity and mystery. It's really simple. With the client's help, I identify all the people he or she works with who see his or her interpersonal challenges on a daily basis. These are the raters. I qualify them with my four commitment questions. And I have them fill out a leadership questionnaire. Sometimes the questions are customized to reflect the company's values and objectives (at GE, for example, there's a high premium placed on cooperation and sharing information across boundaries whereas at another company the premium value might be customer satisfaction).

The questions are simple. Does the executive in question:

- Clearly communicate a vision.

- Treat people with respect.

- Solicit contrary opinions.

- Encourage other people's ideas.

- Listen to other people in meetings.

That sort of thing. I ask people to rate their colleague on a numerical scale. From that, a statistical picture emerges, usually revealing one or two problem areas that we need to address. Surveys show that about 50% of corporate America uses something like this in evaluating employee performance and attitudes. If, somehow, this format has eluded you, I've included a 72-question leadership survey in an appendix to give you a picture of how professionals in this field operate.

But I'm not asking you to become a "feedback professional" here. I have to do it this way because I'm a newcomer at every company I work in. I don't have any history with the client. I've never worked with him. All I know before I meet the client is what his or her boss has told me about him. So I have no alternative but to canvass the troops.

That said, if you've worked in a corporate environment large enough to have three employees in its human resources department, you've probably been a participant in something resembling 360-degree feedback.

Even if you haven't, we're all familiar with feedback—whether or not we label it as such.

We've all endured performance appraisals from our bosses. That's feedback.

We've all gone through salary reviews. That's the most direct feedback.

If we're in sales, we've all read customer surveys of our performance. That's feedback.

We've sat through quarterly sales meetings as our figures are stacked up against our quotas and projections. That, too, is feedback.

We're being told all day long how we're doing. And the reason we accept this feedback and actually attempt to respond to it (e.g., if we're down in sales, we'll try harder to bring the figures up) is that we *accept the process*: An authority figure "grades" us and we are motivated to do better because of it.

It's not like that with interpersonal behavior, which is vague, subjective, unquantifiable, and open to wildly variant interpretations. But that doesn't make it less important. It's my contention—and it's the bedrock thesis of this book—that interpersonal behavior is the difference-maker between being great and near-great, between getting the gold and settling for the bronze. (The higher you go, the more your "issues" are behavioral.)

So, how do we get this much-needed feedback if we have neither the skill nor resources nor opportunity to poll our peers on what they really think about us? We know what feedback is. We don't know how to get it.

Basically, feedback comes to us in three forms: Solicited, unsolicited, and observation. Each of them works well, but not for everyone. Let's look closely at all three to see which one's right for you.

Solicited Feedback, or Knowing How to Ask

Solicited feedback is just that. We solicit opinions from people about what we're doing wrong. Sounds simple, no? I am not always so optimistic.

I'm not saying that you, working on your own, cannot replicate my feedback retrieval methods. It's quite possible that you could corral a dozen people who know you, qualify them with the four commitment test, and have them fill out a questionnaire about what you could be doing better.

My only concern is that we cannot be sure that you will (a) ask the right people, (b) ask the right questions, (c) interpret the answers properly, or (d) accept them as accurate. This harks back to my big issue with negative feedback: We don't want to hear it and people don't want to give it.

In my experience the best solicited feedback is *confidential* feedback. It's good because nobody gets embarrassed or defensive. There are no emotional issues, because you do not know who to blame or retaliate against for attacking you. In the best cases, you have no sense of being attacked at all. You're merely ingesting honest commentary—which you requested!—from blind but well-meaning sources.

The only problem: This is virtually impossible for one person working alone to pull off. To maintain the confidentiality (and avoid the emotionality) you need an unbiased third party to do the polling—someone like me.

Absent that, you have to ask people one-on-one. But that too is fraught with obstacles.

In my experience there are a hundred wrong ways to ask for feedback—and one right way. Most of us know the wrong ways. We ask someone, "What do you think of me?"

"How do you feel about me?"

"What do you hate about me?"

"What do you like about me?"

These are all variations of the same encounter group question designed to elicit honest feelings between people. Well, we're not running encounter groups here.

These types of questions are particularly pernicious in power relationships where the boss is asking the bossed, "What do you think of me?" In a power relationship you have all kinds of issues that influence the answer—because the answer has consequences. People will not tell the truth if they think it will come back to haunt them—and in a power relationship subordinates have no guarantee that the unvarnished truth won't anger the boss, send them back to the end of the line, or worse, get them fired.

When you think about it, these "what do you think of me?" encounter group questions are actually irrelevant. In the workplace you don't have to like me; we don't have to be buddies who hang out together after work. All we have to do is work well together. How we really "feel" about each other is practically moot.

Think about your colleagues at work. How many of them are your friends? For how many of them would you be willing to articulate your true *feelings*? How many of them have you actually thought about in terms of *feelings*? The answer, I suspect, is not that many. A small minority. And yet you probably work well together with a majority of your colleagues. That disconnect—between the small number of *friends* and the larger number of *colleagues* with whom you work well—should convince you once and for all that what people feel or think about you is not the key to getting better.

In soliciting feedback for yourself, the only question that works—the only one!—must be phrased like this: "How can I do better?"

Semantic variations are permitted, such as, "What can I do to be a better partner at home?" or, "What can I do to be a better colleague at work?" or, "What can I do to be a better leader of this group?" It varies with the circumstances. But you get the idea. Pure unadulterated issue-free feedback that makes change possible has to (a) solicit advice rather than criticism, (b) be directed towards the future rather than obsessed with the negative past, and (c) be couched in a way that suggests you will act on it; that in fact you are trying to do better.

Unsolicited Feedback, or the Blindside Event

If we're lucky, every once in a while something or someone comes along who opens our eyes to our faults—and helps us strip away a delusion or two about ourselves. It doesn't happen often, but when it does, we should consider ourselves lucky and grateful.

Psychologists have all sorts of schemata to explain us to ourselves. One of the more interesting ones is a simple four-pane grid known as the Johari Window (named after two real characters, Joe and Harry). It divides our self-awareness into four parts, based on what is known and unknown about us to other people and what is known and unknown about us to ourselves.

As you can see from the illustration on the following page, the stuff that is known about us to others is *public* knowledge. What's known to us and unknown to others is *private*. What's unknown to ourselves and others is, well . . . *unknowable* and, therefore, not relevant.

KNOWN TO OTHERS

Blind Spots
Unknown to us
Known to Others

Public Knowledge
Known to us
Known to Others

UNKNOWN TO SELF   KNOWN TO SELF

Unknowable
Unknown to us
Unknown to Others

Private Knowledge
Known to us
Unknown to Others

UNKNOWN TO OTHERS

The interesting stuff is the information that's known to others but unknown to us. When that information is revealed to us, those are the "road to Damascus" moments that create dramatic change. They are the moments when we can get blindsided by how others really see us, when we discover a truth about ourselves. These blindside moments are rare and precious gifts. They hurt, perhaps (the truth often does), but they also instruct.

I've had a few in my life, but the most significant blindside event came when I was a 28-year-old Ph.D. candidate at UCLA. Back then, in the late 1960s, the era of free love and Woodstock, I thought of myself as being just a little more insightful, more "hip," than the people around me. I believed that I was intensely involved in things like deeper human understanding, self-actualization, and uncovering profound meaning. I was a student in a small class led by a very wise teacher, Dr. Bob Tannenbaum. Tannenbaum was a revered figure not only at UCLA but in psychology circles around the world. He had invented the term "sensitivity training" and had published the most influential papers on the subject. He was a god to me.

In Bob's class we were encouraged to discuss anything we wanted.

I took this as a license to rail against the shallow, materialistic citizens of Los Angeles. For three weeks I delivered a monologue about how "screwed up" people in Los Angeles were—with their sequined blue jeans, gold Rolls-Royces, and manicured mansions. "All they care about is impressing others. They do not understand what is deep and important in life." (It was easy for me to be an expert on the people of Los Angeles. I had, after all, grown up in a small town in Kentucky.)

After enduring my babble for three weeks, Bob asked, "Marshall, who are you talking to?"

"I am speaking to the group," I answered.

"To whom in the group are you talking?"

"I am talking to everybody," I said, not quite sure where Bob was going with this line of interrogation.

Bob said, "I don't know if you realize this, but each time you have spoken you have looked at only one person. You have addressed your comments toward only one person. And you seem interested in the opinion of only one person. Who is that person?"

"That's interesting. Let me think about it," I said. Then (after careful consideration) I said, "You."

Bob said, "That's right. *Me*. There are twelve other people in this room. Why aren't you interested in any of *them*?"

Now that I had dug myself into a hole, I decided to dig even faster. I said, "Dr. Tannenbaum, I think you can understand the true significance of what I am saying. I think that you can truly understand how 'screwed up' it is to run around trying to impress people all the time. I believe that you have a deeper understanding of what is *really* important in life."

Bob asked, "Marshall, is there any chance that for the last three weeks all you have been trying to do is impress me?"

I was stunned by Bob's obvious lack of insight. "Not at all!" I said. "You haven't understood one thing I have said! I have been explaining to you the folly of trying to impress other people. You've totally missed my point and frankly, I am disappointed in your lack of understanding."

He stared at me, scratched his beard, and concluded, "No, I think I understand."

I looked around and saw twelve people scratching their faces and thinking, "Yes, we understand."

I hated Bob Tannenbaum for six months. I devoted a lot of energy into figuring out *his* problems and understanding why *he* was confused. After a half-year of this stewing, it dawned on me that the person with the issue about impressing other people wasn't Bob Tannenbaum or the citizens of Los Angeles. The person with the real issue was me. I looked in the mirror and didn't like the person staring back at me.

I still shudder with shame at the memory of how fatuous I was back then. But we need these painful unsolicited feedback episodes, when others reveal how the world really sees us, in order to change for the better. Without the pain, we might not discover the motivation to change.

This was a blindside event for me not only because it exposed my shallow self-involvement, but it taught me two great lessons that have literally shaped my professional work.

1. It is a whole lot easier to see our problems in others than it is to see them in ourselves.

2. Even though we may be able to deny our problems to ourselves, they may be very obvious to the people who are observing us.

This is the simple wisdom of the Johari Window: What is unknown to us may be well-known to others. We can learn from that.

As human beings we almost always suffer from the disconnect between the self we think we are and the self that the rest of the world sees in us. The lesson that I learned from Dr. Tannenbaum is that the rest of the world usually has a more accurate perspective than we do.

This is the value of *unsolicited feedback*. And in many ways when I work one-on-one with people, I am re-creating that painful realization inspired by Dr. Tannenbaum. I'm trying to blindside them by making them peer through that fourth window to see what is known to others but unknown to them.

If we can stop, listen, and think about what others are seeing in us, we have a great opportunity. We can compare the self that we want to be with the self that we are presenting to the rest of the world. We can then begin to make the real changes that are needed to close the gap between our stated values and our actual behavior.

Although he is no longer with us, I still say, "Thank you, Dr. Tannenbaum."

Observational Feedback, or Seeing Your World Anew

One of my clients—let's call him Barry—told me about one of the more important insights he had at work; it involved a senior executive who was about a half notch above him in the organizational hierarchy.

It's important to know that, because Barry handled a couple of accounts that were near and dear to the CEO, Barry had a slightly closer relationship with the CEO than anyone else in the company. He traveled with the CEO and talked to the CEO at least once a day. Barry's access to the CEO was so good that some of his peers—who weren't as tight with the CEO—resented him for it. They felt that because of his perceived "special relationship" with the CEO, Barry could always go around them and get his way by sucking up to the CEO. It wasn't necessarily true; certainly not to Barry, who had never felt that the CEO had favored him over others. It was envy, pure and simple. But it's important to know that this dynamic may have colored Barry's relationship with his peers. The only strange thing was that Barry had no clue that some of his peers felt that way. He thought they liked him.

Then one day he had a "feedback moment."

In a group meeting Barry noticed that a senior executive named Peter was making a pointed effort to ignore him. Whenever Barry spoke, Peter would look away—as if the sound of Barry's voice was causing him pain. Nobody else in the room noticed this, but Barry did. So he started paying attention to Peter's behavior for the rest of the meeting. And what Barry saw confirmed the first clue. When Peter spoke, he would look around the room making eye contact with everyone—except Barry. Even when the discussion turned to one of Barry's responsibilities, Peter would look away. Everything he said and did gave the impression that Peter wished Barry would simply disappear.

That's when it hit Barry.

"Oh my," he thought, "Peter, who has the power to block some of my initiatives, hates my guts."

"Until that moment," Barry told me, "I had no idea. I thought we were colleagues. I thought we worked well together."

I submit that the subtle signals Barry picked up qualify as significant feedback. Observational feedback—unsolicited, less than explicit, hard to prove—but important feedback nevertheless. Because it taught Barry that he had a fractured collegial relationship that needed immediate attention.

I'm pleased to report that Barry responded brilliantly to this feedback. Instead of being defensive about it—as many of us would be if we learned that someone was harboring a deep animus toward us—he opted to turn the other cheek and begin a campaign to win Peter back to his side.

"I had options in dealing with Peter," said Barry. "I could treat him with kid gloves. Work around him. Ignore him. Start a campaign to undermine *him*. Or I could show him that I'm his friend, not his enemy, because I needed his support. I decided to make him my friend. I would direct business leads his way and go out of my way to bring deals to his division. I would keep him in the loop on everything that touched him and me—by following up and getting his input about stuff I'm working on. I would seek out his advice, show him respect, and hope he responded by no longer ignoring me."

It took Barry more than a year, but this excellent behavior converted the hatred into a working relationship. The two men didn't become instant drinking buddies (that would be asking too much), but Peter no longer hated Barry. More important, they worked well together.

I mention this because it demonstrates (a) that feedback from one person, however abstruse and vague, can be just as important as formal feedback from a group, and (b) not all feedback comes from asking people (solicited) or hearing what they volunteer. Some of the best feedback comes from what you observe. If you accept it and act on it, it's no less valid than people telling you the same thing at point-blank range.

Even if we're only half paying attention, we take in observational feedback all day long.

We shake hands with a neighbor at a party and notice that he doesn't look us in the eye. (Hmmm, we think, what's that all about?)

Coming home after work, we stroll into our living room and our 12-year-old daughter immediately leaves to go upstairs to her room. (Hmm, we think, what did we do to tick her off?)

We try to contact a client or customer and he doesn't return the call. (Hmm, we think, someone's displeased with us.)

Every day, people are giving us feedback, of a sort, with their eye contact, their body language, their response time. Interpreting this casual observational feedback can be tricky; learning that something's not right is not the same as learning what's wrong and how we can fix it.

The good news is that these feedback moments are plentiful and, with some simple drills, we can manipulate them so that patterns emerge to tell us everything we need to know to get started. Here are five ways you can get feedback by paying closer attention to the world around you.

1. Make a list of people's casual remarks about you.

I heard a creativity teacher give her class the following assignment. She sent them out in the street and for one hour had them write down everything they observed people doing in a busy public place. At the end of the hour, each student had compiled more than 150 observations. Then she had them do it again for an hour, except they were only allowed to write down observations *that they found interesting*. The lists were considerably shorter. Suddenly, a man walking across the street wasn't interesting, but a man tossing away a candy wrapper on the pavement—i.e., committing the crime of littering—was. She was trying to make the point that there's a difference between observing and observing *with judgment*.

It's the same in each of our lives. We observe all the time. But we don't often observe with a purpose or with judgment.

For one day, write down all the comments that you hear people make to you about you. For example, "Oh, that was really smart, Marshall." Or, "You're late, Marshall." Or, "Are you listening to me, Marshall?" Any remark that, however remotely, concerns you or your behavior, write it down. At the end of the day, review the list and rate each comment as positive or negative. If you look at the negatives, maybe some patterns will emerge. Perhaps a number of remarks will focus on your tardiness, or your inattention, or your lack of follow up. That's the beginning of a feedback moment. You're learning something about yourself without soliciting it—which means that the comment is agenda-free. It's honest and true.

Then do it again the next day and the next.

Do it at home too, if you want.

Eventually, you'll compile enough data about yourself—without any of your friends and family members being aware that they're giving you feedback—to establish the challenge before you.

When a friend of mine tried this for a week—at work and at home—the remark that popped up most often on his negative list was, "Yes, you said that." In effect people were telling him, "I heard you the first time," which suggested that people found his chronic repetition to be annoying.

An easy issue to fix, but he might never have learned it if he hadn't kept the list and searched for a persisting negative. If you have the courage to face the truth, you can do the same.

2. Turn the sound off.

I sometimes have clients conduct the following exercise. When they're in a team and starting to get bored, I ask them to pretend they're watching a movie with the sound off. They can't hear what anyone is saying. It's an exercise in sensitizing themselves to their colleagues' behavior. They must ask themselves what's going on around them. One of the first things they see is no different than what they hear with the sound on: People are promoting themselves. Only with this newfound sensitization, they see how people *physically* maneuver and gesture to gain primacy in a group setting. They lean forward toward the dominant authority figure. They turn away from people with diminished power. They cut rivals off with hand and arm gestures. It's no different than what people are doing with the sound on except that it's even more obvious with the sound off.

You can do the same for yourself and treat it as a feedback moment. Turn the sound off and observe how people physically deal with you. Do they lean toward you or away? Do they listen when you have the floor or are they drumming their fingers waiting for you to finish? Are they trying to impress you or are they barely aware of your presence? This won't precisely tell you what your specific challenge may be, but if the indicators are more negative than positive, you'll know that you aren't making quite the overwhelming impression on your colleagues that you may have hoped for. You'll know you have some work to do.

A variation on this drill is making sure you are the earliest person to arrive at a group meeting. Turn the sound off and observe how people respond to you as they enter. What they do is a clue about what they think of you. Do they smile when they see you and pull up a chair next to you? Do they barely acknowledge your presence and sit across the room? Note how each person responds to you. If the majority of people shy away from you, that's a disturbing pattern that's hitting you over the head with some serious truth. You have some serious work to do.

The "sound off" drill doesn't quite tell you what you need to change. But at least you'll know where to start asking, "How can I do better?" You can begin with the people in the room.

3. Complete the sentence.

The eminent psychologist Nathaniel Brandon taught me how to apply his sentence completion technique, which is a wonderful exercise for digging deep into creative thought but also works for helping people change.

Pick one thing that you want to get better at. It could be anything that matters to you—from getting in shape to giving more recognition to lowering your golf handicap. Then list the positive benefits that will accrue to you and the world if you achieve your goal. For example, "I want to get in better shape. If I get in shape, one benefit to me is that . . ." And then you complete the sentence.

It's a simple exercise. "If I get in shape, I will . . . live longer." That's one benefit. Then keep doing it. "If I get in shape, I'll feel better about myself." That's two. "If I get in shape, I'll be a better role model for my family and friends." And so on until you exhaust the benefits.

What's interesting about the sentence completion exercise is that as you get deeper into it the answers become less corporately correct and more personal. You start off by saying, "If I become better organized, the company will make more money . . . , my team will become more productive . . . , other people will enjoy their jobs more . . . , and so on." By the end, however, you're saying, "If I become more organized, I'll be a better parent . . . , a better spouse . . . , a better person."

I employed this once with a general in the U.S. Marine Corps. He was a typical hard-nosed Marine who resisted the exercise at first. I'm not sure why. But eventually he relented and played along, saying he wanted to "become less judgmental." As he began, I could see the proud Marine part of him resisting. He completed the first sentence with a cynical crack about "If I become less judgmental, I won't have so much trouble dealing with the clowns at head-quarters." The second sentence was another sarcastic comment. The third time was less sarcastic. By the sixth sentence, I could see tears in his eyes. "If I become less judgmental," he said, "maybe my children will talk to me again."

This may seem like a loopy backward way of giving yourself good feedback. You start with the suggestion and then determine if it's impor-tant. But it works. As the benefits you list become less expected and more personal and meaningful to you, that's when you know that you've given yourself some valuable feedback—that you've hit on an interpersonal skill that you really want and need to improve. That's when you confirm that you've picked the right thing to fix.

4. Listen to your self-aggrandizing remarks.

I don't want to get too psychological here, but have you ever listened to a friend brag about how punctual he is—"You can count on me. I'm al-ways on time."—when you know that being on time is the last thing you can expect from him?

Have you ever heard friends boast about how organized they are, when you know they are unmade beds?

Or how good they are at follow up when everyone thinks their re-sponsiveness is a joke?

In one of those odd bits of reverse psychology, it seems that the stuff people boast about as their strengths more often than not turn out to be their most egregious weaknesses.

None of us is immune to this phenomenon. If it's true about our friends, it's probably true about us. Listen to yourself. What do you boast about? It's quite possible that if you assess this alleged "strength" as closely as your friends do, it's really a weakness. You shouldn't be bragging about it at all. In a perverse way, you've given yourself some of the most honest feedback of all.

I don't want to twist this into knots of psychobabble, but the same les-son might be on display when you make *self-deprecating* remarks.

When a colleague at a meeting starts off by saying, "Maybe I'm no ex-pert on inventory control . . ." you can be sure that the comments that follow will suggest that he does think of himself as an expert on inventory control.

When a friend launches into an argument by saying, "I probably wasn't paying attention . . ." you can be sure that he's planning to show you that he was paying closer attention than you ever suspected.

The one that really perks up my ears is, "I don't have any ego invested in this." You know immediately that the issue is all about ego.

These pseudo-self-deprecating remarks—the ones we say about ourselves but don't believe—are the rhetorical devices and debating tricks of everyday communication that allow us to get an edge on our rivals. Nothing wrong with that. To a student of intracorporate warfare, such self-deprecation from others should put you on high alert. Whatever they say, you know they believe the opposite.

The same could be said of each of us. We should be on high alert when we hear ourselves make self-deprecating remarks—because they might be giving us feedback about ourselves. When you hear yourself make an offhand self-deprecation such as, "I'm not very good at thanking people," it's quite possible that you don't believe it. But it's also possible that it's true, that you're saying something piercingly honest about yourself which you're not yet admitting: You don't thank well.

As I say, I don't want to twist every comment we hear and make into knots. But self-deprecation, pseudo or otherwise, can be one of those honest feedback moments that makes a signal sound in our brain. "Pay attention," it tells us. "This might be something worth *observing*."

5. Look homeward.

Remember the movie *Wall Street* and the character Gordon Gekko? Michael Douglas won an Academy Award for Best Actor for his portrayal of this rude, larcenous wheeler-dealer. Well, I worked with a real-life investment banker who could have inspired the Gekko character.

The man I coached—let's call him Mike—wasn't amoral and unethical like Gekko, but he had some competitive fires burning within his soul that made him treat people like gravel in a driveway. They were the pebbles; he was the SUV. When I finished surveying Mike's colleagues about his interpersonal flaws, Mike's score for treating direct reports and colleagues with respect was an astounding 0.1 percent. That is, out of one thousand managers rated, he was dead last!

But Mike put up equally astounding numbers with his trades. He contributed such vast profits to the firm that the CEO promoted him to the firm's management committee. This should have been the apex of Mike's young career. But it exposed his bad side as well. The firm's leaders, who had been insulated from Mike's behavior, were suddenly in a position to get a firsthand dose of his "lead, follow, or get out of the way" style. In meetings they saw that there was no tollbooth between Mike's brain and mouth. He was surly and offensive to everyone. He would even mouth off to the CEO (his biggest supporter) in meetings. The CEO called me in to work with Mike, to "fix him."

The most obvious thing about Mike when I met him was his delight in his success. He was making more than $4 million a year, so professional validation was coursing through his veins like jet fuel. I suspected that breaking through to Mike by challenging his performance at work would be tough. He was producing and he knew it. So, the first thing I did was sit him down and tell him, "I can't help you make more money. You're already making a lot. But let's talk about your ego. How do you treat people at home?"

He said he was totally different at home, a great husband and father. "I don't bring my work home," he assured me. "I'm a warrior on Wall Street, but a pussycat at home."

"That's interesting," I said. "Is your wife home right now?"

"Yes," he said.

"Let's give her a call and see how different she thinks you are at home than at the office."

We called his wife. When she finally stopped laughing at her husband's statement, she concurred that Mike was a jerk at home, too. Then we got his two kids on the line, and they agreed with their mother.

I said, "I'm beginning to see a pattern here. As I told you, I can't help you make more money. But I can get you to confront this question: Do you really want to have a funeral where you're the featured attraction and the only attendees are people who came to make sure you're dead? Basically, that's where you're headed."

For the first time, Mike looked stricken. "They're going to fire me, aren't they?" he asked.

"Not only are they going to fire you," I said, "but everyone will be dancing in the halls when you go!"

Mike thought a minute, and then said, "I'm going to change, and the reason I'm going to change has nothing to do with money and it has nothing to do with this firm. I'm going to change because I have two sons, and if they were receiving this same feedback from you in twenty years, I'd be ashamed."

Within a year, his scores in terms of treating people with respect shot up past the 50th percentile—meaning that he was above the already-high company norm. He probably deserved even better, since he started so far down in the ditch. He also doubled his income, although I cannot claim a direct cause-effect connection for that.

The lesson: *Your flaws at work don't vanish when you walk through the front door at home.*

The moral: Anybody can change, but they have to want to change—and sometimes you can deliver that message by reaching people where they live, not where they work.

The action plan for leaders (and followers): If you want to really know how your behavior is coming across with your colleagues and clients, stop looking in the mirror and admiring yourself. Let your colleagues hold the mirror and tell you what they see. If you don't believe them, go home. Pose the same question to your loved ones and friends—the people in your life who are most likely to be agenda-free and who truly want you to succeed. We all claim to want the truth. This is a guaranteed delivery system.

These five examples of observed feedback are stealth techniques to make you pay closer attention to the world around you.

When you make a list of people's comments about you and rank them as negative or positive, you're tuning in the world with two new weapons: Judgment and purpose.

When you turn off the sound, you're increasing your sensitivity to others by counterintuitively eliminating the precious sense of hearing.

When you try the sentence completion technique, you're using retrograde analysis—that is, seeing the end result and then identifying the skill you'll need to achieve it.

When you challenge the accuracy of your self-aggrandizing remarks, you're flipping your world upside down—and seeing that you're no different from anyone else.

Finally, when you check out how your behavior is working at home, you realize not only what you need to change but why it matters so much.

The logic behind these drills is simple: If you can see your world in a new way, perhaps you can see yourself anew as well.

Although we've spent a lot of time on feedback here, keep in mind that it is only the baseline of our activity. We are only at the beginning.

If I were an orthopedic surgeon, feedback would be like an MRI. I need the MRI to show deep-tissue damage and identify what's broken. But I still need to perform an operation to fix the problem and the patient still needs weeks of diligent rehabilitation to get better.

If I were an advertising executive, feedback would be the part where the agency studies the data about the client's product. Who's buying it? Why? What's its market share against competing products? But this research feedback isn't a great commercial. I still have to come up with that on my own.

If I were a politician running for office, feedback would be the polling data telling me what's on voters' minds. But I still have to run for election on my own. I still have to convince voters that I'm the right person to deal with their issues. I still have to win votes. Feedback won't do *that* for me.

Feedback tells us what to change, not how to do it. But when you know what to change, you're ready to start changing yourself and how people perceive you. You're ready for the next step: telling everyone you're sorry.

CHAPTER 7

Apologizing

The Magic Move

If it isn't obvious by now, I regard apologizing as the most magical, healing, restorative gesture human beings can make. It is the centerpiece of my work with executives who want to get better—because without the apology there is no recognition that mistakes have been made, there is no announcement to the world of the intention to change, and most important there is no emotional contract between you and the people you care about. Saying you're sorry to someone writes that contract in blood.

In *Harvey Penick's Little Red Book*, there is a brief story titled "The Magic Move." It's Penick's indelible description of the cornerstone of the golf swing—the weight transfer from left to right foot as we take the club back and then the transfer back to the left foot as we bring our right elbow down and swing the club through the ball. If you learn this, says Penick, "you will hit the ball as if by magic."

Well, apologizing is my "magic move." It's a seemingly simple tactic. But like admitting you were wrong, or saying, "Thank you," it's tough for some people to do—but brilliant for those who can.

I can't think of a more vivid example of the magic move's cleansing power than Richard Clarke testifying before the 9/11 commission. Clarke spent hours talking about terrorism to the commissioners, but almost all of his testimony, much of it controversial, was overwhelmed by one moment—when he addressed the 9/11 families to say, "Your government failed you, those entrusted with protecting you failed you, and I failed you." It's an apology that Frank Rich of the *New York Times* suggested "is likely to join our history's greatest hits video reel, alongside Joseph Welch's 'Have you no sense of decency, sir?' "

Some thought Clarke was grandstanding, or that he had no right to apologize, or that he had injected an overwrought emotionality into the otherwise clinical proceedings. But I applauded, because Clarke was doing something that both parties needed. In effect, he was saying, "We can't redo the past. But the worst is behind us, and I am still so sorry." The apology gave him and the people he was addressing a sense of closure, however faint and bittersweet. Closure lets you move forward.

Clarke's apology was replayed on television for days. I'm puzzled that anyone was surprised by the emotional wallop packed into his mea culpa. It's what I try to get my clients to do without thinking. Sometimes the message takes longer to get through than I prefer.

That's what happened with a senior manager named Ted with whom I worked in the late 1990s. Ted was the standard-issue success story: a smart, personable, hard-working, deliver-the-numbers-and-live-the-values type, cherished by his bosses, admired by his colleagues, and loved by his direct reports. There was one recurring flaw in this otherwise perfect picture: Ted was disastrous on follow-up with clients and colleagues. It took years for this flaw to get noticed, which explained why all of Ted's relationships started out ecstatically but eventually drifted into conflict. He alienated the people closest to him—not out of malice or arrogance but out of passive neglect. He failed to return their calls. He would never make the first move to check up on them to see how they were doing. He would only pay attention to them if there was business to be done. This is the kind of benign hurtful pattern that emerges only over time—because you only miss nurturing and caring in their absence. But it was a recurring pattern with Ted. Somewhere along the way, he had to learn how to show people he cared for them as human beings, that he was their friend with or without a deal at stake.

We helped Ted change for the better at work—by applying the magic moves of apologize, advertise, and follow-up. That's not the point though.

Ted and I kept in touch (mostly me calling him, of course), but one day in March 2004 he phoned with exciting news.

"Marshall," he said, "you would have been proud of me. I totally screwed up one of my closest friendships."

"Okay," I hesitated. "And the reason I should be proud of you is . . ."

"Because I apologized and saved the friendship," he said.

The story goes like this: Ted's best friend for 20 years was his neighbor Vince. Over the course of two weeks, Vince had called Ted five times and Ted never called back. (Apparently, the correctives Ted had learned to apply on the job had not quite sunk in in his home life.) Vince, a volatile Sicilian who valued loyalty and friendship above all else, was hurt and stopped talking to Ted. Ted noticed but couldn't bring himself to contact Vince and apologize. Their respective wives tried to arrange a rapprochement: They decided Ted would write a contrite letter to Vince and all would be well. But Ted messed that up too. Because of business and out-of-town trips, several weeks went by without Ted writing the letter that Vince was now expecting. Finally, Vince boiled over and wrote Ted a stinging letter outlining all the slights and offenses that had poisoned their friendship—not returning phone calls, ignoring him at a dinner party, never initiating contact. (This sounds like a soap opera, but bear with me.)

This pained Ted enormously, to the point that he immediately wrote Vince a reply. I quote it here in its entirety because it is a model apologia.

Dear Vince,

As Vito Corleone said when he sat down with the Five Families, "How did it come to this?"

I read your letter a few minutes ago and, in a first effort to change—i.e., being more responsive—I am writing to address the charges. As I see it, there are three.

To the first count of not calling you back, you are right, absolutely right. It is rude. It is not how a friend, or even a solid citizen, behaves. I should know better. It sends an unfortunate and incorrect message that I don't care about you. (If it makes you feel better, I am democratic about this particular failing. I don't call back my mother, my brother, and my in-laws. My wife says, "Me too." This is hardly something to brag about—just a minuscule point of honor on my part to assure you that you are not in the bottom half of some imaginary call-back priority list. Apparently, I don't have one. I treat everyone equally—which is to say, rudely.) For this I apologize to you. And I will change that.

To the second count of being a poor host when you were at my house, I certainly did not intend to ignore you or leave you out of the conversation.

That said, what I remember is not the point. It's what you felt that matters, and this is especially pertinent when the issue is hospitality extended or withheld. As Boston Celtics coach Red Auerbach used to say about coaching his players, "It's not what you say, it's what they hear." You obviously didn't enjoy the evening, and for that I apologize. I like to think of myself as a decent and caring and generous host, and I will take your comments as a signal to do better.

To the third count of my never initiating a phone call to friends, again you are right, absolutely right. Some people, as you say, like to work at friendship. Others don't.

Of all the charges you level at me, the third is the one that pains me most—because it is true and because it is so easily fixed. You are not the first to point this out. I guess I could wander back into my childhood to figure out why I act this way, but looking backward, seeking out scapegoats, is a fool's errand. I'm 52 years old. I can't blame my mother or my upbringing or that lousy tuna sandwich in third grade. All I can do is promise to fix my behavior, one step at a time—by taking my cues from you, by doing the things you say a good friend does. Hopefully, my rehabilitation starts with you.

The evidence notwithstanding, I do value our friendship. Tremendously. We have too many years of laughs and good times and neighboring and genuine caring for each other to let our friendship slip away because I am a schmuck in an area where you least value that kind of behavior. All I can ask is your forgiveness. If you can grant me that, I do not expect us to return to things the way they were. I think we should aim higher. I would want us to return to things as they should be, where I can aspire to the ideal of friendship that you have described in your honest, painfully honest, letter to me.

Shall we discuss this over a bottle of red?

A great letter, right? But not if it goes unread.

Vince sent it back unopened. The wives again interceded, begging Vince to read the letter. When he relented, the process of repairing the friendship was underway—because it is impossible to resist a heartfelt apology.

I always wonder about all those people who, like Ted in his former life, can't bring themselves to admit they're wrong or say they're sorry.

How do they survive in the world? How do they mend damaged relationships? How do they show others what they're really feeling? How can they declare their willingness to alter their annoying ways without first saying, "I'm sorry"?

When I congratulated Ted on his handling of the situation, he said, "You know, if I hadn't gone through this at work I couldn't have apologized to Vince."

"Why can you do it now?" I asked.

"Because I know it works."

That may be a compelling reason to learn the magic move of apology, but the most compelling is this: *It is so easy to do*. All you have to do is repeat these words: "I'm sorry. I'll try to do better."

Try it sometime. It costs you nothing—not even your illusory pride—but the return on investment would make Warren Buffett green with envy. And it will change your life, as if by magic.

How to Apologize

Do you see a pattern here in the examples of Richard Clarke and Ted and Vince? The healing process begins with an apology.

It doesn't matter what we have done or what compels us to apologize. It could be the intense sorrow you feel for causing someone pain. Or the shame of neglecting someone who deserves your attention. Or the heartbreak of losing someone's affection for something you've done. Sorrow, pain, shame, heartbreak. These are powerful emotions, sometimes powerful enough to force an apology out of the hardest heart. But that's not the issue here. Cause and motive do not move me. Whatever forces an apology out of people who normally cannot do it, I'm for it.

Once you're prepared to apologize, here's the instruction manual:

You say, "I'm sorry."

You add, "I'll try to do better in the future." Not absolutely necessary, but prudent in my view because when you let go of the past, it's nice to hint at a brighter future.

And then . . . you say nothing.

Don't explain it. Don't complicate it. Don't qualify it. You only risk saying something that will dilute it. I remember back in 2001 when Morgan Stanley paid a $50 million fine to settle conflict-of-interest charges centering on the firm's research analysts writing favorable reports about companies doing business with the firm. The $50 million payment was supposed to help Morgan Stanley put the scandal behind them and move on to better days. As such, it certainly had the look and feel of an apology. But the firm's CEO, Phil Purcell, blew it the next day in a speech in which he sought to rationalize the fine. He said the firm paid it to get the issue over with; the firm really hadn't done anything wrong, and certainly wasn't as bad as other firms, which had paid even bigger fines. It sounded like he was boasting that his firm had paid the *smallest* fine. That's like bragging that you only served three years of jail time while your cellmates were in for ten.

The media, the Securities and Exchange Commission, and New York's Attorney General immediately leaped on Purcell for his remarks. No matter how much money the firm has, when you write a $50 million penalty check, that's a serious apology. You can't wink while you're apologizing. You can only say you're sorry and keep quiet.

If a sophisticated CEO can mess up a $50 million apology by saying too much, imagine what havoc the rest of us can cause by voicing one word more than "I'm sorry" in our own displays of contrition.

When it comes to apologizing, the only sound advice is *get in and get out as quickly as possible*. You've got plenty of other things to do before you change for the better. The sooner you can get the apology over with, the sooner you can move on to telling the world.

CHAPTER 8

Telling the World,
or Advertising

AFTER YOU APOLOGIZE, you must *advertise*. It's not enough to tell everyone that you want to get better; you have to declare exactly in what area you plan to change. In other words, now that you've said you're sorry, what are you going to do about it?

I tell my clients, "It's a lot harder to change people's perception of your behavior than it is to change your behavior. In fact, I calculate that you have to get 100% better in order to get 10% credit for it from your coworkers."

The logic behind this is, as I've explained in Chapter 3, cognitive dissonance: To recap, we view people in a manner that is consistent with our previous existing stereotypes, whether it is positive or negative. If I think you're an arrogant jerk, everything you do will be filtered through that perception. If you do something wonderful and saintly, I will regard it as the exception to the rule; you're still an arrogant jerk. Within that framework it's almost impossible for us to be perceived as improving, no matter how hard we try.

However, the odds improve considerably if you tell people that you are trying to change. Suddenly, your efforts are on their radar screen. You're beginning to chip away at their preconceptions.

Your odds improve again if you tell everyone how hard you're trying, and repeat the message week after week.

Your odds improve even more if you ask everyone for ideas to help you get better. Now your coworkers become invested in you; they pay attention to you to see if you're paying attention to their suggestions.

Eventually the message sinks in and people start to accept the possibility of a new improved you. It's a little like the tree falling in the forest. If no one hears the thud, does it make a sound? The apology and the announcement that you're trying to change are your way of pointing everyone in the direction of the tree.

Don't Forget the "Dumb" Phase

Any marketer knows that there's no point in creating a great new product if you can't get the message out to the buying public. You have to tell the world, "Hey, I'm over here," and give them a reason to care.

That's the same rationale you must use as you undertake a serious personal initiative. You're about to create a new "you." Do you think people will buy that without a good advertising campaign?

It's not enough to merely let people know what you're doing. You're not running a "one day sale" here. You're trying to create a lasting change. You have to advertise *relentlessly*—as if it's a long-term campaign. You can't assume that people hear you the first time or the second time or even the third. You have to pound the message into your colleagues' heads through repetition that's as steady as a metronome—because people aren't paying as close attention to your personal goals as you are. They have other things on their minds; they have their own goals and challenges to deal with. As a result, your efforts to change may not get instant acceptance from your colleagues. You may have to fight your way through a "dumb phase."

I first heard this phrase as a dinner guest at the home of a wine expert. One of the other guests brought a 12-year-old bottle of red wine from one of the legendary vineyards of France. We were all eager to drink it, but our host politely suggested that it might not be the right time. It's 12 years old. It's ready, we insisted. So we opened the bottle, decanted it, poured it into sparkling crystals, swirled it in the glass, inhaled its profound bouquet, and then eagerly tasted it.

We put down our glasses and looked around at each other. We were all thinking the same thing. This wine has no flavor or character at all.

We tasted again.

Same opinion. The wine was totally bland, as if it had died in the bottle.

Finally, our oenophile host explained that some truly great wines, which can last for decades and tend to improve with age, go through a "dumb period" when the wine goes to sleep for a few years and then wakes up and improves dramatically in the bottle. It happens anywhere from age 6 to 18 years, depending on the wine. Our bottle was still in its dumb period. Like he said, we should have waited.

It's the same with any project you undertake at work, whether it's a campaign of personal change or an initiative that can transform your company. The best ideas are like great wines. They improve with age. But they can also go through a dumb period when they need time to settle and sink in.

Has the following ever happened to you? Your boss gives you a major assignment to find out what's going on at a trouble spot within your company. You do what any well-trained M.B.A. would do. You study the situation, identify the problem, report your findings and recommendations to the boss, outline a new approach, and turn it over to the appropriate people to implement the strategy.

A month goes by. Nothing happens. Another month. Still no progress. Six months later, the trouble spot remains unchanged.

What did you do wrong?

It's simple. You committed "one, two, three, seven."

You failed to appreciate that every successful project goes through seven phases: The first is assessing the situation; the second is isolating the problem; the third is formulating. But there are three more phases before you get to the seventh, implementation.

Unfortunately, a lot of people don't pay close attention to phases four, five, and six—the vital period when you approach your coworkers to secure the all-important political buy-in to your plans. In each phase you must target a different constituency. In phase 4, you woo up—to get your superiors to *approve*. In phase 5, you woo laterally—to get your peers to *agree*. In phase 6, you woo down—to get your direct reports to *accept*. These three phases are the sine qua non of getting things done. You cannot skip or skim over them. You have to give them as much, if not more, attention, as you do phases one, two, three, and seven. If you don't, you may as well be working alone in a locked room where no one sees you, hears you, or knows you exist. That's the guaranteed result of committing "one, two, three, seven."

What's true for getting people to solve a corporate problem is just as true for getting people to help you change for the better. It takes time and relentless persuasion for any idea to gain traction. Think of your "advertising" as recruiting colleagues up, over, and down to buy in to the concept. If you don't, you are committing "one, two, three, seven" on yourself. You can't get to seven without counting from one to six. Anything less is bad arithmetic.

Be Your Own Press Secretary

Wouldn't the world be a better place if we each had our own presidential press secretary to answer tough questions and "spin" our message all day long against any and all adversaries? (It would be great for us perhaps, but I'm not sure I want to live in a world where everyone is "spinning" everyone else.)

That said, there's something to be learned from the methods that politicians employ to stay in power.

Chief among these is staying on message—i.e., knowing what you want to say and then repeating it with extreme discipline and near-shamelessness, until it sinks in. If there's one thing we've learned in this noisy media age, it's that simple, un-nuanced messages break through the clutter and hit home with high impact. (I'm not saying that's always a good thing, but it's a fact of life. Deal with it.)

It's no different when you're attempting to change. Like a politician making headlines for introducing new legislation, if you have a new initiative at work, you have to do something dramatic to announce it. (Reagan taught us that.) For sheer drama, apologizing fits the bill. What could be more theatrical than telling people that you're sorry for some transgression and you'll try to do better in the future, especially people who think *you cannot change*?

Don't stop there. You can't just apologize and say you're trying to do better just once. You have to drill it into people repeatedly, until they've internalized the concept.

It's the reason politicians in a hard election campaign run the same ads over and over again. Repeating their message—relentlessly—works; it sinks the message deeper into our brains.

I don't want to push this political press secretary analogy too far. I'm not asking people to obfuscate or display selective memory or avoid questions, all of which are valuable weapons in the press secretary arsenal. All I'm saying is that you cannot rely on other people to read your mind or take note of the changed behavior you're displaying. It may be patently obvious to you, but it takes a lot more than a few weeks of behavioral modification for people to notice the new you.

That makes it all the more vital that you proactively control the message of what you're trying to accomplish. Here's how to start acting like your own press secretary.

- Treat every day as if it were a press conference during which your colleagues are judging you, waiting to see you trip up. That mindset, where you know people are watching you closely, will boost your self-awareness just enough to remind you to stay on high alert.

- Behave as if every day is an opportunity to hit home your message—to remind people that you're trying really hard. Every day that you fail to do so is a day that you lose a step or two. You're backsliding on your promise to fix yourself.

- Treat every day as a chance to take on all challengers. There will be people who, privately or overtly, don't want you to succeed. So shed the naiveté and be a little paranoid. If you're alert to those who want you to fail, you'll know how to handle them.

- Think of the process as an election campaign. After all, you don't elect yourself to the position of "new improved you." Your colleagues do. They're your constituency. Without their votes, you can never establish that you've changed.

- Think of the process in terms of weeks and months, not just day to day. The best press secretaries are adept at putting out the daily fires, but they're also focused on a long-term agenda. You should too. No matter what happens day to day, your long-term goal is to be perceived as fixing an interpersonal problem—to the point where it isn't a problem anymore.

If you can do this, like the best press secretaries, you'll have your personal "press corps" eating out of your hands.

CHAPTER 9

Listening

JACK NICKLAUS SAID THAT 80 percent of a successful golf shot begins with a proper grip and how you stand over the ball. In other words, success is almost a foregone conclusion before you exert one muscle.

It's the same with listening: 80 percent of our success in learning from other people is based upon how well we listen. In other words, success or failure is determined before we do anything.

The thing about listening that escapes most people is that they think of it as a passive activity. You don't have to do anything. You sit there like a lump and hear someone out.

Not true. Good listeners regard what they do as a highly active process—with every muscle engaged, especially the brain.

Basically, there are three things that all good listeners do: They think before they speak; they listen with respect; and they're always gauging their response by asking themselves, "Is it worth it?" Let's examine each one and see if it makes us better listeners.

Think Before You Speak

The first active choice you have to make in listening is to think before you speak. You can't listen if you're talking. So keeping your mouth shut is an active choice (and as we know, for some people it's tougher to do than bench-pressing 500 pounds).

I don't know anyone better at it than Frances Hesselbein. Frances is one of my all-time heroes—someone I respect, admire, and love on a par with my wife and kids. She was the executive director of the Girl Scouts for 13 years during which she revived a sagging organization, increased enrollment, funding, and diversity, and balanced the budget. She has 17 honorary degrees. She received the Presidential Medal of Freedom in 1998 (America's highest civilian award). Peter Drucker called her the finest executive he's ever known.

Frances Hesselbein does a lot of things well. But she does one thing superbly above all else. She thinks before she speaks. As a result she is a world-class listener. If you asked her if this was a passive gesture, she would assure you that it requires great discipline, particularly when she is upset about what she's hearing. After all, what do most of us do when we're angry? We speak (and not in the carefully measured tones of a diplomat).

What do we do when we're upset? We talk.

What do we do when we're confused or surprised or shocked? Again, we talk. This is so predictable that we can see the other party almost cringe in anticipation of our harsh unthinking autoreflex response.

Not so with Frances Hesselbein. You could tell her the world was about to end and she would think before opening her mouth, not only about what she would say but how she would phrase it.

Whereas most people think of listening as something we do during those moments *when we are not talking*, Frances Hesselbine knows that listening is a two-part maneuver. There's the part where we actually listen. And there's the part where we speak. Speaking establishes how we are perceived as a listener. What we say is proof of how well we listen. They are two sides of the same coin.

I defy you to argue that this approach is anything but a highly active, decisive choice. Telling your brain and mouth not to do something is no different than telling them to do it.

If you can master this, you can listen effectively.

Listen with Respect

To learn from people, you have to listen to them with respect. Again, not as easy to do as you might imagine. It too requires the use of unfamiliar muscles.

Has this ever happened to you? You're reading a book, watching TV, or shuffling papers while your significant other is talking to you. Suddenly you hear, "You're not listening to me."

You look up and say, "Yes I am." And calmly provide a verbatim playback of everything said to prove that you were listening and that your companion in life is . . . wrong.

What have you accomplished by this virtuosic display of your multitasking skills? Was it smart? No. Does your partner think more highly of you? Not likely. Is anyone impressed? Hardly.

The only thing going through your partner's mind is, "Gee, I thought you weren't listening. But now I realize it's a much deeper issue. You're a complete jerk."

This is what happens when we listen without showing respect. It's not enough to keep our ears open; we have to demonstrate that we are totally engaged.

Bill Clinton was the absolute master at this. My wife and I had several opportunities see the President in action in public forums. It didn't matter if you were a head of state or a bell clerk, when you were talking with Bill Clinton he acted as if you were the only person in the room. Every fiber of his being, from his eyes to his body language, communicated that he was locked into what you were saying. He conveyed how important you were, not how important *he* was.

If you don't think this is an active, practically aerobic piece of mental and muscular exertion, try it sometime in a receiving line of 500 people, all of whom regard this brief transaction with you as part of their lifetime highlight reel.

If you've never done it, listening with respect makes you sweat.

Ask Yourself, "Is It Worth It?"

Listening also requires us to answer a difficult question before we speak: "Is it worth it?"

The trouble with listening for many of us is that while we're supposedly doing it, we're actually busy composing what we're going to say next.

This is a negative two-fer: You're not only failing to hear the other person, you're orchestrating a comment that may annoy them, either because it misses the point, adds meaningless value to the discussion, or worst of all, injects a destructive tone into the mix. Not the desired result of listening. Keep it up and soon you won't have to worry about listening—because no one will be talking to you anymore.

When someone tells us something, we have a menu of options to fashion our response. Some of our responses are smart, some are stupid. Some are on point, some miss the point. Some will encourage the other person, some will discourage her. Some will make her feel appreciated, some will not.

Asking "Is it worth it?" forces you to consider what the other person will feel after hearing your response. It forces you to play at least two moves ahead. Not many people do that. You talk. They talk. And so on—back and forth like a beginner's chess game where no one thinks beyond the move in front of them. It's the lowest form of chess; it's also the lowest grade of listening. Asking, "Is it worth it?" engages you in thinking beyond the discussion to consider (a) how the other person regards you, (b) what that person will do afterwards, and (c) how that person will behave the next time you talk.

That's a lot of consequences emanating out of "Is it worth it?"

Think about the last time you floated an idea in a meeting and the most senior person in the room (assuming it wasn't you) ripped you for saying it. It doesn't matter whether your idea was dumb and the other person's response was brilliant—or vice versa. Just think about how you felt. Did you think more highly of the other person saying it? Did it make you appreciate anew that person's tremendous listening skills? Did it inspire you to go back to your work with fresh enthusiasm? Did it make you more eager to speak up the next time you were in a meeting with that person? I'd wager the answers are no, no, no, and no.

That's what happens when you respond without asking "Is it worth it?" People not only think you don't listen, but you have instigated a three-part chain of consequences: (1) they are hurt; (2) they harbor ill feelings toward the person who inflicted the hurt (i.e., they hate you); and (3) in the predictable response to negative reinforcement, they are less likely to repeat the event (i.e., they won't speak up next time).

Keep it up, and here's what will happen: Everyone will think you're an ass (a personal judgment, not necessarily damaging, but certainly not nice). They won't perform well for you (which damages your reputation as a leader). And they'll stop giving you ideas (which reduces your knowledge base). This is hardly the formula for leadership success.

One of my clients was the chief operating officer of a multi-billion dollar company (and now the CEO). His goal was to become a better listener and be perceived as a more open-minded boss. After working with him for 18 months, I asked him what was the major learning kernel he got out of the experience. He said, "Before speaking, I take a breath and ask myself one question, 'Is it worth it?' I learned that 50 percent of what I was going to say was correct—maybe—but saying it wasn't worth it."

He learned what Frances Hesselbein knew—that people's opinions of our listening ability are largely shaped by the decisions we make immediately after asking, "Is it worth it?" Do we speak or shut up? Do we argue or simply say, "Thank you"? Do we add our needless two cents or bite our tongue? Do we rate the comments or simply acknowledge them?

It's not up to me to tell you what to say in a meeting. All I'm saying is that you should consider if it's worth it—and if you believe it is, speak freely.

This is what my client absorbed. As a result, his scores for being a better listener and an open-minded boss skyrocketed. And he became the CEO.

The implications of "Is it worth it?" are profound—and go beyond listening. In effect, you are taking the age-old question of self-interest, "What's in it for me?" one step further to ask, "What's in it for him?" That's a profound consequential leap of thought. Suddenly, you're seeing the bigger picture.

As I say over and over again, this is simple stuff—but it's not easy. If you do it, everything will get better. So much of our interpersonal problems at work are formulaic. You say something that ticks me off. I lash back at you. Suddenly, we have an interpersonal crisis (otherwise known as a fight). It doesn't matter whether we're talking about global warming or whom to hire to make a widget. The content is irrelevant. What matters is how easily we slip into small behavioral patterns that create friction in the workplace—and how just as easily we could assume behavioral patterns that *don't* create friction. That's why simple disciplines—such as thinking before speaking, listening with respect, and asking, "Is it worth it?"—work. They don't require nuance. We just need to do them.

The Skill that Separates the Near-Great from the Great

Two lawyers are sitting at the bar at Spark's Steakhouse in New York City. One is my friend Tom, the other is his law partner, Dave. They're having a leisurely drink, waiting for their table to open up. They're in no rush. Spark's is the kind of place where you don't mind hanging around. It's a landmark steakhouse, with a huge dining room, a world-famous wine list, and a handful of New York's rich, powerful, or glamorous in attendance every night. (It's also notorious as the site where New York crime boss Paul Castellano was gunned down by John Gotti's henchmen.) On this night, the A-list name is superstar attorney David Boies, who has just walked in and immediately makes a beeline to the bar to say hello to lawyer Dave, whom he knows from previous trials. Boies joins Tom and Dave for a drink. A few minutes later Dave gets up to make a phone call outside. It turns into a very long call.

Boies remains at the bar, talking to my pal Tom for 45 minutes.

What the two lawyers discussed is not relevant here.

What's relevant is my friend Tom's recollection of the encounter.

"I'd never met Boies before," said Tom. "He didn't have to hang around the bar talking to me. And I have to tell you, I wasn't bowled over by his intelligence, or his piercing questions, or his anecdotes. What impressed me was that when he asked a question, he waited for the answer. He not only listened, he made me feel like I was the only person in the room."

I submit that Tom's last 13 words perfectly describe the single skill that separates the great from the near-great.

My friend Tom isn't easily impressed. He's vice chairman of a prosperous 300-lawyer firm in New York. His partner Dave is a highly skilled litigator. Boies, of course, is a legal superstar, the attorney the U.S. government hired to argue its antitrust case against Bill Gates and Microsoft, the same attorney Al Gore turned to in 2000 to argue his presidential election challenge in front of the U.S. Supreme Court.

Let's examine what happened at the bar. Tom stayed in his seat. Dave, for inexplicable reasons, disappeared to make a phone call outside. Boies, on the other hand, stuck around and made a lasting positive impression on Tom. There was no reason for him to treat Tom as his new best friend. The two attorneys have different practices; the chances that their paths would cross in court or that they could help each other is virtually nil. In other words, Boies wasn't thinking that there would be some future benefit in being nice to Tom. And yet, he still made my friend Tom feel like the most important person in the room. In showing interest, asking questions, and most important, listening for the answers without distraction, Boies was simply being himself, practicing the one skill that has made him an inarguably great success.

The ability to make a person feel that, when you're with that person, he or she is the most important (and the only) person in the room is the skill that separates the great from the near-great.

Television interviewers like Oprah Winfrey, Katie Couric, and Diane Sawyer, I'm told by people who've met them, have it. When they're talking to you, on camera or off, you feel as if you're the only one who matters to them. It's *the* skill that defines them.

A British acquaintance told me about an aging executive who could always be seen at London restaurants dining with the most beautiful women in the world. It wasn't his looks or animal magnetism. He was short, jowly, overweight, bald, and well into his seventies. But when my acquaintance asked one woman why she was so enthralled with this man, she answered, "He never takes his eyes off me. Even if the Queen walked in, he wouldn't be distracted. He would still be devoting his full attention to me. That's hard to resist."

As I say, Bill Clinton has this skill in spades. Whether you were meeting him for the first time in a receiving line, or dealing with him one-on-one in a private session, Clinton made a point of knowing something positive about you and, without making a big show of it, saying something to let you know he knew it. In effect, he was bragging about you *to you*. That's a very meaningful gesture. (Imagine how you'd feel if, instead of being forced to tell someone how swell you are, they pointed out your swellness to you and to everyone within earshot. Kinda nice, huh? Wouldn't you really respond to that person?) Couple that with a laser-like focus on what you had to say, and you understand why Clinton ascended far from his humble Arkansas origins.

I'm not sure why all of us don't execute this precious interpersonal maneuver all the time. We're certainly capable of doing so when it *really* matters to us.

If we're on a first date with a guy or girl whom we really want to impress, we will be paragons of attentiveness and interest. We will ask all the right questions, and we will pay attention to the answers with the concentration of a brain surgeon operating inside a patient's skull. If we're really smart, we will calibrate the conversation to make sure we don't talk too much.

If we're in a meeting with our boss, we will listen without interruption to every word she says. We will mark the boss's vocal inflections, seeing nuance and meaning that may or may not be intended. We will lock in on the boss's eyes and mouth, searching for smiles or frowns, as if they were significant clues about our career prospects. Basically, we are treating our boss as if she's the most important person in the room (because she is).

Likewise if we're on a sales call with a prospect who could make or break our year. We prepare by knowing something personal about the prospect. We ask questions designed to reveal the prospect's inclinations. We scan the prospect's face for clues about how badly he needs what we're selling. We are at Defcon Five in terms of attentiveness. Full alert.

The only difference between us and the super-successful among us— the near-great and the great—is that *the great ones do this all the time*. It's automatic for them. For them there's no on and off switch for caring and empathy and showing respect. It's always on. They don't rank personal encounters as A, B, or C in importance. They treat everyone equally—and everyone eventually notices.

The weird part here is that all of us, at every level of success, already know this. I've asked my clients point blank, "What interpersonal skill stands out in the most successful people you've met?" In one form or another, they always cite this "make the other person feel singularly special" ability—usually because (like my friend Tom) they're so impressed by people who make *them* feel that way.

So, I don't think I'm promulgating something new or hard to accept here. We already believe it.

The question is: Why don't we do it?

Answer: We forget. We get distracted. We don't have the mental discipline to make it automatic.

That's it in a nutshell.

Ninety percent of this skill is listening, of course. And listening requires a modicum of discipline—the discipline to concentrate. So I've developed a simple exercise to test my clients' listening skills. It's simple—as simple as asking people to touch their toes to establish how limber they are. I ask them to close their eyes and count slowly to fifty with one simple goal: They cannot let another thought intrude into their mind. They must concentrate on maintaining the count.

What could be simpler than that? Try it.

Incredibly, more than half my clients can't do it. Somewhere around twenty or thirty, nagging thoughts invade their brain. They think about a problem at work, or their kids, or how much they ate for dinner the night before.

This may sound like a concentration test, but it's really a listening exercise. After all, if you can't listen to yourself (someone you presumably like and respect) as you count to fifty, how will you ever be able to listen to another person?

Like any exercise, this drill both exposes a weakness and helps you get stronger. If I ask you to touch your toes and you can't, we've revealed that your muscles are tight. If you practice touching your toes each day, eventually you'll become more limber.

That's what this fifty-count exercise achieves. It exposes how easily distracted we can be when we're not talking. But it also helps us develop our concentration muscles—our ability to maintain focus. Do this exercise regularly and you'll soon be counting to 50 without interrupting yourself. This newfound power of concentration will make you a better listener.

After that, you're ready for a test drive.

Put this book down and make your next interpersonal encounter—whether it's with your spouse or a colleague or a stranger—an exercise in making the other person feel like a million bucks. Try to employ the tiny tactics we've outlined here.

- Listen.

- Don't interrupt.

- Don't finish the other person's sentences.

- Don't say "I knew that."

- Don't even agree with the other person (even if he praises you, just say, "Thank you").

- Don't use the words "no," "but," and "however."

- Don't be distracted. Don't let your eyes or attention wander elsewhere while the other person is talking.

- Maintain your end of the dialogue by asking intelligent questions that (a) show you're paying attention, (b) move the conversation forward, and (c) require the other person to talk (while you listen).

- Eliminate any striving to impress the other person with how smart or funny you are. Your only aim is to let the other person feel that *he or she* is accomplishing that.

If you can do that, you'll uncover a glaring paradox: *The more you subsume your desire to shine, the more you will shine in the other person's eyes.* I've seen this happen so many times, it's almost comical. I've watched two people have a discussion where one person is clearly doing all the talking while the other person patiently listens and asks questions. Later on, when I've asked the dominant talker what he thought of the other person, he never regards the other person's relative silence as evidence that he's dull, uninformed, and uninteresting. On the contrary, he invariably says, "What a great guy!"

You'd say the same thing about anyone who brought out the best in you, who made you feel like the most important person in the room.

Please note that this test run is not an exercise in developing newfound charm, or learning the jargon of seduction, or using body language as subtle levers of persuasion. It's nothing more than an exercise in active listening. Active in the sense that there's a purpose to your listening. If your objective is to make people feel like a million bucks in your presence, you'll score a bull's-eye. You already know how to do it—on a first date, on a sales call, in a meeting with your boss. From now on, it's a matter of remembering to *do it all the time*.

CHAPTER 10

Thanking

Why Thanking Works

Thanking works because it expresses one of our most basic emotions: gratitude. Gratitude is not an abstraction. It's a genuine emotion, which cannot be expected or exacted. You either feel it or you don't. But when someone does something nice for you, *they expect gratitude*—and they think less of you for withholding it. Just think about the last time you gave someone a gift. If they forgot to thank you for it, how did you feel about them? Fine human being? Or ungrateful s.o.b.?

Gratitude is a complex emotion—and therefore can be complicated to express. It is frequently interpreted as submissive behavior, slightly humiliating. This may explain why parents must constantly remind their children to say, "Thank you." It's one of the last and hardest things to teach naturally rebellious kids.

One other thing: Saying "Thank you" is a crucial feature of etiquette and being mannerly. As with most rules of etiquette, it can become formulaic; it doesn't have to be sincere. We use the phrase all day long without thinking, often as a form of punctuation in conversation. For example, we'll say "thank you" on a phone call to end the conversation. We may not be conscious that "thank you" in this context really means "We're done here. Now please stop talking." But such is the polite power of "Thank you" that people always obey.

The best thing about saying "Thank you" is that it creates closure in any potentially explosive discussion. What can you say after someone thanks you? You can't argue with them. You can't try to prove them wrong.

You can't trump them or get angry or ignore them. The only response is to utter two of the most gracious, inviting, and sweet words in the language: "You're welcome." It's music to anyone's ears.

Get used to saying, "Thank you." You're going to need this skill as we move on to the final two steps: follow-up and feedforward. But first, a series of thanking drills:

Give Yourself an A+ in Gratitude

I was flying to Santa Barbara, California. Suddenly, the plane took an enormous dip—one of those thrill-ride deep drops that make many passengers grab for the air sickness bag and the rest of us think about the afterlife. The pilot came on the speaker system and announced in his calm Chuck Yeager voice that we had a "minor problem." The landing gear wasn't working and we were going to circle the airport until we ran out of fuel so we could land more safely with the wheels up. It's always disconcerting to be circling in a plane waiting for it to run out of fuel. In those moments, when you're thinking, "I might die!" you begin to ponder your life. You ask yourself, "What do I regret?"

At least that's what I did. I thought about how many people have been good to me in my life. I never thanked them adequately.

I told myself, "If I ever get down on the ground, I will thank these people." This is not an uncommon thought. The number one regret children have when their parents die is that they never told them how much they appreciated all that the parents had done for them.

The plane landed safely. (Believe me, I thanked the pilot and crew.) When I got to my hotel room, the first thing I did was write gushy, mushy thank you notes to at least 50 people who had helped me in my life.

That was the moment I became a connoisseur of gratitude, a virtuoso at thanking. I'm always thanking people now in my e-mails, my letters, my seminars. The last thing I say on most phone calls is not "good-bye" but "thank you," and I really mean it. When it comes to gratitude, I'm a radical fundamentalist. I've even gone so far as to make a list of the top 25 people in both my personal and professional lives to whom I owed thanks. I had special certificates printed up with their names embossed in gold lettering saying, "Thank you. You're one of the top 25 people who have helped me have a great professional life."

I realize this is a bit extreme, but I make no apology for it. I have a lot of deficiencies, but gratitude is not one of them. I regard gratitude as an asset. Its absence is a major interpersonal flaw. I give myself an A+ in gratitude.

That should be your goal, too.

Here's an exercise to get you started (mercifully without the in-flight adrenaline rush of imminent death).

No matter how far along you are in life, think about your career. Who are the people most responsible for your success? Write down the first 25 names that come to mind. Ask yourself, "Have I ever told them how grateful I am for their help?" If you're like the rest of us, you probably have fallen short in this area.

Before you do anything else (including moving on to the next chapter of this book) write each of these people a thank you note.

This isn't just an exercise in making yourself and other people feel good (although that's a worthwhile therapeutic). Writing a thank you note forces you to confront the humbling fact that you have not achieved your success alone. You had help along the way.

More important, it forces you to identify your strengths and weaknesses. After all, when you thank people for helping you, you're admitting that you needed help in the first place—which is one way to pinpoint your deficiencies. If you didn't need to improve in a specific area, you wouldn't have needed another person's help. Think of it as a thank you note's side benefit; it helps you identify your old weak spots (which may still be weaker than you think).

As I write these words, it occurs to me that telling people to write thank you notes is obvious, almost trite. But it's incredible how neglected a practice thanking is. None of us can ever do it enough.

Eventually, you'll come to see that expressing gratitude is a talent—a talent that goes hand in hand with wisdom and self-knowledge and maturity.

A lawyer friend was arguing a case in front of a state supreme court justice. He didn't win the case, but afterwards the judge took him aside and praised him for the quality of writing in his briefs. "They were a pleasure to read," said the judge, "even if they weren't ultimately persuasive."

My friend thanked the judge and explained that he owed his writing skill to an English professor during his undergraduate years at Notre Dame. The professor had taken him aside and in a dozen sessions forced him to write succinctly.

"Did you ever thank him?" asked the wise judge.

"No," said my friend. "I haven't talked to him in twenty years."

"Maybe you should," said the judge.

That night he wrote to the professor, still teaching at Notre Dame, and told him the whole story in a thank you note.

A week later the professor wrote back, congratulating my friend on the timeliness of his note. The professor had been slogging through dozens of term papers, questioning the value of reading them and grading them. "Your note," he wrote, "reminded me that what I'm doing has worth."

That's the beauty and grace of a thank you note. If you can get an A+ in gratitude, nothing bad will ever come of it. Only good.

CHAPTER 11

Following Up

You Do Not Get Better without Follow-Up

Once you master the subtle arts of apologizing, advertising, listening, and thanking, you must follow up—relentlessly. Or everything else is just a "program of the month."

I teach my clients to go back to *all* their coworkers every month or so and ask them for comments and suggestions. For example, that first client who had a problem sharing and including his peers went to each colleague and said the following: "Last month I told you that I would try to get better at being more inclusive. You gave me some ideas and I would like to know if you think I have effectively put them into practice." That question forces his colleagues to stop what they're doing and, once again, think about his efforts to change, mentally gauge his progress, and keep him focused on continued improvement.

If you do this every month, your colleagues eventually begin to accept that you're getting better—not because you say so but because it's coming from *their* lips. When I tell you, "I'm getting better," I believe it. When I ask you, "Am I getting better?" and you say I am, then *you* believe it.

In the late 1970s and early 1980s, New York City's Mayor Ed Koch was famous for touring the five boroughs of New York and asking everyone he met, "How'm I doing?" To the untrained eye, Koch's question seemed like unbridled egotism, a weary hangover from the "Me Decade." Koch knew better. With the gut instinct of a master politician who understood people and perceptions, Koch was executing a crude but fairly sophisticated strategy of follow-up to create change, not only in the city but in its citizens' perception of their mayor.

By asking people, "How'm I doing?" he was advertising the fact that he was trying; that he cared.

By phrasing it as a question, rather than asserting, "I'm doing great," Koch was both including and involving the citizens, telling them in effect that his fate rested in *their* hands.

By repeating the question—turning "How'm I doing" into his personal slogan—Koch was imprinting his efforts in the citizens' minds and reminding them that improving New York City was an ongoing process, not an overnight miracle (which helps explain why he was New York's last three-term mayor).

Most important, "How'm I doing" forced Koch to "walk the talk." If he asked the question and people answered, "Not so great," he had to deal with the answer so he wouldn't hear it the next time he asked, "How'm I doing?"

Follow-up is the most protracted part of the process of changing for the better. It goes on for 12 to 18 months. Fittingly, it's the difference-maker in the process.

Follow-up is how you measure your progress.

Follow-up is how we remind people that we're making an effort to change, and that they are helping us.

Follow-up is how our efforts eventually get imprinted on our colleagues' minds.

Follow-up is how we erase our coworkers' skepticism that we *can* change.

Follow-up is how we acknowledge to ourselves and others that getting better is an *ongoing* process, not a temporary religious conversion.

More than anything, follow-up makes us do it. It gives us the momentum, even the courage, to go beyond understanding what we need to do to change and *actually do it,* because in engaging in the follow-up process, we are *changing*.

Why Follow-Up Works

Let me make an important admission: I didn't start out knowing this about the importance of follow-up. I was preparing training sessions at a Fortune 100 company when the Executive Vice President, perhaps with an eye on the training budget, asked me the perfectly reasonable question, "Does anyone who goes to these leadership development programs ever *really* change?"

I thought about it for a moment, and thought some more, then sheepishly answered, "I don't know."

I had trained thousands of people. I had received glowing reviews about my classes (although it occurred to me that the reviews only meant attendees *thought* my classes were valuable; it didn't prove their value). I had dozens of letters from people who believed they had changed (although I realized that didn't mean *anyone else* believed they had changed). I had worked with some of the best companies in the world and nobody had ever asked me that question. Worse, until that moment, it had never entered my mind.

This was a life-altering moment for me. Until then I had been one of the more successful practitioners of 360-degree feedback, a participative management concept that had workers evaluating their managers rather than the other way around. My personal contribution to the field was the notion of "custom feedback." I created surveys that answered the question, "What makes a great leader in *this particular organization*?" But even though I loved to crunch numbers, I had never gone back to these companies to see if my training sessions had had any effect or if people actually did what they promised to do in the training sessions. I assumed that if they understood the benefit of listening to wise, wonderful, and practical me, they would do what they were told.

Chastened by the executive vice president's piercingly obvious question, I became a follow-up grind for the next two years. I scoured all the research and went back to all my client corporations, assembling data that answered the question, "Does anyone really change?"

The numbers slowly grew into a statistically significant pile that involved eight major corporations, each of which invested millions of dollars a year in leadership development programs. In other words, they took the process of developing executives very seriously. My pool of respondents eventually numbered 86,000 participants.* As I studied the data, three conclusions emerged.

---

* I outlined the complete methodology, statistical results, the companies involved, and my conclusions in "Leadership Is a Contact Sport: The Follow-Up Factor in Management Development," written with Howard Morgan, in *Strategy and Business*, Fall 2004.

The first lesson: Not everyone responds to executive development, at least not in the way the organization desires or intends. Some people are train-able; some aren't. It's not because they don't want to get better. At the eight companies where hundreds of employees have gone through my leadership development training, I asked the participants at the end of each session whether they intended to go back to their job and apply what they had just learned. Almost 100 percent said yes. A year later I asked the direct reports of these same leaders to confirm that their boss applied the lessons on the job. About 70 percent said yes and 30 percent said the boss had done absolutely nothing. This 70/30 split showed up with statistically elegant consistency in each of the eight companies I studied, and it didn't waver whether the executives involved were Amer-icans, Europeans, or Asians. In other words, it reflects human nature, not cultural imprinting.

When I drilled a little deeper to find out why executives would go through training, promise to implement what they learned, and then *not do it,* the answer was incredibly mundane and, again, reflective of human nature. They failed to implement the changes *because they were simply too busy.* After the training session, they all returned to their offices to find piles of messages to return, reports to read and write, clients and customers to call. They were distracted by the day-to-day demands of their job.

This taught me a second lesson: There is an enormous disconnect between understanding and doing. Most leadership development revolves around one huge false assumption: If people understand, then they will do. That's not true. Most of us understand, we just don't do. For example, we all un-derstand that being grossly overweight is bad for our health, but not all of us actually do anything to change our condition.

But this insight didn't really answer my question. It only indicated that 70 percent of all the people who *understand* will actually *do.* It didn't tell me whether the 70 percent who applied the lessons actually got better.

That's when I realized that follow-up was the missing link not only in my training concepts but also in getting people to change. Here I was, telling people that part of the process of changing for the better was fol-lowing up with colleagues and asking, "How'm I doing?" But I had never followed up myself to measure the impact of my clients' follow-up. I rewired my objectives and began measuring people to see not only if they got better but why. My hunch about follow-up being the difference-maker paid off.

I traced five of my eight companies to measure the level of follow-up among their executives. Follow-up was defined as interaction between would-be "leaders" and their colleagues to see if they were, in fact, improving their leadership effectiveness. Follow-up ran through five scales—from "frequent interaction" to "little or none."

The results were astonishingly consistent. At one end of the spectrum, when leaders did little or no follow-up with their subordinates, there was little or no perceived change in the leaders' effectiveness. At the other extreme, when leaders consistently followed up, the perception of their effectiveness jumped dramatically.

My conclusion was swift and unequivocal: *People don't get better without follow-up. That was lesson three.*

In hindsight, it makes perfect sense—and echoes the Peter Drucker prediction that "the leader of the future will be a person who knows how to ask." If nothing else, these studies show that leaders who ask for input on a regular basis are seen as increasing in effectiveness. Leaders who don't follow up are not necessarily bad leaders. They are just not perceived as getting better.

In a way, our work reinforces a key insight from the famous Hawthorne Effect studies, which Harvard professor Elton Mayo conducted among factory workers at the Western Electric Hawthorne Works nearly 80 years ago. The Hawthorne Effect posits that productivity tends to increase when workers believe that their bosses are showing a greater interest and involvement in their work. In its most elemental form, it's the reason employees are more alert at their job when they know the boss is watching. In its more subtle forms, it's the reason entire factory floors work harder with greater morale when they see that their bosses care about their welfare.

The same dynamic was at work in my follow-up studies. Follow-up shows that you care about getting better. Following up with your coworkers shows that you value their opinions. Following up consistently, each month or so, shows that you are taking the process seriously, that you are not ignoring your coworkers' input. That's an important part of follow-up. After all, a leader who sought input from his coworkers but ignored it or did not follow up on it would quite logically be perceived as someone who did not care very much about becoming a better leader.

The whole experience taught me a fourth lesson: *Becoming a better leader (or a better person) is a process, not an event.* Historically, much of executive development has focused on the importance of an *event*—whether it's in the form of a training program, a motivational speech, or an intense executive retreat. My experience with the eight companies proves that real leadership development involves a *process* that takes time. It doesn't happen in a day. Nor can you "get it" in the form of a nitroglycerin tablet.

The process is a lot like physical exercise. Imagine having out-of-shape people sit in a room and listen to a speech on the importance of exercising, then watch some tapes on how to exercise, and perhaps then spend a few minutes simulating the act of exercising. Would you be surprised if all the people in the room were still unfit a year later? The source of physical fitness is not understanding the theory of working out. It is engaging in regular exercise.

Well, that pretty much sums up the value of executive development *without follow-up*. Nobody ever changed for the better by going to a training session. They got better by doing what they learned in the program. And that "doing," by definition, involves follow-up. Follow-up turns changing for the better into an ongoing process—not only for you but for everyone around you who is in the follow-up mix. When you involve other people in your continuing progress, you are virtually guaranteeing your continuing success. After all, if you go on a diet and know that someone who matters to you will check your weight at the end of each month, you're more likely to follow the diet and stay on it.

My Nightly Follow-Up Routine

Let me show you how follow-up works in my life.

I have a coach. His name is Jim Moore, a longtime friend who is a coaching professional. Every night wherever I am in the world, it's Jim's job as my coach to call me and ask me questions. They focus largely on my physical well-being and fitness. They're the same questions each night—and knowing that Jim will call and that I will have to answer the questions honestly is my method of following up on my goal of becoming a healthier individual.

The first question is always, "How happy are you?" Because for me it's most important to be happy. Otherwise, everything else is irrelevant. After that, the questions are:

1. How much walking did you do?

2. How many push-ups?

3. How many sit-ups?

4. Did you eat any high-fat foods?

5. How much alcohol did you drink?

6. How many hours of sleep did you get?

7. How much time did you spend watching TV or surfing the Internet?

8. How much time did you spend writing?

9. Did you do or say something nice for Lyda (my wife)?

10. Did you do or say something nice for Kelly and Bryan (my children)?

11. How many times did you try to prove you were right when it wasn't worth it?

12. How many minutes did you spend on topics that didn't matter or that you could not control?

That's it—my baker's dozen. I realize these questions may sound petty, even shallow. But I don't need help in the deep questions department. I spend most of my working hours talking to people about their relationships and helping them improve in areas that matter deeply to them. I get enough "depth" all day every day.

But I have a lifestyle that wreaks havoc on my physical well-being. I'm on the road, in airports, cars, conference centers, and hotel rooms 200 days a year. If my wife didn't remind me, I wouldn't know what time zone I'm in most days. I don't have the luxury of a "regular" home schedule where

I can eat three square meals each day, sleep in my own bed each night, and follow a fitness regimen that could qualify as a "routine." There is no routine in my life other than the routine of being on the road.

The questions Jim asks me each evening deal with the stuff that's hard for me to do—that requires discipline. They're not petty or shallow to me. They matter. The nightly call is my form of enforced follow-up. (By the way, after I review my questions with Jim, he reviews his questions with me!)

And it works. I'm more disciplined about writing (this book is the proof). I've cut down on my weight, my caffeine consumption, and my time in front of the television. I'm also in better shape than I've been in decades.

As a connoisseur of follow-up's value, I'm not surprised. The key, however, is that *it involves another person besides me*. It's one thing to keep a log each night of the same questions and fill in the answers. That, to me, is not quite follow-up. It's more like entering data in a diary—and considerably less likely to breed ongoing success. (How many of us have started a diary but soon abandoned it?)

But injecting Jim into the mix—a friendly sympathetic human being whom, on the one hand, I do not want to disappoint (that's human nature) and who, on the other hand, provides constant encouragement and input—brings it more in line with the follow-up process I've been describing here. It helps me measure my progress. It reminds people that I'm making an effort to get better. In turn, it provides me with the steady recognition that I *am* getting better. When another person is involved, it's like giving yourself a mirror and being assured that you will like what you see.

You can do this too. You can have your own "Jim Moore." You might think that asking someone to call you each night—without paying them!—is a lot to ask of another human being. It is the rare individual who has the stamina and discipline to call us daily.

Is that so? Many of us perform a variation on this already in our lives.

I know lots of busy adults who, no matter where they are, call their aging parents at the end of each day to see how they're doing.

A group of busy mothers in my neighborhood who have banded together to run marathons and 10K races for charity call each other every night to lock in the time for the next day's run, to map out their training schedules, and to keep each other motivated.

The same with a group of colleagues who have become yoga devotees. They're busy people but somehow they find the time to meet after work at the same yoga class five times a week and then they get together after class to talk about their lives.

We do this because we *care* about our parents, we're *serious* about running and want to excel at it, and we *enjoy* the change in our lives that yoga provides. So we become disciplined about it.

That rigor can—and should—be extended to follow-up in our own lives. After all, isn't changing our behavior and our interpersonal relationships as vital as taking care of our parents or maintaining our physical well-being?

Almost anyone in your life can function as your coach. It could be a spouse, or a sibling, or a son or daughter, or a colleague, or a best friend. It could even be your mother or father. They nagged you when you were a child. I'm sure they'd be delighted to "nag" you again—only this time with your permission.

Your only criteria for picking a coach are:

One, it shouldn't be a chore for your coach to get in touch with you (and with cell phones that's no longer an issue). You never want to have some technical problem as an excuse for not following up.

Two, your coach should be interested in your life and have your best interests at heart. You don't want someone yawning through your checklist as you answer whether you flossed or remembered to take your vitamins. For example, Jim Moore is an old friend, also from my home state of Kentucky. We enjoy talking to each other. It's not a burden for us to call each other.

Three, your coach can only ask the prescribed questions; he or she cannot judge your answers. (Warning: If your coach is a spouse or parent, suspending judgment might be asking a lot of them.)

After that, it's a simple process. Pick an issue in your life that you're not happy with and that you want to improve. Make a list of a dozen small daily tasks—nothing so major that it overwhelms the rest of your day— that you need to do to improve in your chosen area. And have your "Jim Moore" ask you about each task at the end of each day. That's it. As with any exercise, you won't see results immediately. But if you stick to it with daily follow-up, you will do all the tasks on your list. The results will appear. You will change. You will be happier. And people will notice.

CHAPTER 12

Practicing Feedforward

You've identified the interpersonal habit that's holding you back.

You've apologized for whatever errant behavior has annoyed the people who matter to you at work or at home. You've said, "I'm sorry. I'll try to do better." And they've accepted that.

You've continued to advertise your intention to change your ways. You've remained in steady contact with the people who matter, regularly reminding them that you're trying to do better. You do this by bringing up your objectives and asking point-blank, "How am I doing?"

You have also mastered the essential skills of listening and thanking. You can now listen to people's answers to your questions without judging, interrupting, disputing, or denying them. You do this by keeping your mouth shut except to say, "Thank you."

You've also learned how to be more diligent about follow-up, seeing the process as part of an ongoing, never-ending advertising campaign to (a) find out from others if you are, in fact, getting better and (b) remind people that you're still trying, still trying.

With these skills, now you're ready for feedforward.

As a concept, as something to do, feedforward is so simple I almost blush to dignify it with a name. Yet some of the simplest ideas are also the most effective. Since they're so easy to do, you have no excuse not to try them.

Feedforward asks you to do four simple steps:

1. Pick the one behavior that you would like to change which would make a significant, positive difference in your life. For example, *I want to be a better listener.*

2. Describe this objective in a one-on-one dialogue with *anyone* you know. It could be your wife, kids, boss, best friend, or coworker. It could even be a stranger. The person you choose is irrelevant. He or she doesn't have to be an expert on the subject. For example, you say, *I want to be a better listener.* Almost anyone in an organization knows what this means. You don't have to be an "expert" on listening to know what good listening means to you. Likewise, he or she doesn't have to be an expert on you. If you've ever found yourself on a long flight seated next to a perfect stranger and proceeded to engage in an earnest, heartfelt, and honest discussion of your problems with that stranger—or vice versa—you know this is true. Some of the truest advice can come from strangers. We are all human beings. We know what is true. And when a useful idea comes along, we don't care who the source is. (If you think about it, a stranger—someone who has no past with you and who cannot possibly hold your past failings against you or, for that matter, even bring them up—may be your ideal feedforward "partner.")

3. Ask that person for two suggestions *for the future* that might help you achieve a positive change in your selected behavior—in this case, becoming a better listener. If you're talking to someone who knows you or who has worked with you in the past, the only ground rule is that there can be no mention of the past. Everything is about the future.

    For example, you say, *I want to be a better listener. Would you suggest two ideas that I can implement in the future that will help me become a better listener?*

    The other person suggests, *First, focus all your attention on the other person. Get in a physical position, the "listening position," such as sitting on the edge of your seat or leaning forward toward the individual. Second, don't interrupt, no matter how much you disagree with what you're hearing.*

These two ideas represent *feedforward*.

4. Listen attentively to the suggestions. Take notes if you like. Your only ground rule: You are not allowed to judge, rate, or critique the suggestions in any way. You can't even say something positive, such as, *"That's a good idea."* The only response you're permitted is, *Thank you.*

That's it. Ask for two ideas. Listen. Say thank you. Then repeat the process with someone else. In seeking feedforward ideas, you're not limited to one person. That would be like restricting your initial feedback (the one that told you where you needed to improve) to talking to one person; it would dramatically lessen the chances of getting an accurate picture of what you're doing wrong. You can do feedforward with as many people as you like. As long as people are providing you with good ideas that you can use or discard (but which don't confuse you), feedforward is a process that never needs to stop.

All I've outlined here, really, are the ground rules for a conversation that *should* and *could* take place in the workplace all day long every day. These conversations rarely happen—precisely because in most workplace conversations we *aren't* working with these restrictions: Ask for two ideas; listen; say thank you. Even if we behave within the normal parameters of politeness and etiquette in the workplace, we think we have an obligation to be totally honest in every discussion. For some reason, when we're "engaged" in frank talk with another person, we interpret this to mean that we are locked in a debate. Because we like to succeed, we assume we have to win the debate. We think we have a license to use every debating trick to win, including bringing up the past to bolster our side of the "argument."

Is it any wonder that even in the least toxic environments, honest well-intentioned dialogues devolve into hurt feelings, misunderstandings, and counterproductive resentments?

Feedforward solves this dilemma.

In my scheme of things, feedforward is a dramatic improvement on what we traditionally think of as feedback. It grew out of a discussion I had with Jon Katzenbach in the early 1990s. We were frustrated with the limitations of the usual corporate feedback mechanisms to find out areas of improvement in an organization, such as the questionnaires that forced people to relive the past over and over again—the discussions among colleagues that descended into nightmarish arguments about who did what to whom way back when. As I hope I made clear in my brief history of feedback in Chapter 6, feedback has its virtues. It's a great tool for determining what happened in the past and what's going on in an organization. It's no different than reading history, which teaches us how we all arrived here right now in this moment. Like reading history, it provides us with facts about the past but not necessarily ideas for the future.

Feedforward, on the other hand, is feedback going in the opposite direction. That is, if feedback, both positive and negative, reports on how you functioned in the past, then feedforward comes in the form of ideas that you can put into practice in the future. If feedback is past tense, then feedforward is future perfect.

The best thing about feedforward is that it overcomes the two biggest obstacles we face with negative feedback—the fact that successful people in dominant positions don't want to hear it (no matter what they say, bosses prefer praise to criticism) and that their subordinates rarely want to give it (criticizing the boss, no matter how ardently he or she tells you to "bring it on," is rarely a great career move).

Feedforward shrinks the discussion down to the intimate parameters of two human beings. If it isn't obvious yet (and if it isn't then one of us has not been paying attention), this book and its process for getting better hinges on one inalterable concept.

I don't establish what you need to do to change for the better.

You don't establish it either.

They do.

Who are they?

Everyone around you. Everyone who knows you, cares about you, thinks about you, has you pegged.

Let's say you want to do a better job of listening. It's possible that a coach can explain to you how to be a better listener. The advice will be true, supportable, and impossible to dispute. But it will be generic. It's much better to ask the people around you, "What are some ways I can do a better job of listening to you?" They'll give you specific, concrete ideas that relate to them—how they perceive you as a listener—not the vague ideas a coach would give. They may not be experts on the topic of listening, but at that moment in time, they actually know more about how you listen, or don't, than anyone else in the world.

Until you get everyone who is affected by your behavior on your side and working to help you change, you haven't really begun to get better.

This is why the concept of feedforward is so important.

Feedforward eliminates many of the obstacles that traditional feedback has created.

It works because, while they don't particularly like hearing criticism (i.e., negative feedback), *successful people love getting ideas for the future.* If changing a certain type of behavior is important to them, they will gobble up any ideas that are aimed at changing that behavior. And they will be grateful to anyone who steps forward with an idea, not resentful. There's no arguing with this. Successful people have a high need for self-determination and will tend to accept ideas about concerns that they "own" while rejecting ideas that feel "forced" upon them.

It works because *we can change the future but not the past.* It doesn't deal in wishes, dreams, and conquering the impossible.

It works because *helping people be "right" is more productive than proving them "wrong."* Unlike feedback, which often introduces a discussion of mistakes and shortfalls, feedforward focuses on solutions, not problems.

On the most elemental level, it works because *people do not take feedforward as personally as feedback.* Feedforward is not seen as an insult or a putdown. It is hard to get offended about a suggestion aimed at helping us get better at what we want to improve (especially if we are not forced to implement the suggestion).

On a purely technical level, it works because when we receive feedforward, all we have to do is function as a listener. We can *focus on hearing without having to worry about responding.* When all you're allowed to say is "Thank you," you don't have to worry about composing a clever response. You also are not permitted to interrupt, which makes you a more patient listener. Practicing feedforward makes us "shut up and listen" while others are speaking.

However, feedforward is a two-way street—and it is designed to protect as well as bring out the best in the people who are providing it.

After all, who among us doesn't enjoy giving helpful suggestions when asked? The key is when asked. Feedforward *forces us to ask*—and in doing so, we enlarge our universe of people with useful ideas. Asking, of course, *gives the other person a license to answer.* I cannot overestimate how valuable this license can be. I'm sure that all of us are surrounded by smart well-meaning friends who "understand" us better than we "understand" ourselves. I suspect they would love to help us; most people like to help others. But they hold back because they think it is rude or intrusive to try to help someone who has not asked for our assistance. Asking solves this.

Also, there's no threat of pain in the process. If you're giving me two ideas that I've asked for, you will only receive my gratitude. Not resentment. Not an argument. Not punishment. On top of that, you don't even have to be right. You don't have to prove that your suggestions are good ideas—because I'm not judging them. All I can do is accept them or ignore them. A clever scheme that eliminates fear and defensiveness, don't you think?

More than anything, feedforward creates the two-way traffic I love to see in the workplace, the spirit of two colleagues helping each other rather than a superior being providing a critique. It's the feeling that when we help another person, we help ourselves.

Leave It at the Stream

If feedforward sounds like some eating technique you'd see advertised on late-night TV, guaranteeing weight loss with a faster metabolism, I apologize. Feedforward won't make you thinner.

But it may make you happier. The concept really is as simple as it sounds. Instead of rehashing a past that cannot be changed, feedforward encourages you to spend time creating a future by (a) asking for suggestions for the future, (b) listening to ideas, and (c) just saying thank you. Its strongest element, by far, is that it doesn't permit you to bring up the past—ever. It forces you to let go of the past.

That's important when you consider how many hours of organizational time and productivity are lost in the endless retelling of our coworkers' blunders, or how much internal stress we generate reliving real or imagined slights, or how often team-building sessions degenerate into, "Let me tell you what you did wrong" slugfests rather than, "Let me ask you what we can do better" love-ins.

An old Buddhist parable illustrates the challenge—and the value—of letting go of the past.

Two monks were strolling by a stream on their way home to the monastery. They were startled by the sound of a young woman in a bridal gown, sitting by the stream, crying softly. Tears rolled down her cheeks as she gazed across the water. She needed to cross to get to her wedding, but she was fearful that doing so might ruin her beautiful handmade gown.

In this particular sect, monks were prohibited from touching women. But one monk was filled with compassion for the bride. Ignoring the sanction, he hoisted the woman on his shoulders and carried her across the stream—assisting her journey and saving her gown. She smiled and bowed with gratitude as the monk splashed his way back across the stream to rejoin his companion.

The second monk was livid. "How could you do that?" he scolded. "You know we are forbidden to touch a woman, much less pick one up and carry her around!"

The offending monk listened in silence to a stern lecture that lasted all the way back to the monastery. His mind wandered as he felt the warm sunshine and listened to the singing birds. After returning to the monastery, he fell asleep for a few hours. He was jostled and awakened in the middle of the night by his fellow monk.

"How could you carry that woman?" his agitated friend cried out. "Someone else could have helped her across the stream. You were a bad monk."

"What woman?" the sleepy monk inquired.

"Don't you even remember? That woman you carried across the stream," his colleague snapped.

"Oh, her," laughed the sleepy monk. "I only carried her across the stream. You carried her all the way back to the monastery."

The learning point is simple: When it comes to our flawed past, *leave it at the stream.*

I am not suggesting that we should *always* let go of the past. You need feedback to scour the past and identify room for improvement. But you can't change the past. To change you need to be sharing ideas for the future.

Race car drivers are taught, "Look at the road, not the wall."

That's what feedforward does. Who knows? Not only may it help you win the race, but you'll definitely have a better trip around the track.

Pulling Out the Stops

In which leaders learn how to apply the rules of
change and what to stop doing now

CHAPTER 13

Changing: The Rules

IF I HAD TO rank my best client, in terms of magnitude of improvement in the shortest amount of time, it would have to be the division chief at a major manufacturing company. Let's call him Harlan.

Harlan had 40,000 employees under his command and he was doing a great job within this enormous division. Harlan was considered a great leader by his direct reports. Harlan's boss, the CEO, desperately wanted him to focus more on reaching out across the organization and providing leadership for the *entire* company.

I went through the drill with Harlan—commit to changing, apologize to all the people who gave you feedback, tell them you're trying to change, and follow up with them regularly to find out how you're doing in their eyes. When I say Harlan's my best client, one of the things I remember is how quickly he "got it." He bought my methods lock, stock, and barrel— and put them into action immediately. I was thinking this would be the standard 18-month assignment, but after 12 months Harlan's feedback was already posting the biggest improvement scores I'd ever seen in the shortest amount of time.

I flew to Harlan's headquarters, strolled into his office, and said, "We're done. You have the biggest improvement scores I've ever seen!"

"Whaddayamean? We barely got started."

"Well, I spent a lot of time with your colleagues assembling the feedback. Let's not forget that. And, yes, our time together was brief. But these scores prove that any issues you had with your colleagues last year have evaporated. They see you as being incredibly inclusive and working to benefit the entire company.

"Don't forget, you're earning several million dollars a year. Your time is valuable, more valuable than mine. Where do you think your CEO would rather have you spending your valuable time? Making money for the company or shooting the breeze with me? I think we know the answer to that one. I'm not in the time-spending business. I'm in the getting-better business. And you're better."

Harlan conceded the point. I was feeling pleased with myself (about two ticks short of smug if you want the truth) so I opted to waste some of his valuable time to ask, "What do you think you've learned from this whole process?"

He surprised me with his answer.

"I've learned that the key to your job, Marshall, is client selection. You 'qualify' your clients to the point where you almost can't fail. The deck is totally stacked in your favor."

It surprised me because he wasn't talking about himself. He was turning the tables on me. Then he said something more profound.

"I admire that kind of selectivity because that's what I do here. If I have the right people around me, I'm fine. But if I have the wrong people, not even God can win with that hand."

I guess that's another reason Harlan is a great client. He saw through all the bells and whistles of my admittedly simple methodology and honed in on my little secret: I make it easy on myself. I don't place sucker bets. I only work with clients who have an extremely high potential of succeeding. Why would anyone want to operate any other way?

Jack Welch once told *Esquire* magazine what he had learned playing sandlot baseball as a kid. He said, "When you were small, you were always the last one picked for the team and put out in right field. The years passed, and then *you* were putting guys out in right field. You learned one thing as you got older: You picked the best players and you won."

As you go through life, contemplating the mechanics of success and wondering why some people are successful and others are not, you'll find that this is one of the defining traits of habitual winners: They stack the deck in their favor. And they're unabashed about it.

They do this when they hire the best candidates for a job rather than settle for an almost-the-best type.

They do this when they pay whatever it takes to retain a valuable employee rather than lose him or her to the competition.

They do this when they're fully prepared for a negotiation rather than winging it.

If you study successful people, you'll discover that their stories are not so much about overcoming enormous obstacles and handicaps but rather about avoiding high-risk, low-reward situations and doing everything in their power to increase the odds in their favor.

For example, have you ever wondered why the most successful people at the top of your organization tend to have the best personal assistants? Simple answer: Successful executives know that a great assistant can shield them from dozens of daily annoyances that would otherwise distract them from doing their real job. If you think all the top executives have top assistants because of luck rather than design, you need a few more lessons in stacking the deck in your favor.

This winning strategy is so obvious to successful people, I feel almost sheepish mentioning it—as if it will elicit a chorus of "duhs!" from readers. But it's amazing how some people go out of their way to unstack the deck against themselves.

When you're talking about interpersonal behavior, people's common sense gets fuzzy and opaque. They lose sight of their true mission in life. They have trouble identifying or accepting the behavior that's holding them back. They don't know how to choose a strategy to fix the problem. And they often pick the wrong thing to fix. In other words, they stack the deck against themselves.

The following seven rules will help you get a better handle on the process of change. If you obey them, you'll be stacking the deck in your favor.

Rule 1. You Might Not Have a Disease That Behavioral Change Can Cure

I was asked to coach the CEO of a top medical company some years ago. His feedback report was quite a remarkable document. His peers and direct reports genuinely loved this fellow. No one who came in contact with him had anything negative to say about him. I had never seen such perfect marks in interpersonal relations.

"What's going on?" I asked. "Why am I here?" The CEO said he felt completely at sea about the technological innovations that were changing the company, and as a result had trouble communicating with some subordinates.

"You're a great guy," I said. "I'd love to work with you. But you don't have a disease that I can cure. What you need is a technology wizard to sit by your side and mentor you. You don't need me." He was a little like a hypochondriac with a pain in his rib cage. He thinks he has lung cancer when all he has is a little muscle pull.

Sometimes we confuse interpersonal problems with something else. In the medical company case, it was obvious. But the line between a behavioral flaw and a technical shortcoming can get blurry.

I was called in to work with the CFO of a major investment bank. Let's call him David. This fellow was an interesting case—a young, ambitious, hard-working, motivated, hit-the-numbers type who was *not* an arrogant, know-it-all jerk. In fact, David was admired and beloved. In the poker game of life, David had drawn four aces and a nine (he wasn't perfect, but damn close). You could see this in the way people in the office related to him. The females swooned around him. The direct reports snapped to attention. His colleagues from other divisions felt comfortable enough around him to engage in the friendly towel-snapping banter you see among ex-jocks who genuinely like and would kill for each other. David seemed to work in a perfect world where everything fell into place the moment he walked into the room.

I thought, "Why am I here?"

When I studied David's feedback, a disorienting picture emerged. No significant problems on any of the usual interpersonal flaws. Except the consensus opinion was that David could be a better listener. He wasn't hearing them out and he didn't seem to understand their true accomplishments.

This didn't jibe with all of David's positives. Executives who share, inspire loyalty, and are well liked don't score low on listening. It's an integral part of their interpersonal portfolio.

When I dug deeper, though, a more complicated picture emerged. It turned out that David, as CFO, was the firm's frontman with the media. Every quarter he had to talk with analysts and the financial press to highlight the firm's achievements. The firm had fallen prey to the same ethical lapses that many financial services companies were guilty of in the early part of the new millennium. But whereas other firms were getting decent press treatment under the circumstances, David's firm was getting mauled. Every day was a new headline that damaged the firm's reputation. And David took the heat for it.

David's people wondered why he wasn't getting the message out properly. "We're great," they thought. "We're not getting recognized for our greatness. David's in charge of delivering that message to the public and failing at it. Therefore, David's not hearing us."

A logical train of thought, if you're the direct reports.

But not if you're David.

David's problem wasn't that he ignored what people told him. As CFO, he knew the results better than anyone. David's problem was that he wasn't very good at "spinning" the media.

That's not a behavioral problem. It's a skill problem. David needed a coach all right—a media coach. But he didn't need me.

You have to be careful with feedback. Conducted properly, feedback is not deceptive. It reveals what's on people's minds. But it can be misinterpeted (you see only what you want to see) or misread (you see something that isn't there).

Keep this in mind. Sometimes feedback reveals a symptom, not a disease. A symptom is a headache; give it time and it goes away. A brain tumor, on the other hand, can't be ignored. It needs treatment. I see this in organizations that have endured a temporary downturn; the feedback reveals angry employees lashing out at scapegoats. Angry employees need to be heard and dealt with.

Sometimes, as in David's case, feedback reveals a problem that's one or two steps removed from anything that the individual is doing wrong. Be careful, then. You may be trying to fix something that isn't broken, doesn't need fixing, or can't be fixed by you.

Rule 2. Pick the Right Thing to Change

One of the first things I have to face with clients is the difference between miswanting and mischoosing. It's subtle, but real. Wanting, after all, is different from choosing. So are those moments when we get either process wrong, when we miswant or mischoose.

The distinction comes from psychologists studying the science of shopping. We want a sweater, for example. Then we choose a certain sweater based on the thought matrix that went into wanting it. For example, there are all sorts of reasons people want a certain type of sweater. They might want it for warmth. They might want it for its feel. They might want one that looks great, or is reputedly the best in the world, or the most expensive (or cheapest), or the most au courant in style, or that complements the color or their eyes. The reasons for wanting a sweater are almost infinite. Basically, we want a sweater because we think it will make us happier. Miswanting occurs when we discover that what we wanted *did not make us happy.*

Choosing is slightly different. Once we decide what sweater we want, we must choose among a vast array of options that fit the bill. Will it be the blue cashmere sweater with the Armani label and $1000 price tag? Or the blue wool from Land's End for $49? Both will keep us warm and accent our eye color (if that's what we wanted), but if we're on a limited budget, the latter is a wiser choice than the former.

The same distinction arises with people deciding to change for the better. One of my first tasks is helping them distinguish between what they want in life and how they choose to reach that goal. Again, the difference is one of wanting and choosing. And I don't get involved in the wanting part. It's none of my business. To weigh in with an opinion on some individual's goal in life would mean passing a value judgment on his or her reason for living. I won't do that. (And in turn I wouldn't want them passing judgment on my goals.) That's what I mean by being mission neutral.

However, I do have strong opinions about how people *choose* to reach their goals. There I'm not neutral. After all, if they make the wrong choice, they'll fail—which means I'm a failure too, and that is decidedly not my mission in life. (See above.)

So I spend serious time with people helping them decide what they need to change.

The first thing we do is review what they're doing right and what they may need to change. Successful people, by definition, are doing a lot of things right. Nothing to fix there.

Then we narrow it down. Not every challenge needs to be addressed. Assuming that I have gotten an individual to commit to changing for the better and changing *something,* I often have a hard time convincing successful people that not everything needs improving. Successful people have a glaring tendency to overcommit. If you outline seven flaws, they'll want to tackle all of them. It's one reason they're successful—and the impetus behind the cliché, "If you want something done right, give it to a busy person." So, my first task is to tell them, "Don't overcommit," and get them to believe it.

I also know that giving people unlimited choices only confuses them. Faced with too many options, they go back and forth among the options, trying to maximize their choice. Successful people hate being wrong even more than they like being right. This can easily turn into paralysis; in their never-ending quest for the best option, they end up deciding nothing.

So I turn their attention to the one vital flaw that needs fixing. In most instances I treat it as a pure numbers game.

Let's say you come to me for coaching. We go through your menu of five documented areas for improvement: 10 percent of your coworkers say you don't listen; 10 percent say you don't share information; 20 percent say you're bad at meeting deadlines; 40 percent say you gossip too much; and 80 percent say you get angry.

Which single issue should we focus on changing? Objectively speaking, it's a no-brainer. You have a serious issue with anger. Four out of five coworkers think you have a hot temper. We need to change that first.

You'd think that would be obvious. What's interesting, though, is how often the people I work with try to ignore that in-your-face problem and instead tackle one of the other flaws. I'm not sure why. Maybe it's denial (although at this point in the process, where you're committed to changing, denial should be long behind us). Maybe it's our natural urge to take the path of least resistance, to start with an easy fix first. Maybe it's just contrariness. Whatever the reasons, my job as a coach is to make you see that you have to improve at controlling your emotions. The other issues are moot, off the radar. More than half your colleagues didn't even mention them as an issue. That's how you pick the right thing to change.

In a way, I can see why people have problems choosing what needs fixing. In golf, for example, it is common wisdom that 70 percent of all shots take place within 100 yards of the pin. It's called the short game, and it involves pitching, chipping, hitting out of sand traps, and putting. If you want to lower your score, focus on fixing your short game; it represents at least 70 percent of your score. Yet if you go to a golf course you'll see very few people practicing their short game. They're all at the driving range trying to hit their oversized drivers as far as they can. Statistically, it doesn't make sense because over the course of 18 holes, they'll only need their drivers fourteen times (at most) whereas they'll pull out their short irons and putters at least 50 times. Athletically it doesn't make sense either. The short game demands compact delicate small-muscle movements; it is much easier to master than the violent big-muscle movements of driving off the tee. Nor does it make sense competitively. If you improve your short game, you *will* shoot lower scores—and beat the competition.

The numbers don't lie, and yet even the most avid golfers hide from the truth and refuse to fix what really needs fixing. (My hunch is that hitting balls out of sand traps all day is simply not as much fun as taking big swipes at the ball off the tee. But who am I to judge?) If golfers really wanted to stack the deck in their favor, they'd spend three hours on their short game for every hour they spend trying to hit the ball a mile. Still few do. It would take a stern golf teacher standing over them every day to enforce the practice routines they know they should be pursuing.

If you think it's hard to get people to fix their flaws in golf, which (let's not forget) is a highly pleasurable game totally within our control, imagine how tough it is getting people to change at work, where the stakes are higher but the results are not completely under your control. That's one reason I take this stuff so seriously. When people commit to getting better, they are doing something difficult and heroic. In truth, I applaud my clients when they *begin* the process of fixing their flaws, not at the *end*. If they commit and follow my advice, their success is a foregone conclusion. I don't need to applaud a fait accompli.

Rule 3. Don't Delude Yourself About What You *Really* Must Change

I was called in to work with a Chief Financial Officer named Matt. The problem, as usual, revolved around Matt's interpersonal skills. Nothing wrong with his CFO skills. Matt could read a balance sheet, outmuscle bankers, and keep his company financially viable with the best of them. In fact, as the fellow guarding the company's cash flow, Matt had accumulated more power than any CFO in the company's history. If you wanted to pursue any idea that cost money, you had to run it up the flagpole in Matt's office. Matt, almost as much as the CEO, could bless or kill any initiative.

That was the problem. Matt had developed an overweening sense of self-importance. It came out in brusque comments, dismissive opinions, and an increased inaccessibility to his direct reports.

That's when I showed up.

"Matt, we need to make changes," I said.

Matt cut me off.

"What I'd really like to do is lose twenty pounds and firm up my body."

"Are you serious?" I asked, thinking I'd get some resistance to changing his executive style but not expecting a discussion about physical fitness.

"Yes," he said. "Dead serious."

"You'd rather get a six-pack than get better at work?" I asked.

"That's what makes me unhappy," he said. "And that's why I'm so grouchy. If I can fix that, maybe everything else will improve, too."

I had to admire his honesty, if not his logic. It fit with his feedback, which said he was self-involved to the point of vanity. He thought he knew all the answers. That's what he needed to change.

At the same time, I knew the old saw, that if you don't have your health, nothing else matters. So maybe Matt was right. Maybe if he felt better about his looks, his health, and his vigor, everything else would fall into place.

So I went with it.

I said, "Look, it says here you need to be more sensitive to other people, less abrupt, less self-absorbed. On the other hand, you're so into yourself, you want to fix your stomach muscles. Which do you think is easier to accomplish? A six-pack or one less interpersonal flaw at work?"

"A six-pack," he said. "It's just a matter of discipline, following a routine, and sticking with it."

"Hmmm . . ." I thought. "Can't argue with that. If you follow a routine and stick with it, you'll get results. You'll achieve your goals."

Only problem: It's very tough to do. Even tougher to maintain. But Matt wasn't seeing that.

I've spent 3000 nights in the last two decades in hotel rooms, jet lagged and wide awake with only the television to keep me company. In other words, I have seen my share of late-night infomercials hawking the latest fitness gadgets. I know all the hard sell promises.

"How much would you pay to have a body like this?"

"In one week you could be feeling great."

"It feels terrific. Let us show you how easy it is."

"In eight minutes a day, tighten your flabby abs into the sexy six-pack you always wanted."

I knew why Matt thought acquiring a bodybuilder's abs was easier to achieve than being a little more civil to his colleagues. His mind had been warped by the constant media promises that anyone can get in world-class physical shape with a little effort and willpower.

I wasn't questioning Matt's goal.

I was worried about his understanding of how we set and achieve goals. And why.

I've studied the research on goal-setting and goal achievement. A lot of it centers on diet and fitness because (a) there's a huge population of people interested in such goals, (b) it's easy to measure, and (c) with record numbers of Americans either obese or out of shape, there's a huge (and compelling) history of failure in this area. I've learned that there are five reasons people do not succeed with their diet and fitness goals. They mistakenly estimate:

- *Time:* It takes a lot longer than they expected. They don't have time to do it.

- *Effort:* It's harder than they expected. It's not worth all the effort.

- *Distractions:* They do not expect a "crisis" to emerge that will prevent them from staying with the program.

- *Rewards:* After they see some improvement, they don't get the response from others that they expected. People don't immediately love the new improved person they've become.

- *Maintenance:* Once they hit their goal, people forget how hard it is to stay in shape. Not expecting that they'll have to stick with the program for life, they slowly backslide or give up completely.

This is what I explained to Matt in his office. I wasn't trying to talk him out of his six-pack. (If it makes him happy, I'm cool with it.) I was trying to make him see that he was a little delusional about his goal.

Getting in shape was eminently doable. Lots of people have done it. But it would not be easy. For one thing, it would take *time* away from his job. It would probably take more *effort* than all those infomercials, exercise books, and personal trainers at the gym suggested. There was a good chance that some *distractions* at his superbusy CFO job or at home might sidetrack him. More important, even if he achieved his goal, there was no guaranteed *payoff* that it would make him less grouchy. On the contrary, it might make him even more vain, self-satisfied, and insufferable. And there was certainly no guarantee that his colleagues would suddenly admire him for his newfound physique (they might even resent it).

I could see this last point got to Matt. He was already in a hole with his colleagues. It never occurred to him that some private effort to look and feel better could somehow backfire and put him in a *deeper* hole with those same colleagues. But it could—because it loudly and specifically excluded them. It was just another example of Matt being self-involved.

Even though I didn't walk into Matt's office expecting to talk about abs and crunches, the meeting had a serendipitous benefit—because the reasons we miscalculate our diet and health goals apply to any goal achievement. If you want to succeed at goal setting, you have to face the reality of the effort and the payoff before you begin. Realize that the "quick fix" and the "easy solution" may not provide the "lasting fix" and the "meaningful solution." Lasting goal achievement requires lots of time, hard work, personal sacrifice, ongoing effort, and dedication to a process that is maintained over years. And even if you can pull that off, the rewards may not be all that you expect.

This may not be the best support for a late-night infomercial, but it is great material for achieving any real change.

"Now," I asked Matt, "are we ready to talk about what your colleagues think of you?"

Rule 4. Don't Hide from the Truth You Need to Hear

I am in my late 50s. At my age, the most important feedback I need is called an annual physical examination. As feedback, it's literally life-or-death information. I managed to avoid this feedback for seven years. It's not easy to avoid a doctor's visit for seven years, but I did it by telling myself, "I will get a physical after I go on my 'healthy foods' diet. I will get the exam after I begin my exercise program. I will get that exam after I get in shape."

Who was I kidding? The doctor? My family? Myself?

Have you ever avoided a physical exam and told yourself the same thing? Almost half the executives I've worked with have.

How about the trip to the dentist? After putting off the appointment as long as possible, do you orchestrate a frenzy of dental flossing two days before visiting the dentist's office?

Admittedly, a little bit of the impulse behind this behavior is our need to achieve. We want to score well in the doctor's or dentist's "test," so we prepare for it.

However, a much bigger reason for this behavior is our need to hide from the truth—often from what we already know. We know we need to visit a doctor or dentist, but we don't because we might not want to hear what he has to say. We figure if we don't seek out bad news about our health or teeth, there can't be any bad news.

We do the same in our personal life. For example, when I'm working in a large sales organization, I always throw a spot quiz at the sales force.

"Does your company teach you to ask customers for feedback?"

A chorus of yeses.

"Does it work? Does it teach you where you need to improve?"

Another yes chorus.

Then I focus on the men: "How many times do you do this at home? That is, ask your wife, 'What can I do to be a better partner?'"

No yes chorus. Just silence.

"Do you men believe this stuff?" I ask.

Back to the yes chorus. "Of course!" they say in unison.

"Well, I presume your wife is more important to you than your customers, right?"

They nod.

"So why don't you do it at home?"

I can see their collective wheels turning as the truth dawns on them: They're afraid of the answer. It might hit too close to home. And, worse, then they'd have to do something about it.

We do the same with the truth about our interpersonal flaws. We figure if we don't ask for critiques of our behavior, then no one has anything critical to say.

This thinking defies logic. It has to stop. You are better off finding out the truth than being in denial.

Rule 5. There Is No Ideal Behavior

Benchmarking—the notion that there is a performance ideal exemplified by people and organizations—is one of the biggest hazards in getting people to change for the better. It's not that there isn't something to be gained from modeling ourselves against the best in their category. But it can do more harm than good if applied poorly. Sometimes the desire for "perfect" can drive away "better."

In my line of work, there are a lot of benchmarks for successful behavior, but they are composites. They are usually made from multiple people and multiple examples. The perfect benchmark human being, like the perfect benchmark organization, does not exist. That colors how people think. They believe that there is an ideal executive out there—and that they should be like him or her.

You can't be and don't have to be all things to all people. If there were a list of 39 successful attributes for the model executive, I would never argue that you have to be the perfect expression of all 39 of them. All you need are a few of them. No matter how many of the 39 attributes you *don't* embody, the real question is, how bad is the problem? Is it bad enough that it merits fixing? If not, don't worry about it. You're doing fine.

I take great comfort in the fact that Michael Jordan, to many the best basketball player to ever play the game, was a mediocre baseball player in the minor leagues and, as a golfer, would have a tough time keeping up with at least twenty golfers who live within an 800 yard radius of my home in San Diego. If Michael Jordan, a preternaturally superb athlete and competitor—in fact, *the* benchmark for other basketball players— could only excel at one sport, what makes you think you can do better?

It's not just sports. I work with a lot of clients in the financial services sector. When I check the annual rankings of how the firms are doing against their rivals, one firm is ranked #1 at investment banking, a different firm is #1 at mergers and acquisitions, yet another is #1 at fixed income securities, and so on through a dozen categories. No firm is #1 at everything, and very few firms are even tops in two categories. In an environment where all the big firms are loaded with the best and brightest out of the top business schools, the competition is too stiff for one firm to dominate all categories.

It's no different in the workplace. Take a look around your office. Someone's the best salesman. Someone else is the best accountant. Someone else is the best manager. No one is the best at everything.

This isn't a license for mediocrity. It's a reality check. It's your permission to deal in trade-offs and pick one thing to improve upon rather than everything.

Even in my narrow profession of executive coaching, I've further narrowed my ambition to one thing: Helping people achieve long-term positive behavioral change. I don't do strategy. I don't do innovation. I don't coach information technology or media relations or industrial psychology. The list of what I don't do could fill several dozen books. I can live with that, because I've chosen to try to be the best I can be in my admittedly narrow corner of the coaching fiefdom. If I'm shooting for the gold at this, I have to come to terms with the fact that I ain't even stepping up to the starting blocks in everything else.

The same applies to your task of changing your behavior. Pick one issue that matters and "attack" it until it doesn't matter anymore. If you're a bad listener, choose to become a better listener—not the best listener in the world (whatever that means!). If you don't share information, get better at sharing until it's not an issue anymore (but realize that you will never be perfect in everyone's eyes, and you don't need to be).

Benchmarking is great because it teaches us to aim high. But when we apply it to ourselves, we often overreach. This is the "ready, fire, aim" school of self-improvement. We don't discriminate among benchmarks. We want to be the best at everything.

When it comes to creating long-term positive change in ourselves, we have one gun, one bullet. You can't hit more than one target with that ammunition.

P.S. There's a bonus to ignoring benchmarks. People commonly fear that if they get better at X they'll get worse at Y—as if improvement is a zero-sum game. Not true. Statistically, if you get better at X, it helps everything else get better, too. I have 20,000 feedback reports confirming this. If you're a bad listener who learns to listen more, then you are perceived as treating people with more respect. In deferring to their views, you probably hear their ideas better. Good ideas don't fall through the cracks because of your benign neglect. This is turn makes you appear as a more involved, concerned leader, which improves morale—and surely has an effect on delivering better numbers. Everything gets better with one change. That's a statistical fact.

Rule 6. If You Can Measure It, You Can Achieve It

Most of us in business spend a great deal of time measuring. We measure sales, profits, rate of growth, return on investment, income versus outgo, same-store sales from quarter to quarter, etc. In many ways, part of being an effective manager and leader is setting up systems to measure *everything*. It's the only way we can know for sure *how we're doing*. Given our addiction to measurement—and its documented value—you'd think we'd be more attuned to measuring the "soft-side values" in the workplace: How often we're rude to people, how often we're polite, how often we ask for input in a meeting rather than shut people out, how often we bite our tongue rather than spit out a needlessly inflammatory remark.

These are the "soft" values that are hard to quantify but, in the area of interpersonal performance, are as vital as any hard number we can come up with. They demand our attention if we want to alter our behavior—and get credit for it.

About ten years ago, I decided I wanted to be a more attentive father. So I asked my daughter, "What can I do to be a better parent?"

She said, "Daddy, you travel a lot, but I don't mind that you're away from home so much. What really bothers me is the way you act when you *are* home. You talk on the telephone, you watch sports on TV, and you don't spend much time with me. One weekend, when you'd been traveling for two weeks, my friends were having a party. I wanted to go, but Mom wouldn't let me. She said I had to spend time with you. So I stayed home, but you didn't spend any time with me. That wasn't right."

I was hurt and stunned, because (a) she nailed me and (b) I was an oafish dad who had needlessly caused his daughter pain. There's no worse feeling in the world, I can assure you. You never want to see your children in any pain. And you certainly don't want to be the source of it.

I recovered quickly—and reverted to a simple response that I teach all my clients.

I said, "Thank you. Daddy will do better."

From that moment I started keeping track of how many days I spent at least four hours interacting with my family without TV, movies, football, or the telephone as a distraction. I'm proud to say I got better. The first year I logged in 92 days of unencumbered interaction with my family. The second year, 110 days. The third year, 131 days. The fourth year, 135 days.

Five years after that first conversation with my daughter, I was spending more time with my family and my business was more successful than it had been when I was ignoring them. I was beaming with pride—not only with the results but also with the fact that, like a skilled soft-side accountant, I documented them. I was so proud, in fact, that I went to my kids, both teenagers by this time, and said, "Look kids, 135 days. What's the target this year? How about 150 days?"

Both of them said, "No, Daddy, you have overachieved."

My son Bryan suggested paring down to 50 days. My daughter Kelly agreed. In the end both voted for a massive cutback in time with Daddy.

I wasn't discouraged by their response. It was as eye-opening as that first conversation with my daughter five years earlier. I was so focused on the numbers, on improving my at-home performance each year that I forgot that my kids had changed, too. An objective that made sense when they were nine years old didn't make sense when they evolved into teenagers.

Everything is measurable if we're clever enough to see that it needs measuring—and can devise a way to track it. For example, no matter how busy you are or how much you travel for your job, it's easy to measure how many days a year you spend at home. All you have to do is look at the calendar—and count. Yet how many of us, especially the spouses and parents among us who feel guilty about our frequent absences from our loved ones, ever think about tracking our days at home?

The strange thing is we do this habitually in so many other parts of our lives outside the workplace. Runners training for a race constantly measure how fast they are running and keep a log of the miles they cover each week. Even a casual athlete trying to get in shape will go to the gym and maintain a rough memory that he lifted x amount of weight yesterday, so that three weeks later he would want to lift x weight plus 20 percent. So why don't we apply the same metrics to goals that really matter?

Once you see the beauty of measuring the soft values in your life, other variables kick in, such as the fact that setting numerical targets makes you more likely to achieve them. For example, another measurement I injected into my home life was seeing if I could spend 10 minutes each day engaging my wife and each of my kids in a one-on-one conversation. Ten minutes is not a long time, but it's a significant improvement on zero. I found that if I measured the activity I was much more likely to do it. If I faltered, I always told myself, "Well, I get a credit towards the goal and it only takes me ten minutes. Maybe I'm tired, but what the hell. I can just go ahead and do it." Without that measurable goal, I was much more likely to blow it off.

Rule 7. Monetize the Result, Create a Solution

The same metrics you apply to yourself to change behavior can be applied to other people, especially if money is part of the equation.

For example, when he noticed all the trash talk and vulgarity his children brought home from school, a friend of mine established a "swear jar" for the family. Every time anyone uttered a profanity, they had to donate a dollar to the jar. The first thing the father noticed, after depositing several dollars a day for the first week, was how foul-mouthed he was around the children. He learned where they were picking up the bad habit: from him. Monetizing the punishment does that. When you actually have to pay for your mistakes, you notice them more acutely. Unless you like losing money for no reason, you eventually change your ways. Within a month, the vulgarity had vanished.

There are all sorts of ways to incentivize people to change their behavior—and I approve of anything that works from bonuses to fines to gifts to vacations. It's a simple idea, but it's amazing how few people think of attaching a financial reward to ending a problem. I've been coaching executives for two decades now, but it was only in 2005 that one of my clients introduced a financial incentive into the process. He was one of the top officers at a West Coast industrial company, a real hard charger whose big issue was not sharing information. The company CEO assured me that, no matter how harsh the feedback and how severe the resistance from employees, I would collect my fee. "This guy will get better," said the CEO. "He would rather die than fail—at anything."

The CEO was right. This guy was a pleasure to work with because he was so determined to get better. He quickly picked up that neither he nor I was the important constituency in the process. The people who worked with and for him were. So he did something I'd never seen before. He concluded that the most vital person in the process was his executive assistant. She was the one who saw him day in and day out. She knew his faults best and she would have the strongest opinions about what he needed to do to get better. She was also in the best position to see if he was mending his ways as well as remind him when he was backsliding. So he made *his* improvement become as important to her as to him. He told her, "If Marshall gets paid, you get a $2,000 bonus."

Within 12 months she collected her bonus.

I'd never thought of this or seen it done before, but you can be sure that I'm mentioning it to all future clients.

You can monetize the punishment and end the problem. Or you can monetize the result and create a solution. Either way, it works.

Rule 8. The Best Time to Change Is Now

As I've written, of the tens of thousands of business people who have come to my lectures and classes, only 70 percent ever followed through on what they learned and actually did something about it. I am not ashamed of this fact—which means a 30 percent noncompliance rate. Actually, I'm proud of my noncompliance rate and amazed it isn't much higher.

If you've gotten this far in this book, I am sure you believe that you will do at least something (if only one simple thing) that is advised herein. (For example, how tough can it be to stop punishing the messenger?) But I'm resigned to the fact that while many readers will do this, many will not.

We have interviewed hundreds of people who have participated in our training programs one year later. We asked the people who did nothing why they did not live up to the commitments that they made after they attended leadership training. As far as we can tell, most people who do nothing are no worse as human beings than the people who change. They are no less intelligent. They have about the same values.

Then, why don't they do what they committed to do?

The answer can be found in a dream. It's a dream I have often—and you may, too. It goes something like this:

You know, I am incredibly busy right now. In fact, I feel about as busy today as I have ever felt. Some days I feel overcommitted. In fact, every now and then my life feels out of control.

But we are working on some unique and special challenges right now. I feel like the worst of this is going to be over in a couple or three months. After that, I am going to take a couple of weeks, take a little time off, get organized, spend some time with the family, and start working out. Everything is going to change. This time will be here soon. After that, it won't be crazy anymore!

Have you ever had a dream that sounds vaguely like this? How long have you been having this dream? How's that working for you?

Perhaps it's time to stop dreaming of a time when you won't be busy. Because the time will never come. It's your dream—but it's also a mirage.

I have learned a hard lesson trying to help *real* people, change *real* behavior in the *real* world. There is no "couple of weeks." Look at the trend line! Sanity does not prevail. There is a good chance that tomorrow is going to be just as crazy as today.

If you want to change anything about yourself, the best time to start is *now*. Ask yourself, "What am I willing to change now?" Just do that. That's more than enough. For now.

CHAPTER 14

Special Challenges for People in Charge

Memo to Staff: How to Handle Me

For years one of the most popular talk radio programs in the U.S. has been *Imus in the Morning* with Don Imus. The daily program is a curious mix of current events, satirical songs, rants by Imus, interruptions by his staff, and interviews with call-in guests who range from powerful politicians to network anchors to authors promoting their books to ordinary citizens. Imus's only rule for guests is, You cannot be boring.

Imus's on-air persona (which may or may not be real) is that of a curmudgeon. He's always mad about something—whether it's government hypocrisy or the air quality in the studio. You can't tell if Imus is liberal or conservative, Democrat or Republican, hard-line on moral issues or soft. Nor can you predict how he will treat his guests. He's an equal opportunity offender. Sometimes he's polite and deferential, other times rude, calling people "morons" and "weasels" and "liars" while they're on the air. The one thing you can be sure of listening to Imus is that at some point *you* will get upset. Imus gets away with this antisocial behavior because every once in a while he explains to the audience what he's up to. "The only thing you have to understand about this show," he says, "is that everything I say is jive. You cannot take it seriously. You'll know I'm serious only when I say the following six words: 'You have to stop that now.' Everything else is jive."

It's a little like the Surgeon General's warning on a cigarette pack—and brilliant. In effect, he's instructing the audience on how to deal with him. Perhaps as a result, *Imus in the Morning* is consistently one of the highest rated shows in its highly competitive time slot.

It's a technique every boss should learn.

Wouldn't it be great if all bosses came with similar product warnings? Wouldn't it be even better if, like Imus, they were sufficiently self-possessed that they could write the warnings themselves?

Imagine a workplace where the boss tells you, "Listen, I like to punish the messenger, so be very careful when you're bringing me bad news. I'll probably bite your head off, even though I know it's not your fault."

Or, "No matter how terrific your idea and how thoroughly you've thought it out, I'm going to add my two cents to it in order to improve it. Your first impulse will be to listen to me and act on my suggestion. Please don't. Just nod your head and pretend you're listening. If you're as smart as I thought you were when I hired you, you'll ignore me and do it your way."

A lot of bosses are already doing some variation on this with their employees. I know one self-made man who has a volcanic temper. He doesn't fly off the handle too often. But he leads a very busy schedule, starting at 4 A.M. with dictation to his secretary, phone calls to distant time zones, and not one but two breakfast meetings. By the time the rest of us begin our workday, he's already worked a full day—and begun another one. As a result, he's chronically tired, which means he's chronically testy. The slightest annoyance can set him off. The good news is that he knows this about himself. He's not putting on a show—like a baseball manager throwing a fake hissy fit over an umpire's bad call. He's genuinely mad. But the rage dies down as quickly as it erupted. To him, the tantrum acts as a release valve. I've seen him when he's lost it, and it's not a pretty picture. Employees have been to known to burst into tears during one of his tirades. To his credit, he regains his composure instantly and always tells his staff, "I'm not mad at you. I'm just mad. And now it's over and forgotten. I'm sorry you had to be here to witness it." A little bit of this is phony (he probably is angry at something a staffer has done) but he's smart enough to let them know that he's behaving like a jerk and they ought to ignore it.

This sort of candor is admirable—because it features a boss trying to get better by admitting to a managerial shortcoming, telling his colleagues, and helping them deal with it. (If I were his coach, I'd also have him soliciting suggestions—i.e., feedforward—from his staff on how he could correct this shortcoming, but let's take it one step at a time.)

Some years ago I worked with a public relations executive who was having a hard time hanging on to personal assistants. He'd hire perfect candidates, but they'd quit after six or seven months on the job. I wasn't able to track down this bevy of former assistants to get their feedback on why they left, so I tried an experiment. I asked the executive to imagine the feedback I would have gotten from all his departed assistants. What would they say good and bad about him? Then I asked him to write it down as if it were a memo to his next prospective assistant titled "How to Handle Me." Here's what he wrote:

I'm good with people and even better with ideas. If clients have a problem, it's my job to come up with a creative solution. I'm bad at everything else. I hate paperwork. I find it hard to perform the usual courtesies that clients expect of a personal services business. I don't follow up with thank you notes. I don't remember birthdays. I dread picking up the phone, because it's always someone with a problem, never someone calling to say that a huge check is on its way to me or that I've won the lottery. You need to know this about me. I have a pretty good idea how the business is doing, but I don't like budgets and expense reports and projections. People think I'm an unmade bed as a manager, and they're right. I'm not bragging or being self-deprecating. It's the truth.

On the personal side, I'm a decent, polite human being. I'll never yell at you. When things are going well and we've pulled off a few miracles in a row, I begin to think I'm one of the funniest, most charming people on earth. You may find my humor caustic at these times. Please don't take it personally. Better yet, tell me I'm out of line. I have a relaxed laissez-faire personality, and the more hectic things get, the calmer I get. That's my peculiar reflex to pressure. Don't misinterpret this cool demeanor to mean that I don't care. I care a lot. I only expect one thing of you: I want you to do as much of my job as you can handle. The less I have to do the better. Do that and we will succeed magnificently together.

He handed this document to his new assistant, a bubbly graduate fresh out of the University of Michigan named Michelle, on her first day at work. When I saw him again about 18 months later, I was dying to know if he was making progress with his so-called assistant-retention issues.

"Are things working out with Michelle?" I asked.

"Oh yes," he said.

"How can you tell?" I asked, ever the skeptic.

"Because last Christmas every client sent her—not me—a lavish fruit basket or bottle of champagne to thank her. When I told her that I wanted an assistant to do my job for me, she took it to heart. Apparently, she's been shielding me from almost every problem that comes across her desk—and solving it herself. That wouldn't have happened if I hadn't told her how to handle me."

What's interesting (and reassuring) about this story is that it's an example of a boss accurately assessing his shortcomings *and* his employee agreeing with him. That isn't always the case. Sometimes the gap between what a boss says about himself and what the staff believes is wide, very wide.

The most obvious disconnect is when the staff concludes that the boss's opinion of how he wants to be handled is either fantasy or wishful thinking. I saw this some years ago with a division chief who prided himself on his fairness and the fact that he didn't play favorites. He never wrote it down in a "How to Handle Me" memo to staff, but he was always warning employees that he didn't like yes men and suck-ups, that you earned your way on to his first team purely on performance. Unfortunately, his staff considered this self-assessment to be about 180 degrees removed from the truth. The man was a sucker for sycophants. He hated to be challenged and he habitually rewarded those who agreed with him at the expense of those who did not. What should have been an opportunity to bring boss and employees in sync actually became a toxic joke that divided both sides further.

The other disconnect is more subtle. It occurs when the boss's self-assessment is accurate but irrelevant.

I saw this with the CEO of an energy company who was famous for being a stickler for details, even to the point of correcting people's grammar and punctuation in memos and letters. He had been an English teacher who had switched to corporate law, where his attention to detail made him a great success. The energy company had been a client, and when he skillfully guided the company out of bankruptcy, again in part because of his fanatic attention to detail, the board appointed him CEO. That's when the trouble began.

He never wrote a "How to Handle Me" memo. (The idea had yet to occur to me.) But then again, he didn't have to. Every time he took a red pencil to one of his senior staff's writings, he was sending an unmistakable signal that "this matters to me." Word spread quickly through the executive ranks that if you wanted to make a favorable impression on the new CEO, all you had to do was write memos with perfect grammar and punctuation. If he didn't change his ways, he would either have a mutiny on his hands or an executive suite filled with gifted grammarians.

That's when I was called in. You can imagine the problem. The boss was sending a signal on what he expected from his executives. And it had the added virtue of being true. But the executives thought it was silly, that this was no way to run a company or judge executive talent. I went over his staff's feedback. The first comment was, "Five million dollars a year is a lot to pay for an editor." Second comment: "Put away the red pencil." Third comment: "This is no longer the first grade." And so on. It took me months to make the CEO accept that correcting grammar in internal memoranda was a poor—and humiliating—use of his time. What mattered to him did not matter to the troops. That was a dangerous disconnect that neither he nor the company could afford.

I mention this because writing a memo to staff on "How to Handle Me" is not only an admirable exercise in self-examination, but a surefire method for stimulating dialogue with the troops. But be careful. Your memo has to be brutally honest. Your employees have to believe it is accurate. And most important, they must believe it matters. Anything less on all three counts and you may as well keep your instructions to yourself.

Stop Letting Your Staff Overwhelm You

One of the great pleasures of being the boss (any kind of boss, whether you're running a three-person staff or a division of 30,000 employees) is that you get to call the shots—all the shots. Meetings begin when you say they begin. They take place where you want them to take place. They end when you say they're over. Whether you're a great boss or a bad one, you answer to no one who's under your charge. They all answer to you.

There's a dangerous underside to this, which eludes many bosses once they get inside their comfortable cocoon of all-powerfulness.

As a boss, you alone know how much you depend on your people. Without their loyalty and support, you are nothing. (You know this, and if you're a wise leader, you remind your people repeatedly that you know how much you need them.) But you should never forget that it's a two-way street. Just as you are dependent on your staffers, they're dependent on you—in ways that may have nothing to do with on-the-job performance. They crave your attention, your approval, your affection. If you've got any sort of charisma as a leader, they literally gauge their status in the organization by how much face time they get with you.

There's nothing wrong with this. What better way for the troops to develop than by getting face time with their leaders so they can observe and then emulate their behavior? But this codependency can develop into trouble.

I know the editor-in-chief of one of the top women's magazines. An incredibly well-organized woman, she took pride in her ability to juggle her high-pressure job and still maintain a sane home life with her husband and two young kids. She was pretty close to being a perfect boss: fair, egalitarian, kept her door open to everyone. (She was even fair to people after she fired them, always helping them land new jobs.)

The payoff for perfection, however, was not what she expected. As a dedicated having-it-all mom, she tried to be home by 6:30 each night to be with her children. Over time she noticed that she was making more and more excuses for working late, to the point that within two years she was regularly at her desk until 9:30 or 10 P.M. At first she thought it was simply because she loved her job (running a glamorous money-making magazine can be a ton of fun). But as she analyzed the problem, she realized it had nothing to do with her. Her staff depended on her too much. A lot of it could be blamed on her openness and availability. She had created an environment where it was easy to get face time with the boss. So everyone naturally wanted face time. Of course, this put her in a never-ending upward spiral where she could never leave the office. People were always coming in to her at the end of the day, saying, "I need 10 minutes of your time." Being the perfect boss, she would give it to them. Paradoxically, she was losing control *because she was in control.*

To regain control, she gathered her staff and announced, "From now on my door is closed after 5:45. After that it's 'get-out-of-my-face time.' Only my kids get face time."

That only solved half the problem. She got home by 6:30 every night. But her staff felt lost and abandoned. That's when I got involved.

Making the staff less dependent on her, I said, was a good thing. But they still needed leadership. They still needed to be re-directed.

I had her arrange discussions with each of her direct reports—to discuss two things:

One, I wanted her to ask each of them, "Let's look at your responsibilities. Are there areas where you think I need to be more involved and less involved?" She was making them define the areas where they could legitimately ask for face time with her—and areas where it was not legitimate. In effect, she was delegating more responsibility to them, but in a generous and empowering way. She was allowing *them* to determine how much responsibility they could take.

Two, I wanted her to say, "Now let's look at my job. Do you ever see me doing things that a person at my level shouldn't be doing, such as getting involved in details that are too minor to worry about?" She was forcing them to come up with ideas for how she could become more disengaged. In effect, she was letting them help her get home by 6:30. What better gift can a leader present to his or her troops? And vice versa.

I didn't have to remind her to say, "Thank you."

Remember this the next time you find yourself trapped by a needy, demanding staff. If they need too much of your time, you can't just tell them to stop bothering you. You have to wean them away and make it seem like it's their idea. Let them figure out what they should be doing on their own. Let them tell you where you're not needed. There's a fine line between legitimate face time and get-out-of-my-face time. It's up to you as boss to make the troops face that.

Stop Acting as if You Are Managing You

Telling staff how to handle the boss is admirable, but it doesn't completely solve one of the great unappreciated ironies of the boss vs. bossed dynamic. It is this: A lot of managers assume that their staff should be exactly like them—in behavior, in enthusiasm, in intelligence, and most especially, in how they apply that brainpower. You can't blame them. If

I were a super-successful boss, I'd be inclined to populate my organization with clones of . . . *me*. What better way to assure that everything gets done *my* way? This, by the way, is a perfectly natural inclination. Given the choice, we all favor hiring people who closely resemble the person we see in the mirror every day.

At the same time, we're also smart enough to know that an organization stocked with clones marching in lockstep doesn't create diversity in an organization. You need different voices, different mindsets, different personalities in the mix. In my experience, it's the odd out-of-left-field dissenting voices, the ones challenging groupthink and the status quo, that make an organization hum and thrive.

Also, a staff of clones does not guarantee fluid teamwork. For example, if I were Michael Jordan starting a basketball team from scratch, I'd be glad to have one player like me, but I'd still need two or three taller, stronger players to man the front line and a smaller, lightning-quick player to feed me the ball. A basketball squad of five Michael Jordans, intriguing as it sounds, is surely a recipe for dysfunction.

Most bosses are smart enough to know this and therefore resist the temptation to hire only mirror images of themselves. But that doesn't mean the message sinks in completely. Sometimes I have to remind even the most sensitive, tuned-in bosses, "You are not managing you."

This hit me when I began working with the CEO of a large service company. Let's call him Steve. Steve prided himself on being a great leader who lived the values he encouraged all his employees to follow. In fact, he considered himself the role model for his company's leadership values.

As with all of my clients, I let Steve know what all of his coworkers thought of him. While they were generally ecstatic that Steve was the CEO, they were in general agreement that he stifled the flow of open communication. In this one area, his behavior was inconsistent with his message. He was not practicing what he was preaching.

A simple problem, I thought, easily solved if Steve is willing to change. I would get him to listen more and ask people for input. I would tell him that he cannot end any meeting without asking everyone present if they felt like they had a fair hearing of *their* views. If he did that consistently over 12 months or so, the no-dialogue rap would fade away.

It wasn't that simple. As I studied the feedback from Steve's staff, something didn't add up. On the one hand, the feedback said he killed open discussion. On the other hand, it said he was always changing his mind. That was confusing, because people who kill open discussion are not usually people who are always changing their mind. The two flaws tend to be mutually exclusive.

To make the situation more perplexing, when I talked to Steve, he practically laughed at the feedback. "I may have a lot of issues," he said, "but killing dialogue is not one of them. I'm always talking things out with my people."

I recalled interviewing one of Steve's directors, who said, "You have to understand, this fellow is the world champion at arguing with himself. He was a star debater in college."

Now the feedback made sense.

Time and time again, an employee would come to Steve with an idea. Being a debate champion, Steve's first reaction was to go into debate mode and shoot holes in the idea. The employee's reaction, as a direct report, was to shut down in the face of the verbal onslaught from the boss. Two people, two different perspectives. Steve thought he was having an open debate. The employee thought that he had just been blown away.

Steve compounded the problem by debating with himself as well. Someone would say, "Why don't we try this?" and Steve would approve. He inspired his whole staff to get behind the suggestion. But a few days later, after he had enough time to debate his decision strenuously with himself, he'd change his mind, saying, "Maybe that wasn't such a good idea." In his head, he was being open-minded. In his staff's collective brain, he was confusing them.

Let's not get into the fact that you can't do that in a leadership position. You can't motivate 200 people to conquer a hill and, when they all start charging, say, "Wait a minute. Maybe this isn't such a smart plan." Do that a few times, and no one's going to be inspired to take hills for you. They will just sit there and wait.

Let's focus on making Steve see the problem, which I like to call The Golden Rule Fallacy. You see it in situations where the boss makes the logical inference that the people being bossed are just like him and, in strict obedience to the Golden Rule, like to be treated the same way that the boss likes to be treated. *I like it when people treat me this way, therefore I will treat everyone else this way.*

When I pointed out to Steve that he liked heated debate because it played to his strengths, he agreed. "I like it when people do that for me, mix it up and argue."

"That's nice, but they aren't you," I said.

"What's wrong with it?" he asked. "What's wrong with me expressing an opinion, and someone else expressing an opinion, and we have a healthy debate? I love that."

I said, "Well, yes, but you are the boss—and they aren't. You were the star debater at college—and they weren't. This isn't a fair fight! All you're doing to them is saying, 'You lose. I win.' Their odds of beating you at this game are zero. So they opt not to play."

"That's not true," he countered. "I have someone on staff who loves it as much as I do."

"That's the problem," I said. "Sometimes your debating style works, particularly with people who enjoy arguing both sides of every issue and don't back down from the verbal jousting. If everybody on your staff was like this one person, you wouldn't have a problem. Unfortunately, 99 percent of your team is not like that guy. Your one success is not being replicated with anyone else. Why? Because that single exceptional employee is just like you. But you are not managing you."

True to form, Steve the debating champion had lured me into a heated debate. Luckily, the "you're not managing you" line hit home. Suddenly he got it. He saw that he was operating under a bogus assumption that what was good for him was good for everyone else.

From that moment on, Steve's improvement was a sure thing. He paid close attention to his debating urges, and stifled them when they put his staff at a huge disadvantage. He apologized to everyone for the mistakes in his past, and promised to do better in the future. He routinely invited people to voice their opinions in meetings, and thought once, twice, three times before challenging them. (Nothing wrong with challenging people. His goal was to open up the dialogue, not become a doormat for every silly opinion.) He followed up with people, reminding them that he was trying to improve in this area. Lastly, he asked them for suggestions that could help him get even better.

It didn't happen overnight. These transformations require time to take hold with the people assessing you. As I say, you have to change 100 percent to get 10 percent credit for it. So, after 18 months, Steve was perceived as a better boss. He was the same guy in most ways. He still loved to argue with himself and anyone else in the room. The only difference: He now accommodated the fact that his staffers didn't necessarily feel the same way as he did.

Since my session with Steve, I've been more alert to this it's-not-a-fair-fight dynamic between bosses and the bossed.

A friend once told me about her boss and his obsession with documentation. He had been trained as a lawyer, someone who was slavishly devoted to evidence and paperwork and perfectly maintained files. When he started his marketing consulting business, he did not abandon his fondness for paper. He still saved everything. This was fine except he expected everyone else to be as obsessed with retaining documents as he was. He would call meetings during which everyone knew he would haul out some ancient letters and memos as evidence to chastise someone for letting things fall through the cracks.

I interpreted this behavior as typically wrongheaded management, classic Golden Rule Fallacy at work. This great entrepreneur overlooked the fact that as owner of the company, he had access to any and all documents, whereas his subordinates did not. He did not appreciate that he was instigating a fight that only he could win. He loved documents and documentation, and wrongly assumed everyone else did too.

See it once and you begin to see it everywhere.

By all means, do unto others as you would have them do unto you. But realize that it doesn't apply in all instances in management. If you manage your people the way you'd want to be managed, you're forgetting one thing: You're not managing you.

Stop "Checking the Box"

I was meeting with a chief executive recently, listening to him express puzzlement that his employees did not understand the company's mission and overall direction.

"I don't get it," he said. "I've spelled it out for them in meetings. I've summarized it in a memo. See, here's the memo. It's very clear. What more do the employees want?"

For a moment there, I thought he was kidding—that he had a very refined sense of irony. Making people understand the company's mission and vision doesn't happen by fiat, or by memo. It also doesn't happen overnight. Surely this smart CEO knew that. By the pained expression on his face, I could tell he was dead serious and (if only in this one area of management) clueless.

"Let's review the situation," I said. "How was this memo distributed?"

"By e-mail," he said. "It went to everyone in the company."

"Okay," I said, "but my hunch is that the method of distribution is all you know about this. How many people actually opened the e-mail and *read* the memo?"

"I don't know," he said.

"Of those, how many do you think *understood* the memo?"

"I have no idea," he said.

"Of those who understood it, how many *believed* it?"

He shook his head.

"Of this dwindling group of believers, how many *remembered* it?"

Another sorry head shake.

"That's a lot of unknowns for something you regard as vital to your company's existence," I said. "But that's not the worst part. Once you eliminate all the people who either didn't receive, or read, or understand, or believe, or remember the memo—and it's quite possible there's no one left—how many people do you think will adopt the memo's contents? How many will begin living and breathing the company's mission because of your memo?"

I think I heard the CEO mutter a contrite "I dunno," but it was hard to tell because by now his voice was nearly inaudible.

It's not my mission in life to deflate or depress clients, so I tried to revive his spirits by changing the subject—by pointing out that the problem was *him*, not his memo.

"The only thing you're guilty of," I said, "was checking the box!"

"Huh?" he said.

"You thought your job was done when you articulated the mission and wrote the memo—as if it were one more item on your to-do list for the day. You checked the box, and you moved on. Next."

I could see the scales slowly lifting from his eyes, so I pressed on with my theory about what may be the most egregious source of corporate dysfunction: the failure of managers to see the enormous disconnect between understanding and doing. Most leadership development revolves around one huge false assumption—that if people understand then they will do. That's not true. Most of us understand, we just don't do. As I said in Chapter 11, we all understand that being grossly overweight is bad for our health, but not all of us actually do anything to change our condition.

This CEO is no different from most executives who believe their organizations operate with strict down-the-chain-of-command efficiency. The boss says, "Jump." The subordinates ask, "How high?" In a perfect world, every command is not only obeyed, but obeyed precisely and promptly, almost as if it were a fait accompli. The boss doesn't have to follow up *ever*—because he said it and it was done. After all, he checked the box.

I'm not sure why bosses persist in thinking this way. Maybe their ego can't fathom that their orders might not be strictly followed. Maybe they're too lazy to investigate whether people did their bidding. Maybe they're too disorganized to adhere to strict follow-up procedures. Maybe they think that following up is beneath them. Whatever the reason, they blindly assume that if people understand, they will do.

The good news here for every manager, including my CEO client, is that this false belief has a simple cure. It's called follow-up. Once you send out a message, you ask people the next day if they heard it. Then you ask if they understood it. Then a few days later, you ask if they did something about it. Believe me, if the first follow-up question doesn't get their attention, the next one will, and so will the final one.

Stop Being Prejudiced About Your Employees

I spend most of my professional life trying to change people's behavior in the workplace. I tell people that change is a simple equation: Stop the annoying behavior and you'll stop being perceived as an annoyance. It's so easy, I'm amazed I get paid to teach it.

I wish I could say the same about changing the way people *think*. But lately that's become a critical part of my practice, too. The big reason for it is that there's been a radical shift in the way employees regard their roles in and their relationship to an organization. The magazine *Fast Company* nailed it in 1998 when it ran a notorious cover story titled "Free Agent Nation." It posited the then-radical notion that the "organization man" was dead, that the best performers in a company were no longer interested in sacrificing their lives for the good of the organization. The smart ones believed that their corporation would "drop them in a flash" when they no longer met the company's needs, so they in turn were willing to "drop the company" when it no longer met *their* needs. Free agency meant that each employee was operating like a small self-contained business rather than a cog in the wheel of a large system.

It took a while for this free agent virus to spread. But trust me, it's an epidemic now, a sweeping pathology that demands a change in the way bosses think.

The first thing I do with managers who are overwhelmed or confused by this workplace shift is make them see that they are *prejudiced* about their employees. This always gets their attention. "Me. Prejudiced? Get outta here!" But if prejudice means harboring inflexible, intolerant beliefs about a group of people that do not coincide with reality or how that group sees itself, it's true. Managers who are blind to the changes in this new cohort of free agents are operating like dangerous, deluded executive bigots. (It's no different than a manager refusing to hire a young married woman because he believes she will leave her job eventually to have babies and, therefore, is not serious about her career. It's easy to forget that there was a time not too long ago when almost everyone thought this way.) The prejudice against free agents takes many forms, but here are four that any of us can easily fall into.

1. I know what they want.

This is the biggest prejudice. And the easiest to understand. Almost every economic model has historically assumed that money is the key motivator for any employee. And so bosses assume that if they pay their people top dollar, they will get top performance and loyalty in return. Sorry, it doesn't work that way anymore.

There's no denying that money matters in everyone's career calculus. But at some point, the top performers achieve a level of financial comfort, however tenuous, when other considerations begin to dominate. As economist Lester Thurow pointed out in *Building Wealth,* free agents must wrestle with the paradox that the economic value of their experience falls rather than rises in the course of a career. The shelf life of knowledge, especially technical knowledge, is continuously shrinking. And so free agents respond by moving on to new challenges that enhance their knowledge and let them outpace the shrinking value of their experience—and in turn reward them with more satisfaction and, quite possibly, more money.

If you've ever been puzzled by a talented employee who left you to work at another company in a different job for less money, blame it on this prejudice.

This prejudice, carelessly or ruthlessly applied, can actually drive good people away. I remember a multimillionaire entrepreneur telling me in amazement about a well-paid writer on his staff who could never meet a deadline. The entrepreneur liked the writer, but wanted to change his cavalier attitude toward deadlines. So he instituted a seemingly simple carrot-and-stick scheme: Every time the writer made his monthly deadline, he'd get a $500 bonus. To no effect. The writer still missed his deadlines. Apparently, he was making enough money so that an additional $500 a month didn't make that much difference to him. It was no different when the entrepreneur increased the bonus to $3000. Still no improvement. Only when the boss resorted to *deducting* $3000 from the writer's paycheck did he change his ways. Economists would call this "loss aversion"—the phenomenon that we hate losing something more than we enjoy gaining its equivalent. I would call this prejudice—a failure to understand what motivates an employee. The writer did indeed meet his deadlines for a few months, but he left the company within six months.

Apparently, although the writer didn't care about the rewards for good performance, he felt strongly about being punished for poor performance. The bonus didn't motivate him. The deduction, though, insulted him. The entrepreneur figured out how to change his employee's behavior, but he also drove him away. They're a complicated lot, these free agents. And if you think you know what makes them tick, you first need to check your prejudices at the door.

This I-know-what-they-want delusion extends far beyond money. As a general rule, people in their 20s want to *learn* on the job. In their 30s they want to *advance*. And in their 40s they want to *rule*. No matter what their age, though, understanding their desires is like trying to pin down mercury. You have to find out what they want at every step—by literally asking them—and you can't assume that one size fits all. The person who sees the noble goal of "work-life balance" as irrelevant at age 24 may find it critical at 34.

Consider the still-young career of shortstop Alex Rodriguez. At age 20 he won a batting title with the Seattle Mariners. Four years later he moved to the Texas Rangers for the staggering salary of $25 million a year, where he was the American League MVP and three-time home run champion. Four years later, at the tender age of 28, he moved to the New York Yankees. He was by general consensus the best player in the game, and yet two teams let him go! Actually, the organization didn't let him go. He left the organization—the first time for more money, the second time for a shot at the World Series with the perennial front-running Yankees. This is classic "free agent nation" in action (in large part because baseball "invented" free agency in 1975 after a legal battle that let players move freely among the teams). It's an example of (a) the employee calling the shots, (b) the employee using the organization to fulfill *his* needs, and (c) those needs changing over time.

As for the entrepreneur and the writer above, I don't know what I would have done—other than to assure the entrepreneur that the traditional carrot-and-stick approach doesn't work anymore. Clearly, dangling the carrot of more money for meeting deadlines didn't work. But that doesn't mean that beating the writer with the stick of a salary deduction would appeal to him either.

2. I know what they know.

The days when managers know how to do every job in the company better than anyone else are over. The reason Peter Drucker said that the manager of the future will know how to ask rather than how to tell is because Drucker understood that knowledge workers would know more than any manager does. Well, the future is here with a vengeance. And smart managers need to shed the overconfident bias that they know as much as their employees know in specific areas. It's a blind spot that diminishes their employees' abilities and enthusiasm, and ultimately shrinks the boss's stature.

3. I hate their selfishness.

How many times has an employee come to you complaining that he or she isn't happy or fulfilled in a job, and the initial thought balloon hanging over your head is, "Quit griping, you selfish oaf! I pay you a lot of money to do a job, not to be happy. Get back to work."

How many times has an employee come to you with an outside job offer, hoping that you will counter the offer because he or she doesn't want to leave you or the company, and your initial response is to question the employee's loyalty, to regard him or her as an ingrate and traitor?

I contend that these crude Neanderthal responses are instances of prejudice, too. And it's easy to see why managers feel this way. They have decades of bias training on their side. Historically, large U.S. companies have benefited from a one-sided proposition. While the *company* was supposed to maximize return for itself and shareholders, the *individual* was expected to discount his or her self-interests and focus on the good of the company. It was considered outrageous for employees to openly demand, "What's in it for me?"

I hope we can all agree that in the new world order—where the organization man has been replaced by the highly mobile free agent—no manager should be taken aback by employees who are looking out for themselves. You certainly shouldn't resent them for it, or brand them as selfish. Actually, you should embrace it, because it's a relatively easy problem to handle if you can beat the employees to the punch.

A talent agent once told me about an eye-opening encounter he had with Jack Welch when he was chairman of General Electric. The agent's firm had just concluded a long-term contract renewal, with an eye-popping raise and stock options, for an on-air broadcaster at GE's NBC broadcasting unit.

Welch mentioned the broadcaster's name in the meeting and the agent half-proudly, half-sheepishly said, "Yes, I'm afraid we took you guys to the cleaners with that one."

Welch's eyes flared for a second, and the agent feared that he had needlessly insulted the legendary CEO. In solemn, serious tones, Welch said, "You don't understand. You didn't hose us. We *wanted* to give him the money. We would have done anything to keep him happy."

Let that be your model for dealing with needy, demanding, allegedly "selfish" employees. To ignore them and resent them is to misunderstand them—and eventually lose them. You're committing the corporate equivalent of a hate crime.

4. I can always get someone else.

In the past, the key to wealth may have been control of land, materials, plants, and tools. In that environment, the worker needed the company more than the company needed the worker. Today the key to wealth is *knowledge*. As a result, the company needs the knowledge worker far more than the knowledge worker needs them. To make matters worse, the workers know this! They see themselves as fungible assets—no longer at the mercy of company whim—rather than dispensable commodities. The difference is subtle but real: As a fungible asset, the free agent sees himself as always getting a better job somewhere else; if he were merely a commodity, anyone could replace him (which, we know, is not true anymore).

Managers at smart companies are catching on. They're beginning to see that their relationship with top talent resembles a strategic alliance rather than a traditional employment contract. They know free agents can leave anytime. When I polled the top 120 executives at one of the world's leading high-tech companies, "Can the highest potential leader who works for you leave the company and get another job *with a pay raise* in one week?" all 120 executives said yes!

I'm sure this was the managerial prejudice at play when the Orlando Magic let Shaquille O'Neal slip out of their hands in 1995 and go off to the Los Angeles Lakers. (This is like Microsoft letting Bill Gates go elsewhere, or Sony Music letting Bruce Springsteen slip away from their recording label. Some talent is not replaceable.) Sure, Shaq was expensive to keep, but Orlando must have thought he was replaceable, that they could spend the money to buy another player just like him. That's a costly prejudice. The facts are that Orlando turned into a second-tier team when O'Neal left, and the Lakers won three world championships soon after he arrived.

I cite sports examples here because the information is public and readily available, not because it's free agent behavior at its most extreme. Believe me, this same extreme "what's in it for me" attitude goes on thousands of times a day in companies across America. People unhappy. People running off resumes at Kinko's. People testing the job market. People leaving good jobs for better ones. All because their bosses were blind to the real reasons they came to work each day. If that blindness isn't prejudice, I don't know what else to call it. But it's happening. The only difference is we don't read about each individual case in the newspaper.

If none of these examples hits home yet, let me hit you where it can really hurt.

If you continue to harbor these prejudices and ignore the changing realities in your workplace, it can cost you your job. It can cost you your job even if you're the top dog and are putting up great numbers.

I'm not saying that managers have been completely stripped of their authority. In most places, the top-down chain of command structure is still intact. People still obey their bosses' commands. But there's been a subtle shift in power in the workplace, and some of it now resides in the free agents. More of it than managers imagine. That's one reason I have a job. When I work one-on-one with a manager, it's often because he or she has done something to tick off his direct reports. Some are so annoyed that they leave the company. In effect, the departing employees are voting with their feet. At some point, if enough of them cast similar votes, the free agent workers' response to the manager registers as a serious problem. That's when I get called in—to find out what's annoying the employees, share that with the boss, and get him to change his ways.

Casey Stengel liked to point out that on any baseball team, one third of the players loved the manager, one third hated him, and one third were undecided. "The secret to managing a ballclub," said Stengel, "was to keep the third who hated you from getting together with the third who were undecided."

That's the real peril today in free agent nation. One employee can't bring a good manager down. But a bunch of employees can gang up and topple even the most productive bosses.

Remember this as you gently or brutally navigate your way through the ever-shifting management landscape of free agent nation. Take a temperature reading on your prejudices from time to time. Are you responding to your employees with outdated biases? Or are you meeting the new free agent mindset on its own terms? In the context of this book, accepting the new terrain can make you a more successful boss—and quite possibly save your job.

Your people are changing constantly and it's right in front of your eyes. If you don't change accordingly, you may as well be managing with your eyes wide shut. That's the most unforgivable prejudice of all.

Stop Trying to Coach People Who Shouldn't Be Coached

In the same way that some of your problems do not need fixing because they are an issue to only a small minority of people, as a boss you should stop trying to change people who don't want to change.

This may sound harsh, but some people are unsalvageable. You're only banging your head against a wall if you think you can fix them.

Believe me, I know. It's taken me years to appreciate that some problems are so deep and systemic and strange that they are impervious to my particular ministrations. Through trial and error, I have shed all illusions about my methods, and concluded that some flaws can't be coached away by any boss, especially with the following employees.

Stop trying to change people who don't think they have a problem. Have you ever attempted to change the behavior of a successful adult at work who has no interest in changing? How much luck have you had with this conversion activity? The answer is always the same: No luck. Now bring it closer to home. Have you had any luck trying to change a spouse, partner, or significant other who has no interest in changing? Again, same answer. My mother went to college for two years and was a superb and much-admired first grade teacher. She was so dedicated that she saw no line of demarcation between how she behaved in the classroom and in the real world. She talked to everyone with the same slow patient cadence and simple vocabulary that she employed with her six-year-olds each day. Mom lived in a world entirely populated by first graders. I was always in the first grade. Her siblings were always in the first grade. All of our relatives were in the first grade. My father was in the first grade. Mom was always correcting everyone's grammar. One day she was correcting my father (for the ten thousandth time). He looked at her, sighed, and said, "Honey, I'm 70 years old. Let it go."

If your people don't care about changing, don't waste your time.

Stop trying to change people who are pursuing the wrong strategy for the organization. If they're going in the wrong direction, all you'll do is help them get there faster.

Stop trying to change people who should not be in their job. Some people feel they're in the wrong job at the wrong company. Perhaps they believe that they were meant to be doing something else. Or that their skills are being misused. Or that they they're missing something. If you have any sensitivity, you have a good idea who these people are. Even if you pick up only a tiny molecule of this vibe, ask them, "What if we shut down today? Would you be surprised, sad, or relieved?" More often than not, they will choose "relieved." Take that as your cue to send them packing. You can't change the behavior of unhappy people so that they become happy. You can only fix the behavior that's making the people around them unhappy.

Finally, stop trying to help people who think everyone else is the problem.

I once dealt with an entrepreneur who, after a few high profile employee departures, was concerned about employee morale. He ran a dominant company in a fun business. People loved working there. But the feedback said the boss played favorites in the way he compensated people. Some employees were handsomely paid; others got whatever he thought he could get away with. The only way to get a big raise was to put a gun to his head—i.e., threaten to quit and mean it.

When I reported this back to the entrepreneur, he surprised me by agreeing with the charge and defending it. Like many self-made men, he regarded every nickel he paid an employee as a nickel that didn't go into his pocket. He paid people according to a Darwinian scale of what he thought they were worth in the marketplace. If they could get more elsewhere, they'd have to prove it to him first.

I'm not a compensation strategist. I wasn't equipped to solve this problem. But he had another surprise in store for me. It turned out the entrepreneur hadn't called me to help *him* change. He wanted me to fix the employees.

In moments like this I tend to run, not walk, away. It's hard to help people who don't think they have a problem. It's impossible to fix people who think someone else is the problem.

You should, too. People like this will never give up on their near-religious belief that any failure is someone else's fault. They hold this belief as firmly as if it were their religion. Trying to convert them would like trying to convert an ardent Democrat into a Republican—or vice versa. Not gonna happen. So save time and skip the heroic measures. This is an "argument" you will never win.

You Are Here Now

TAKE A BREATH. Take a deeper breath.

Imagine that you're 95 years old and ready to die. Before taking your last breath, you're given a great gift: The ability to travel back in time—the ability to talk to the person who is reading this page, the ability to help this person be a better professional and lead a better life.

The 95-year-old you understands what was really important and what wasn't, what mattered and what didn't. What advice would this wise "old you" have for the "you" who is reading this page?

Take your time and answer the question on two levels: personal advice and professional advice. Jot down a few words that capture what the old you would be saying to the younger you.

Once you've written these words down, the rest is simple: Just do whatever you wrote down. Make it your resolution for the rest of the current year, and the next. You have just defined your "there."

I cannot define "there" for you. I cannot dictate it and I'm certainly not going to judge it as being worthy or noble. To do so would not only be presumptuous, it's none of my business.

But I can make a rough prediction about what some features of your "there" will look like—because a friend of mine actually had the opportunity to interview people who were dying and ask them what advice they would have had for themselves. The answers he got were filled with wisdom.

One recurring theme was to "reflect upon life, to find happiness and meaning now," not next month or next year. The Great Western Disease lies in the phrase, *I will be happy when* . . . As in, *I will be happy when I get that promotion*, or *I will be happy when I buy that house*, or *I will be happy when I get that money*. The wise old you has finally realized that the next promotion, the next achievement, the next move to a larger house or a more attractive corner office won't really change your world that much. Many older people say they were so wrapped up in looking for what they didn't have that they seldom appreciated what they did have. They often wish they would have taken more time to enjoy it.

A second recurring theme was "friends and family." Consider this: You may work for a wonderful company, and you may think that your contribution to that organization is very important. When you are 95 years old and you look at the people around your deathbed, very few of your fellow employees will be there waving good-bye. Your friends and family will probably be the only people who care. Appreciate them now and share a large part of your life with them.

Yet another recurring theme was the reflection to "follow your dreams." Older people who have tried to achieve their dreams are always happier with their lives. Figure out your true purpose in life, and go for it! This doesn't apply just to big dreams; it is also true for little dreams. Buy the sports car you always wanted, go to that exotic locale that's always held your fascination, learn how to play the piano or speak Italian. If some people think your vision of a well-lived life is a bit goofy or off-beat, who cares? It isn't their life. It's yours. Few of us will achieve all of our dreams. Some dreams will always elude us. So the key question is not, "Did I make all my dreams come true?" The key question is, "Did I try?"

I conducted a research project for Accenture involving more than 200 high-potential leaders from 120 companies around the world. Each company could nominate only two future leaders, the very brightest of its young stars. These are the kinds of people who could jump at a moment's notice to better-paying positions elsewhere. We asked each of these young stars a simple question: "If you stay in this company, why are you going to stay?" The three top answers were:

1. "I am finding meaning and happiness now. The work is exciting and I love what I am doing."

2. "I like the people. They are my friends. This feels like a team. It feels like a family. I could make more money working with other people, but I don't want to leave the people here."

3. "I can follow my dreams. This organization is giving me a chance to do what I really want to do in life."

The answers were never about money. They were always about happiness, relationships, following dreams, and meaning. When my friend asked people on their deathbeds what was important to them, they gave exactly the same answers as the high-potential leaders I interviewed.

Use that wisdom now. Don't look ahead. Look behind. Look back from your old age at the life you hope to live. Know that you need to be happy now, to enjoy your friends and family, to follow your dreams.

You are here.

You can get there!

Let the journey begin.

Appendix

This leadership inventory was developed as part of a research project (sponsored by Accenture) involving 200 specially selected high-potential leaders from 120 companies around the world. Respondents are asked to rate leaders on a five-point scale, ranging from Highly Satisfied to Highly Dissatisfied.

Global Leadership Inventory

Consider your own (or this person's) effectiveness in the following areas. How satisfied are you with the way he or she (or you) . . .

Thinking Globally

1. Recognizes the impact of globalization on our business

2. Demonstrates the adaptability required to succeed in the global environment

3. Strives to gain the variety of experiences needed to conduct global business

4. Makes decisions that incorporate global considerations

5. Helps others understand the impact of globalization

Appreciating Diversity

6. Embraces the value of diversity in people (including culture, race, sex, or age)

7. Effectively motivates people from different cultures or backgrounds

8. Recognizes the value of diverse views and opinions

9. Helps others appreciate the value of diversity

10. Actively expands her/his knowledge of other cultures (through interactions, language study, travel, etc.)

Developing Technological Savvy

11. Strives to acquire the technological knowledge needed to succeed in tomorrow's world

12. Successfully recruits people with needed technological expertise

13. Effectively manages the issue of technology to increase productivity

Building Partnerships

14. Treats coworkers as partners, not competitors

15. Unites his/her organization into an effective team

16. Builds effective partnerships across the company

17. Discourages destructive comments about other people or groups

18. Builds effective alliances with other organizations

19. Creates a network of relationships that help to get things done

Sharing Leadership

20. Willingly shares leadership with business partners

21. Defers to others when they have more expertise

22. Strives to arrive at an outcome *with* others (as opposed to *for* others)

23. Creates an environment where people focus on the larger good (avoids sub-optimization or "turfism")

Creating a Shared Vision

24. Creates and communicates a clear vision for our organization

25. Effectively involves people in decision-making

26. Inspires people to commit to achieving the vision

27. Develops an effective strategy to achieve the vision

28. Clearly identifies priorities

Developing People

29. Consistently treats people with dignity

30. Asks people what they need to do their work better

31. Ensures that people receive the training they need to succeed

32. Provides effective coaching

33. Provides developmental feedback in a timely manner

34. Provides effective recognition for others' achievements

Empowering People

35. Builds people's confidence

36. Takes risks in letting others make decisions

37. Gives people the freedom they need to do their job well

38. Trusts people enough to let go (avoids micromanagement)

Achieving Personal Mastery

39. Deeply understands her/his own strengths and weaknesses

40. Invests in ongoing personal development

41. Involves people who do not have strengths that he/she does not possess

42. Demonstrates effective emotional responses in a variety of situations

43. Demonstrates self-confidence as a leader

Encouraging Constructive Dialogue

44. Asks people what he/she can do to improve

45. Genuinely listens to others

46. Accepts constructive feedback in a positive manner (avoids defensiveness)

47. Strives to understand the *other person's* frame of reference

48. Encourages people to challenge the status quo

Demonstrates Integrity

49. Demonstrates honest, ethical behavior in all interactions

50. Ensures that the highest standards for ethical behavior are practiced throughout the organization

51. Avoids political or self-serving behavior

52. Courageously "stands up" for what she/he believes in

53. Is a role model for living our organization's values (leads by example)

Leading Change

54. Sees change as an opportunity, not a problem

55. Challenges the system when change is needed

56. Thrives in ambiguous situations (demonstrates flexibility when needed)

57. Encourages creativity and innovation in others

58. Effectively translates creative ideas into business results

Anticipating Opportunities

59. Invests in learning about future trends

60. Effectively anticipates future opportunities

61. Inspires people to focus on future opportunities (not just present objectives)

62. Develops ideas to meet the needs of the new environment

Ensuring Customer Satisfaction

63. Inspires people to achieve high levels of customer satisfaction

64. Views business processes from the ultimate customer perspective (has an "end to end" perspective)

65. Regularly solicits input from customers

66. Consistently delivers on commitments to customers

67. Understands the competitive options available to her/his customers

Maintaining a Competitive Advantage

68. Communicates a positive, "can do" sense of urgency toward getting the job done

69. Holds people accountable for their results

70. Successfully eliminates waste and unneeded cost

71. Provides products/services that help our company have a clear competitive advantage

72. Achieves results that lead to long-term shareholder value

Written Comments

What are your strengths? Or if you are evaluating someone, what does this person do that you particularly appreciate? (Please list two or three *specific* items.)

What *specifically* might you do to be more effective? Or if evaluating someone, what suggestions would you have for this person on how she or he could become even more effective? (Please list two or three *specific* items).

Index

Contents

Preface

This book focuses on practitioners' perspectives of how structural social work theory is utilized in practice settings. It is the first time that a social work text has combined the efforts of academics and practitioners in the crafting of each individual chapter. This has enabled the book to link theory and practice in a unique way. Using concrete examples, the chapters detail the "how to" side of using structural social work theory. Much of the literature to date discusses how the theory ought to be utilized in practice rather than describing how it *is* used in practice. The book goes beyond discussing how practitioners should work against oppression across multiple and intersecting differences. It details how practitioners are challenging economic, social, and political structures while simultaneously helping individuals, families, groups, and communities. It does not discuss oppression in a vacuum, but directly links it to concrete structures.

This book has used its own theory in its construction. It is the result of the work of a collective beyond that of the listed editors. The idea for the book began at a structural social work conference at Ryerson University in the fall of 2006, and many of the authors in this text attended the conference. Individual chapters were written by teams that comprised academics and practitioners. Each chapter was then reviewed by two members of the collective—often a practitioner and an academic—before it was reviewed by the editors. We constantly challenged each other to look deeply at how the everyday lives of situated clients and practitioners are inextricably linked to structures and how this link shifts our practice of social work.

This is a book of optimism. All too often in academia we are focused on writing critiques. We critique social policies, practice approaches, analyses of social issues, and so on. The goal is always to further develop or improve what we are critiquing or to suggest alternatives, but in the process we often focus on the criticism and stop short of writing about what works. Students will sometimes talk about course readings and their feelings of frustration and hopelessness, stating that it seems like nothing is going right and that things are never going to change. While critiques are still important, this book starts from a different premise. Using concrete examples, it illustrates the ways in which structural social work theory is successfully being implemented in social work practice; it is about what works, rather than what is not working. In giving examples of what *does* work in structural social work practice, it offers hope to others that this work is not only possible, but that it is happening, it is effective, and the rest of us can do it too.

We begin in Part 1 by setting the backdrop for the main focus of the book. Murray and Hick begin by highlighting the tenets and some of the history of structural social work theory. Included is a brief overview of current issues in the structural social work field, including the role of postmodernism, the challenges of a focus on multiple oppressions, and questions of blurred boundaries between structural social work theory and related perspectives such as radical, critical, and anti-oppressive theories and approaches. Next, current structural approaches are discussed in the context of Maurice Moreau's early work in researching and writing about the use of structural social work theory in practice. The challenges of achieving the two structural goals of alleviating the effects of structural oppression while working toward social transformation are also discussed. Olivier offers guidelines for assessing our work in light of these goals. Lastly, barriers and catalysts to the successful integration of theory and practice are organized in a new conceptual framework of theory–practice integration. Through this framework, there is a discussion of the literature on theory–practice integration that largely focuses on the so-called gap between theory and practice. In this chapter, Peters suggests that one of the goals of the conceptual framework is to be able to identify ways in which theory–practice integration is supported and encouraged, thus increasing the likelihood of its success. Using the framework as an organizing tool, Peters outlines the chapters in Part 2, highlighting the diverse ways in which structural social work theory is effectively supported in practice.

The chapters in Part 2 provide practice examples, and they are the heart of this book. They display the depth and complexity of the myriad of ways in which structural social work is being successfully practised across Canada. The authors write about their work with various populations, including children;

women; youth; lesbian, gay, bisexual, transgender, two-spirited, queer, and intersex people; new immigrants; people with mental health issues; and others. The authors also write about a variety of fields of practice, including work with sexual abuse survivors, violence against women, organizational development, environmentalism, (dis)ability rights, and the education of social workers and peers on issues of oppression.

Although there are many lessons to be learned from these practitioners, there are four themes in particular that stand out. First, all of these practitioners are sharing how structural social work theory is being successfully incorporated into practice. Second, structural theory states that social problems arise from oppressive social structures, thus linking the micro, mezzo, and macro. True to the theory, the practitioners in this book describe a variety of ways in which they are continuously working across all of these levels. Third, the examples of practice experiences demonstrate that structural social workers use creative ways of incorporating mainstream and other skill sets into a structural approach. Last, and perhaps most optimistically, over and over again the chapters identify numerous ways in which their structural practice is effective, encouraged, and affirmed. This gives us a map for how we can repeat, encourage, and expand the use of structural social work theory elsewhere.

Part 3 closes with a discussion of the future of structural social work and the threads that are woven through the chapters. Lysack challenges social workers to understand and incorporate environmental issues into our practice. This is a laudable goal, and we need to begin a dialogue on how structural social work can do this. The concluding chapter suggests that future directions for structural social work need to include working with like-minded colleagues from other disciplines and re-integrating social justice values into our Canadian Association of Social Workers' Code of Ethics.

A final important success of this book is that it begins to address the criticism that structural social work theory is a romantic ideal that cannot be translated into practice skills; that it is un-doable. In Chapter 2, Olivier acknowledges that the goal of social transformation is a laudable but challenging one that is difficult to measure. All of the chapters describe the steps involved in naming and addressing structural oppression, and toward educating people about the structural roots of social issues. Several of the chapters identify concrete ways in which their work has directly led or contributed to changes in legislation, social policies, municipal by-laws, and societal attitudes. This is social transformation. It is possible, and it is actually happening. And so we have hope. Hope that a structural approach is actually possible, and that it can achieve social change. And hope that if this group of practitioners can do it, then so can others.

Heather I. Peters,
Tracy London,
Tammy Corner,
and Steven F. Hick

Acknowledgements

General Acknowledgements

In the spirit of structural social work, this book was a collective effort. The chapters were reviewed not only by the four listed editors, but also by an editorial collective. The collective comprised Bessa Whitmore, Anita Vaillancourt, Tara LaRose, Purnima George, and Si Transken. A mention of these reviewers in the acknowledgements does not do justice to their efforts. They provided detailed feedback and constructive suggestions to contributors, and without them this book would not have attained such a high standard.

This is the first time that we know of where individual chapters have been written by teams comprising academics and practitioners. We would like to acknowledge the efforts of the practitioners in taking time from their busy schedules and contributing their ideas and insights. We believe it has provided a unique perspective for this book. We would like to acknowledge all of the practitioners who go to work each day, striving to provide support to clients while challenging and changing societal structures. A special thank you is owed to the authors who contributed to this book for their willingness to take the time to share examples from their work. Their experiences are an important contribution to the field of structural social work theory and its practical application.

We would also like to thank Bessa Whitmore for her work to get this project off the ground and for her support throughout the process.

Steven Hick

First, I have to recognize the central help freely given by the editorial collective. Their help greatly improved the chapters they reviewed. Finally, a warm thank you to my partner, Vaida, and my children, Kristina and Justin, for being supportive as I sat at my computer for yet another evening.

Heather Peters

I was fortunate to grow up in a family whose members espouse and live social justice values in all aspects of their lives, including their volunteer and paid work. I would like to acknowledge my family, including my parents, Ione and Adolph Peters, my sister, Crystal Peters, and my brother-in-law, Dave Fast, for what they have taught me about social justice and for their ongoing support of me and my work. I would especially like to thank my life partner, Bruce Self, for his strong social justice stance, and his encouragement and support of me. His unwavering belief in the importance of this project was demonstrated many times over as he carried much of our work at home so that I could spend more time on the book. Thank you for the ways in which you care for me.

Tammy Corner

I would like to acknowledge, and thank, Bessa Whitmore for obtaining funding and organizing the 2006 structural social work conference at Ryerson University in Toronto titled, *Honouring Our Past, Considering Our Present, Envisioning Our Future*. This conference launched the idea for this text. Thank you also to all the individuals, including academics and practitioners, who are making a difference by challenging structures that oppress while inspiring and holding a vision of hope for a just world. Through the media, we are often inundated with negative stories of injustice and frequently do not hear the good news stories. This text is an example of some of the actions that are creating positive change.

Tracy London

I am deeply appreciative of the support and mentorship of my fellow editors, Steven Hick, Heather Peters, and Tammy Corner—colleagues who have inspired me through their commitment to structural social work.

PART 1

Introduction

CHAPTER 1

Structural Social Work:
Theory and Process

KATE M. MURRAY AND STEVEN F. HICK

Introduction

The structural approach to social work emerged during the mid 1970s as an alternative to what was seen as a pathologizing and individual-oriented focus in social work practice at the time. The approach has continued to re-define itself as new research and insights emerge, but its key feature remains: the approach's critical historical analysis examines how structures are often the root cause of social problems. It does not ignore individual problems or psychology, but scrutinizes these as linked to exploitative social arrangements. Thus, structural social work not only addresses individual difficulties, but also seeks to transform society toward values of freedom, humanitarianism, collectivism, equality, self-determination, popular participation, and social justice.

Structural social work has been criticized for neglecting *practice* in favour of *theory*, offering few concrete guidelines—especially in clinical contexts. In response, this text portrays the structural approach in action: contributors outline the practice of structural social work *on the ground*. However, we cannot ignore theory altogether! This first chapter provides the conceptual scaffolding for the practice-oriented chapters in this book. Drawing on our recent summary of the approach (Hick & Murray, 2008), we conduct an overview of key features and theoretical foundations of structural social work, and critically assess issues that enrich and challenge the approach.

Structural social work is informed by many—sometimes competing—perspectives, including Marxism, feminism, anti-racism, post-colonialism, radical humanism, radical structuralism, and postmodernism (Carniol, 2005c; Lecomte, 1990; Lundy, 2004; Mullaly, 2007; Payne, 2005). This multi-faceted origin poses practical and theoretical challenges. First, structural social work is inconsistently referenced in some literature, suggesting a need to clarify its position and its vision of transformation. Second, the subsumption of feminist, class-based, anti-racist, and other critical analyses under one *unifying* framework is thought to jeopardize the distinct contribution of each analysis. Third, there is debate about the integration of postmodern insights.

The Development of Structural Social Work

Structural social work was developed in Ottawa, Canada, by Carleton University Social Work Professor Maurice Moreau, with input from Gisele Legault (University of Montreal); Pierre Racine and Michele Bourgon (Université du Québec); Helen Levine, Mike Brake, Peter Findlay, Roland Lecomte, Allan Moscovitch, and Jim Albert (Carleton University); and Peter Leonard (Warwick and McGill Universities) (Carniol, 1992).

The profession of social work in Canada (and North America) developed out of two distinct and contradictory perspectives of social issues, which can be traced back to the late 1800s (Lundy, 2004; Mullaly, 2007). The first is the Charitable Organization Society movement, which identified an individual focus for explaining and solving social issues. The second, the Settlement House movement, saw the causes and solutions to social issues as residing in societal structures. In the 1940s, the newly developed social work profession in Canada aligned itself with the individual focus by identifying *social casework* as the dominant approach to clinical social work practice (Mullaly, 2007). This pseudo-medical methodology for *diagnosing* and *treating* individual problems incorporated Freudian psychoanalytic principles. However, in the 1960s and 1970s, economic and political upheaval and the heightened consciousness of second-wave feminist, gay and lesbian, environmental, labour, Quebec separatist, and First Nations' activism increased focus on collective aspects of social problems. In response, numerous progressive and conflict-based sociological theories based in Marxism and feminism emerged to criticize dominant institutions and existing social relations (Moreau, 1988).

The anti-psychiatry movement and critical sociological theories—especially labelling and deviancy theories—highlighted the social control functions of social work and challenged traditional professional definitions (Moreau, 1988). In response, many progressive social workers turned to more holistic general systems theory. However, others took up materialist and feminist critiques, noting systems theories' failure to adequately address interpersonal and structural power imbalances (Moreau, 1988). Embracing these critiques, Carleton University students demanded the school's recognition of institutional injustice, fostering structural social work's simultaneous focus on individual change and longer-term structural transformation (Moreau & Leonard, 1989). However, despite the energetic birth of the approach and its continued prominence at Carleton University (and a handful of other schools), conservative global trends in the 1980s led to the declining visibility and perceived impracticality of transformative approaches throughout this decade.

In the 1990s, radical approaches to social work experienced a revival. In 1993, Mullaly situated structural social work as providing a nuanced analysis of contemporary socio-political and economic issues, and a coherent framework for radical practice. Fook's (1993) radical casework theory advanced transformative methods for practice. Subsequently, there have been several noteworthy contributions to this literature (e.g., Carniol, 1992, 2005a, 2005b, 2005c; Dominelli, 1997; Hick, Fook, & Puzzuto, 2005; Ife, 1997, 2001; Leonard, 1997; Lundy, 2004; Mullaly, 1997, 2007; Pease & Fook, 1999; Reisch & Andrews, 2002). Nonetheless, Reisch and Andrews have cautioned that progressive approaches remain the minority in the United States, representing "the road not taken" by the social work profession (2002, p. 226).

Theoretical Influences and Key Features

Structural social work's influences include critical social theories, feminism, and—more recently—postmodernism, multicultural, and queer theory. Each of these takes a *conflict* perspective of society (Agger, 2006). A more liberal *order* perspective views social problems as a disruption of society's natural equilibrium, suggesting institutional fixes to re-establish stability (i.e., *level the playing field*). In contrast, conflict or *change* perspectives view society as composed of numerous individuals and groups, between which there are complex tensions and areas of agreement and disagreement wherein power is always implicated.

In the 1920s, critical theory became specifically associated with German thinkers of the Frankfurt School; in essence, however, critical theories are any that criticize society (Mann, 2007). Agger (2006) listed general features of critical theories (summarized here):

- opposition to conventional *positivist* conceptions of truth and a *natural* social order;
- envisioning potential for a positive future informed by the past and present;
- viewing domination as structural;
- questioning of *false consciousness*, *hegemony*, and *ideology*;
- linking of personal experiences and social change;
- viewing agency–structure interaction as dialectic; and
- focusing on both the *means* and *ends* of change.

Based on its critical influences, structural social work is among those approaches described as *progressive*, *radical*, or *transformative*—in contrast to those considered *conventional*. Depending on their theoretical foundations, conventional approaches often emphasize inner exploration, personal adjustment, or behaviour change. Such approaches include cognitive behaviour therapy, solution-focused or brief therapy, psychodynamic therapy, or eclectic approaches based on system theory. The structural approach may draw from conventional approaches, but ultimately privileges analysis of social structures and relations.

Key features of structural social work include critique of dominant structures and a vision of transforming society, a focus on power, and attention to person–structure dialectics.

A Critique of Dominant Social and Economic Structures

The ongoing globalization of neo-liberal capitalism is coincident with a transfer of wealth from poor to rich countries and from the less affluent to the wealthy (see Seabrook, 2002). Based on a historical and contemporary critique of dominant social orders, structural social work rejects the inevitability of such trends. The approach highlights how social structures are constructed and reinforced by powerful elites, ensuring their continued dominance while exploiting less powerful groups. Drawing on a materialist (especially Marx's historical and dialectical materialist) perspective, which emphasizes physical and economic conditions as pivotal elements of the social world, structural social work understands the capitalist economic organization of paid and unpaid work to purposefully maintain patriarchy (male dominance), profits, and private property.

Rights, resources, and rewards are allocated differentially on the basis of, *inter alia*, gender, class, and race (Moreau & Leonard, 1989).

Structural social work adopts a Marxist theory of ideology as "a material force and significant arena of political struggle" (Moreau, 1988, p. 4), wherein dominant belief systems reinforce powerful interests. Following from theorist Antonio Gramsci (1971), Moreau and Leonard (1989) described how participation in capitalist social relations is reinforced by institutions of socialization, including schools, churches, media, the family, and social agencies. Such structures cultivate belief in *meritocracy*, suggesting that anyone can *get ahead* through skill, hard work, and a positive attitude—even though this is not the case for many people (see Seabrook, 2002). Drawing on Smith (1990), Hick (2005) described how ideological processes allow *beliefs* to overrule, and replace, the lived experience of individuals. Also required are institutions of regulation and correction, including police, armed forces, courts, and social services. Institutions and policies reinforce particular forms of group living and sexuality that bolster the economic structure— for instance, nuclear families and heterosexuality (Moreau & Leonard, 1989).

Within social work, increased economic and modernist rationalism (Ife, 1997) has corresponded with an emphasis on *efficiency*, privatization, and characterizing clients as *consumers*. In practice, this means larger caseloads, job instability, and less pay for workers, and reduced quality and accessibility for individuals seeking assistance (see Carniol 2005b; Ife, 1997; Lundy, 2004; Mullaly, 2007). Less profitable services are delivered as temporary, bare-minimum supports—just enough to quell widespread demand for change. This residual, *charity* model is also a mechanism through which wealthier individuals can ease their conscience and corporations can improve their public image. Via its critical social lens, structural social work addresses seemingly *individual* difficulties in a multifaceted way.

The Vision and Work of Radical Transformation

This critique of dominant institutions reveals possibilities for their dismantling and suggests a vision of transformation. Mullaly (2007) framed progressive social work values as fundamentally incompatible with contemporary capitalism; he advocated social transformation through government intervention resulting in public control of the economy, resources distributed equitably or according to need, participatory democracy, and recognition of social problems as inherent in a capitalist society. In addition, Carniol (1979) emphasized multidisciplinary and holistic (including spiritual) support to individuals.

Mullaly (2007) advanced Mishra's (1981) structural model of welfare, or Social Welfare State, which pursues full employment through government–union cooperation; comprehensive environmental planning; solidaristic wages to counter concentrations of wealth; equality of living conditions through the public, universal provision of services such as health care and education; and full participation in society. This vision of transformation is dauntingly broad. However, some have highlighted actual, incremental moves toward such possibilities. Carniol (1979, 2005c) described alternative—often feminist—organizations wherein community members participate directly in organizational consensus-based decision-making (even staff hiring and evaluation), and salaries are determined according to need. Ife (1997) highlighted alternative economic and currency schemes, such as Local Exchange Trading Systems (Dobson, 1993 and Dauncey, 1988 in Ife, 1997).

A Focus on Power: Multiple Forms of Oppression

The central concern of structural social work is power—both personal and political—and how society's rich and powerful define and constrain the less powerful (Moreau, 1979). Structural social work uses multiple critical analyses to highlight how dominant structures decrease access to opportunities, resources, and power for certain groups, resulting in individual and collective experiences of oppression. Feminists underscore the pivotal insight that the "personal is political"; that is, *private* interactions and roles are shaped by, and reinforce, larger, gendered, dominant institutions and relations of power (e.g., C. Baines, Evans, & Neysmith, 1998). Others (including critics of Marxism and feminism) illustrate how language, religion, nationality, ancestry, and skin colour continue to be the basis of exploitation and inequality (hooks, 1989; Ing, 1991; Satzewich, 1998); racism is often invisibly embedded within taken-for-granted structures and assumptions of *whiteness* (Frankenberg, 1993). Indigenous peoples' perspectives emphasize a historical analysis of colonialism as central to understanding present conditions of oppression (Baskin 2003; Carniol, 2005b). Others expose social structures as infused with heterosexism and homophobia based on assumed heterosexuality and gender *norms* (Carabine, 1996; O'Brien, 1994; Richardson, 1996). (Dis)ability movement activists emphasize how *disability* is socially constructed through assumptions of the able-bodied, young, male *norm*; existing supports for this norm are defined as *entitlements*, while people requiring different kinds of help are assumed needy or dependent (Wendell, 1996). By attending to those who document such experiences of oppression, structural social work recognizes the many categories by which individuals are exploited. This multiplicity of perspectives enriches the approach's understanding of how emancipation might occur and the inclusive transformation to which it aspires.

Structural social work's view of multiple oppressions has emerged as an innovative, defining feature. The structural approach is equally critical of all oppression and concerned with all oppressed groups. Moreau (1988) described the political and theoretical basis of structural social work as resting on "a contemporary Marxist analysis profoundly influenced by feminism and criticisms of both Marxism and feminism for their ignorance of the dynamics of racism" (p. 4). This class analysis critiques the monopolization of economic power by a decreasing number of wealthy elites. However, unlike in orthodox Marxism, class is not singularly prioritized. Instead, "the approach places alongside each other the divisions of class, gender, race, age, ability/disability and sexuality which are not placed in a hierarchy of importance, but are seen to generate 'highly interconnected but irreducible social forces' within advanced, patriarchal capitalism" (Moreau, 1988, p. 4). Thus, the approach explores the existence (or non-existence) and interplay of these forces in each particular case (Moreau, 1988); experiences of oppression are seen as multi-faceted—often shared collectively, but also unique to individual circumstances (Lundy, 2004). Carniol (2005b) highlighted the significance of this contribution, noting that Moreau "expanded the scope of radical social work in Canada by … arguing that multiple oppressions were interwoven into the structures of systemic inequality. He warned about the futility of debates trying to show that any one particular oppression was … more central than another" (p. 60).

Like Moreau, Mullaly (2002) described a "total system of oppression" composed of interrelated structural, cultural, and personal levels; *internalized oppression* describes how marginalized individuals or groups may become influenced by ideologies that characterize them as *undeserving*, and thus begin to accept their exploited position (e.g., Moreau, 1979, 1990; Moreau & Leonard, 1989; Mullaly, 2002, 2007). Via these multiple levels, organized illegitimate privilege is achieved by certain groups at the expense of others (Carniol, 2005b). Structural social work theorists and practitioners continue to refine this analysis, promoting exploration of these points of intersection among different forms of oppression, which Lundy (2004) described as multiplied "tangled knots."

Many recent contributions in this area incorporate postmodern and post-structural thought. Postmodern and post-structural theories are difficult to define. Generally, these ideas emerged in the 1990s to critique modernity's emphasis on *science, reason,* and *grand theories* (including Marxism). Postmodernism has a diffuse (vs. state-centred) view of power and its intimate link to knowledge (e.g., Foucault, 1980). Both oppression and resistance are seen to have multiple sources: a diversity of positions, perspectives, and identities are expressed through specific interactions in local arenas (Carniol 2005b, 2005c). Instead of *truth*, realities are co-constructed from diverse, fragmented, and sometimes conflicting stories (Fook, n.d., in Carniol 2005b; Mullaly, 2007). Respect for individual *voice* requires attention to self-definition and language, and rejects notions of *one linear track* to emancipation (Carniol, 2005c). Postmodern thinking criticizes classical clinical models that suggest *experts* can understand the client "other" through techniques of empathy (Tremblay, 2003); instead, the location and subjectivity of clients and workers are acknowledged, enabling transformed relationships and solidarities (Carniol, 2005c). Carniol (2005c) suggested that postmodernism and post-structuralism enable probing of complex layers of internalized oppression and privilege that are based in local-to-global, multi-interactive structures. Hick (2005) characterized the postmodern view of power as reflexive, assembled, and coordinated—rather than simply possessed—revealing more possibilities for empowerment within structural social work practice.

A Dialectical Approach

The perceived duality between *individual* and *structural* causes of human experience is a recurring theme in social theory (Mann, 2007). In conventional social work, this assumed personal–social duality can mean an emphasis on self-determination and *self-help* capacity, but also enables personal blame for problems. Elsewhere, this supposed duality has led to structural determinism, wherein individuals are cast as *victims of structures that cannot be changed*. Pease has cautioned how this latter outlook negates the possibility for emancipatory social work practice (in Moreau & Leonard, 1987).

Instead of this perceived duality, structural social work takes a *dialectical* approach wherein *individual agency* and *social structures* are understood to be engaged in a mutually reinforcing relationship; each organizes and perpetuates the other. Not static or immovable, oppressive structures are subjectively constituted by human actions through particular ideologies and power relations. Dialectical principles can be summarized as follows (adapted from Naiman in Mullaly, 2007, pp. 237–238):

- Everything is related; nothing can be understood in isolation.
- Change is constant. Nothing is absolute or immutable; new forms replace old forms while preserving some older, viable elements.
- Change is gradual, incremental, and cumulative; small changes eventually aggregate into radical transformations.
- Change results from the unity and struggle of opposites. There is commonality even within binaries (e.g., good/bad, true/false, capitalist/socialist); that which seems unified contains opposing tensions. These tensions or contradictions become the basis for social change.

Thus, the formation of structures is viewed as dynamic and shifting, involving both individual and collective elements composed of multi-layered structural, cultural, and personal forces.

To conceptualize this individual–structure dialectic, Marx described exploitative economic exchanges between workers and owners within capitalism as *social relations* (Hick, 2005). Smith (1987) defined social relations as "concerted sequences or courses of social action implicating more than one individual whose participants are not necessarily present or known to one another" (p. 155). Smith suggested that social relations are evident in everyday settings as people act competently, but unconsciously, to coordinate their actions with others, according to standards or expectations. Understanding the *personal* as *political*, structural social work advances social and political change beginning within everyday social relations, such as in sexuality, family roles, and the workplace.

A dialectical approach also responds to the question of whether one should make change *from within*, or work *outside, against the system*. Social workers are rarely hired as activists; most work in government-funded institutions or agencies. Thus, some argue that politics and social work should not mix, that professional non-directiveness and value-neutrality requires radicals to "leave their politics at home." Others question whether a sanctioned profession is capable of any action that fundamentally challenges the dominant social order in which it is embedded (Meyer, 1981; Pincus & Minahan, 1973). However, structural social work challenges this perceived separation between *professional* and *personal* life. The approach advocates simultaneous, even coordinated, action both *within* and *outside* institutions. Even while acting as agents of government, structural social workers can facilitate social change by using contradictory relations to provide oppressed groups with access to knowledge and state power.

Despite this dialectical understanding (and perhaps owing to the approach's title), authors continue to critique structural social work as deterministic, over-emphasizing structure at the expense of personal, lived context (Hart, 2001, in Harris, 2006) or viewing consumers as "blank slates" who are "awaiting inscription by a politically aware social worker" (Rossiter, 1996, p. 26). Irrespective of whether these criticisms are well informed, inadequate treatment of individual–agency interaction is a theme that permeates many of the approach's critiques and challenges.

Research, Knowledge, and Education

Wachholz and Mullaly (1997) described a dearth of material on research methodology in structural social work. Consequently, the authors advanced guidelines based on feminist research principles: reflexivity, consciousness-raising, rejection of objectivity, ethical concern for research participants, and emphasis on personal empowerment and social transformation. Additionally, Hick's (1997) *quadrant continuum* of participatory research aimed to help structural social workers critically locate their participatory methods. More recently, Bellefeuille and Hemingway (2006) outlined a participatory cooperative inquiry exploring structural social work students' ethical decision-making in field education, and George, Coleman, and Barnoff (2007) involved service-users in evaluating structural social work as a model of service. A few other recent studies have not specifically advanced structural social work research methods, but have incorporated the approach in a theoretical framework (e.g., Hillian, 2000; Le Camp, 2006; Murphy, 2007). Baskin (2003) viewed structural social work research on Aboriginal peoples as promising if undertaken *by* Aboriginal people—recognizing oral traditions and Aboriginal concepts of *validity*.

Without specifically addressing structural social work research, many authors have highlighted important considerations regarding the construction and application of knowledge—especially given post-structural awareness of *power-knowledge* (Foucault, 1980). Using postmodern ideas, Todd and Burns (2007) emphasized bodily knowledge, language, and uncertainty; Baskin (2003) emphasized a historical perspective, rejecting culture as *static*. Many contemporary structural social work thinkers have highlighted the approach's rejection of *objective, positivistic* social science, noting that social workers are constantly implicated in constructing knowledge about people and issues (George, Preston, & Coleman, 2007; Hick, 2005). Thus, critical self-awareness of social location is key to structural social work (Carniol, 2005b; Ewashen, 2003). To illustrate, Baskin (2003) emphasized powerful assumptions inherent in social work education: "The choice of subject matter cannot be neutral. Whose history and perspective is taught and whose ignored? Which groups are included and which are left out of the reading list or text? From whose point of view is the past and present examined? Which theories are emphasized and which are not?" (p. 70).

Structural social work educators advocate experiential and creative methods, drawing on Freire's (1970) critical ideas of *praxis* (action–reflection–action), dialogical rapport, and consciousness-raising. Authors have suggested pedagogical and substantive features, including reflecting on social location and identifying with those who appear different (Tremblay, 2003); interdisciplinary or multi-organization collaboration in community-based popular education (George, Preston, & Coleman, 2007); a move from the traditional, Western focus on binaries to exploration of context, values, and critical thinking within ambiguity (Bellefeuille & Hemingway, 2006); and a shift from pedagogy (child teaching and learning) to andragogy (adult teaching and learning) (Hillock & Profitt, 2007). However, challenges in structural social work education arise due to tension (including anger, guilt, and powerlessness) that arises when discussing power and privilege, and contrasts between radical teachings and the approach of students' practice settings (Ewashen, 2003; George, Preston, & Coleman, 2007).

Structural Social work in Practice

Structural social work has been criticized for failing to teach practical social work skills such as assessment and interviewing. This relates to the approach's development in reaction to the dominant over-emphasis on *casework skills* in the 1950s and 1960s (Moreau & Leonard, 1989). In response, authors have highlighted that structural social work can adapt and enhance existing methods. Moreau and Leonard (1989) suggested that many existing techniques are acceptable, provided they do not psychologize or depoliticize problems or mystify clients. Moreau (n.d.) provided an assessment guide for family intervention, and Lundy (2004) gave an overview of genograms, contracts, and communication skills from a structural perspective. However, Moreau and Leonard (1989) re-framed the assumed need for practice tools. They suggested that over-concern with *skills* reinforces dominant beliefs that locate social problems—and solutions—within the realm of the individual; responsibility for problem-solving thus becomes centred within a social worker's expertise in a particular *technique*.

Structural social work practice is guided by a political assertion that people can *participate* in social change toward a possible future free of domination. Influenced by Paolo Freire's (1970) techniques of emancipatory popular education, Moreau and Leonard (1989) identified four practices of structural social work; Moreau et al. (1993) added a fifth to produce the following list:

1. Defence: maximizing access to rights and resources.
2. Collectivization: encouraging the development of collective consciousness.
3. Materialization: grounding problems in access to resources.
4. Increasing the client's power in the worker–client relationship.
5. Enhancing the client's power through personal change: encouraging disruption of destructive thoughts, feelings, and behaviours.

Some authors have suggested additional activities (e.g., social action); Carniol (1992) and Hick (1998) each discussed six practice elements, while Mullaly (1993) described eight. However, the above five practice objectives, outlined in Chapter 2 of this text, are most commonly associated with structural social work. Nonetheless, many practice-related critiques remain; structural social workers navigate numerous theoretical and practical challenges within the increasingly complex terrain of real-world diversity, subjectivity, and power. This text explores such challenges through an *applied* examination of both new and existing practice principles and skills that are congruent with structural social work.

Critiques and Challenges

As we have noted here and elsewhere (Hick & Murray, 2008), structural social work is seen to have features that distinguish it from other radical and progressive approaches. Indeed, there has recently been a marked increase in publications that develop the approach (e.g., Baskin, 2003; Bellefeuille & Hemingway, 2006; Coates & Sullivan, 2005; DeClark, 2007; Ewashen, 2003; George, Coleman, & Barnoff, 2007; George & Marlowe, 2005; Hick et al., 2005; Le Camp, 2006; Lundy, 2004; Mullaly, 2007; Murphy, 2007; Todd & Burns, 2007).

Lack of Clarity

Despite its contemporary popularity, however, the approach appears somewhat lost, or blurred, within a string of similar approaches, including critical, political, progressive, radical, anti-discriminatory, and anti-oppressive social work. The term "structural social work" was first used by Middleman and Goldberg (1974), who identified the environment as the source of social problems, but attributed this to the liberal notion of *disorganization* rather than critiquing dominant socio-economic structures or envisioning social transformation (Mullaly, 1997). However, authors using both Moreau's transformative approach and Middleman and Goldberg's systems approach continue to publish referencing *the* Structural Approach (e.g., Goldberg Wood & Middleman, 1991; Goldberg Wood & Tully, 2006). Thus, it is perhaps not surprising that Harris (2006) characterized structural social work as "in the 'systems/ecological' category," "aligned with radical theory," and seeking "to transform ... conditions and social structures," but concluded that the approach does not "necessarily challenge the status quo" (p. 9). Furthermore, structural social work has been variously described as a precursor, an example, or a critique of radical social work (e.g., Bellefeuille & Hemingway, 2006; Campbell, 2005; Mullaly, 1997). Elsewhere, it is not clear if anti-oppressive social work or anti-oppressive practice (AOP) encompasses and builds on structural social work, or if this is a new, interchangeable term (e.g., D. Baines, 2007; Barnoff, George, & Coleman, 2006; Campbell, 2005; Carniol, 2005c).

D. Baines (1999) critiqued the early development of structural social work as having an "amorphous and ill-defined 'left', liberal theoretical base." She stated, "This lack of a firm critical theoretical underpinning weakened the potential of structural social workers to practise and develop our theory in emancipatory ways" (p. 457). Indeed, it is questionable whether the vision of transformation is adequately developed or clear in either structural social work or AOP. Carniol (1979) noted that incorporation of Marxist analysis has enabled a critique of the influence of the corporate elite over the government (including social welfare), economy, and communications media; however, he stated that Marxism's broad, generic application has come to include stereotypes and/or to be equated with oppressive regimes. Thus, Carniol noted, it fails to be convincing on the question of alternatives—an issue of great relevance to those seeking to be progressive. Hillock and Profitt (2007) suggested that social workers are often "unclear and imprecise about what we mean by structural change and how we can make these changes happen" (p. 39); they cautioned against using vague and catch-all ideas, and emphasized the need for specificity, questioning our motives and assumptions, and clarifying our political and theoretical perspectives.

A Unifying Framework?

Structural social work is thought to potentially act as a unifying approach within radical social work (Carniol in Hick & Murray, 2008; Mullaly, 1993). AOP has made similar claims (D. Baines, 2007). Carniol (B. Carniol, personal communication, March 10, 2007) cites the structural approach's receptivity to new areas of critical awareness during its formulation in the1970s. These have included critique of historic and contemporary colonialism, use of illegitimate privilege as an analytic tool, recognition of spirituality as one source of personal inspiration to resist structural injustices, and calls to transform international trade structures. In addition, Carniol notes the advantage of "remaining open to all theoretical advances that bring social justice closer to reality" (2005b, p. 67), suggesting that practitioners may *pick and choose* helpful perspectives and discard the rest. Structural social work has been seen to enable the integration of various concepts and practices, such as radical and feminist approaches (Fook, 1993). This disrupts conventional, artificial distinctions between *direct intervention, community development*, and *policy analysis*, and the perceived choice between working *within* or *against* the system. Recent publications have described the complementary use of structural social work with queer theory (Coates & Sullivan, 2005; Murphy, 2007), postmodern feminism (Murphy,

2007; Todd & Burns, 2007), family systems therapy and ecological systems theory (Coates & Sullivan, 2005), and Aboriginal perspectives (Baskin, 2003). The use of structural social work as a *complementary* approach is seen to offer the potential for a more flexible and/or nuanced analytical framework (George, Preston, & Coleman, 2007; Murphy, 2007; Todd & Burns, 2007).

However, others have cautioned that the attempted *amalgamation* of several theoretical perspectives under a single umbrella may obscure, leave out, or risk the integrity of these important critiques. Razack and Jeffery (n.d. in Carniol, 2005b) asserted that there has been a dangerous weakening of focus on racism and the oppressive ideology of whiteness as "core analyses of race have been quickly cloaked under the rhetoric of anti-oppression, diversity, cross-cultural approaches, and multiculturalism" (p. 62). D. Baines (1999) stated that Mullaly's (1997) epistemology of structural social work does not adequately reflect feminism, and is instead a "broad Marxist approach with a few gestures at social work as a female terrain" (p. 457). Furthermore, differences exist even *within* the many perspectives encompassed by structural social work. Working class, racialized, and queer women have challenged the feminist myth of *universal sisterhood* and feminism's ability to represent Aboriginal women (Monture-Angus, 1999 in Ewashen, 2003), and have highlighted discrepancies among liberal, radical, and socialist feminisms (e.g., Berg, 2002). Similarly, D. Baines (2003) noted that the racisms faced by, for instance, Chinese, African, or Jewish Canadians, are multiple and distinct. Tester (2003a) asserted that diverse experiences of oppression require different analytical and practice tools, warning that combining these as elements of an *umbrella* theory can suggest false equivalencies and lead to confusion or conflict.

Increasingly, authors have demanded that structural social work acknowledge the distinct experiences of Aboriginal peoples (Baskin, 2003; George, Preston, & Coleman, 2007), emphasizing that despite the interconnectedness of different forms of oppression, oppression experienced by First Nations peoples is unique among oppressed groups (Baskin, 2003). With the exception of Carniol (2005b), key structural social work publications (e.g., Lundy 2004; Moreau, 1979, 1990; Moreau & Leonard, 1989; Mullaly, 1993, 1997, 2007) have been somewhat superficial in addressing First Nations' experiences. Colonialism and Aboriginal peoples are generally (but not always) listed amongst *dominant structures* and *oppressed groups*, but there is little sense of a deep infusion of Aboriginal perspectives on cooperation versus competition, giving versus accumulation, respect to elders and children, attention to holism and balance—especially spiritual elements—in healing, focus on group and clan versus individualism, relationship versus task orientation, and the struggle for decolonization (Baskin, 2003; Harris, 2006). While many of these values are incorporated, they are generally attributed to socialist and/or feminist analyses.

Postmodern Uncertainty

The emergence of postmodern theories has brought a new challenge for structural social work. We have touched on various postmodern contributions to understanding oppression; however, others have identified apparently irreconcilable differences between postmodern theories and key elements of structural social work. There is a concern that postmodernism's denial of universal phenomena, diffuse understanding of power, and deconstruction of *categories* obscures structural domination through capitalism and along the lines of, *inter alia*, skin colour, gender, and sexuality (Ife, 1997). An uncritical acceptance of multiple truths is thought to enable an *anything goes* relativism, resulting in failure to condemn hurtful actions (Lundy, 2004). Others have asserted that postmodernism limits opportunities for solidarity and coherent action for progressive change. Mullaly (2007) suggested that Harvey's (1989) analysis of disjointed postmodern temporal structures reduces the utility of *history* and *continuity* within social movements. Finally, Brotman and Pollock (1997) and Mullaly (1997) asserted that the postmodern over-emphasis on difference, localism, and fragmentation plays into the divide-and-rule tactics employed by the privileged, while, in contrast, local contexts have been increasingly subjugated through globalized capital accumulation. Hick (2005) noted that the "elusiveness" of postmodernism described by Foucault (1973) poses difficulties for a dialogue with structural social work. Nonetheless, Hick ultimately viewed critical and postmodern theories as able to inform one another.

The Problem of *Oppression*

D. Baines (1999) and others have critiqued structural social work for failing to generate a model to understand the dynamics of multiple oppressors. Proponents of the approach concur there is need for theoretical development to explicate multiple identities, fluidity of group membership, contextual variables, personal or psychological variables, and individual variations in experience. Social workers must acknowledge group heterogeneity and oppression both between and *within* oppressed groups (Carniol, 2005b; Mullaly, 2002). Conceptualizations of intersecting modes of oppression include Ng's (1993) gender-saturated view of *class* as "any group of people's relationship to reproduction and production, as well as reproduction's relationship to production" (in D. Baines, 2003, p. 55). Likewise, Hart (1994 in Geller, 2004) used *heteropatriarchy* to theoretically link the heterosexual imperative with patriarchal gender ascription. D. Baines (1999) called for a comprehensive model of how multiple axes of injustice collude, collide, cooperate, and contest—both theoretically and in everyday life. Meanwhile, Hillock and Profitt (2007) suggested that the conceptualization of oppression cannot depend on moments of *democracy, equality, justice,* or *emancipation* that are unattainable because they assume a shared utopia.

However, Tester (2003a) recommended that the framework of *oppression* should be reconsidered altogether, given its *problem* focus and potential reduction to binary definitions of *oppressor–oppressed.* He suggested that social workers— especially students—are vulnerable to being "paralysed by the thought, not so much of being oppressed, but of being at least to some degree the oppressor" (Tester, 2003a, p. 131). He questioned the idea of *internalized oppression*— warning that designating another's perception as a "false framework" is disempowering. However, he did not advocate accepting injustice because those involved are not aware. There is extensive documentation of oppression as experienced by, *inter alia,* Indigenous peoples though colonial genocide, female survivors of patriarchal violence, low-paid, *disposable* workers within capitalism, and sexual minorities within heterosexism (B. Carniol, personal communication, May 22, 2008). Hence, there is a need for nuanced analysis. Carniol has suggested that structural social work challenges the oppressor–oppressed binary by viewing those in the oppressor role as capable of and responsible for choice, but simultaneously as subject to social structures that facilitate exploitative relations. He has asserted that instead of paralyzing, this analysis invites social workers to acknowledge when we are colluding with oppression—an awareness central to the development of critical consciousness and change strategies (B. Carniol, personal communication, May 22, 2008). Instead of debating what is *true or false,* Tester (2003a, 2003b) advocated pursuit of redistributive social justice, and honouring differing cultural perspectives through moral and philosophic deliberations about values, inclinations, strengths, and common ground.

Theory in Action

What does this mean for social workers *on the ground*? While Moreau and others have responded to critiques of the approach's impracticality by outlining various practice principles, many contemporary social work educators, students, and practitioners appear to need less surety. Todd and Burns (2007) noted that "all theories are partial, illuminating some aspects of the world while obscuring others" (p. 24); thus, many have advocated a thoughtful combination of often interdisciplinary approaches (Coates & Sullivan, 2005; George, Preston, & Coleman, 2007) and *relational thinking* (Anderson & Collins, 2001), which understands experiences as simultaneously unique, yet linked. Some have proposed an *indeterminate, critical* postmodernism (Agger, 2006; Hick, 2005), treating postmodernism more as a *turn* than a complete break from modernity (Best & Kellner, 1997; Hick et al., 2005). Many social workers appear more accepting of tensions, and see constructive potential in uncertainty. This absence of *positive reference* (Todd & Burns, 2007) requires practitioners to critically and carefully deliberate on issues of culture, value, and commitment within the specific realities of diverse and complex practice contexts.

Correspondingly, a recent structural social work conference culminated in a call for discovery of how structural social work is actually *being done*: "Day-to-day, creative practices need to be understood and shared widely with others in the social work community.... We need to document creative approaches and bring this information [back] regarding structural social work practice" (George, Preston, & Coleman, 2007, p. 14). In this vein, D. Baines (2007) has offered a practice-oriented text on AOP. Furthermore, George and Marlowe (2005) described a structural approach taken in rural India, wherein many years of practice allowed one grassroots organization to both alleviate immediate poverty and violence, and facilitate the systemic abolishment of *untouchability*. However, such a detailed account of structural social work is uncommon. Educators, students, and practitioners describe the need to document *how to survive* as a structural social worker in the real world of mainstream agencies and regressive, restrictive state policies; this survival requires a balancing of critical analysis and practice with *hope* (George, Preston, & Coleman, 2007).

Respecting the importance and emotionality of language, there has been a collective call to create a *safe space* for dialogue and continuing education about social work practice. Along with several publications we have cited, it is our hope that this text provides such a space.

References

Agger, B. (2006). *Critical social theories: An introduction.* Boulder, CO: Paradigm Publishers.

Anderson, M.L., & Collins, P.H. (2001). *Race, class and gender: An anthology.* Belmont, CA: Wadsworth Publishing.

Baines, C., Evans, P., & Neysmith, S. (Eds.). (1998). *Women's caring: Feminist perspectives on social welfare.* Toronto, ON: Oxford University Press.

Baines, D. (1999). [Review of the book *Structural social work: ideology, theory and practice* (2nd ed.)]. *Canadian Review of Sociology & Anthropology, 36*(3), 457–458.

Baines, D. (2003). Race, class, and gender in the everyday talk of social workers: The ways we limit the possibilities for radical practice. In W. Shera (Ed.), *Emerging perspectives on anti-oppressive practice* (pp. 43–64). Toronto, ON: Canadian Scholars' Press Inc.

Baines, D. (2007). *Doing anti-oppressive practice: Building transformative politicized social work.* Halifax, NS: Fernwood Publishing.

Barnoff, L., George, P., & Coleman, B. (2006). Operating in survival mode: Challenges to implementing anti-oppressive practice in feminist social service agencies in Toronto. *Canadian Social Work Review, 23*(1/2), 41–58.

Baskin, C. (2003). Structural social work as seen from an Aboriginal perspective. In W. Shera (Ed.), *Emerging perspectives on anti-oppressive practice* (pp. 65–79). Toronto, ON: Canadian Scholars' Press Inc.

Bellefeuille, G., & Hemingway, D. (2006). A co-operative inquiry into structural social work students' ethical decision-making in field education. *Journal of Social Work Values and Ethics, 3*(2).

Berg, S. (2002). The PTSD diagnosis: Is it good for women? *Affilia, 17*(55), 55–68.

Best, S., & Kellner, D. (1997). *The postmodern turn.* New York: Guilford Press.

Brotman, S., & Pollock, S. (1997). Loss of context: The problem of merging postmodernism with feminist social work. *Canadian Social Work Review, 14*(1), 9–21.

Campbell, C. (2005). Anti-oppressive social work. In F.J. Turner (Ed.), *Canadian encyclopaedia of social work* (pp. 14–15). Waterloo, ON: Wilfred Laurier University Press.

Carabine, J. (1996). Heterosexuality and social policy. In D. Richardson (Ed.), *Theorizing heterosexuality* (pp. 55–74). Buckingham, UK: Open University Press.

Carniol, B. (1979). A critical approach in social work. *Canadian Journal of Social Work Education, 5*(1), 95–111.

Carniol, B. (1992). Structural social work: Maurice Moreau's challenge to social work practice. *Journal of Progressive Human Services, 3*(1), 1–20.

Carniol, B. (2005a). Analysis of social location and change: Practice implications. In S. Hick, J. Fook, & R. Pozzuto (Eds.), *Social work: A critical turn* (pp. 153–165). Toronto, ON: Thompson Educational Publishing.

Carniol, B. (2005b). *Case critical: Social services and social justice in Canada* (5th ed.). Toronto, ON: Between the Lines.

Carniol, B. (2005c). Structural social work (Canada). In J.M. Herrick & P.H. Stuart (Eds.), *Encyclopaedia of social welfare history in North America* (pp. 391–393). Thousand Oaks, CA: Sage Publications.

Coates, J., & Sullivan, R. (2005). Achieving competent family practice with same-sex parents: Some promising directions. *Journal of GLBT Family Studies, 1*(2), 89–113.

DeClark, R. (2007). *Alienation and marginalisation: A case study of the social experiences of men in the LifeHouse program.* Unpublished master's thesis, Carleton University, Ottawa, Ontario, Canada.

Dominelli, L. (1997). *Anti-racist social work* (2nd ed.). London, UK: Macmillian.

Ewashen, A.M. (2003). *Walking the maze: The labyrinth between privilege and structural social work practice.* Unpublished master's thesis, University of Northern British Columbia, Prince George, British Columbia, Canada.

Fook, J. (1993). *Radical casework: A theory of practice.* St. Leonards, Australia: Allen & Unwin.

Foucault, M. (1973). *The order of things.* New York: Vintage Books. (Original work published 1966)

Foucault, M. (1980). *Power/knowledge* (C. Gordon, Ed.) (C. Gordon, L. Marshall, J. Mepham, & R. Soper, Trans.). New York: Pantheon Books.

Frankenberg, R. (Ed.). (1993). *White women, race matters: The social construction of whiteness.* Minneapolis, MN: University of Minnesota Press.

Freire, P. (1970). *Pedagogy of the oppressed* (M.B. Ramos, Trans.). New York: Continuum International Publishing Group. (Original work published 1968)

Geller, T. (2004). Queering Hollywood's tough chick: Subversions of sex, race, and nation in *The Long Kiss Goodnight* and *The Matrix*. *Frontiers, 25*(3), 8–34.

George, P., Coleman, B., & Barnoff, L. (2007). Beyond "providing services": Voices of service users on structural social work practice in community-based social service agencies. *Canadian Social Work Review, 24*(1), 5–22.

George, P., & Marlowe, S. (2005). Structural social work in action: Experiences from rural India. *Journal of Progressive Human Services, 16*(1), 5–24.

George, P., Preston, S., & Coleman, B. (2007). *Structural social work: Honouring our past, considering our present, envisioning our future. September 28 & 30, 2006, Ryerson University, Toronto, Conference Report.* Toronto, ON: Ryerson School of Social Work.

Goldberg Wood, G., & Middleman, R.R. (1991). Advocacy and social action: Key elements in the structural approach to direct practice in social work. *Social Work with Groups, 14*(3–4), 53–63.

Goldberg Wood, G., & Tully, C.T. (2006). *The structural approach to direct practice in social work: A social constructionist perspective.* New York: Columbia University Press.

Gramsci, A. (1971). *Selections from the prison notebooks* (Q. Hoare & G. Nowell Smith, Trans., Eds.). New York: International Publishers.

Harris, B. (2006). A First Nations' perspective on social justice in social work education: Are we there yet? (A post-colonial debate). *The Canadian Journal of Native Studies, 26*(2), 229–264.

Harvey, D. (1989). *The condition of postmodernity: An enquiry into the origins of cultural change.* Oxford, UK: Blackwell.

Hick, S. (1997). Participatory research: An approach for structural social workers. *Journal of Progressive Human Services, 8*(2), 63–79.

Hick, S. (1998). *Elements of structural social work. Module 16: structural social work.* Retrieved October 23, 2008, from www.socialpolicy.ca/52100.

Hick, S. (2005). Reconceptualizing critical social work. In S. Hick, J. Fook, & R. Pozzuto (Eds.), *Social work: A critical turn* (pp. 39–54). Toronto, ON: Thompson Educational Publishing.

Hick, S. Fook, J., & Pozzuto, R. (Eds.). (2005). *Social work: A critical turn.* Toronto, ON: Thompson Educational Publishing.

Hick, S., & Murray, K. (2008). Structural social work. In M. Gray & S. Webb (Eds.), *Thinking about social work.* London: Sage Publications.

Hillian, D.A. (2000). *How the parents of boys experience the youth justice system.* Unpublished master's thesis, University of Victoria, Victoria, British Columbia, Canada.

Hillock, S., & Profitt, N.J. (2007). Developing a practice and andragogy of resistance: Structural praxis inside and outside the classroom. *Canadian Social Work Review, 24*(1), 39–55.

hooks, b. (1989). *Talking back. Thinking feminist. Thinking Black.* Cambridge, UK: South End Press.

Ife, J. (1997). *Rethinking social work: Towards critical practice.* Melbourne, Australia: Longman.

Ife, J. (2001). *Human rights and social work: Towards rights-based practice.* Cambridge, UK: Cambridge University Press.

Ing, R. (1991). Sexism, racism and Canadian nationalism. In J. Vorset (Ed.), *Race class, gender: Bonds and barriers* (pp. 12–26). Toronto, ON: Garamond Press.

Le Camp, J. (2006). *Adolescent women's perspectives of homelessness in the Canadian North.* Unpublished master's thesis, University of Northern British Columbia, Prince George, British Columbia, Canada.

Lecomte, R. (1990). Connecting private troubles and public issues in social work education. In B. Wharf (Ed.), *Social change and social work in Canada* (pp. 31–51). Toronto, ON: McClelland & Stewart.

Leonard, P. (1997). *Postmodern welfare.* London, UK: Sage Publications.

Lundy, C. (2004). *Social work and social justice: A structural approach to practice.* Peterborough, ON: Broadview Press.

Mann, D. (2007). *Understanding society: A survey of modern social theory.* Toronto, ON: Oxford University Press.

Meyer, C.H. (1981). Social work purpose: Status by choice or coercion? *Social Work, 26*(6), 69–70.

Middleman, R.R., & Goldberg, G. (1974). *Social service delivery: A structural approach to social work practice.* New York: Columbia University Press.

Mishra, R. (1981) *Society and social policy: theories and practice of welfare*. London: Macmillan.

Moreau, M.J. (n.d.). *Family "therapy"/intervention using a structural approach: A suggested assessment guide*. Unpublished manuscript.

Moreau, M.J. (1979). A structural approach to social work practice. *Canadian Journal of Social Work Education, 5*(1), 78–94.

Moreau, M.J. (1988). *Practice implications of a structural approach to social work*. Unpublished manuscript.

Moreau, M.J. (1990). Empowerment through advocacy and consciousness-raising: Implications of a structural approach to social work. *Journal of Sociology & Social Welfare, 17*(2), 53–67.

Moreau, M.J., Frosst, S., Frayne, G., Hlywa, M., Leonard, L., & Rowell, M. (1993). *Empowerment II: Snapshots of the structural approach in action*. Ottawa, ON: Carleton University Press.

Moreau M.J., & Leonard, L. (1989). *Empowerment through a structural approach to social work: A report from practice*. Ottawa, ON: Carleton University.

Mullaly, B. (1993). *Structural social work: Ideology, theory and practice*. Toronto, ON: McClelland & Stewart.

Mullaly, B. (1997). *Structural social work: Ideology, theory, and practice* (2nd ed.). Toronto, ON: Oxford University Press.

Mullaly, B. (2002). *Challenging oppression: A critical social work approach*. Toronto, ON: Oxford University Press.

Mullaly, B. (2007). *The new structural social work* (3rd ed.). Toronto, ON: Oxford University Press.

Murphy, P. (2007). *The qualitative experiences of queer women accessing mental health services in Ottawa*. Unpublished master's thesis, Carleton University, Ottawa, Ontario, Canada.

O'Brien, C.A. (1994). The social organization of lesbian, gay, and bisexual youth in group homes and youth shelters. *Canadian Review of Social Policy, 34*, 37–57.

Payne, M. (2005). *Modern social work theory* (3rd ed.). Chicago, IL: Lyceum Books.

Pease, B., & Fook, J. (Eds.). (1999). *Transforming social work practice: Postmodern critical perspectives*. London, UK: Routledge.

Pincus, A., & Minahan, A. (1973). *Social work practice: Model and method*. Itasca, IL: F.E. Peacock.

Reisch, M., & Andrews, J. (2002). *The road not taken: A history of radical social work in the United States*. New York: Brunner-Routledge.

Richardson, D. (1996). Heterosexuality and social theory. In D. Richardson (Ed.), *Theorizing heterosexuality* (pp. 1–20). Buckingham, UK: Open University Press.

Rossiter, A.B. (1996). A perspective on critical social work. *Journal of Progressive Human Services, 7*(2), 23–41.

Satzewich, V. (Ed.). (1998). *Racism and social inequality in Canada: Concepts, controversies, and strategies of resistance*. Toronto, ON: Thompson Educational Publishing.

Seabrook, J. (2002). *The no-nonsense guide to class, caste & hierarchies*. Oxford, UK: New Internationalist Publications.

Smith, D.E. (1987). *The everyday world as problematic: A feminist sociology*. Toronto, ON: University of Toronto Press.

Smith, D.E. (1990). *The conceptual practices of power: A feminist sociology of knowledge*. Toronto, ON: University of Toronto Press.

Tester, F. (2003a). Anti-oppressive theory and practice as the organizing theme for social work education: The case against. *Canadian Social Work Review, 20*(1), 127–132.

Tester, F. (2003b). Difference, dissent and common ground: A rebuttal. *Canadian Social Work Review, 20*(1), 137–138.

Todd, S., & Burns, A. (2007). Post-structural possibilities: Beyond structural practice in child protection. *Canadian Social Work Review, 24*(1), 23–38.

Tremblay, G. (2003). Understanding multiple oppressions and how they impact the helping process for the person requesting assistance. In W. Shera (Ed.), *Emerging perspectives on anti-oppressive practice* (pp. 65–79). Toronto, ON: Canadian Scholars' Press Inc.

Wachholz, S., & Mullaly, B. (1997). Human caring: Towards a research model for structural social work. *Canadian Social Work Review, 14*(1), 23–43.

Wendell, S. (1996). *The rejected body: Feminist philosophical reflections on disability*. New York: Routledge.

CHAPTER 2

Operationalizing Structural Theory:
Guidelines for Practice

CLAUDE OLIVIER

Introduction

As a social worker, I have grappled with the question of whether my approach to social work is truly structural. This deliberation gets played out in the selection and application of practices and activities at both micro and macro levels, as well as in assessing the outcomes of my work. Answering the above question is important to me because the structural approach to social work captures my commitment to assisting people in their struggles with oppressive and unjust social structures, while at the same time working to change these structures. This commitment stems from my own experiences of oppression as a gay man, and has only been strengthened through social work with people who are negatively affected by oppressive social relations, ideologies, and structures. In practice, however, answers are not always easily attained and I am not always certain if my work has contributed to individual empowerment and structural change. For example, I have sometimes found it difficult to determine if program or policy changes that I have been involved in have produced strategic steps toward social transformation or have instead remained at a level of social reform with no real movement toward structural change. Similarly, I have not always been able to assess if my work with individuals has fostered personal liberation and empowerment, or rather has reinforced people's uncritical adaptation to the prevailing social order.

In this chapter, I draw upon my practice experience and the structural social work literature in outlining (1) the operationalization of theory in structural social work practice; and (2) guidelines for determining the congruency between practice approaches, their intended aims, and structural social work. This application of theory and guidelines provides me with direction and reassurance in my practice, while countering moments of self-doubt and discouragement. I find that self-doubt and discouragement can creep in if I fail to recognize the opportunities to apply structural social work theory and the impact of my work. The direction and reassurance, however, comes from my ongoing praxis of identifying opportunities to apply structural theory and then assessing, reflecting upon, and fully recognizing the outcomes of my social work practice.

Structural Social Work Practice: Operationalizing Theory

Practice approaches and activities should be congruent with the overall goals of structural social work. Bob Mullaly (2007) stated that "The goal of structural social work is two-fold: (1) to alleviate the negative effects on people of an exploitative and alienating social order; and (2) to transform the conditions and social structures that cause these negative effects" (p. 245). It follows that practice should be designed "to meet the goals of immediate tension relief for victims of oppression as well as longer term struggle to eliminate the real sources of oppression" (Moreau et al., 1993, p. 3). A number of structural and more broadly radical social work scholars over the past three decades have developed practice principles and approaches consistent with the above goals. I will discuss the writings of several of these authors whom I find especially helpful in guiding my own social work practice.

Jan Fook (1993) has identified potentially radical elements of social casework or direct practice. She emphasized that assessment should identify how the inadequacies of socio-economic structures, such as power imbalances, ideological role restrictions, and social labelling, cause personal problems. The goal of radical casework is then to assist individuals in changing their social situation by taking increased control over the direct effects of these socio-economic structures. Individuals increase their control by exercising more power, rejecting ideological restrictions, and resisting the effects of social labelling. Suggested strategies to bring about change and increase control include social education, such as teaching new skills in the context of an awareness of social factors; the active use of resources and teaching how to access services and resources; social empathy, including empathy of feelings, experiences, and perceptions of the social world; social support, particularly in trying alternatives; developing critical awareness through consciousness-raising; and empowerment, advocacy, and a casework relationship based on equality and sharing.

Mullaly (2007) made many of the same suggestions for carrying out social work practice with individuals. He emphasized consciousness-raising through such means as political education linking the personal to the political, critical questioning of socially conditioned assumptions concerning the causes of client problems, social empathy and normalization to bring attention to the fact that many others of the same social grouping share the same problem or concern, and re-defining problem definitions to illuminate their structural origins. He also stressed the importance of collectivization and connecting people who share similar social challenges, not only as a means of consciousness-raising, but also as a step toward collective social action. Overarching all of these social work practices is the goal of fostering client empowerment and a dialogical worker–client relationship (Mullaly, 2007). The latter refers to a relationship "wherein all participants in the dialogue are equals, wherein each learns from the other and teaches the other" (Mullaly, 2007, p. 317).

Mullaly (2007) also explained how alternative services and organizations, social movements and coalition building, progressive unionism, professional associations, and electoral politics can bring about structural change and offer potential involvement for social workers. Mullaly thus illustrates the practice of structural social work at both micro and macro levels, as well as within one's workplace and beyond. Colleen Lundy (2004) also outlined practice approaches that encompass individuals and their families, small groups, and communities. In this respect, structural social work calls for an integration of work at these various levels. As Moreau (1990) pointed out, "Work within agencies from a structural perspective must ... be linked to related struggles for social change outside agency walls" (p. 57).

Moving from a more theoretical discussion of practice to what social workers actually do, Moreau et al. (1993) analyzed taped client sessions submitted by self-identified structural social workers. They organized the skills demonstrated by these workers into five practice objectives:

1. Defence: maximizing the client's access to resources and rights in relation to a structure, organization or agency representative.
2. Collectivization: helping the client move beyond an individualistic understanding of their problem situation and solution.

3. Materialization: grounding "the client's problem situations in their access to resources as determined by their position in society" (p. 198).
4. Increasing the client's power in the worker–client relationship: the worker making his or her own power explicit, while enhancing the client's power within the worker–client relationship.
5. Enhancing the client's power through personal change: maximizing the client's "potential to change thoughts, feelings, and behaviours that are self-destructive and/or destructive to others, while acknowledging the impact of the societal context" (p. 238).

In their study report, Moreau et al. (1993) listed over 50 practice skills organized under the above five objectives. Table 2.1 outlines the three most frequently used skills within each of the five objectives.

They also analyzed the data through grouping frequently used interventions and summarized that "Workers are primarily helping people develop and elaborate a new understanding of thoughts, feelings and behaviours ... engaging in various facets of contracting ... validating clients ... helping to operationalize, coach and support new strategies with people ... and gathering data on and making links to material conditions" (p. 309). Integral to the use of all of the skills is a critical social analysis, linking the client's problem situation to the broader social context. Moreau et al. stressed that all of the five objectives contain skills that can contribute to client empowerment. While not intentionally applied in a prescriptive manner, the skills illustrate how a structural approach can be put into practice. I find it critical to apply these skills in the context of a dialogical relationship to prevent imposing my own structural assessment onto a client and discounting his or her understanding of the problem situation. My goal is to explore the problem in context with the client, and not to try to convince him or her of my perspective. It is also important to keep in mind that the skills outlined by Moreau et al. focus on direct practice and, therefore, are not meant to encompass the skills or activities associated with other levels of practice. I have found, however, that collectivization practices frequently lead to the involvement of clients in macro change processes.

In addition to developing its own applied literature, a related strength of structural social work is its willingness to be informed by other practice theories. Moreau (1979) cautioned, however, that the integration of other practice

TABLE 2.1: The most frequently used practice skills (adapted and reproduced with permission from Moreau et al., 1993).

Defence practices (p. 163)
1. Workers give information to clients concerning their rights and entitlements. 2. Workers coach clients to defend themselves against a structure, organization, or person representative thereof. 3. Workers initiate with clients the questioning of rules of institutional systems. (From a total of 11 identified practices)
Collectivization practices (p. 181)
1. Workers point out to clients that their physical condition, thoughts, feelings, behaviour, or situation is similar to that of others. 2. Workers refer clients to similar others, groups/networks, and/or community organizations related to their situation. 3. Workers initiate with clients efforts to build alliances and coalitions. (From a total of 8 identified practices)
Materialization practices (p. 199)
1. Workers gather data on possible determining links between clients' problem situations and their working and living conditions. 2. Workers give attention to clients' needs for material resources: (i) money, (ii) goods (shelter, food, clothing), (iii) services (e.g., day care, lawyer), and (iv) time. 3. Workers initiate with clients the making of links between thoughts, feelings, and behaviours to material and ideological conditions. (From a total of 8 identified practices)
Increasing the client's power in the worker–client relationship practices (p. 221)
1. Workers make a clear work contract with clients. 2. Workers share the rationale behind their interventions, questions, and interpretations of clients' situations. 3. Workers attempt to reduce distance between themselves and their clients by discussing the most comfortable use of names, location of meetings, and accessibility, by chitchatting, and so on. (From a total of 15 identified practices)
Enhancing the client's power through personal change practices (p. 239)
1. Workers help clients identify thoughts, feelings, or behaviours that are congruent with a new understanding (self, other, in context) of their problem situation. 2. Workers help clients make links between their thoughts, feelings, and behaviours and their problem situation, given the context. 3. Workers help clients make links between the thoughts, feelings, and behaviours of others and the client's problem situation, given the context. (From a total of 13 identified practices)

theories should not be done in a way that depoliticizes clients' problems or mystifies the helping process. Fook (1993) coined the term "radical extension" to describe the use of more conventional social work practices in a manner consistent with structural social work. Furthermore, structural social work's two-fold goal of helping individual clients and of working toward the transformation of societal structures suggests the potential for using practice methods associated with all levels of social work practice.

While I find the structural social work literature, supplemented with broader social work literature and my own practice wisdom, fairly sufficient in guiding my social work practice, I also find myself still questioning the congruency of my work with the overall goals of structural social work, particularly when it comes to bringing about structural change. Mullaly (2002) contended that "anti-oppressive social work practice at the structural level attempts to change those institutional arrangements, social processes, and social practices that work together to benefit the dominant group at the expense of subordinate groups" (p. 193). He added, "social reform is not a part of social transformation unless it represents one step in a long-range strategy for more fundamental change" (p. 193). While I agree that structural social work must move us beyond limited reform, this goal has at times led me to question or doubt the value of my work—leading me back to my question: "Is my approach to social work truly structural?" In the following section, I outline guidelines and criteria that have helped me to answer this question. I elaborate on what I have found useful in thinking about my own social work practice and its fit with the process and goals of structural social work.

Guidelines for Determining the Congruency between Practice Approaches, Their Intended Aims, and Structural Social Work

A structural social work approach to practice requires the integration of its theory base in both problem assessment and intervention or action. The following are common themes or principles found in the structural and radical social work literature that I use to inform the analysis of problems and to develop subsequent responses (Carniol, 1992, 2005; Fook, 1993; Healy, 1993; Hick, Fook, & Pozzuto, 2005; Moreau, 1979, 1990; Mullaly, 2007; Payne, 2005).

1. Analysis of causes of problems experienced by client groups and of barriers encountered in addressing problems:
   • causes of problems traced to the structural level of society, that is social institutions (e.g., schools, government, medical services) or oppressive social relations (e.g., class division, sexism, racism, ageism, heterosexism); and
   • critique of dominant, underlying ideologies that determine social institutions and relations.
2. Responses to problems experienced by client groups:
   • protection of individuals against the effects of oppression by more powerful groups and structures (e.g., addressing immediate needs for resources);
   • fostering clients' understanding of the links between personal problems and oppression by societal structures;
   • recognition of potential social control functions of social welfare agencies and acting to reduce worker–client power imbalances;
   • fostering collectivization of individuals who share common struggles and problem situations; and
   • working toward goals of social transformation such as the removal of inequality and injustice, and replacement with structures that are more egalitarian and reflective of the equality of all social groupings.

These themes or principles serve as guidelines that I apply in working with individual clients or client groups throughout all phases of the helping process from initial assessment to ending reflections. Although I have found them invaluable in guiding my social work practice, I have had to consider two additional criteria for assessing the outcomes of my work. The measures that I use to determine the congruency between what I do and the principles of structural social work are whether the change process helped to, at a minimum,

1. "alleviate the negative effects on people of an exploitative and alienating social order" (Mullaly, 2007, p. 245)—the first element of Mullaly's two-fold goal of structural social work; and
2. surface the structural root causes of people's problems.

The alleviation of the negative effects of an oppressive social order can be attained through activities such as helping an individual client to obtain needed resources or advocating with a client group for program or policy change. The second criterion relates to raising awareness about the need for structural change without requiring the certainty of social transformation. I find that raising awareness of root causes of structural problems can be done at both micro and macro levels of practice. In fact, goals that I develop with an individual client generally do not include attaining structural change, but our work does frequently involve discussion of the root causes of the client's problem or concern. This discussion often results in new insights on both our parts. At the macro level, the goal of the group that I am working with may be structural change. However, it has been my experience that often we can only be sure of drawing attention to root causes of social problems and the need for social change, without ever knowing the eventual outcome of this increased critical awareness. As stated earlier, it may not be possible to distinguish between program or policy changes that result in limited reforms versus steps toward social transformation. Nevertheless, attention can be still drawn to the structural reasons for the needed change. I believe that raising awareness in and of itself is an important step toward social change. These two criteria—immediate assistance and critical awareness—have proved useful in assessing the outcome of my work and have brought me closer to answering the question—is my work truly structural?

In the remainder of this chapter, I will present two case examples to illustrate the use of the two assessment criteria, along with the application of the practice guidelines listed under the analysis of and responses to problems experienced by client groups. The first case example reflects micro-level practice, while the second is more macro in scope.

Case Study 1:
Group Work with Persons Living with HIV/AIDS

Since the late 1980s, I have been involved either as a staff member or volunteer with community-based AIDS organizations. This involvement has included facilitating support groups for persons living with HIV/AIDS. The most recent group that I facilitated consisted of four members who met every two weeks for eight sessions. In one of the first sessions, the group members established an overall group goal: "To provide a comfortable, friendly, and respectful atmosphere/environment where group members can socialize with others living with HIV/AIDS and share/

discuss their experiences." Many of the process aspects of delivering this group fit well with my compilation of guidelines for structural social work practice.

The group itself was a vehicle for collectivization and resulted in many benefits associated with mutual aid. The relationships that formed in the group tended to be interdependent and based on reciprocity. This can be a very empowering process that is especially beneficial to a person living with HIV/AIDS, who may have lost the sense of having control over his or her life, having self-worth, and being able to contribute. A typical meeting would commence with an informal and often spontaneous check-in. This would be followed by an open discussion. Frequently, a group member would introduce a specific topic that he or she was having difficulty with and the other members would offer assistance in the form of empathy, information, suggestions, and advice. Fostering mutual aid (vs. relying only on worker-to-group member support and assistance) was one means of reducing the worker–client power imbalance. Another means was involving the group members in decisions around group goals and purposes, meeting dates and times, the length of the meeting, and group discussion topics and activities.

Throughout the group discussions and activities, I always remained alert for opportunities for social analysis, tracing causes of members' problems to social institutions and relations, and their underlying ideologies, and fostering members' understanding of the links between personal problems and oppression by societal structures. I did this in a dialogical fashion through asking questions, sharing information, or voicing an opinion whenever I assessed that such contributions would add to the group's analysis of the issue, or exploration of the root causes of their problems or challenges. I used a technique of bringing in narratives from other persons living with HIV/AIDS (with their permission) to stimulate discussion and enhance critical consciousness. The following are examples of "pieces" of narratives that I have used:

- In relation to low-income: "I've had people say 'Oh, let's go out to go get a coffee' or 'Let's go out to lunch' and it's like, you know, 'I don't have the time right now.' You know that wasn't the truth at all. I had lots of time. I just didn't have the money to do it."
- In relation to family relationships: "We didn't have a close relationship when I was growing up. But we started to and then I was infected ... because it's such a social stigma ... they just backed off."

- In relation to friends and new acquaintances: "Sometimes I always get the feeling from some people … especially at the very first … that I wasn't going to be here that long anyway, you know. So it's almost like you're kind of marginalized and that … it's like you're a person without a future. So you're kind of existing for the moment right? I don't feel like I want to tell people … 'cause I don't want people to feel sorry for me or I don't want it to set up barriers and obstacles because people feel or think that because of my condition I'm not capable or less capable of doing things."
- In relation to HIV disclosure and potential romantic/sexual relationships: "When do you tell? You know you don't want to invest a whole lot of time and energy and then find out they're not interested. And for that reason you think, 'Well, I should tell them fairly early on,' but if you tell them fairly early on they're not that invested in you and so why would they want to take that on? So you can't have a casual date 'cause there's … this big issue to face."

This sharing of "voices" often led to rich discussion. At times, it also alleviated the negative effects of oppression through surfacing root causes of problems. For example, discussions of low income often led to a critical assessment of income assistance programs and the conclusion that inadequacies rest with these programs and not with the individual. The topic of personal relationships would often include discussion of the beliefs and attitudes held by others. Group members would share their own interpretations of the narratives, along with their own stories and experiences.

Sometimes I would share my perspective in a dialogical manner if I thought it might be helpful. For example, in one discussion a group member described being rejected by someone when the other person found out that she was HIV positive. Another group member replied that she should not feel bad because of the other person's "ignorance." I shared that sometimes I still feel hurt, even when I recognize that I have no responsibility for how the other person has treated me. So these discussions would result in much interpersonal sharing, and sometimes people would leave with new explanations and understandings of their experiences and challenges, explanations that often included greater insight into the structural contributions to problems. This sharing and discussion overlaps with the principle of protection of individuals against the effects of oppression through the reduction of self-blame and fostering of personal liberation.

In the post-group evaluation that I conducted, group members described benefits related to meeting new people and establishing friendships, gaining new information and learning from others, and having the opportunity to socialize. They enjoyed the opportunities to share that involved both listening to others' stories and telling their own: "being able to connect with other people" and "getting insight into other people's perspectives." Group members described benefits from having their feelings and experiences normalized and from being able to vent frustrations and negative feelings: "It was nice to hear that you're not alone in this world and that you're not the only person that, that's got HIV or AIDS." The group overall, as well as the more focused narrative activity, met the two criteria that I use to assess the outcome of my work: (1) the group was helpful to the group members in countering some of the negative effects of oppressive structures and relations, and (2) the process helped to surface root causes of their problems.

Case Study 2:
Social Action with a Gay and Lesbian
Rights Organization

In the early to mid 1990s, I was very involved in a human rights coalition whose main goal was to attain the inclusion of sexual orientation in New Brunswick's *Human Rights Act*. My work for this organization was as a volunteer, illustrating that social workers also contribute toward social change outside of their primary workplace. Although the organization was primarily focused on gay and lesbian rights issues, it spearheaded the formation of a coalition with other organizations to lobby the government for a review and broadening of the provincial human rights legislation. The legislation was insufficient in a number of areas, such as affording women protection against discrimination based on pregnancy. The formation of the coalition was an effective strategy for broadening support for human rights reform and for making links between various sources of oppression. My involvement in the coalition encompassed strategy development, speaking to the media, and directly lobbying politicians. Part of the coalition's work also involved research with the provincial gay/lesbian/bisexual community to document the prevalence and types of discrimination experienced. This research was used to inform the lobby efforts, and served a collectivization and consciousness-raising function within the gay and lesbian community.

The coalition was successful in persuading the government to undergo a review of its human rights legislation and eventually to prohibit sexual orientation as grounds for discrimination. In relating the coalition's efforts to guidelines for structural social work practice, a number of key principles were met. The analysis included underscoring the discriminatory practices of social structures, even within the province's own *Human Rights Act*, and the heterosexist ideology that shapes social institutions and relations. The coalition's efforts were aimed at protecting individuals against the effects of oppression, fostering understanding of the links between personal problems and oppression, fostering collectivization, and working toward goals of social transformation. With respect to the last of these points, I believe that the coalition's education efforts changed not only the legislation, but also public opinion. In assessing the outcomes of this work, the two criteria of (1) alleviating the negative effects of oppression and (2) surfacing structural root causes of people's problems were met.

Conclusion

I believe that the guidelines and criteria that I use to assess my social work practice, activities, and outcomes are realistic and provide both direction and reassurance. This is important for two reasons: the necessity of having guidelines to inform practice and to reassure one that one's work is meaningful. In addition to having guidelines and criteria, however, is the ability to recognize opportunities for structural practice and to have the conviction and courage to then follow through. I have found following through particularly challenging in environments that may dismiss my ideas as either too radical or too naïve. In this respect, it is important to apply a structural analysis to the context in which one practices. Fook (1993) stated, "It is particularly important that a critical theory of society should include a realistic assessment of the limitations of professional social work power within present institutional systems. The radical caseworker needs to be aware of what avenues for action are possible within the existing structure, and what actions may be presently possible to change that structure" (pp. 29–30). A realistic understanding of context will help to foster a celebration of gains made at the same time as reducing self-blame for not bringing about structural change where such change lies largely outside of one's control. Having said this, I remain encouraged by the ongoing opportunities that I have to apply a structural approach and the many successes at both micro and macro levels, and in settings ranging from small community organizations to larger institutions. The bigger question of contributing to social transformation still remains somewhat elusive, but perhaps this in itself is good because it fuels reflexive practice on seizing the opportunities that present themselves while recognizing imposed structural limitations. Chapter 3 may further assist in responding to this uncertainty through situating structural social work theory and practice in a model of theory–practice integration.

References

Carniol, B. (1992). Structural social work: Maurice Moreau's challenge to social work practice. *Journal of Progressive Human Services, 3*(1), 1–20.

Carniol, B. (2005). *Case critical: Social services and social justice in Canada* (5th ed.). Toronto, ON: Between the Lines.

Fook, J. (1993). *Radical casework: A theory of practice*. St. Leonards, Australia: Allen & Unwin.

Healy, B. (1993). Elements in the development of an Australian radical social work. *Australian Social Work, 46*(1), 3–8.

Hick, S., Fook, J., & Pozzuto, R. (Eds.). (2005). *Social work: A critical turn*. Toronto, ON: Thompson Educational Publishing.

Lundy, C. (2004). *Social work and social justice: A structural approach to practice*. Peterborough, ON: Broadview Press.

Moreau, M.J. (1979). A structural approach to social work practice. *Canadian Journal of Social Work Education, 5*(1), 78–94.

Moreau, M.J. (1990). Empowerment through advocacy and consciousness-raising: Implications of a structural approach to social work. *Journal of Sociology & Social Welfare, 17*(2), 53–67.

Moreau, M.J., Frosst, S., Frayne, G., Hlywa, M., Leonard, L., & Rowell, M. (1993). *Empowerment II: Snapshots of the structural approach in action*. Ottawa, ON: Carleton University Press.

Mullaly, B. (2002). *Challenging oppression: A critical social work approach*. Toronto, ON: Oxford University Press.

Mullaly, B. (2007). *The new structural social work* (3rd ed.). Toronto, ON: Oxford University Press.

Payne, M. (2005). *Modern social work theory* (3rd ed.). Chicago, IL: Lyceum Books.

CHAPTER 3

Situating Practitioners' Experiences in a Model of Theory–Practice Integration

HEATHER I. PETERS

Challenges in linking theory or knowledge with social work practice have been documented in the literature for many years (Bailey & Lee, 1982; Lewis, 2003; Mullaly, 2007; Payne, 2005; Pilalis, 1986; Reynolds, 1942, 1963; Secker, 1993; Sheldon, 1978). While some of the problems in linking theory with practice relate to social work theories in general (Healy, 2005; Pilalis, 1986; Reynolds, 1963; Secker, 1993), other issues are specific to structural social work theory or to broader critical social work theories, including anti-oppressive, radical, feminist, anti-racist, and other related theories, as discussed by Murray and Hick in Chapter 1 (Moreau & Leonard, 1989; Mullaly, 2007; Payne, 2005). This chapter begins with a brief discussion of the literature on the perceived gap between theory and practice in general. The majority of the chapter describes a model or conceptual framework[1] through which the integration of structural social work theory and practice can be organized and understood. The model creates a context to better understand the many progressive ways in which the practitioners and authors of this text are bridging the gap between structural social work theory and practice.

The Gap between Theory and Practice

A review of the literature on theory–practice integration indicates that the primary focus currently and over the years is that the utilization of theory in practice is problematic (Peters, 2007). Writers have argued that the gap between theory and practice is a common challenge in the social work discipline (Bogo & Vayda, 1998; Harre Hindmarsh, 1992; Hearn, 1982; Lewis, 2003; Pilalis, 1986). Other research suggests that theory–practice integration is a problem for social work students from the time they begin their field placements (Bogo &

Vayda, 1998; Vayda & Bogo, 1991). Although a logical place to bridge theory and practice is during social work education, instructors struggle with how to assist students in making this link (Boisen & Syers, 2004; Reay, 1986).

Two related dilemmas are common to discussions of theory and practice integration. The first is the debate over whether abstract theory is useful in practice settings (Lee, 1982; Mullaly, 2007; Smith, 1971). The second debate is about which is more appropriate and useful in a practice context: an eclectic use of theory or the use of one specific theoretical approach in which one has an expertise (Mullaly, 2007; Poulter, 2005; Robbins, Chatterjee, & Canda, 1999). Both of these debates are issues in other professional disciplines as well (Harre Hindmarsh, 1992). The division in the first debate is typically one of academics arguing in favour of the use of theory, and of direct-practice social workers stating that practice experience should be foremost in shaping one's interventions (Lee, 1982; Smith, 1971). Others argue, however, that all practitioners utilize theory, whether they are aware of it or not (Mullaly, 2007; Reay, 1986). This occurs as practitioners examine their experiences for patterns that then guide future actions, essentially creating informal theories (Mullaly, 2007; Reay, 1986). Since such experiential theories are rarely subjected to conscious analysis and research, practice based on experiential assumptions can, at the least, result in chaotic work with clients and, at the worst, cause damage or distress to the people with whom one is working (Loewenberg, 1984; Mullaly, 2007; Reay, 1986; Robbins et al., 1999). Mixing and matching bits of various theories in an eclectic approach is also problematic. This tactic often results from a superficial understanding of theory and can result in the misuse of theory in practice settings (Mullaly, 2007; Robbins et al., 1999).

This book brings practitioners and academics together to address the question of integrating structural social work theory into social work practice. Rather than focusing on the problems with integrating theory into practice, the chapters start from the perspective of practitioners who are successfully incorporating structural theory into their work. In these chapters it is practitioners, often together with academics, who indirectly address the two debates above through the sharing of their work experiences. First of all, the chapters indicate that the use of structural theory in practice benefits clients in many ways that may be less likely to occur without this theoretical perspective. Second, practitioners focus on the use of structural theory specifically in their practice, rather than an eclectic approach, although some also incorporate perspectives complementary to structural theory, such as Africentric theory discussed by Thomas Bernard and Marsman in Chapter 12 and the use of progressive (dis) ability models discussed in Chapter 9 by MacDonald and Friars. Thus, this book intends to turn the traditional problematic approach to theory–practice integration on its head by focusing instead on the varied ways in which the incorporation of structural theory into practice successfully results in positive outcomes for clients, practitioners, and society as a whole.

A Model to Understand Theory–Practice Integration

One difficulty in making sense of the literature on the integration of structural theory into practice is that often the problems of integration are discussed one at a time and without reference to other potential concerns. Yet a review of the literature suggests that there are a number of different concerns, all of which may hinder or facilitate theory–practice integration, and all of which are interrelated (Peters, 2007). In order to make sense of the varied nature of the literature on this topic, I have utilized the idea of a concept map to develop a visual picture or model of theory–practice integration (Maxwell, 2005). The model assists in better understanding the spaces between abstract theory and the point of praxis, where, from the perspective of a structural theoretical framework, social work practitioners put social justice transformation into practice. These spaces may operate as either barriers or catalysts to the implementation of structural social work theory in practice. The model is a useful step in challenging barriers and creating additional supports, thereby increasing the effective use of structural theory in practice. Although the model can be utilized to organize and understand the integration of theories in general at a practice level, it also allows for an exploration of the unique conditions inherent to the integration of specific theories in practice, such as that of structural social work theory, which is examined here. The conceptual framework identifies five spaces between structural theory and practice, where the integration of the two may be either challenged or encouraged (see Figure 3.1). These spaces are described in the following section, and the chapters of this book are outlined in the context of the framework.

FIGURE 3.1: Conceptual Framework: The spaces between theory and practice.

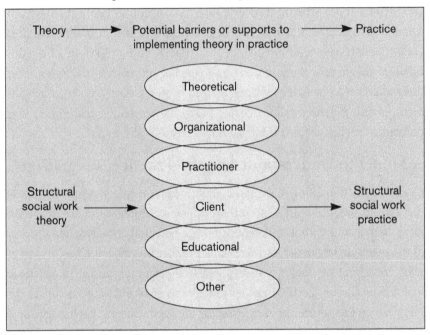

Spaces in the Theory–Practice Integration Model
Theoretical Space

The first space between theory and practice is that of the theory itself, and the ways in which it is and is not conducive to being operationalized at the practice level. Moreau's research into the use of structural social work theory in practice asked participants about the benefits and limitations of the theory (Moreau & Leonard, 1989). Participants identified the following as theory strengths: a broad analysis with a focus on structural change, empowerment of clients, and a decrease in client blame. Limitations of the theory were described as a lack of emphasis on client change and limited connection of the theory to specific practice skills. Structural theory has also been criticized for emphasizing the structural roots of social and individual issues to the exclusion of individual responsibility and agency (Finn & Jacobson, 2003; Rossiter, 1996). This should not be the case since the agency–structure dialectic is a key component of structural theory; however, it may be that this concept has not yet been adequately translated into practice activities and skills. In Chapter 1, Murray and Hick discuss this and other criticisms of structural social work theory. In Part 3, Future Directions, Lysack (Chapter 13) suggests that an environmental consciousness and practice perspective is missing and should be added to the theory. While no theory is perfect, and all theories are dynamic and changing, one of the achievements of this book is the description of many concrete ways in which structural theory is actively being translated into effective practice.

The authors of this book are participating because they are successfully utilizing structural theory in their work, and so they see the theory as being useful, relevant, and practical. Yet they demonstrate that there are diverse ways in which structural theory benefits practice. One of the commonalities across chapters is that all touch on the ways in which their work operates from a position of respect and empowerment of service users. The objective of collectivization (Moreau et al., 1993; Mullaly, 2007; Olivier, Chapter 2) has provided direction for the growth and development of a sexual assault centre in a northern community (Hemingway, Johnson, & Roland, Chapter 5); a women's centre and a youth centre (Burrill & Peters, Chapter 6); a safe place for youth who identify as lesbian, gay, bisexual, transgender, two-spirited, queer, or intersex (LGBTTQI) (Brown, Richard, & Wichman, Chapter 10); and a grassroots collaboration of progressive youth organizations (Wright, Sayani, Zammit, & George, Chapter 11). For all of the criticism about the difficulty in actualizing structural social work's principle of social transformation (Olivier, Chapter 2), several of the authors have identified ways in which their work has changed provincial government legislation (Olivier, Chapter 2; Thomas Bernard & Marsman, Chapter 12) or moved municipalities and communities toward more inclusive policies and actions (Burrill & Peters, Chapter 6; Hemingway et al., Chapter 5). Wright et al. (Chapter 11) argue that their work has created a shift in funders' views of youth and has pressured funders toward projects that see youth in a positive light rather than categorizing them as "at risk."

Structural theory is also useful in work with individuals and families. Feehan, Boettcher, and Quinn (Chapter 4) start their chapter with a defence of the use of structural analysis in their 20 years of practice within the field of child sexual abuse. They state that many people are initially offended by their ideas. Some express concern that a structural approach does not hold perpetrators accountable for their behaviour or, worse, that victims of abuse come to blame themselves for what has happened to them. However, when practice incorporates the structure–agency dialectic, a cornerstone of structural theory, it allows for a dynamic approach that can place perpetrator responsibility in a societal context, and remove blame from victims while giving them skills to defend themselves in the future. Feehan et al.'s discussion of the respectful ways in which they bring this concept into their work is insightful, eye-opening, and counters the criticism that structural theory ignores individual power and agency.

FIGURE 3.2: Theoretical space.

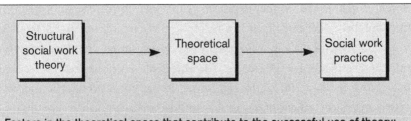

Factors in the theoretical space that contribute to the successful use of theory:

- Operationalization of abstract constructs into practice skills and guidelines
  (Olivier, Chapter 2)

- The incorporation of the agency–structure dialectic by balancing change in societal structures with change in individuals
  (Feehan et al., Chapter 4; Murray & Hick, Chapter 1; Olivier, Chapter 2)

- Principles of respectful ways of practising and empowerment of service users
  (all chapters)

- Collectivization principle to guide development of organizations and support groups
  (Burrill & Peters, Chapter 6; Brown, Richard, & Wichman, Chapter 10)

- Goal of social transformation to support activity to change government policies
  (Burrill & Peters, Chapter 6; Olivier, Chapter 2; Thomas Bernard & Marsman, Chapter 12)

Organizational Space

The second space that has an important effect on the use of theory in practice is the organizational space. Social workers tend to utilize theories supported by the organization in which they work (Chan & Chan, 2004). Thus, the organizational space can be particularly problematic for the use of critical social work theories (Harre Hindmarsh, 1992). Alternatively, organizations with a progressive understanding of social problems can create spaces in which structural social work practice thrives (Carniol, 2005; George & Marlowe, 2005; Mullaly,

2007). Research by Moreau found that two of the most important factors in supporting the use of the structural approach to practice are (1) support from management, and (2) support from peers in the agency or the larger community (Moreau & Leonard, 1989). Another factor is the ideology of organizations' funding sources. The current neo-conservative climate (or neo-liberal according to some writers) is in contradiction to the social democratic worldview of structural social work (Mullaly, 2007). In this climate, organizations are often pressured to provide services and programs within a traditional paradigm instead of a structural paradigm. The pressure comes from government funding agencies, be it through contract directives or funding cuts targeting progressive programs (Barnoff, George, & Coleman, 2006; Razack, 2002).

The chapters in this book describe a variety of ways in which organizations support the use of structural social work in practice. Although Carniol and Del Valle (Chapter 8) and Wright et al. (Chapter 11) echo the concern that funding cuts can put pressure on workers to ignore structural issues, they acknowledge the importance of the organization and workplace in supporting work from a structural perspective, even when it means taking additional time to build rapport and trust with service users (Chapter 8) or turning down funding that does not fit with structural perspectives (Chapter 11). Brown et al. (Chapter 10) describe how structural analyses guided the very development of the Youth Project for LGBTTQI youth. Ongoing governance of the non-profit organization is through the Youth Board; goals of empowerment and collectivization mean that the youth whom the centre serves also control the organization's decision-making. Similarly, Peters (Chapter 6) joined the NOOPA (No Ordinary People Allowed) Youth Centre in its early stages, and used structural principles to work with the board and staff to develop organizational policies, procedures, values, and a mission statement. These founding policies were all drafted to embody structural principles, and to guide the ongoing work of the organization toward a structural approach. The creation of the Association of Black Social Workers (ABSW) and the restructuring of the Women's Contact Society along structural lines have also resulted in the support of structural practice in all aspects of these organizations (Thomas Bernard & Marsman, Chapter 12; Burrill & Peters, Chapter 6).

However, not all organizations support a structural approach to practice. While it is helpful when this does occur, it is still possible to engage in structural social work practice in organizations that operate from positions contrary to structural understandings, such as the medical model inherent in mental health institutions (Schwartz & O'Brien, Chapter 7) and the highly structured hospital environment described in one case study by MacDonald and Friars (Chapter 9). On the other hand, several of the case studies in Chapter 9 also identify structurally oriented colleagues as being supportive in advocating for services to meet client needs.

FIGURE 3.3: Organizational space.

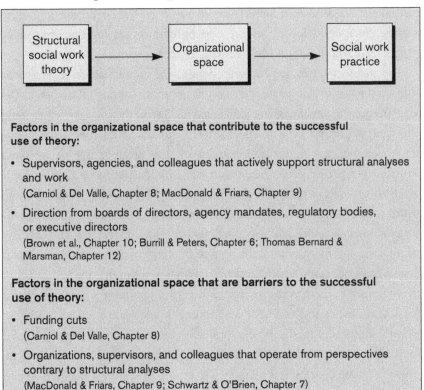

Factors in the organizational space that contribute to the successful use of theory:

- Supervisors, agencies, and colleagues that actively support structural analyses and work
  (Carniol & Del Valle, Chapter 8; MacDonald & Friars, Chapter 9)

- Direction from boards of directors, agency mandates, regulatory bodies, or executive directors
  (Brown et al., Chapter 10; Burrill & Peters, Chapter 6; Thomas Bernard & Marsman, Chapter 12)

Factors in the organizational space that are barriers to the successful use of theory:

- Funding cuts
  (Carniol & Del Valle, Chapter 8)

- Organizations, supervisors, and colleagues that operate from perspectives contrary to structural analyses
  (MacDonald & Friars, Chapter 9; Schwartz & O'Brien, Chapter 7)

Practitioner Space

The third space between theory and practice is at the personal level of the practitioner. Practitioners tend to seek out and utilize theories that fit with their worldview (Barbour, 1984; Chan & Chan, 2004), and this is particularly true for the use of structural social work theory (Moreau & Leonard, 1989). In one research study, it was found that practitioners have difficulty in practising from a critical perspective if they have an incomplete understanding of the theory and its application to practice (Baines, 2000, 2003). Practitioners also need to develop their own critical consciousness, as well as a knowledge of their own biases and power issues, to be effective in addressing oppression in their work (Pitner & Sakamoto, 2005; Prilleltensky & Nelson, 2002).

Several of the authors in this book articulate specific details on the importance of personal growth and incorporating structural concepts into their own lives. Olivier sets the stage for this early in the book in Chapter 2. He begins by admitting that he struggles with whether his practice is truly structural, saying that the goal of social transformation is a difficult one to judge. In his grappling of this issue he articulates two questions that he asks himself of his work: (1) does it lead to a better public understanding of the root causes of social issues, and (2) does it assist in alleviating the effects of oppression on people's lives. This honest, ongoing examination of his practice is a part of his personal growth that contributes to effective structural practice.

Several of the authors identify personal growth and self-awareness as crucial components of effective structural practice. Carniol and Del Valle (Chapter 8) speak about how the practitioner's personal and professional understanding of ideologies contributes to a better understanding of these issues as faced by clients. The example discussed in Chapter 8 is a powerful demonstration of how the social worker's personal critical consciousness allows him or her to empathize and, therefore, to work more effectively with the client in addressing issues of oppression. Feehan et al. also begin their chapter with a discussion of how a structural practitioner must begin by looking inward to become consciously aware of one's own values, beliefs, and worldview (Chapter 4). They indicate that a lack of awareness of one's perspective will lead to a client–worker relationship that simply reproduces the power imbalances inherent in societal structures, thereby undoing any attempts to address oppression with clients. Lysack (Chapter 13) suggests that practitioners need to locate themselves in the web of life in order to understand the importance of environmental issues to social justice work and to work effectively in addressing environmental concerns. Wright et al. (Chapter 11) describe how structural workers strategically position themselves as allies working with youth, rather than as experts working on youth issues. In the chapter describing work with LGBTTQI youth, the authors sum up their suggestions for practice in this field with the admonishment to "do your own work" first, including scrutinizing your own values, understanding how you contribute to the oppression of LGBTTQI people, and educating yourself on LGBTTQI issues, contexts, and appropriate ways of practising with this group of people (Brown et al., Chapter 10).

FIGURE 3.4: Practitioner space.

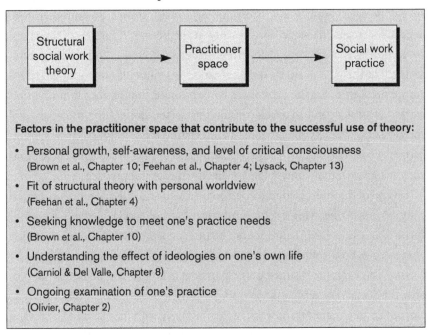

Factors in the practitioner space that contribute to the successful use of theory:

- Personal growth, self-awareness, and level of critical consciousness
  (Brown et al., Chapter 10; Feehan et al., Chapter 4; Lysack, Chapter 13)
- Fit of structural theory with personal worldview
  (Feehan et al., Chapter 4)
- Seeking knowledge to meet one's practice needs
  (Brown et al., Chapter 10)
- Understanding the effect of ideologies on one's own life
  (Carniol & Del Valle, Chapter 8)
- Ongoing examination of one's practice
  (Olivier, Chapter 2)

Client Space

The fourth space between theory and practice is that of the client. Social workers indicate that they modify their theories and skills to meet the needs and interests of clients (Barbour, 1984; Chan & Chan, 2004). Client empowerment is a key component of structural social work (Moreau, 1990; Mullaly, 2007). Thus, clients should have direct and ongoing involvement and decision-making power in the interactions between themselves and the social worker. Moreau found that the use of social analysis in direct practice with clients was determined in part by the stage of the intervention, the receptiveness of clients, and the gender and age of clients. However, client factors were not as important in the utilization of structural theory as other factors, such as those found in the organizational and practitioner spaces (Moreau et al., 1993). While clients may discourage the use of structural theory, they can also be encouraging of a critical or collective approach to practice (McNicoll, 2001, 2003).

One theme through all of the chapters in this book is that of working from a place of respect and empowerment of clients. This means that clients are equal partners in their work with a social worker; therefore, the client's perspective on the use of a structural approach is important. One demonstration of this partnership is with the Youth Project (Brown et al., Chapter 10), where the youth served by the organization also comprise the Youth Board responsible for the decision-making of the organization. While it is unlikely that clients would actively disagree with an approach that treats them with respect and supports them in controlling decisions about their own lives, it is possible that clients may disagree with a structural analysis of the issues facing them. Carniol and Del Valle (Chapter 8) write that sharing power occurs simultaneously with educating clients about the roots of oppression: "We do more than support client strengths because we challenge client attitudes, feelings, and behaviours when clients express stereotypes or assert privileges that are harmful to themselves or to others." Clients are then given room to think about these challenges and make their own decisions about them: "My re-framing efforts were aimed at critical consciousness-raising. Then I

FIGURE 3.5: Client space.

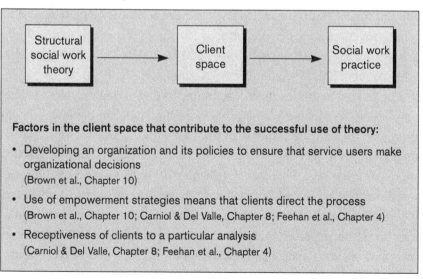

Factors in the client space that contribute to the successful use of theory:

- Developing an organization and its policies to ensure that service users make organizational decisions
  (Brown et al., Chapter 10)

- Use of empowerment strategies means that clients direct the process
  (Brown et al., Chapter 10; Carniol & Del Valle, Chapter 8; Feehan et al., Chapter 4)

- Receptiveness of clients to a particular analysis
  (Carniol & Del Valle, Chapter 8; Feehan et al., Chapter 4)

was deliberately quiet to allow Carolina to process my input." Ensuring that clients have space to make their own decisions about the causes of oppression in their lives is also described in Chapter 4. Feehan et al. describe a three-circle model that they use to help sexual abuse victims understand structural connections to their context. Clients and workers then examine the model together, with the understanding that clients will identify for themselves those aspects of the model that are most relevant to their experiences.

Educational Space

Last is the educational space, the places where practitioners learn about structural social work. Social work education is a common starting point in the literature for examining theory–practice integration issues (Bogo & Vayda, 1998; Boisen & Syers, 2004; Campbell, 1999, 2002, 2003b; Fook, Ryan, & Hawkins, 1994, 2000; Lam, 2004; Marchant, 1986; Rossiter, 1995, 2001; Vayda & Bogo, 1991; Walden & Brown, 1985). Factors in the educational space include instructors' choice of theories to teach, interest in critical theories, and ability to connect critical theories to practice (Razack, 2002; Rossiter, 1995). Agency-based field supervisors are also in a position to support or undermine the use of structural or other critical theories in field placements (Finch et al., 2003; Razack, 1999). Research has found that, particularly when teaching structural and related theories (including anti-oppressive, feminist, anti-racist, and anti-heterosexist theories), pedagogical practices and teaching styles must match the perspective that is being taught. As a result, students see the perspective in action and are better able to take it into practice themselves (Campbell, 1999, 2003a, 2003b; Dore, 1994; Nyland, 2006; Wehbi, 2003; Woodford & Bella, 2003; Zapf et al., 2003).

The authors in this text have few comments to make on the role of educational institutions in their use of theory in practice, probably because the focus is on practice activities rather than how the authors came to use structural theory. However, there are two connections to educational institutions that are of particular note. Brown et al. (Chapter 10) write that the Youth Project was developed as a field placement at Dalhousie University by a lesbian faculty member together with a lesbian student. In this case, the university, or at least one faculty member, understood structural contexts of LGBTTQI issues and creatively developed a structural solution to one aspect of these issues.

In Chapter 12, Thomas Bernard and Marsman identify work done by ABSW to educate social work practitioners and students on anti-racism and cultural sensitivity. This suggests that such training was not adequate in schools of social work at this time, but that some schools were at least open to ABSW's efforts to educate students about racism and anti-racist practices. Thus, educational institutions may support structural practices and analyses in the larger community or, alternatively, may undermine them by excluding such perspectives from curricula.

While most of the chapters do not discuss institutional forms of education, many do describe work to educate clients, colleagues, institutions, and the public about the structural causes of social issues as a regular part of their practice activities (Burrill & Peters, Chapter 6; Feehan et al., Chapter 4; Hemingway et al., Chapter 5; MacDonald & Friars, Chapter 9; Schwartz & O'Brien, Chapter 7; Thomas Bernard & Marsman, Chapter 12; Wright et al., Chapter 11). While this is sometimes described as consciousness-raising or client advocacy, it also necessarily entails a teaching component. Wright et al. (Chapter 11) also describe their extensive efforts to educate funders regarding structural analyses of issues facing youth, and through these efforts seek to transform funding opportunities. Educational institutions do not have an exclusive hold on education, as learning and teaching take place in many

FIGURE 3.6: Educational space.

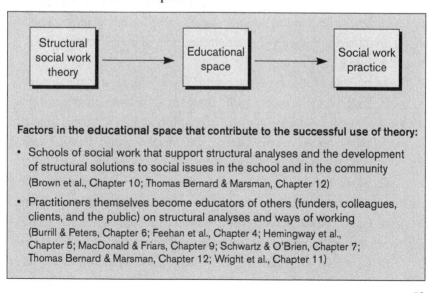

Factors in the educational space that contribute to the successful use of theory:

- Schools of social work that support structural analyses and the development of structural solutions to social issues in the school and in the community (Brown et al., Chapter 10; Thomas Bernard & Marsman, Chapter 12)

- Practitioners themselves become educators of others (funders, colleagues, clients, and the public) on structural analyses and ways of working (Burrill & Peters, Chapter 6; Feehan et al., Chapter 4; Hemingway et al., Chapter 5; MacDonald & Friars, Chapter 9; Schwartz & O'Brien, Chapter 7; Thomas Bernard & Marsman, Chapter 12; Wright et al., Chapter 11) different formal and informal spheres. It is important that the process of structural analysis is shared across disciplines and in society as a whole in the work toward social transformation. As more people understand the theory, it leads to more support for structural practices in the field.

Additional Comments on the Conceptual Framework

There are two additional comments regarding the framework. First of all, there is one final space called "other," which is intended to acknowledge that there may be additional supports or barriers not covered in the five spaces. One such factor is that of historical antecedents, as discussed by Brown et al. (Chapter 10). These authors point out that there are a number of historical events and societal values that, although many have changed over time, may continue to have negative repercussions on the lives of LGBTTQI seniors today. A structural approach to practice must be flexible in working in this context. Likewise, history also holds positive changes in societal attitudes, social policies, and structures regarding a number of oppressions, many of which have opened up opportunities for current structural practice. Historical materialism, a cornerstone of critical analysis, has been described as a dance through time (Ollman, 2004). In this dance, the vision for the future begins with an understanding of the past and the seeds of change it contains, which can guide our work in the present to move us toward a progressive and socialist vision for the future (Harvey, 2004; Ollman, 2004). The importance of historical materialism to critical and structural theories suggests that historical antecedents are an important factor in theory–practice integration, as in the example given by Brown et al. in Chapter 10.

The second comment on the conceptual framework regards the important role of the dialectic in the model itself. These spaces between theory and practice are described as separate in order to establish an initial understanding of the model. However, as in any dialectic, the interaction and dialogue among components means that there is significant overlap between the spaces and that each space affects and is affected by each of the others. The interactions among the spaces add to the framework such that the whole is greater than the sum of the parts. This is consistent with critical postmodern approaches that acknowledge diversity and complexity as well as general structures (Ife, 1997; Mullaly, 2007). In this model, organizations, practitioners, clients, and the other spaces between theory and practice are dynamic, growing, and constantly changing, just as are theory and practice themselves. As well as the overlap between the spaces, the effects of the dominant ideology and issues of power and oppression (as well as anti-oppressive analyses) infiltrate all of the spaces and thus affect the ways in which theory and practice are integrated. The chapters give the best demonstration of this dialectic and overlap of the spaces between theory and practice. Rather than containing dry lists of activities, the authors share vibrant, complex, and dynamic experiences of structural practices that change workers and organizations, empower clients, and challenge unjust structures in communities and society.

From a Gap toward a Bridge between Structural Social Work Theory and Practice

The distinguishing factor between a neo-liberal approach and a socialist or structural approach to social work practice is that the former has a goal of alleviating the negative issues facing individuals that are caused by societal structures, while the latter has goals of both alleviating negative effects while working to change those structures that are causing the problems in the first place (Moreau et al., 1993; Mullaly, 2007; Olivier, Chapter 2). As Olivier points out in Chapter 2, it is sometimes difficult to see if our social work practice is doing only the first, or if it is making small steps of change that will eventually turn into the latter goal of social change and transformation. The social work practice experiences shared in this book demonstrate examples of working toward both goals by challenging and changing oppressive laws, policies, and ideological worldviews of decision-makers; creating safe places from which to strategize about ways to challenge oppressive structures; and alleviating the effects of oppression and educating people on structural foundations of social problems.

Thus, the chapters demonstrate the many varied ways that structural social workers are successfully bridging theory and practice. Focusing on a bridge instead of a gap gives us permission to move forward in our social work practice. We no longer need to be stuck in a place of defending structural practice against allegations that it is idealistic, unrealistic, and un-doable. We know that it is possible. We know that every day, social workers are quietly going to work and passionately transforming their small corner of the world. Those small transformations add up to larger transformations and, slowly, change happens.

We can see it take place in the lives of the practitioners who have shared their work with us in the pages of this book.

Endnote

[1] The terms "model" and "conceptual framework" are used interchangeably in this chapter.

References

Bailey, R., & Lee, P. (Eds.). (1982). *Theory and practice in social work*. Oxford, UK: Blackwell.

Baines, D. (2000). Everyday practices of race, class and gender: Struggles, skills and radical social work. *Journal of Progressive Human Services, 11*(2), 5–27.

Baines, D. (2003). Race, class, and gender in everyday talk of social workers: The ways we limit the possibilities for radical practice. In W. Shera (Ed.), *Emerging perspectives on anti-oppressive practice* (pp. 43–64). Toronto, ON: Canadian Scholars' Press Inc.

Barbour, R.S. (1984). Social work education: Tackling the theory–practice dilemma. *British Journal of Social Work, 14*, 557–577.

Barnoff, L., George, P., & Coleman, B. (2006). Operating in survival mode: Challenges to implementing anti-oppressive practice in feminist social service agencies in Toronto. *Canadian Social Work Review, 23*(1/2), 41–58.

Bogo, M., & Vayda, E. (1998). *The practice of field instruction in social work: Theory and process* (2nd ed.). New York: Columbia University Press.

Boisen, L., & Syers, M. (2004). The integrative case analysis model for linking theory and practice. *Journal of Social Work Education, 40*(2), 205–217.

Campbell, C. (1999). Empowering pedagogy: Experiential education in the social work classroom. *Canadian Social Work Review, 16*(1), 35–48.

Campbell, C. (2002). The search for congruency: Developing strategies for anti-oppressive social work pedagogy. *Canadian Social Work Review, 19*(1), 25–42.

Campbell, C. (2003a). Principles and practices of anti-oppressive pedagogy as represented by Dr. Terri Swice. In W. Shera (Ed.), *Emerging perspectives on anti-oppressive practice* (pp. 393–411). Toronto, ON: Canadian Scholars' Press Inc.

Campbell, C. (2003b). *Struggling for congruency: Principles and practices of anti-oppressive social work pedagogy*. Ottawa, ON: National Library of Canada.

Carniol, B. (2005). *Case critical: Social services and social justice in Canada* (5th ed.). Toronto, ON: Between the Lines.

Chan, K.L., & Chan, C.L.W. (2004). Social workers' conceptions of the relationship between theory and practice in an organizational context. *International Social Work, 47*(4), 543–557.

Dore, M.M. (1994). Feminist pedagogy and the teaching of social work practice. *Journal of Social Work Education, 30*(1), 97–106.

Finch, J.B., Bacon, J., Klassen, D., & Wrase, B.J. (2003). Critical issues in field instruction: Empowerment principles and issues of power and control. In W. Shera (Ed.), *Emerging perspectives on anti-oppressive practice* (pp. 431–446). Toronto, ON: Canadian Scholars' Press Inc.

Finn, J.L., & Jacobson, M. (2003). *Just practice: A social justice approach to social work.* Peosta, IA: Eddie Bowers Publishing Co.

Fook, J., Ryan, M., & Hawkins, L. (1994). Becoming a social worker: Educational implications from preliminary findings of a longitudinal study. *Social Work Education, 13*(2), 5–26.

Fook, J., Ryan, M., & Hawkins, L. (2000). *Professional expertise: Practice, theory and education for working in uncertainty.* London, UK: Whiting & Birch.

George, P., & Marlowe, S. (2005). Structural social work in action: Experiences from rural India. *Journal of Progressive Human Services, 16*(1), 5–24.

Harre Hindmarsh, J. (1992). *Social work oppositions: New graduates' experiences.* Aldershot, UK: Avebury.

Harvey, D. (2004). The principles of dialectics. In W.K.E. Carroll (Ed.), *Critical strategies for social research* (pp. 125–132). Toronto, ON: Canadian Scholars' Press Inc.

Healy, K. (2005). *Social work theories in context: Creating frameworks for practice.* Basingstoke, UK: Palgrave Macmillan.

Hearn, J. (1982). The problem(s) of theory and practice in social work and social work education. *Issues in Social Work Education, 2*(2), 95–118.

Ife, J. (1997). *Rethinking social work: Towards critical practice.* Melbourne, Australia: Longman.

Lam, D. (2004). Problem-based learning: An integration of theory and field. *Journal of Social Work Education, 40*(3), 371–389.

Lee, P. (1982). Some contemporary and perennial problems of relating theory to practice in social work. In R. Bailey & P. Lee (Eds.), *Theory and practice in social work* (pp. 15–45). Oxford, UK: Blackwell.

Lewis, C.H. (2003). Concepts of theory, practice, and integration in social work: The student perspective. *The Journal of Baccalaureate Social Work, 9*(1), 113–130.

Loewenberg, F.M. (1984). Professional ideology, middle range theories and knowledge building for social work practice. *British Journal of Social Work, 14*, 309–322.

Marchant, H. (1986). Gender, systems thinking and radical social work. In H. Marchant & B.E. Wearing (Eds.), *Gender reclaimed: Women in social work* (pp. 14–32). Sydney, Australia: Hale & Iremonger.

Maxwell, J.A. (2005). *Qualitative research design: An interactive approach* (2nd ed., vol. 41). Thousand Oaks, CA: Sage Publications.

McNicoll, P. (2001). Putting social justice on the agenda: Addressing habitual and social barriers. In C.J. Carson, A.S. Fritz, E. Lewis, J.H. Ramey, & D.T. Sugiuchi (Eds.), *Growth and development through group work* (pp. 91–102). New York: The Haworth Press.

McNicoll, P. (2003). Current innovations in social work with groups to address issues of social justice. In N.E. Sullivan, E.S. Mesbur, N.C. Lang, D. Goodman, & L. Mitchell (Eds.), *Social work with groups: Social justice through personal, community, and societal change* (pp. 35–50). New York: Haworth Press.

Moreau, M.J. (1990). Empowerment through advocacy and consciousness-raising: Implications of a structural approach to social work. *Journal of Sociology & Social Welfare, 17*(2), 53–67.

Moreau, M.J., Frosst, S., Frayne, G., Hlyma, M., Leonard, L., & Rowell, M. (1993). *Empowerment II: Snapshots of the structural approach in action.* Ottawa, ON: Carleton University Press.

Moreau, M.J., & Leonard, L. (1989). *Empowerment through a structural approach to social work: A report from practice.* Ottawa, ON: Carleton University.

Mullaly, B. (2007). *The new structural social work* (3rd ed.). Toronto, ON: Oxford University Press.

Nyland, D. (2006). Critical multiculturalism, whiteness, and social work: Towards a more radical view of cultural competence. *Journal of Progressive Human Services, 17*(2), 27–42.

Ollman, B. (2004). Why dialectics? Why now? Or, how to study the communist future inside the capitalist present. In W.K.E. Carroll (Ed.), *Critical strategies for social research* (pp. 133–143). Toronto, ON: Canadian Scholars' Press Inc.

Payne, M. (2005). *Modern social work theory* (3rd ed.). Chicago, IL: Lyceum Books.

Peters, H.I. (2007). *A review of the literature: Mapping the spaces between theory and practice.* Unpublished paper submitted for post-doctoral comprehensive examinations, School of Social Work, University of British Columbia, Vancouver, British Columbia, Canada.

Pilalis, J. (1986). The integration of theory and practice: A re-examination of a paradoxical expectation. *British Journal of Social Work, 16*(1), 79–96.

Pitner, R.O., & Sakamoto, I. (2005). The role of critical consciousness in multicultural practice: Examining how its strength becomes its limitation. *American Journal of Orthopsychiatry, 75*(4), 684–694.

Poulter, J. (2005). Integrating theory and practice: A new heuristic paradigm for social work practice. *Australian Social Work, 58*(2), 199–212.

Prilleltensky, I., & Nelson, G. (2002). *Doing psychology critically: Making a difference in diverse settings.* New York: Palgrave Macmillan.

Razack, N. (1999). Anti-oppressive social work: A model for field education. In G.-Y. Lie & D. Este (Eds.), *Professional social service delivery in a multicultural world* (pp. 311–329). Toronto, ON: Canadian Scholars' Press Inc.

Razack, N. (2002). *Transforming the field: Critical antiracist and anti-oppressive perspectives for the human services practicum.* Halifax, NS: Fernwood Publishing.

Reay, R. (1986). Bridging the gap: A model for integrating theory and practice. *British Journal of Social Work, 16*, 49–64.

Reynolds, B.C. (1942). *Learning and teaching in the practice of social work.* New York: Rinehart & Company.

Reynolds, B.C. (1963). *An uncharted journey: Fifty years of growth in social work.* New York: The Citadel Press.

Robbins, S.R., Chatterjee, P., & Canda, E.R. (1999). Ideology, scientific theory and social work practice. *Families in Society, 80*(4), 374–384.

Rossiter, A.B. (1995). Teaching social work skills from a critical perspective. *Canadian Social Work Review, 12*(1), 9–27.

Rossiter, A.B. (1996). A perspective on critical social work. *Journal of Progressive Human Services, 7*(2), 23–41.

Rossiter, A.B. (2001). Innocence lost and suspicion found: Do we educate for or against social work? *Critical Social Work, 2*(1), 1–7.

Secker, J. (1993). *From theory to practice in social work: The development of social work students' practice.* Aldershot, UK: Ashgate Publishing.

Sheldon, B. (1978). Theory and practice in social work: A re-examination of a tenuous relationship. *British Journal of Social Work, 8*(1), 1–22.

Smith, G. (1971). On everyday theory in social work practice. *Social Work Today, 2*(3), 25–28.

Vayda, E., & Bogo, M. (1991). A teaching model to unite classroom and field. *Journal of Social Work Education, 27*(3), 271–278.

Walden, T., & Brown, L.N. (1985). The integration seminar: A vehicle for joining theory and practice. *Journal of Social Work Education, 21*(1), 13–19.

Wehbi, S. (2003). Beyond the role play: Alternative teaching methods in an anti-oppressive classroom. In W. Shera (Ed.), *Emerging perspectives on anti-oppressive practice* (pp. 363–380). Toronto, ON: Canadian Scholars' Press Inc.

Woodford, M., & Bella, L. (2003). Are we ready to take a stand? Education about heterosexism—fostering anti-oppressive practice. In W. Shera (Ed.), *Emerging perspectives on anti-oppressive practice* (pp. 413–430). Toronto, ON: Canadian Scholars' Press Inc.

Zapf, M.K., Pelech, W., Bastien, B., Bodoy, R., Carriere, J., & Zuk, G. (2003). Promoting anti-oppressive social work education: The University of Calgary's access learning circle model. In W. Shera (Ed.), *Emerging perspectives on anti-oppressive practice* (pp. 447–465). Toronto, ON: Canadian Scholars' Press Inc.

PART 2

The Practice of Structural Social Work

CHAPTER 4

The Societal Context of Child Sexual Abuse

*RICHARD FEEHAN, MAUREEN BOETTCHER,
AND KATHALEEN S. QUINN*

As social workers in the field of child sexual abuse, we have been bringing a structural social work perspective into a clinical setting for 20 years. Typically, this area of practice is assumed to reflect an individualist pathology perspective in which the consequences and causes of child sexual abuse are centred in the internal life of the victim and perpetrator. In contrast, we have been using a model of treating abuse that is anchored in contextual understanding, which allows us to add dimension to our understanding of sexual abuse and to show how the abuse reflects societal factors, which both survivors and perpetrators can identify and master in their own lives. Consistent with the clinical narrative approach to "externalizing the problem" (White & Epston, 1990), our model allows for a strengths orientation to practice, but, more importantly, it introduces a variety of structural understandings to the limited clinical world. This has been particularly important in our work with numerous communities in which multiple incidents of abuse have occurred.

Within this chapter, we argue that structural practice in the field of child sexual abuse requires a process of both looking outward to the external context of our world and inward at the structures of practice itself. To look outward means to attend to the social processes that invite both perpetration and victimization. It requires a practice of deconstructing attitudes and values that contribute to oppression and taking an active role in a collaborative process with our clients in challenging those oppressions and reconstructing a newer and healthy reality. Looking inward means making active choices about how we ourselves will engage in clinical work, and defining that work not as simple one-to-one practice, but as clinical involvement with social institutions, community organizations, and the society in which we live.

As we begin the process of describing our practice, we know from previous experience that it is essential to address a number of "gut" issues that interfere with the reader's ability to be open to hearing our perspective. When introducing our model to students, community groups, and other professionals, we begin by making the declaration that child sexual abuse is not an abnormality in our society. In fact, to the alien observer, it would appear that child sexual abuse is a routine part of our world, at least as much so as most of the other activities we engage in, such as water skiing and bowling. Statistical evidence suggests that one in three girls and one in four boys is sexually abused by the age of 18 years (Committee on Sexual Offences Against Children and Youth, 1984). Given this evidence, we are forced to admit that abuse is not an aberration to the norm, but a common part of the structure of our society. Having declared that child sexual abuse is "normal," however, we do not imply on any level that it is acceptable. The essence of structural social work is that we understand that the origins of problems are routinely rooted in the very structures of society, and that the dominant processes of our world contain within them the oppressions that lead to individual suffering. Acknowledging and analyzing these sufferings, and their root causes, in no way suggests complacency. As structural social workers, whenever we note that many individuals share a collective form of injury, we immediately ask: In what way is the personal political? How are the unconscious social relations of people's everyday lives complicit in the oppression? (See Murray & Hick, Chapter 1.) Just as in the past we have found that poverty, racism, sexism, and the oppression of sexual orientation can be shown to be systemic, so we apply the same analysis to child sexual abuse.

Immediately, of course, many people are offended. Are we saying that perpetrators do not have individual responsibility for their actions or, worse, are we suggesting that victims are somehow part of the problem? Coming solely from an individualist perspective, these questions make a great deal of sense. While we agree that a perpetrator remains 100 percent responsible for his (or, less frequently, her) behaviour and that the victim in no way "deserved" or contributed to their own abuse, we believe that the dichotomization of individual and social realities is both false and dangerous. It does not limit the responsibility of the offender to suggest that the structures of society "invite" offending behaviour, behaviour that they can control, in part, by learning to decline these invitations. It is the traditional individualist philosophy that suggests that a problem originating outside of yourself is not your responsibility. The structuralist approach merges responsibility for the transformation of the person and the society. Furthermore, helping survivors to recognize and disarm the many traps set out before them has the effect of empowerment, not blame. The "problematization" of the dominant social structures (Murray & Hick, Chapter 1) provides us with a focus for intervention that recognizes the humanity of both the survivor and the offender while providing an avenue for personal empowerment and transformation.

When we began our practice, we were all trained as clinical social workers, deeply influenced by mainstream knowledge in the field, including the works of Badgley (Committee on Sexual Offences Against Children and Youth, 1984), Briere (1992), Courtois (1988), Finkelhor and Browne (1985), Gil (1988), Sgroi (1985), and many others. As all the initial therapists in our practice were experienced as child welfare workers, we understood that child sexual abuse is prevalent and has enormous consequences for children and their families. Given our feminist orientation to practice, we understood that the act of child sexual abuse was not simply a sexual act, but an abuse of power. As a result, the way in which the practice was established needed to reflect our understanding of the problems endemic to child abuse. We believed that setting up practice without analyzing our position vis-à-vis the social political structures within which our practice was embedded would be unwise. Many of the therapists we knew—and who we made referrals to as child welfare workers—simply followed a model of providing one-on-one treatment to victims, with the goal of personal healing separate from its context.

As structural social workers, we believe the first "skill" of practice is to conduct an analysis of the "context" of our work. The purpose of this analysis is two-fold. First, we acknowledge that we bring into our practice a personal identity, cultural orientation, and worldview. Examining and remaining conscious of your own values and beliefs is imperative to guard against the client becoming disempowered. Otherwise, the relationship between the social worker and the client simply becomes a reflection of the dominant narratives of power in society. Second, the purpose of our analysis of social context is to draw from it the relevant implications for the structure of our own practice. In the case of child sexual abuse, for example, decisions need to be made about the gender of therapists seeing both male and female clients. Furthermore, the question of treating both males and females in the same facility, and treating both victims and offenders in the same facility, is a reflection of values. If you believe that offenders offend because of individual pathology, and you believe that victims can only view offenders from the perspective of their own vulnerability, you are unlikely to want them in the same building. If, however, you believe that victimization and offending behaviour are both rooted in larger societal structural causes, then integrating the treatment of both may be appropriate. This, of course, means that social workers must have a clear idea of how they will address the issue of emotional safety for the survivors.

In our practice, we decided to work with whole families within which sexual abuse had occurred, and subsequently decided to keep the work together. This is particularly important when working with adolescent offenders who have victimized younger siblings. In these families, rejecting the perpetrator and cutting off all future contact is not typically an option. If we were working with unrelated offenders and victims, it is likely that we would take a different course. It was apparent that our work needed to be simultaneously grounded in the best clinical ideas possible and reflective of social context. To do this, we needed to articulate our model of understanding about how social structures are intimately tied to child sexual abuse. The following section outlines that model, as pictured in Figure 4.1.

Our Model

Through our analysis, three general areas of societal structures were delineated: patriarchal systems, depersonalization within the Western dominant culture, and cultural attitudes toward sex. In the next few pages, we will describe many of the factors we believe to be related to each of these spheres of influence. Consistent with Moreau's emphasis that exploitative social divisions not be placed in hierarchical importance (Moreau & Leonard, 1989), we view the effect of these influences to be complex and unique to each individual. Furthermore, these attributes of our society are not assumed to be directly causal of child sexual abuse, but rather are "invitations" to the possibility of sexual abuse occurring in any given family. In general, it is the intersection of these factors that is associated with the likelihood of the occurrence of child sexual abuse, and the existence of their opposites that is associated with healthy, non-abusive families.

Patriarchal Systems

In our first circle, three aspects of our patriarchal culture are highlighted: gender socialization, devaluation of the feminine, and the assumption of hierarchy as

FIGURE 4.1: Patriarchal systems

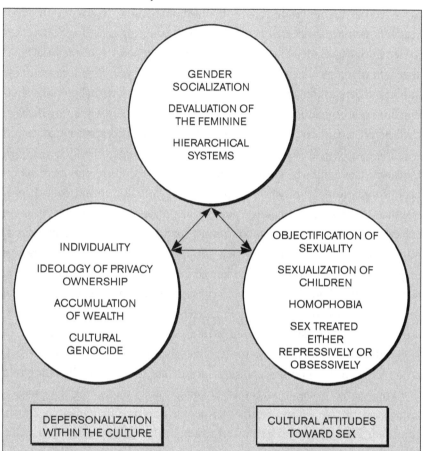

inevitable. For years, authors have argued that the relationship between gender and sexual violence is not accidental and must be considered in any attempt to prevent or decrease acts of sexual violence (Kimmel, 1990; Kokopeli & Lackey, 1990; Miedzian, 1991; Thorne-Finch, 1992). Brannon and David (in Kimmel, 1990, p. 8) identified four axioms of learned masculinity:

- Masculinity is demonstrated by distance from the feminine.
- Masculinity is measured by success and status.
- Men must be confident, secure, reliable, impressive, and utterly cool.
- Men must exude a manly air of violence, aggression, and daring.

These axioms of male gender socialization show us how abuse may be an expression of attempting to achieve the ideal masculinity in a world in which gender is narrowly defined in a binary manner. Distancing oneself from the external feminine allows men to disregard women's personhood. A hierarchical belief system in which men are better than women creates an invitation for men to use or abuse others as they please. Devaluing the feminine internally means shutting down the emotions and the capacity for empathy because they are "female" characteristics. The absence of empathy and poor emotional expression are linked with the offender's ability to overcome internal inhibitions (Finklehor, 1984). Measuring masculinity by status and success ensures that men must be in a competition for power over others. Only one man can be at the top and, as such, only one man can achieve the required power. The power derived from sexual abuse enhances the offender's motivation to abuse, particularly when he is unsuccessful in other areas. The dominant view that men are controlling and aggressive may give strength to both the offender's ability to overcome his inhibitions and to reducing the child's belief in his or her power to seek help. These ideas about masculinity have particular potency in a society that also has strong attitudes linking sexuality and violence (Kokopeli & Lakey, 1990; Stoltenberg, 1989).

Raising women in a society that devalues their gender also creates an invitation for women to be susceptible to sexual abuse. Continually being told that your gender is less than the other gender, and establishing the expectation that your role is to nurture other people's needs rather than your own, contributes to a sense of disempowerment in the face of oppressive behaviour. Furthermore, the belief that you are personally responsible for resolving someone else's feelings—as women often are—has the effect of engendering both a sense of personal culpability for having been abused and the long-lasting effects of the feeling of shame that the abuse was a consequence of your failure to meet your role expectations.

Depersonalization within the Culture

In addition to the invitations that are provided through the structures of our gender socialization, a number of cultural values associated with capitalist structures are also seen to be significant to the existence of child sexual abuse. These include individuality, privacy, accumulation of wealth, and cultural abuse. In our present society, there are strong notions of individuality that suggest that we, as people, derive our value not through our relationships and communal efforts, but through a competitive, zero-sum game in which one person's gain of esteem results in a loss to another. Pitting people against each other in this way invites the idea that it is acceptable to take your needs from someone else, particularly those lower in the hierarchy. This individualistic attitude is typified by a sense of privacy and ownership. When you have ownership of something you may do with it as you wish. Interference from the outside is viewed as a violation of privacy. To the degree to which we view our children as objects of ownership, we believe that we have free rein to do with them as we please. Structurally speaking, respecting the privacy of others frequently results in the absence of protective factors in the face of offending behaviour.

In a capitalist society, the ultimate definition of success is the accumulation of wealth. However, it is not simply having wealth, but having comparatively greater wealth than others that frequently provides a sense of personal success. Individuals who adhere strongly to this value system inevitably live with a sense of failure because someone else always has more than them. The cumulative effect of failures to rise up the hierarchy may be a contributing factor to an offender's motivation to abuse. A system in which your personal value is limited to your role as a "cog in the machine" or the achievement of a paycheque does not support a deeper and more spiritual sense of self.

Depersonalization is further exacerbated for individuals whose cultural or racial identification is not consistent with the dominant culture. Living in a society that either actively rejects your worldview or structurally dismisses your perspective inevitably leads to personal trauma and heightens the invitations to both power-seeking behaviour and vulnerability to others. The strongest example of this cultural factor is the colonization experience of the Aboriginal people in Canada. Through the imposition of oppressive structures, including residential schools, the indiscriminate apprehension of children, and the failure to uphold treaty rights, the Native population of Canada has experienced collective trauma reflected in disproportionate rates of addiction, incarceration, family violence, and child sexual abuse.

Cultural Attitudes toward Sex

The third sphere of influence relevant to child sexual abuse is our cultural attitudes toward sexuality in general and the sexuality of children in particular. Of particular concern is the reduction of sexuality to a tool for profit, and a tool of interpersonal control. In many ways, the social messages regarding sexuality invite people away from viewing sexuality as a relationship defined by consent, equality, respect, trust, and safety (Maltz & Holman, 1987) and toward viewing sexuality as a commodity to be possessed. Sex is frequently portrayed as the ultimate goal of interpersonal interaction. Adolescent males find themselves feeling shame for not having the appropriate number of sexual conquests and the invitation exists to achieve this need, at the expense of other people. When age-appropriate partners are not readily available or willing then adolescents who view themselves, in part, as children may readily turn to younger children without a sense of being an oppressor. This is exacerbated by the fact that, in our society, sexuality is frequently defined in a narrow manner, reflective of the sexuality typical of young dating people. While we would agree that all individuals are sexual from the time of birth, a problem arises when sexuality appropriate to 20-year-olds is attributed to much younger children. Frequent images of sexualized children in the media legitimize children as objects of sexual acts.

The existence of homophobic attitudes in society further contributes to the possibility of child sexual abuse, insofar as it heightens the anxiety of men to prove their heterosexuality. When homosexuality is vilified, the need to avoid being labelled as a homosexual may result in an increased motivation to engage in sexual conquests. Adolescent males frequently have limited opportunities to experiment with sexuality at an age-appropriate level and are vulnerable to opportunities to sexually exploit younger children.

A second significant issue is the problem of members of the public confusing the sexual abuse of children by adults of the same gender with homosexuality. This results in two problems: the unfair attribution of violence to people in the gay/lesbian/bisexual and two-spirited community and a misdirected focus on sexual orientation rather than on the sexual abuse of power.

The absence of a strong, healthy attitude toward sexuality in our society is a further structural failure leading to child sexual abuse. Frequently, sexuality is treated either oppressively or obsessively. On the one hand, sex may be viewed as a sin, shutting down healthy discussion and creating a sense of secrecy that increases the possibility that sexual activity will reflect the desires of the individual with the greatest power. On the other hand, sex may be viewed obsessively, focusing on sexual experience as the ultimate goal of all human interaction, using sex to sell music, movies, and soft drinks, stripping it of its more complex aspects, and providing heightened confusion and stress, leading to increased vulnerability for both perpetration and victimization.

Implications for Practice

When patriarchal systems, depersonalization within the culture, and cultural attitudes toward sexuality are viewed as structures in society that invite the possibility of abuse, the implications are clear. Each of the factors that can be identified within this model has a direct application to work with both victims and offenders, as well as for families, communities, and society at large. Society and individuals can change their relationships and ideas about how we socialize our children, how we value success, and how we express our sexuality. Mullaly (2002) stated that the levels of a social structure are interdependent and mutually reinforcing, and that change is required within three spheres: the substructural level, the social institutional level, and the level of social relationships. More commonly, these levels are referred to as the personal, organizational, and cultural levels (Dominelli, 2002). In this next section, we will look at the particular skills and activities that can be employed to address each of these levels. First, we will address work with both victims and offenders of child sexual abuse. Then our focus will shift to work with institutions such as group homes, foster parents, and the child welfare system. Finally, practice at the level of social relationships will be addressed, with an emphasis on working with large communities.

Structural Practice with Victims of Child Sexual Abuse

The primary application of structural practice with victims of child sexual abuse is clinical engagement. This may be a surprising statement to people who imagine that structural work can only be performed at the policy or community development levels. However, one of the central goals of structural social work is "to alleviate the negative effects on people of an exploitative and alienating social order" (Mullaly, 2002, p. 124), and much of this work is done at the substructural level through critical consciousness-raising and psycho-educational work. A number of suggestions for "radical" therapy exist in the literature (Barnoff & Coleman, 2007; Dominelli, 2002; Baines, 2007). In each of these models, practitioners are instructed in breaking down the rigid barriers between the three levels of work to create a holistic practice. At the clinical level, it is essential that clients are supported in deconstructing, resisting, challenging, and reconstructing the structures of society that affect them (Fook, 2002). In Chapter 1, Murray and Hick identified five practices of structural social work that can all take place in the clinical setting. All of these practices are reflected in clinical work when the focus is on re-defining clients' experiences with an emphasis on claiming personal power and defining the self in a manner different to the one invited within the arena of unconscious social relations. Clients work in the client–worker relationship, in groups with others who have had similar experiences, and within their families and communities to transform both themselves and the structural invitations that reproduce trauma.

In our practice, clients are introduced to the three-circle model of patriarchal systems, depersonalization within the culture, and objectification of sexuality. Structural practice is neatly coupled with clinical practice. Our structural understanding provides the clinical work with a specific direction and reminds the therapist that their work must be guided by an understanding of the context of abuse as much as the details of the abuse. At the same time a great demand is placed on the clinical skill set, because it is very important that the structuralist themes be handled in the work in a manner that does not either re-victimize the client for not sharing our structural analysis, or turn the therapy into a positivist pursuit of the absolute truth from the structuralist perspective. Following from a feminist orientation, introduction of the themes must recognize that each of the ideas may have greater or lesser relevance to an individual client, and that no one truth, particularly one brought to the session by the therapist, is the correct one. For many clients, particular themes will simply not be true, at least at this time or in this situation.

We have found that a narrative (White & Epston, 1990) orientation to practice is highly consistent with a structuralist perspective. People who have been victimized have frequently had created for them a dominant story of personal blame, deep shame, and powerlessness. The skill of inviting alternatives to the dominant story of sexual abuse is in part accomplished by introducing the client to a structuralist understanding of the invitations to abuse in the dominant culture. Therapeutically, this involves the narrative strategies of externalization and validating alternative client narratives. For example, when addressing the issue of patriarchy, our children's groups are often asked to make collages from magazines depicting images of masculinity and femininity found in the dominant culture.

This is then followed by discussions and games focused on identifying and challenging the rules and assumptions associated with each gender. The goals of our groups are fully consistent with the structuralist belief that people who are oppressed by the structures need to gain support from each other and develop personal skills in identifying and challenging power. For example, one of our groups had the following goals: reduce feelings of isolation and stigmatization, recognize the right to control over one's own body and life, develop a level of comfort with issues relating to one's own body and sexuality, learn to trust oneself, become knowledgeable about sexual abuse and healthy sexuality, increase self-esteem, increase awareness of societal attitudes toward men and women, develop direct and clear communication, and learn to care for oneself. While these goals will be familiar to anyone working in the area of child sexual abuse, the manner in which these concepts are introduced and handled in the group helps to identify it as structuralist work. Children in our groups soon learn that we are not blaming them for not having particular skills. Rather, they identify these skills as something that can be learned to assist in recognizing when the external world is inviting either victimization or perpetration, and develop the ability to decline those invitations. Taking this perspective has some particular advantages. Children who learn to recognize the problems as external to themselves have a greater likelihood of separating themselves from the blame, shame, and stigma associated with abuse. In addition, as they develop the skills to identify these invitations, and to decline them, they develop a mastery that helps them overcome powerlessness, which is an essential part of the process of preventing a child going from "victim to victimizer" (Ryan, 1989).

Being able to identify a variety of oppressive, but non-sexually abusive behaviours—typically referred to as grooming behaviours—allows a child and his or her parents to develop strategies of safety, which can be addressed far before actual sexual touching occurs. This is quite important when a child is likely to have ongoing contact with the individual who committed the sexual abuse, such as an older sibling.

Structural Practice with Perpetrators of Sexual Abuse

In much the same way as with the survivors of sexual abuse, work with people who commit sexual abuse is defined by the belief in structural invitations and is resolved, in part, by locating the source of oppression in the structures that invite it. To some degree, this eliminates the simplistic binary understanding of oppressor and oppressed that is opposed by Tester (see Murray & Hick, Chapter 1, p. 19). Following from the work of Alan Jenkins (1990) and the narrative therapists, our adolescent offenders are taught to identify the structural invitations that act as "restraints" to the development of healthy dominant stories. Again, the specific intervention begins with introducing the three-circle model to our clients and spending a great deal of time processing the ideas. A variety of games and activities have been developed to address each of the ideas in the model. For example, younger children are assisted in developing a board game in which a variety of articles must be obtained. Each of the articles represents an aspect of a final goal. Children seeking to become a knight might need to obtain a horse, helmet, shield, mantle, and so on. In order to obtain the articles, children proceed around the board (which they have created) and answers question cards about invitations to offending behaviour. Gathering the articles and becoming a knight is part of the creation of a new understanding and a new set of behaviours.

Again, it is important to address the question of whether acknowledging structural invitations to abuse is a way of avoiding personal responsibility for abuse. It is clear in our work with adolescents that simply demanding they take full responsibility leads to feelings of guilt and shame, which typically exacerbate the cycle of offending behaviour. If, instead, we can help children to identify that they are responsible for allowing the "restraint" of abusiveness and invite them to argue for a non-violent relationship, then we succeed in stopping the oppression of both the victim and the victimizer. They are indeed responsible because they have not identified the structural invitations and taken responsibility to prevent the influence of these invitations on their lives. Identifying these external aspects of perpetration increases offenders' mastery and increases the opportunity for them to take personal responsibility. Clearly this is not the only work done with adolescent offenders, but it is the piece of work relevant to our discussion of structuralist social work practice.

Structuralist Practice with Child Sexual Abuse on the Community Level

In addition to these ideas on how a structuralist understanding can be implemented within the clinical context of treating children who have been sexually abused, it is essential that social workers must also reach beyond the therapeutic realm to the pursuit of change in the larger environment. Introducing structural thinking into the one-on-one work, the group work, and the family work is only the beginning. Within our private practice, we have always felt it important that we have significant engagement with the community systems surrounding our clients and their families, and furthermore that we have a significant role in the transformation of society itself.

Doherty and Beaton (2000) outlined five levels of community engagement possible for clinical social workers. In this model, social workers can work to progress from a minimal level of involvement to full participation in transformative community associations. Community work involves proactive connections with community systems, which means that the structural social worker pursues a relationship with the child welfare system, the hospitals, the policing system, and the schools to develop positive protocols for the handling of child sexual abuse cases. In the complex realm of interacting systems, it is quite possible for children to be re-victimized by a loss of personal power and voice over their own treatment. In part, this involves working with community systems to ensure gaps are filled and procedures are predictable and supportive. It also means we have attempted to extend our structural understanding by providing professional development opportunities to our peers in the community and workshops to community groups throughout the year.

Particularly in settings with staff members who are expected to follow internal protocols, we have found a tendency for the rules to reflect the needs of the provider rather than the residents. The circle that we refer to as "depersonalization within the culture" is particularly relevant here. If the children with whom we are working have consistent experiences of disempowerment in their homes, then not much of what we work on in therapy will be particularly useful. On the other hand, if the children do hear a message of empowerment, but the institution is not part of the overall work, then you may be setting children up for conflict and punishment. It is important that childcare staff and foster parents are included in the structural analysis and every attempt is made to create a living environment consistent with the empowerment and transformational message of structural social work. For example, in one of our workshops with childcare staff, they were able to identify that a new rule that forced adolescents to take a bath at only one time during the day, rather than as they wanted to throughout the day, was depersonalizing.

In addition to the dissemination of our structural understanding, a number of our activities have been focused on providing an alternative for each of the structural invitations to abuse. For example, one of the authors has produced a newsletter entitled "Man to Man," which addresses new definitions of masculinity. As well, workshops have been provided through the local Personal Development Centre called "Men and Self-Esteem." These positive activities are not seen as an adjunct to the clinical work, but as a fulfillment of our structural approach.

In the First Nations community, it is essential that clinical work is supported by the establishment of relationships with chiefs, council, and community elders. In reserve communities, sexual abuse is often significantly widespread and affects not only the individuals involved, but also the community, which often shares a common sense of shame, guilt, and powerlessness. Providing opportunities for the community to come together to learn about structural invitations to sexual abuse and to develop community-level responses is an essential part of social work practice and is an important part of differentiating our practice from other counselling professions. The focus of these workshops is on a variety of pieces of information that enhance the community's understanding of both the issue of sexual abuse and the tools for responding to abuse. In the many workshops we provide, we introduce the idea of analyzing context for structural invitations to abuse, we teach clinical models of understanding sexual abuse, and we provide opportunities for community members to have input into developing action plans for community-level responses.

Furthermore, providing services close to or in the communities of concern, rather than requiring individuals to leave their community to seek help, further enhances the sense that the community is a place of support and healing. In our practice, therapists traveled on a weekly basis to small towns, and on one occasion, a team member was hired to move to a northern community for a year to deal locally with a situation in which many children were abused by a priest. Ultimately, it is critical that we support the shift toward empowering Aboriginal people to work within, and on behalf of, their own communities.

Conclusion

Structural social work requires practitioners to both analyze and respond to oppressive structures in the larger context and to create intentional structures within their work. These tasks begin long before you actually engage in work with service users. Sitting down, before you open your clinic doors, to carefully delineate the specific ways in which the oppressive structures of society have a direct effect on you as a practitioner and on your clients is essential. In our work, we have outlined a number of factors that we believe contribute to the existence of abuse and to the extent of harm created by sexual abuse. Having a clear understanding of these factors affects both the choices we make in engaging our clients, and the ultimate goals of therapy. Additionally, being a structuralist practitioner demands that our work is not limited to one-to-one practice. To be a clinical social worker in this field also means to be a public educator, a community developer, and an advocate for social transformation.

References

Baines, D. (2007). *Doing anti-oppressive practice: Building transformative politicized social work*. Halifax, NS: Fernwood Publishing.

Barnoff, L., & Coleman, B. (2007). Strategies for integrating anti-oppression principles: Perspectives from feminist agencies. In D. Baines (Ed.), *Doing anti-oppressive practice: Building transformative, politicized social work* (pp. 31–49). Halifax, NS: Fernwood Publishing.

Briere, J. (1992). *Child abuse trauma: Theory and treatment of the lasting effects*. Thousand Oaks, CA: Sage Publications.

Committee on Sexual Offences Against Children and Youth (Badgley). (1984). *Sexual offences against children*. Ottawa, ON: Department of Supply and Services.

Courtois, C. (1988). *Healing the incest wound*. New York: Norton.

Doherty, W., & Beaton, J. (2000). Family therapy, community and civic renewal. *Family Process 39*(2), 149–161.

Dominelli, L. (2002). *Anti-oppressive social work theory and practice*. Basingstoke, UK: Palgrave Macmillan.

Finkelhor, D. (1984). *Child sexual abuse: New theory and research*. New York: Free Press.

Finklehor, D., & Browne, A. (1985). The traumatic impact of child sexual abuse: A conceptualization. *American Journal of Orthopsychiatry, 55,* 530–541.

Fook, J. (2002). *Social work: Critical theory and practice*. London, UK: Sage Publications.

Gil, E. (1988). *Treatment of adult survivors of sexual abuse*. New York: Launch Publishing.

Jenkins, A. (1990). Invitations to responsibility. Adelaide, Australia: Dulwich Centre Publications.

Kimmel, M. (1990). *Men confront pornography*. New York: Meridian.

Kokopeli, B., & Lackey, G. (1990). More power than we want: Masculine sexuality and violence. In F. Abbott (Ed.), *Men and intimacy* (pp. 8–15). Berkeley, CA: Crossing Press.

Maltz, W., & Holman, B. (1987). *Incest and sexuality: A guide to understanding and healing.* Lanham, MD: Lexington Books.

Miedzian, M. (1991). *Boys will be boys: Breaking the link between masculinity and violence.* New York: Doubleday.

Moreau, M.J., & Leonard, L. (1989). *Empowerment through a structural approach to social work: A report from practice.* Ottawa, ON: Carleton University.

Mullaly, B. (2002). *Challenging oppression: A critical social work approach.* Toronto, ON: Oxford University Press.

Ryan, G. (1989). Victim to victimizer: Rethinking victim treatment. *Journal of Interpersonal Violence, 4,* 325–341.

Sgroi, S. (1985). *Handbook of clinical intervention in child sexual abuse.* New York: Simon and Schuster.

Stoltenberg, J. (1989). *Refusing to be a man: Essays on sex and justice.* New York: Meridian.

Thorne-Finch, R. (1992). *Ending the silence: The origins and treatment of male violence against women.* Toronto, ON: University of Toronto Press.

White, M., & Epston, D. (1990). *Narrative means to therapeutic ends.* New York: Norton.

Addressing the Immediate Needs of Service Users as Part of Fundamental Structural Change:
Complementary or Contradictory Processes?

DAWN HEMINGWAY, CLARIE JOHNSON, AND BRENDA ROLAND

Early in 1984, after unsuccessful efforts to find help for a family member who disclosed childhood sexual abuse, a local woman placed an advert in a Prince George newspaper to see if others were grappling with similar situations. The response was overwhelming and, with three founding members taking the lead, the Survivors of Sexual Abuse Society (now Surpassing Our Survival [SOS] Society) was born. Although there was little funding and no professionally trained staff, SOS had strong experiential leadership and substantial support from the local community, and quickly became a northern voice for those concerned about sexual violence. From the outset, the organization sought to change people's lives by providing direct services while organizing for policy and political change. Situated in northern British Columbia, far away from the centres of political power, it was not surprising that self-advocacy and community activism were considered essential components to meet the needs of northern residents. Although not labelled as such, SOS operated from a structural, transformative perspective before anyone with formal social work education was part of the organization. Similarly, SOS was influenced by the women's movement of the day, but had no explicitly articulated feminist perspective. Principles that guided its work were very much in sync with structural social work, as depicted in Part 1 of this text and described by Moreau (1979, 1990), Mullaly (2002, 2007), Carniol (1992, 2005), Fook (1993), and other structural educators and practitioners. This character of SOS is reflected in its mission statement and goals, which read in part:

> We advocate for societal change that does not tolerate oppression, exploitation or violence in any form ... [we seek] to develop and strengthen

effective partnerships with organizations whose vision it is to end violence in all its forms and work at a local, provincial and national level to improve social policy and promote social justice ... (Surpassing Our Survival Society, 2007)

SOS is continually challenged to uphold its structural perspective within a social and health-care system that tends to pathologize individuals rather than look to systemic roots and solutions. This chapter provides glimpses of the day-to-day undertakings of SOS, including aspects of our organizational development, our role and relationship with the broader community in seeking to create a more just and equitable society, and how a structural perspective is central to working with individuals who access SOS services. Ongoing efforts to address immediate needs as an integral part of creating conditions for longer-term structural change reveal potentially contradictory and complementary aspects of our practice. As the authors of this account, we wish to acknowledge that each of us was involved in the women's movement and addressing sexual violence long before completing any formal social work education. Decades of community and political organizing provide the backdrop for the work we undertake today and for the story we are about to tell.

Organizational Leadership and Staffing

In the 1980s, without a university north of Vancouver, degreed social workers in northern British Columbia were a minority and most practicsed in established government agencies such as the Ministry for Children and Families. Non-profit community organizations relied heavily on staff without much post-secondary education to organize, implement, and sustain their work. SOS was no exception. Both staff and society board members tended to be community organizers with a feminist, social activist perspective and/or direct experience with sexual violence. Over the years, new educational standards for staffing became prerequisites to access operational funding. These educational requirements, coupled with opening the University of Northern British Columbia (and its School of Social Work), led to a shift in staffing at SOS with social work graduates playing a pivotal role. The nature of the board also shifted to one that now consists of a wide range of community members and professionals, with and without direct experience with sexual violence. Like their predecessors, these staff and board members seek to provide critical services in ways that meet immediate needs, but that do so in a context that both acknowledges and strives to lay groundwork for fundamental structural change.

Transition in the makeup of the staff and board brought to the fore some delicate questions and initiated discussion with respect to the role of, and necessity for, professional training, experiential knowledge, and grassroots organizing skills. How do professionalism, social activism, or experience with sexual violence fit with a structural, transformative perspective? Would introducing formal social work educational requirements undermine the activist nature of this grassroots organization? There were (and continue to be) multiple and complex views. Is direct experience with sexual violence essential for working in this field or can others also work effectively? Is the critical theory and thinking that is foundational to structural social work education a requirement for genuinely progressive practice? Can a profession with a history of providing band-aid solutions and seeking to "make the system work" truly be the harbinger of structural change? Ultimately, the experience and practice of SOS came to embrace a breadth of experiential and clinical knowledge and education across staff and board members, with an implicit structural perspective (captured in our mission, guiding principles, and goals) as the glue that binds everyone and all aspects of work together. Potentially divisive approaches to tackling sexual violence have become more complementary than contradictory.

Not surprisingly, name changes were part of this development process. In 1988, in order to better reflect the breadth of services offered, the Survivors of Sexual Abuse Society became the Prince George Sexual Assault Centre Society. More recently, in 2007, the centre became the Surpassing Our Survival Society to capture the significance of moving beyond survival.

Seeking Structural Change: Exemplars of Community Practice

From its inception, SOS has embraced and practised the philosophy of "the personal is political." Work with both adults and children and all aspects of service provision at SOS are anchored in identifying and acknowledging power imbalances that lead to sexual violence and the socio-economic structures that perpetuate this violence. To be true to structural practice with service users, SOS is inescapably enmeshed in the broader change processes within northern

British Columbia and beyond. These involvements are not "one of" or "add-ons," but are integral to the day-to-day life and work of the organization. The following are representative highlights of this work.

Take Back the Night/Take Back the Highway

Our commitment to structural change is reflected in unrelenting public education work linked to collective action. One of the most visible manifestations is the leadership SOS provides in organizing Take Back the Night (TBTN), an internationally recognized event in which women and children march through the streets to highlight their right to live without fear of violence, harassment, and sexual assault. An annual event in Prince George since 1994, TBTN addresses realities and issues of the time—from poverty to international solidarity, to honouring elders, grandparents, and foremothers, to highlighting violent deaths of northern women.

An exciting development in this work was the 2005 launch of Take Back the Highway (TBTH). SOS, organizing the Prince George component, joined with First Nations and community organizations across the North to demand action concerning women (mostly Aboriginal) who had been murdered on, or gone missing from, Highway 16 between Prince Rupert and the Alberta border—the Highway of Tears. Marches, dancing, drumming, and prayers took place simultaneously on the highway near Burns Lake, Hazelton, Houston, Kitimat, Prince George, Prince Rupert, Smithers, Terrace, Fort St. James, and Vanderhoof. This powerful public awareness campaign (Lheidli T'enneh First Nation, Carrier Sekani Family Services, Carrier Sekani Tribal Council, & Prince George Native Friendship Centre, 2006, pp. 10, 12), coupled with the 2006 Highway of Tears Symposium and ongoing work in local communities, made outrage about the missing women so visible that it could no longer be ignored. The RCMP began to use a new computer database to examine possible links between unsolved cases; a private investigator became involved; the number of confirmed missing women doubled from nine to 18; politicians began to pay attention, and some attended TBTH; government funding (albeit a very limited amount) was provided for a Highway of Tears Coordinator; and the Highway of Tears became known internationally (Woodard, 2005). But there remains a long way to go.

Taking on a Powerful Public Official

A provincial court judge in Prince George who used the power of his position to sexually assault Aboriginal girls aged 12–16 years was identified because of the incredible strength and courage of his young victims. Despite their own unbelievably difficult circumstances trying to survive on the streets of Prince George, they came forward and shared their horrific experiences at the hands of Judge David Ramsey. Several years of confidential and behind the scenes work ultimately resulted in charges being laid. During Ramsey's trial and sentencing, SOS provided a supportive presence in the community. In collaboration with the Violence Against Women in Relationships Committee, we initiated a local emergency meeting to provide a community-wide response and press release to address the violence and imbalance of power that Ramsey's actions represented. Our collaborative response was made widely available not only to the media, but also via email listservs and other community networks. The initiative of these young girls laid the groundwork for a far more open community discussion about sexual violence and provided the momentum for other young women facing abuse to come forward.

Advocating for Optional Third-Party Reporting

Victims of sexual violence can be reluctant to report their experiences to police because of fears that they will not be believed, will be blamed or judged, or will face retaliation from the perpetrator. However, many women who access support services and choose not to report the violence they experience speak about being haunted, wondering if another woman will later be sexually assaulted by the same man responsible for their attack.

Third-party reporting (TPR) allows adults who experience sexual assault to anonymously report their offenders. A third party, such as SOS, collects the information and provides it to police, who can then review the information, create assailant profiles, look for any trends, and take whatever actions might be appropriate. SOS has practised TPR on an informal basis since it was founded in 1984. After years of development, a TPR questionnaire and protocols with local RCMP were launched in Prince George in September 2005 during Sexual Violence Awareness Month, and training for service providers began with SOS playing a leadership role. As one of only a few communities in British Columbia that had an established protocol and practice of TPR, the Prince George process was an initial exemplar used in the process of developing a standardized province-wide process. SOS joined with the Women's Safety Program subcommittee of the British Columbia Association of Specialized Victim Assistance and Counselling Programs to create a provincial template, launched in spring 2008 (Community Coordination for Women's Safety, 2008). This template facilitates all British Columbia law enforcement agencies in collecting and entering data in a standardized way that allows comparisons and profiling across the province. It is hoped that this province-wide initiative will enhance the capacity for police to identify serial perpetrators much earlier in the investigative process than happened, for example, with the missing women on the Downtown Eastside of Vancouver. We hope it will also contribute to solving the cases of women missing and murdered along Highway 16. In addition to helping identify and indict an offender, women themselves have disclosed that writing down exactly what happened to them can be therapeutic.

Quilting: The Power of Storytelling through Art

During the time of the Pinochet dictatorship in Chile (1973–1990), quilting became a way for women to gather for support and comfort, tell the stories of disappearing loved ones and of pain and hunger, and form a visual expression of resistance to the oppression of the Pinochet regime (Agosin,1996). Inspired by these Chilean Arpilleras, the Children's Program Coordinator at SOS initiated a women and children's quilting project in conjunction with the TBTN march in 2002. This ongoing project, which began as a means of non-traditional therapeutic self-expression, has become much more. Quilting workshops and displays have become an integral part of resistance to oppression and organizing for social justice within our community. Four beautiful, powerful quilts with dozens of squares have been completed and are now displayed at SOS and a local women's shelter. These quilts are a representation not only of the experience of sexual violence and the suffering endured, but also of hopes and dreams for a future without violence.

We hope these few examples provide a sense of SOS's involvement in and contribution to local community work involving sexual violence. The totality of these involvements inform, and are informed by, the direct services SOS provides to those who have experienced sexual violence.

Linking Immediate Needs to Structural Change: Exemplars of Practice with Individuals

The following themes highlight some of the education provided and interventions utilized when working with individuals who seek assistance at SOS. Each provides a sense of how work at SOS is informed by and inseparable from a structural perspective.

Identifying and Speaking to Mother-Blaming

Caregivers accompanying children to our counselling services are often mothers, guilt-ridden and blaming themselves for their child's victimization. Self-blame is further perpetuated by the judgment of others. Mothers have reported being asked by professionals, including child protection workers, doctors, teachers, police, and counsellors, questions such as, "Where were you?" "Why did you have a male babysitter?" and "How did you not know?"

Through structural social work practice, SOS challenges the wider cultural expectation and unfounded belief that mothers always know what is happening for and to their children. Research indicates that in the vast majority of child sexual abuse cases, mothers do not know about the abuse (Barnett, Miller-Perrin, & Perrin, 1997; Breckenridge & Baldry, 1997; Caplan, 1989), making it essential to acknowledge just how effectively the offender's schema for secrecy is maintained. By blaming the mother we alienate her, lose sight of offender accountability, and obscure other significant influences such as poverty, patriarchy, and racism. Insight into mother-blaming and its systemic roots helps provide a context for mothers to better understand the situation they and their children face and can assist them in taking the steps necessary to move forward.

During one intake session, a mother was trying to be very stoic and talked about feeling guilty for not protecting her daughter and feeling inferior because she did not know how to be supportive or how to "fix things." The counsellor provided the comparison about how in other realms of our lives, whether it is an illness or a mechanical problem with our vehicle, we access doctors or mechanics and we are not considered inferior or lacking in any way; we just require a particular skill set. To address the feelings of guilt, the counsellor used a drawing of a queen's cloak and the analogy of wearing a "cloak of responsibility." The mother then wrote out all the reasons she felt responsible for her child's victimization. The counsellor and mother discussed the covert and insidious nature of mother-blaming and how it contributes to the heaviness of the cloak. After exploring the elements of her daughter's disclosure, the mother was able to identify that her guilt did not have sufficient logic and that ultimately the alleged offender was responsible for the abuse and the betrayal of her trust. The mother wept with relief as she ripped up the drawing of her "cloak of responsibility."

Victim-Blaming: Where Does Responsibility Lie?

Victims of property crime may be frequently questioned about their failure to take necessary precautions: "Don't you have an alarm system?" or "Were your doors locked?" With sexual violence, the level of scrutiny is such that the onus is entirely on the victim to prove her victimization and face the court of judgment about her character. Is she moral or immoral? Was she in the wrong place at the wrong time or did she "ask for it"? Myths rooted in the oppression and exploitation of women declare that sexual assault is inevitable and part of the natural order of things; that women are assaulted only because they have poor judgment, put themselves in dangerous situations, follow a particular lifestyle, wear a short skirt, or have a drink or two. Even implementation of the 1983 Rape Shield Law (Sutton, 1999), intended to restrict court testimony regarding a woman's sexual history or character, has failed to halt accusations and innuendo that blamed the victim. Women continue to be silenced.

A vital piece of the work at SOS is to lay the groundwork for an environment in which critical thinking can develop and myths can be exposed and dispelled. In one-on-one and group sessions we talk with women about victim-blaming and walk with them through their own experiences. We talk about the steps forward that have been taken: the young women who stood up to Judge Ramsey; the option of TPR; how quilting can give a voice to victims; the impact of TBTN and TBTH. We also acknowledge the challenges still to be faced, such as recent scrutiny of the actions of the women missing on Highway 16. After it came to light that a number of these young women had been hitchhiking, comments were made that "… if they would just quit hitchhiking," instead of "… if killers would just stop murdering women." The onus continues to be placed on women to restrict their behaviour in the false hope that behaviour change will somehow put an end to the sexual violence they experience. Yet we know that systemic racism, tacit acceptance of the inevitability of violence against women, the feminization of poverty, and the lack of adequate and affordable transportation are but a few of the underlying problems contributing to the disappearance and murder of northern women—not the action of hitchhiking.

Challenging Silence and Misconceptions

To address the silent nature of sexual violence from a structural perspective is complex and involves much more than just working with the victims. First it is necessary, at a societal level, to educate (e.g., Sexual Violence Awareness Month) and acknowledge that such abuse exists, that it is a problem, and, further, that fictitious and contrived beliefs can perpetuate and facilitate violence with sex as a weapon. Only a fraction of the abuse happening to adults and especially to children in our community is visible via the news media and other statistical sources. What is reported often continues to profile misconceptions and especially "stranger danger," despite research clearly indicating that both children and adults are most likely to be sexually abused by someone known to them (Ogrodnik, 2007).

We are a confusing society with seemingly hypocritical views of sex and sexuality. Although we are daily bombarded with toxic and degrading images of women and young girls being sexually objectified through television, movies, music, advertisements, and so on, there remains, for example, a level of hesitancy about providing children with age-appropriate sex education. Sexist elements in the media become commercial commodities that influence accepted cultural standards (Bergeron & Bissonnette, 2007; Jhally & Kilbourne, 2002). Practice at SOS encourages those who access our services to look at the media through a new lens, as well as challenging other service providers and the general public to do the same.

Two examples highlight this work. The first involves a 10-year-old girl who was making a collage to depict her feelings prior to, during, and after disclosing her abuse. While flipping through magazines for images and words, she came across an advertisement for scented tampons that had a sample of the scent attached. She smelled it, wrinkled up her nose and passed the sample to the counsellor. After smelling it, the counsellor looked at her and said, "I wouldn't want my vagina to smell like that." The child burst into a fit of giggles because talking about "S-E-X" was embarrassing. After collecting herself, she said, "Neither would I." The remainder of the session continued with critiquing advertisements and discussing how the media can make girls and women feel bad about themselves and their bodies.

The second example involves SOS responding to a newspaper article that focused attention on a picture of young women having a good time at a teen video dance party. The picture evoked reader letters and comments with regard to how these young women were dressed and implied that they were "inviting" sexual advances. SOS responded with a letter that stated in part:

> When do you start holding the media accountable for objectification of the female body and the creation of fashions that teens will emulate? When do we begin to demand high profile individuals be leaders in being positive fashion role models for female youth, instead of expecting our youth to tread through unspoken rules of societal stereotypes about what a woman is or is not, what is "easy" or "trashy" and what constitutes "asking for it"? … When do we stop blaming girls, teens and women? (Prince George Sexual Assault Centre, 2006)

This one letter completely changed the tone of the discussion from one that critiqued and blamed the young women to one that began to examine the accountability of the media and broader society.

Trying to Cope: Survival Mechanisms

SOS works with a wide range of adults from all walks of life who have experienced sexual violence. Many feel intense shame—that they are dirty, that nobody should (or does) care about them, or that they have no value. To numb these feelings, or at least cope with them, some turn to substance abuse or other forms of self-harm, such as eating disorders or cutting themselves. From a structural, feminist lens we seek to better understand these behaviours as survival mechanisms used to cope with the effects of sexual violence. It is not surprising that sometimes women find themselves unable to function, to follow through with getting assistance from potential support services, or to attend appointments once made. Too often we expect those who have experienced sexual violence to fit into established programs, procedures, and a nine-to-five work day without fully taking into account the specific situations they face. SOS staff work together with these women to find a way forward, always beginning from the particularities of each individual woman's circumstances. We meet women in coffee shops, advocate for transportation, are available after hours, go to a woman's home if requested, and have met teens at the high-school counsellor's office.

Poverty can amplify the exceedingly difficult situation already faced by victims of sexual violence. For some women, even beginning to think about healing themselves and their family is a foreign concept when they don't have a roof over their heads or food for their children. One woman and her children walked for 45 minutes (one way) in –40°C weather to access services. Yet, when SOS staff approached the income-assistance office to seek travel funding, a disturbing comment was overheard: "Even if we give them extra money, they don't use it for transportation anyway." Are we really in a position to judge if a struggling mother uses money allocated to transportation for another purpose? The SOS staff member took time to talk with the financial assistance worker about her comment and ultimately received the funding requested.

Women who have left violent relationships or who are trying to overcome other forms of sexual violence have a lot to deal with, and those who access services at SOS face the additional challenges of living in rural, remote, or northern communities that tend to have fewer supports and services available. These daily encounters with living examples of the feminization of poverty are a huge impetus for SOS to continue and escalate its work for structural change, but also to fight for daily reforms to improve the lives of women now. To this end, we have become strong advocates for and with our clients. We have successfully advocated with elected officials to have hydro and water services restored to a mother who left a relationship because her teenage daughter was being abused and, in the process, lost her job. When a man from an outlying area was without access to sexual assault services in his own town, and also without the funds to travel to Prince George, we advocated for him to access the health authority bus service, normally restricted for medical appointments only. We have supported a woman in her self-advocacy efforts to receive services from SOS because she knows the counsellor in her own town and wishes anonymity.

What about Men?

There tends to be a focus on women as the victims of sexual violence, and this chapter is no exception. This reflects the reality that most victims continue to be women (Statistics Canada, 2007). However, both women and men are sexually assaulted and SOS has always had a men's program to provide services for male youth and adult men who have been sexually abused as children or sexually assaulted as adults. A structural social work perspective is imperative to break down the barriers that prevent men from giving voice to their experiences of sexual violence. Freeing this voice requires challenging dominant, rigid gender roles that suggest men can't be victims of sexual violence, only perpetrators. SOS plays an active role within the community to raise awareness of male victims of sexual violence, including working to increase access to services for men. We also have a children's program that includes both girls and boys. At the same time, it is important to recognize that sexual violence is a gendered crime. The reality is not that men are not victims of sexual violence; it is that they are almost always the perpetrators of sexual violence against both women and men (Ogrodnik 2007; Statistics Canada 2007). Although SOS does not provide direct services to offenders, we advocate for and work with other community agencies to ensure that offenders receive the support necessary to take responsibility for their actions and move ahead with their lives in a positive way.

Our community has always elected to have a women-and-children-only TBTN march. Men are respectfully asked to understand the need for women-only space or events, but are encouraged to show their support in other ways. A local group, Men Against Violence Against Women, advertises the event and hosts the post-march reception. Other men show support by providing childcare so that partners, sisters, and mothers can participate. We are often challenged by those who consider our approach a form of reverse discrimination. But SOS, as well as other organizations on the planning committee, maintains that what is important to remember is that by virtue of the real and continuing power differences in society between men and women as groups, the occasional exclusion of men by women has a very different meaning than the historical exclusion of women by men. At the same time, we recognize that sexual violence is fundamentally rooted in a capitalist, patriarchal system and that structural change is necessary in order to create an environment in which all human beings are valued and sexual violence no longer has a place.

Victim to Warrior

In the 1970s, a second wave of feminists initiated a vital public conversation about sexual violence. The efforts of early-day sexual assault survivors in northern British Columbia increased social awareness, reduced trauma for other survivors, and were the harbinger of essential prevention and intervention programs still to come. Along with increased consciousness of the problem came the provision of preventative and clinical services as well as a discussion of larger issues, including the systemic roots of sexual assault and the language used to describe those who have experienced it. When a crime has been committed against a person, the common and legal term for his or her status is "victim." This language has also been adopted for victims of interpersonal crimes such as sexual violence. However, due to the passive connotation associated with the term "victim," it was soon replaced with "survivor," a word that emphasizes the capacity of those who have experienced sexual violence to surpass being mere victims and move on with their lives—to survive. "Survivor" is viewed as empowering the individual and reflects the person's inner strength and inherent abilities. Sandra Butler (1978), author of *Conspiracy of Silence: The Trauma of Incest*, speaks of healing as a journey from victim, to survivor, to warrior. Some dislike the word warrior, but few have walked their own healing path without reaching a stage where further progress requires taking action to change the situation that caused the victimization in the first place. For example, many who have sought services at SOS ultimately talk about feeling liberated through participation in events such as TBTN, TBTH, or Prevention of Violence Against Women Week. This excerpt from a letter sent to SOS by a young client says it all:

> Just walking along that path was so symbolic for me ... I was taking it back. I was taking back what they had taken from me. My creativity, my imagination, my childhood, my power, and most of all my self ... Words cannot explain what I felt walking along with all you empowering and courageous women.... (Lucier, 2005)

The journey from victim to survivor to warrior is a journey that belongs to everyone, although not all are currently able to complete the journey. Changing our name from the Prince George Sexual Assault Centre to Surpassing our Survival reflects the journey of our organization to seek out and embrace the warrior in all of us.

Conclusion

We hope that this chapter has provided a sense of how SOS threads a structural perspective through its practice and that the aspects we have highlighted will help engender critical discussion about practice in a sexual assault agency. Some have told us that SOS should focus solely on strengthening clinical counselling and intervention skills and leave the larger political issues to the politicians. We fully understand the importance of day-to-day work that addresses critical, immediate needs. It must be done. But, ultimately, meeting these immediate needs is not very meaningful if not carried out in the context of fighting for longer-term fundamental changes that will eradicate sexual violence. In practice and of necessity, these potentially contradictory approaches are, in fact, concurrent and complementary undertakings. Our belief, borne out by nearly 25 years of practice, is that you cannot successfully do one without the other.

References

Agosin, M. (1996). *Tapestries of hope, threads of love: The Arpillera Movement in Chile, 1974–1994*. Albuquerque, NM: University of New Mexico Press.

Barnett, O.W., Miller-Perrin, C., & Perrin, R. (1997). *Family violence across the lifespan: An introduction*. Thousand Oaks, CA: Sage Publications.

Bergeron, P. (Producer), & Bissonnette, S. (Writer/Director). (2007). *Sexy Inc.: Our children under influence* [Documentary]. National Film Board of Canada.

Breckenridge, J., & Baldry, E. (1997). Workers dealing with mother blame in child sexual assault cases. *Journal of Child Sexual Abuse, 6*(1), 65–80.

Butler, S. (1978). *Conspiracy of silence: The trauma of incest*. San Francisco: New Glide Publications.

Caplan, P. (1989). *Don't blame mother: Mending the mother–daughter relationship*. New York: Harper & Row.

Carniol, B. (1992). Structural social work: Maurice Moreau's challenge to social work practice. *Journal of Progressive Human Services, 3*(1), 1–20.

Carniol, B. (2005). *Case critical: Social services and social justice in Canada* (5th ed.). Toronto, ON: Between the Lines.

Community Coordination for Women's Safety. (May 2008). *Community agency third party reporting procedures: Version 1*. Vancouver, BC: BC Association of Specialized Victims and Counselling Programs.

Fook, J. (1993). *Radical casework: A theory of practice*. St. Leonards, Australia: Allen & Unwin.

Jhally, S. (Producer/Director), Kilbourne, J. (Creator). (2002). *Killing us softly 3: Advertising's image of women* [Documentary]. Northampton, MA: Media Education Foundation.

Lheidli T'enneh First Nation, Carrier Sekani Family Services, Carrier Sekani Tribal Council, & Prince George Native Friendship Centre (16, June 2006). *A collective voice for the victims who have been silenced: The Highway of Tears Symposium Recommendations Report.* Retrieved October 23, 2008, from http://www.ubcic.bc.ca/files/PDF/highwayoftearsfinal.pdf

Lucier, S. (2005, September 17). *A letter to SOS and the TBTN organizing committee.* Unpublished.

Moreau, M.J. (1979). A structural approach to social work practice. *Canadian Journal of Social Work Education, 5*(1), 78–94.

Moreau, M.J. (1990). Empowerment through advocacy and consciousness-raising: Implications of a structural approach to social work. *Journal of Sociology & Social Welfare, 17*(2), 53–67.

Mullaly, B. (2002). *Challenging oppression: A critical social work approach.* Toronto, ON: Oxford University Press.

Mullaly, B. (2007). *The new structural social work* (3rd ed.). Toronto, ON: Oxford University Press.

Ogrodnik, L. (Ed.). (2007). *Family violence in Canada: A statistical profile.* Ottawa, ON: Canadian Centre for Justice Statistics.

Prince George Sexual Assault Centre. (2006, February 27). Mixed messages for teenage girls [Letter to the editor]. *Prince George Citizen*, p. 4.

Statistics Canada. (2007). *Measuring violence against women, statistical trends 2007.* Ottawa, ON: Statistics Canada.

Surpassing Our Survival Society. (2007). *Policy manual.* Prince George, BC: Surpassing Our Survival Society.

Sutton, T. (1999). *Sexual assault in Canada.* Retrieved October 23, 2008, from http://web.viu.ca/crim/sutton.htm

Woodard, S. (2005, October 21). Communities unite to reclaim the Highway of Tears. *Indian Country Today.* Retrieved October 23, 2008, from http://www.highwayoftears.ca/news.htm#Communities_unite_to_reclaim_the_Highway_of_Tears

CHAPTER 6

Community Development and Administration in the Structural Tradition:

Mezzo and Macro Levels of Practice

ANNE BURRILL AND HEATHER I. PETERS

Introduction

Our experiences of mezzo and macro social work are as executive directors of two community-based, grassroots organizations in Williams Lake, a small community in the central interior of British Columbia. As directors of these organizations, we have had the opportunity to create organizational spaces that are supportive of structural analyses of social issues, and to work at community, policy, and political levels to address those issues. We have sought to create an awareness of the connections between structural and personal issues and to encourage individual, group, and societal change and social action. The focus of the chapter is on practising structural social work in the context of our administrative and community work at a women's centre and a youth centre. The chapter begins with a brief discussion of what macro and mezzo levels of social work practice look like and how they are important components of structural social work theory, and of our work. We describe the organizations in which we have worked, and share our experiences as structural social workers in administrative positions.

Mezzo and Macro Practice

While many helping professions and professionals choose to focus on micro-level practice by providing services to individual clients and families, structural social work seeks to understand how personal, familial, and social issues are intricately and inextricably connected to social policies and structures (Carniol, 1992, 2005; Lundy, 2004; Moreau & Leonard, 1989; Mullaly, 1997, 2007). From a structural perspective, traditional clinical practice with a focus on the individual alone does not achieve social change. Structural social workers need to integrate micro, mezzo, and macro levels of work in their practice in order to create awareness of the importance of these structures on our lives and to work toward a less oppressive society. Defining these levels is important because traditional definitions may work against structural analyses and practice. Barker's definition of micro practice is work with "individuals, families and small groups" (2003, p. 272). Mezzo practice includes working with "families and small groups" and may involve "educating ... and bringing people together" (Barker, 2003, p. 272). Macro practice has been defined as narrowly as "helping communities, neighbourhoods or organizations" (Heinonen & Spearman, 2006, p. 49) and as broadly as "bringing about improvements or changes in the general society" (Barker, 2003, p. 257). The first of these macro definitions ignores structural practice because it is about helping groups rather than making social change. Research and policy development as macro practice activities are conspicuously absent from both of the above definitions, while community development activities may fall in either the mezzo or macro levels, depending on which definition is used.

Rather than define mezzo and macro practice narrowly, we have opted to use a broad definition that is consistent with a structural approach to social work. As executive directors of non-profit organizations, our administrative work is traditionally included in macro practice definitions (Barker, 2003; Heinonen & Spearman, 2006). However, we see organizational social work as occurring at both the mezzo (as in community development work within the agency or larger community) and macro levels (such as policy change at municipal and provincial levels).

Our mezzo-level practice starts with a focus on the immediate group we are working with, or on the community in which our clients[1] live, such as a neighbourhood or the social community of a person or group. Community work also extends to working with, or at the level of, the city or larger region or district. When we use the terms "community" or "mezzo-level practice," these are typically defined by the people we are currently working with and in a way that is relevant to each particular practice experience, and thus they may change across situations. Since we seek to link personal issues with community and societal contexts, the definition of mezzo grows with each client or group as they start to understand the larger structural connections to what they initially understood as a personal trouble. "Mezzo-level practice" is also used here to describe community development and organizational activities. "Macro-level practice" includes policy development, administrative activities, research, political advocacy, social action, consciousness-raising at a societal level, and other activities designed to create and support social change.

While this chapter focuses on our mezzo and macro activities, it is important to understand that while doing this work we are also engaged in micro-level activities. For example, as administrators we may still at times work directly with clients. In addition to this, skills typically associated with micro activities (such as communication skills and rapport building) are important in mezzo and macro work such as working with agency staff, connecting with others in the community, and political advocacy. The examples we provide also demonstrate how all levels of practice are integrated in the structural tradition.

The Organizations

The discussions of mezzo- and macro-level structural social work practice in this chapter will be based on our experiences as executive directors at two non-profit organizations. Heather Peters worked as the Executive Director of the NOOPA (No Ordinary People Allowed) Youth Centre (operated by the Boys and Girls Club of Williams Lake and District) and Anne Burrill as the Executive Director at the Women's Contact Society.[2] Williams Lake is a small community (population of approximately 10,000) in the central interior of British Columbia, although it is a service centre for a much larger region. It is economically dependant on resource industries, primarily forestry but also mining and ranching. Originally a frontier settlement in Northern Secwepemc (Shuswap) territory, it maintains an image of a tough western town. When this is combined with a sense of independence and the business focus of the city councillors and larger community, it often results in a conservative approach to social problems. While there are community members who were empathetic to the introduction of a structural perspective, there were also times when we faced opposition.

The NOOPA Youth Centre

The need for a youth-friendly space within Williams Lake was initially identified by youth who brought their suggestions to various local service providers. These youth and service providers began meeting as the Youth Network to find a creative solution to meeting the recreational and social needs of youth. The NOOPA Youth Centre was born out of this group in 1994. The centre is aimed at youth ages 12–18 years, although various programs and activities include younger and/

or older youth, depending on the purpose and goals of each activity. Peters joined the centre as the Executive Director shortly after its inception, and worked with youth and the Youth Network for seven years to develop the organization.

From its inception, the organization was interested in working at larger mezzo and macro levels, as well as the micro level, to address the needs of youth. The centre offers youth a safe place to gather for fun activities and to talk about their interests and what they want from the organization and the larger community. Out of this have come many different programs and events, including those promoting individual growth such as recreational and social activities, cooking and nutrition programs, HIV/AIDS prevention programs, an advocacy outreach program, and employment search support. Community development and social change activities are also a regular part of the youth centre, including forums for youth to engage politically with mayoral candidates; opportunities for youth to share their opinions with community leaders; support for youth to lobby for youth-friendly infrastructure (such as a skateboard park); creation and publication of a magazine by, for, and about local youth; and a regular art show and coffee house to showcase youth talent and present a positive view of youth to the community. These activities are flexible because they change to meet the needs identified by the youth accessing the centre at any given time.

Women's Contact Society

The Women's Contact Society was formed in the late 1970s, originally as a self-help support group. By 1982 it was established as a non-profit organization focused on connecting women and supporting them to deal with a range of issues. Much of the work of the early organization was focused on employment re-entry programs for women who were returning to the workforce. The organization evolved as women's needs in the community changed, and by the mid 1990s was focused on addressing childcare issues as well as meeting the needs of marginalized women, particularly those living in poverty (Burrill, 2003).

Burrill joined the organization in 1996 as Executive Director and led the organization during the following eight years. During that time, the Women's Contact Society operated a day care for young parents, a childcare provider support and training program, a housing and income assistance advocacy program, and a wide range of other short-term projects. Some of these projects focused on the delivery of micro-level services such as smoking-cessation programs, women's health workshops, and early child development programs. In addition, a number of mezzo- and macro-level projects were undertaken to make changes at the community, societal, and policy levels. Some of these projects included women's safety assessments of local neighbourhoods; community-based research projects to better understand and address local women's issues (such as spousal violence, childcare, mental health, and menopause); and policy analysis, focusing primarily on provincial health and social welfare issues (such as income assistance policies, childcare policies, health policies, and access to legal aid). One example of community consciousness-raising was a production of *The Vagina Monologues* to educate the community on gender, sexuality, and sexual violence.

Agency Administration and Service Delivery
Setting the Stage within the Organizational Structure

While a highly formalized and hierarchical organization can perpetuate power and oppression, an informal, flat, consensus-based organization can also utilize power and oppression in an implicit way. Thus, the latter is not necessarily more aligned with a structural approach. In order to establish a structural approach to agency administration, agency leaders and staff must understand how power and oppression exist in an agency structure, and be able to engage in an analysis of how the personal and political connect. It is important that an awareness of agency structures and power be developed across the whole organization from front-line staff through to the board of directors. This sets the tone for service delivery and work with clients.

At the Women's Contact Society, Burrill began her tenure by using micro-level skills to work with existing staff and board members to establish individual relationships. This assisted with gaining an understanding of the role each person played in the organization and the values, priorities, and approaches they brought to their work. Acknowledging the power differences that existed between the various positions within the organization brought people together and allowed relationships to grow. Staff meetings and individual meetings with staff members and directors were opportunities for shared decision-making, demonstrating concern about the personal lives and issues of staff (including gender-related issues), creating awareness of structural connections for staff issues, and encouraging a work- and home-life balance. This translated into assisting staff to begin to make links between their own lives, the lives of their clients, and the broader societal contexts that affect all people. In addition, Burrill instituted annual staff/ board planning events and staff development retreats that focused on building relationships, as well as organizational strategic and program planning. These provided opportunities to reflect on the approaches the organization was taking to the work they were doing. These events strengthened the sense of shared power and collaboration in making change at all levels within the organization, and facilitated an understanding of structural analyses across the organization. One of the direct results of the improved structural understanding of staff and board members was the creation of a new mission statement for the organization that more clearly reflected a structural approach: to promote social awareness of women's issues and to strive for change in ideas, laws, and situations that deny equality to women (Burrill, 2003, p. 2).

At the youth centre, Peters also took a direct approach to integrating structural approaches. Her tenure began within three months of the organization opening its doors and so there was substantial opportunity to integrate a structural approach from the ground up. One of her first tasks was to develop organizational policies and procedures. Instead of working exclusively with the board on this task, which is normal in many organizations, Peters gathered policy and procedure examples from other similar organizations and then shared options with staff, asking for their thoughts on what would work best to support them in their work. The document that went to the board for discussion and approval was therefore based on the realities of front-line work and had the support of staff. This process became a model for the organization, and particularly for staff, who were then encouraged to develop programs and services together with youth in order to ensure that services were the best possible fit with youth needs.

Although executive directors take direction from the board, boards rely on executive directors to be experts on the field in which they work and to provide background information to assist the board in making decisions. This allows executive directors the opportunity to explain and promote a structural approach to service delivery to board members, so that this can become integrated into the very foundations of the organization such as in the mission statement and guiding principles. In one of the youth centre's first strategic planning sessions with the board and staff, the understanding of structural connections to youth well-being was discussed and then recognized in the development of the mission statement:

> Youth are a part of the community, and their well being determines the health of future communities. It is, therefore, the NOOPA Youth Centre's primary goal to work together with youth to ensure that this community meets the needs and interests of young people. (Cariboo Youth Online: NOOPA Youth Centre, 1998)

Thus, the mission statement does not focus on helping youth improve themselves, but on ensuring that the community meets the needs of youth—this larger goal creates a context for improving youth health and well-being, while improving community and society well-being simultaneously. This structural perspective acknowledges that issues facing youth are often not just within the purview of youth. Rather, youth issues are created and/or exacerbated by community and societal policies and attitudes. Therefore, in order to address the root causes of these issues, the larger focus encompassed in the mission statement is important.

Service Delivery

Integrating a structural approach into the very foundation of the organization sets the stage for a structural approach to client services and for interactions with the larger community. As services are developed, planned, evaluated, and restructured, a structural analysis can be employed to begin building in opportunities to broaden the focus of the services. This moves the focus from simply assisting individual clients to making links with community and structural issues, understanding social policy implications, and working toward mezzo- and macro-level change. Once this focus shifts, the use of empowerment and consciousness-raising approaches can be integrated in the micro-level practice with clients. Using a structural approach to working with individuals to help them cope with particular life circumstances means shifting from simply focusing on the role of the individual in the problem to broadening the understanding the client has to include an analysis of the societal and structural systems, systems of power and oppression, and social policies that make an impact on the life of that person. This must be done in a way that empowers the client, rather than leaving the person with a sense that it is hopeless to try to make change. Therefore, micro-level skills are critical in balancing shared resolution of client's issues with the realities of structural oppression.

Bringing people with similar concerns together, consciousness-raising, and empowerment are three structural tools in working with clients, as described by Olivier in Chapter 2. These tools are also valuable in facilitating the development of staff and directors, within an agency, as demonstrated in the section above. Consciousness-raising is a process that is closely associated with structural social work as well as with other anti-oppressive and social justice movements (Bishop, 2002; Fook, 2002; Mullaly, 2002, 2007). Critical consciousness is built on the understanding that popular beliefs and ways of thinking encourage a view of problems that focuses on the weaknesses of individuals; in this context, individual change is the natural solution to these problems. As a result, social structures that benefit some people in power, and which create the conditions for social problems, are accepted as the norm and are not challenged. The goal of consciousness-raising is to develop an understanding of the links between societal structures and social issues, thereby setting the stage for people to come together to challenge structures (Bishop, 2002; Fook, 2002; Mullaly, 2007). Mullaly (2002) suggested that consciousness-raising is most effective when people with similar concerns are brought together in order for people to see that they are not alone. Once people recognize that there are others facing similar challenges, empowerment strategies can be used to engage people individually and collectively in making change. These empowerment strategies are about assisting people to identify and develop the tools and skills they need to successfully challenge and change structures (Bishop, 2002).

The NOOPA Youth Centre used the tools of consciousness-raising, empowerment, and collectivity (bringing people together) in its engagement of youth skateboarders at a time when skateboarding was viewed with hostility by much of the community. As there was no formally sanctioned skateboard location in Williams Lake, skateboarders were forced to turn to public locations, such as parking lots and stairs. Business owners were increasingly frustrated with patrons having to dodge skateboarders and loose skateboards in order to access local businesses. Signs saying "skateboarding prohibited" were going up quickly and businesses began lobbying city council for a by-law banning skateboarding in public places. As the sport was outlawed in more locations, youth who engaged in the activity became increasingly identified as problem youth who flaunted rules and were a danger to others. Thus, the issue was defined as a problem with "bad kids." Individual skateboarders brought the issue to the attention of the youth centre staff. As a first step the youth centre brought skateboarders together at a meeting to give the youth space to discuss their concerns. The youth centre then worked with a core group of self-identified skateboarders to take steps toward solving the problem.

The first component of consciousness-raising in this example was to work with youth to assist them in understanding that the issue was occurring at the community and municipal level, and that as citizens they had a right to have access to space in which to participate in their sport. Consciousness-raising with the youth in terms of identifying the issue as a community issue was quite straightforward! However, other elements of understanding were needed before the problem would be solved. Work with the youth included not only re-framing the problem, but also identifying possible proactive solutions that would meet the needs of the youth while addressing this issue of the larger community. Consciousness-raising with the youth included identifying Williams Lake City Council as a group who had the power to make the problem worse (by passing a by-law banning skateboarding) or to make it better (by participating in the creation of a skateboard park). Youth also learned that it would be useful to have at least some local businesses on their side in the battle for their own space, rather than treating all businesses as the opposition.

Thus, the work with skateboarders had several structural components. Bringing youth skateboarders together to share their joint concerns as a collective was the first step. Consciousness-raising with youth to re-define the issue and to re-define places of support was another key piece. Empowerment of youth to develop and work toward their own solutions to the problem came out of consciousness-raising activities.

Community and Political Development
Community Work

A commitment to community engagement and social change work is a necessary extension of practising structural social work in the context of agency administration. Linking the personal and political in the context of organizational structure and micro-level practice positions the organization to be a leader in addressing social issues in community and political contexts. Some organizations have community development workers who take on the bulk of these responsibilities. However, in our situations this position did not exist.

As executive directors we were engaged with the larger community in many different ways already, and so community development activities were a natural extension of our other responsibilities. In addition, as executive directors we encouraged all staff to take on community development activities that were identified as important issues through their work with women and youth. Sharing community development activities with all agency staff means that this work is not segregated, but rather is integrated into all aspects of the organization and into all micro-practice activities.

At the Women's Contact Society, this was strategically approached by identifying personal/political issues at the micro level and then initiating community development and social change initiatives to move those issues to the mezzo and macro levels. At least one major community development or social change project was undertaken by the organization each year to address an issue identified in micro-level practice. Many of these projects incorporated service delivery, research, and social change components.

One such project developed out of the centre's work with women who had been victims of violence, both intimate partner violence and more public incidents. In less than one year, two women were violently murdered in the community and several women were assaulted physically or sexually. This led the Women's Contact Society to bring women together to talk about their fears and the need to address issues of community safety. A Take Back the Night march was organized to raise awareness of the violence in the community. A funding proposal was developed and a women's safety initiative began surveying women's perceptions of safety in their neighbourhoods, workplaces, schools, and public spaces. The results of this survey were used to support requests for additional funding to conduct a women's safety audit, which involved women and community leaders walking through particular areas of the community during late evening hours to identify specific risks and potential solutions.

A report on each audit was developed and the outcomes were used to lobby city council and other organizations to make changes to infrastructure that would support increased safety for women and, by extension, for the whole community. The city implemented the majority of recommendations, including increased lighting, removing hiding places such as fences and shrubs, and changing entry and access points for public buildings.

Consciousness-Raising and Advocacy at Community and Political Levels

In our work, consciousness-raising and advocacy occur at all of the levels of practice: micro, mezzo, and macro. Activities within the larger community included consciousness-raising efforts to help political decision-makers and the public better understand the ways in which community and government contribute to social problems, and the ways in which structural changes will address these issues. Regular and ongoing networking with community leaders and politicians is an important first step to opening doors for advocacy and awareness-raising on future issues, and this may be especially beneficial in smaller communities (Brownlee, Graham, & Dimond, 1997). Although community functions can seem superficial or status-oriented at times, having a personal relationship with various community leaders can allow quick access to a person who may have the ability to support or undermine an important resource for the organization and clients (Brownlee et al., 1997). In Williams Lake, connections within the leadership arena meant that executive directors of local non-profit organizations were invited to a "meet and greet" opportunity with British Columbia cabinet ministers when they were in the city on a working retreat. Peters and Burrill both attended this event and took the opportunity to lobby key ministers regarding youth and women's issues. A discussion with one minister was followed several weeks later by the reinstatement of funding for a local youth program.

One instance of community-level consciousness-raising at the youth centre is a continuation of the previous example of work with skateboarders. Once the youth and centre staff had a clear understanding of the skateboarding problem as a community-level issue, the next step was to work with youth to change the views of the larger community. The first goal was to identify that the problem was a lack of community space for skateboarders, rather than a problem with youth. Staff and youth worked together to identify potentially skateboard-friendly professionals and businesses in the community and went to talk with business owners about how the tension between businesses and skateboarders could be addressed through the development of a public skateboard park in the city. While some business owners were not supportive, many saw this solution as win–win and began assisting the youth in lobbying city council for the development of a skateboard park. Youth and staff also engaged the local media in their attempts to bring the larger community on board in supporting a skateboard park. The local newspaper in particular was helpful in sharing the message that the community did not have a problem with "bad youth," but that the real issue was the lack of an adequate place in which skateboarders could participate in their sport.

The next step was to lobby city council for two things. The first was to encourage city council to reject a by-law banning skateboarding, which would have criminalized a group of youth for a sports activity. The second was to secure city council's commitment to provide land and partial funds for a public skateboard park. As Executive Director, Peters had been developing professional relationships with city councillors for several years over other youth issues. These relationships were useful because time could be spent informing individual city councillors of the importance of the above two points. In addition to utilizing personal relationships with councillors to create an awareness of the situation, youth and staff arranged to appear before council to speak to the issues. The skateboarders identified several key youth to appear as the main speakers, with one youth centre staff member also speaking briefly in support of the youth and the proposed skateboard park. Youth had also asked several business owners to speak in favour of the skateboard park and the ways in which it would benefit the whole community.

The work of the youth and the youth centre was successful and ultimately the city donated land, in a youth-approved location, and contributed financially to the park, with the youth centre raising the rest of the funds from community partners. While the development of a skateboard park seems like a common-sense solution, the problem was compounded by a city council that typically held pro-business views and who had a history of solving other issues with by-laws banning behaviour rather than supporting a more proactive approach. Thus, the successful resolution of this issue, and the movement of city council and the larger community toward acknowledging their role in creating and maintaining youth-friendly spaces, was a turning point in the consciousness of the community and municipal government.

Policy Analysis and Political Advocacy

Policy analysis can occur at organizational, community, provincial, and federal governmental levels within the context of a local organization. Over time, our work included analysis at all of these levels. Political advocacy and social actions are often more effective when like-minded groups come together collaboratively in a united front. As Executive Director of the women's centre, Burrill joined with women's organizations and childcare programs across British Columbia to analyze the impacts of, and actively oppose, sweeping program and funding cuts instituted by the Campbell Liberal government in 2001 and 2002. At the provincial level, Burrill worked with other women's centres to lobby provincial government to continue funding childcare, legal aid, and women's services. Locally she spoke at public rallies, was interviewed by the media, and lobbied the local member of the legislative assembly to oppose the cuts. While many of the service cuts went ahead as planned, this collective action was successful in getting funding for childcare support programs reinstated just prior to the closure of those programs across the province.

Conclusion

Structural social work theory insists that we move beyond just an individual (micro) approach to also working at community (mezzo) and societal, policy, and political (macro) levels (Mullaly, 2002, 2007). Social work is both critical and active, and we must maintain a focus on understanding and addressing the root causes of oppression and marginalization while attending to the lives of individual clients. To do so, we must be able to link the personal with the political, and keep one foot in each world: understanding the realities of people's lives (individual/micro) and working to effect change in the systems and structures that create those realities (mezzo/macro). Our examples demonstrate that engaging structural social work analyses and practices in the context of organizational and administrative work offers exciting opportunities to create structural organizations, to raise the consciousness of individuals and communities regarding root causes of community issues, and to successfully challenge and change structural causes of social problems.

Endnotes

[1] We are reluctant to use the word "clients" for the sense of separation between "us" and "them" that is suggested in the term. In addition, the people with whom we work are not necessarily clients in a traditional sense. However, the term is used because it is cumbersome to repeat the phrase "the people with whom we work."

[2] This chapter is based on our personal goals and experiences during our work, and is not written from the perspective, or on behalf, of the organizations for which we worked. Therefore, the ideas expressed here are our own, and should not be attributed to these organizations.

References

Barker, R.L. (2003). *The social work dictionary* (5th ed.). Washington, DC: National Association of Social Workers' Press.

Bishop, A. (2002). *Becoming an ally: Breaking the cycle of oppression in people* (2nd ed.). Halifax, NS: Fernwood Publishing.

Brownlee, K., Graham, J.R., & Dimond, P. (1997). Strategies for community assessment. In K. Brownlee, R. Delaney, & J.R. Graham (Eds.), *Strategies for northern social work practice* (pp. 113–128). Thunder Bay, ON: Lakehead University Centre for Northern Studies.

Burrill, A. (2003). *The good food box: Project proposal.* Unpublished manuscript.

Cariboo Youth Online: NOOPA Youth Centre. (1998). *Mission statement.* Retrieved June 8, 2008, from http://hp.bccna.bc.ca/~aa015/noopa.htm#mission

Carniol, B. (1992). Structural social work: Maurice Moreau's challenge to social work practice. *Journal of Progressive Human Services, 3*(1), 1–20.

Carniol, B. (2005). *Case critical: Social services and social justice in Canada* (5th ed.). Toronto, ON: Between the Lines.

Fook, J. (2002). *Social work: Critical theory and practice.* London, UK: Sage Publications.

Heinonen, T., & Spearman, L. (2006). *Social work practice: Problem solving and beyond.* Toronto, ON: Nelson.

Lundy, C. (2004). *Social work and social justice: A structural approach to practice.* Peterborough, ON: Broadview Press.

Moreau, M.J., & Leonard, L. (1989). *Empowerment through a structural approach to social work: A report from practice.* Ottawa, ON: Carleton University.

Mullaly, B. (1997). *Structural social work: Ideology, theory, and practice* (2nd ed.). Toronto, ON: Oxford University Press.

Mullaly, B. (2002). *Challenging oppression: A critical social work approach.* Toronto, ON: Oxford University Press.

Mullaly, B. (2007). *The new structural social work* (3rd ed.). Toronto, ON: Oxford University Press.

CHAPTER 7

Injustice Can Happen Whether You're Psychotic or Not:

Incorporating Structural Social Work Theory in a Mental Health Setting

KAREN SCHWARTZ AND ANN-MARIE O'BRIEN

Introduction

Each field of practice brings its own challenges for the structural social worker. In the area of mental health, one of the first challenges is reconciling the medical model with a critical approach that brings together elements of Marxism, radical social work, feminism, and anti-oppressive practice. Service users of the mental health system are often oppressed and stigmatized (Kirby, 2006). In her book on structural social work, Colleen Lundy says that "sustained feelings of powerlessness, uncertainty, and loss of control over decisions that influence one's life create high levels of damaging stress that negatively impact on mental and physical health," (Lundy, 2004, p. 87). Experiences of service users in the mental health field highlight the difficulties and frustrations when decisions about one's life are controlled by well-meaning others. Structural social work involves analyzing the structures that oppress service users. In order to do this it is important to understand the history and policy context of mental health services. The recent incorporation of compulsory treatment options into mental health law is particularly challenging for social workers (Campbell et al., 2006). Community treatment orders (CTOs) prescribe a course of treatment in the community with severe consequences for not following them. Thus, a psychiatric setting is a challenging but important place to operate from a structural perspective.

This chapter focuses on the use of structural social work skills when working with a client on a CTO. Our case study illustrates how social structures and oppressive social relations work against the service user, and how the social worker can employ various practice skills to combat this process. The specific skills that will be discussed are the structural social work tasks identified by Maurice Moreau (Moreau & Leonard, 1989).

Diverse Explanations of Mental Illness and a Discussion of Terminology

The medical establishment views mental illness as a biochemical imbalance in the brain that is best treated by bio-psychosocial interventions including medication, counselling, and development of the service user's social support network. At the opposite end of the continuum, characterized by the anti-psychiatry movement (Szasz, 1987), is the belief that mental illness is a socially constructed concept that encourages discrimination against and marginalization of segments of the population who seem unable to compete in the increasing globalized, capitalist world environment. A social construction is an institutionalized entity in a social system invented or constructed by members of a dominant culture or society that exists because people agree, usually unconsciously, to believe as if it exists or follows certain conventional rules (Berger & Luckmann, 1966). Social workers believe that a biomedical approach alone is insufficient to understand, address, and act in complex human situations, such as those faced by people who use mental health services (Heinonen & Metteri, 2005). It is limiting because, on its own, this perspective does not take into consideration or address the social institutions that cause, create, or exacerbate ill health. Some people may have greater vulnerabilities to developing mental health problems due to medical, nutritional, genetic, or other factors. Research has shown that the social factors that play a major role in contributing to vulnerability to breakdown or distress include systemic oppression or disadvantage, physically and psychologically invasive acts, abandonment, bereavement, and witnessing domestic violence (Tew, 2005). These types of trauma can render the person a powerless victim and unable to negotiate boundaries or relationships with others (Tew, 2005).

"Service user" is a recent term used to describe people who use the services provided in mental health settings. In the past, these people would have been referred to in extremely derogatory terms such as "lunatic," or simply by their diagnosis (e.g., schizophrenic, manic), Everett (2000). "Patient" eventually replaced lunatic and, while potentially less stigmatizing, this word also includes the connotation of someone who is not as powerful as the psychiatrist who determines the diagnosis. It is important to note that changes in nomenclature from "lunatic" to "patient" were originally driven by mental health-care professionals. More recent changes to "consumer," "survivor," and "service user" have been driven by people who use mental health services (Reaume, 2002). The term "service user" implies a sense of power, in that a user of services has the right to object if the service they receive does not meet their standards for service. "How a person with a psychiatric history chooses to self identify has a lot to do with how one views public policy on mental health care as well as personal experiences and expectations of mental health treatment" (Reaume, 2002, p. 425). Many authors (e.g., Moreau, Lundy, and Oliver) use the word client, so when they are quoted we will use client. In our writing we will use the term service user.

The *Mental Health Act* of Ontario and Community Treatment Orders

"Few recent changes in psychiatry have polarized the various stakeholders in the mental health system as much as the propriety of issuing community treatment orders" (O'Reilly, 2004, p. 579). The purpose of CTOs in Ontario, as defined by its *Mental Health Act* (s. 33.1–33.9), is to provide a person who suffers from a serious mental disorder and has a revolving-door pattern of admissions with a comprehensive plan of community-based treatment that is less restrictive than being detained in a psychiatric facility. The foundation of the CTO is a plan that describes the obligations of the various players and is agreed to by the physician, the service user, and any community agencies providing service under the plan. The goals of this plan are to create the necessary conditions to prevent repeated hospitalizations and help the service user live successfully in the community. A CTO is in effect for six months, at which time it can be withdrawn or renewed. Upon a second renewal, a mandatory review of the case by the independent Consent and Capacity Board, must take place.

If a service user is non-compliant with the CTO, and the physician believes that he or she continues to meet the criteria for issuance, the physician may issue an Order for Psychiatric Examination and must make reasonable attempts to inform the service user of this process. If the service user does not comply, the Order for Psychiatric Examination authorizes the police to apprehend the service user and return him or her to the physician for examination (s. 33.3 [2]). The physician then examines the service user to determine if he or she meets the criteria for an involuntary admission, or if the service user should be released.

Seven years after the introduction of CTOs in Ontario there remains a paucity of research on their effectiveness. Given that the purpose of CTOs is to provide a comprehensive plan of community-based treatment that is less restrictive than being detained in a psychiatric hospital, one area of evaluation is to examine their effectiveness at reducing hospital admissions. There is a dearth of Canadian studies on CTOs, but worldwide studies have shown that CTOs were effective in reducing the number and length of hospital admissions (Dreezer & Dreezer, 2005); associated with moves to more supportive housing arrangements (O'Brien & Farrell, 2005); effective for engaging otherwise resistant people in their treatment and recovery (Hunt et al., 2007); and respected patients' autonomy (Dawson, et al., 2003). Other provinces with similar legislation include Saskatchewan and Nova Scotia.

The Service User

Agnes is a 60-year-old woman. She is single and lives in a supervised residence. Agnes has many strengths. She is resilient, engaging, very social, and has a good sense of humour. Agnes is divorced and has two adult children. She has also been diagnosed with schizophrenia and is required to take medication. Because of numerous involuntary hospitalizations and difficult behaviour, Agnes is under a CTO. Many official bodies have an impact on her life. Her psychiatrist decided that she lacked capacity to make treatment decisions. The office of the Public Guardian and Trustee, a division of the Attorney General's office, acts as substitute decision-maker for Agnes. In Ontario, the public guardian makes treatment decisions when there is a finding of incapacity and no family members are willing or able to take on this role.

Agnes believes that the root cause of most of her difficulties is that aliens control her brain. Many other people in her life believe that the root cause is a serious mental illness called schizophrenia. Agnes does not follow recommended treatment plans because she does not accept the idea that she is mentally ill. Without medication, Agnes' behaviour drew the attention of others, who called the police. She was then handcuffed and taken to hospital for an involuntary admission, an experience that led to continued feelings of powerlessness. A CTO was issued for Agnes to increase the probability of compliance with treatment and decrease the number of involuntary admissions. The CTO requires Agnes to keep regular appointments with her psychiatrist and her case manager and to take medication.

Structural Social Work Skills

Maurice Moreau defined four objectives of a structural social work practitioner: defence of the client, collectivization of social problems, materialization of social problems, and client empowerment (Moreau & Leonard, 1989). In Chapter 2, Claude Oliver fleshes out these objectives and the practice skills associated with them. It is important to understand that these are not mutually exclusive—any of these tasks can be conceived of as a means to reach the others and the use of any one may involve the use of the others (Moreau & Leonard, 1989). We will discuss these tasks in reference to Agnes.

Defence of the Client

The structural social work task of defence of the client refers to the work of "maximizing the client's access to resources and rights" (Murray & Hick, Chapter 1). While Agnes believes that there is little she can do to address the problem (as she sees it) of aliens controlling her brain, it is the structural social worker's role to help her identify aspects of her life that she can influence and control, and resources available to assist her with this process.

The first opportunity for empowerment was establishing a therapeutic alliance with Agnes. Initially, Agnes was angry, irritable and dismissive. She had once again been brought to the hospital against her will. She had lost her housing and was separated from her friends. The social worker understood and respected Agnes' emotions in this social context. Social work contacts with Agnes were brief and respectful, but frequent. As trust was established, Agnes began to engage with the social worker. At that point, the social worker discussed with Agnes what she needs to do to stay out of hospital and let Agnes know that part of her job as a social worker is to ensure that these elements are represented in the community treatment plan. How often would Agnes like to meet with her service providers? Where would she like to meet with them? Agnes negotiated these issues with the social worker. At first this required a great deal of help from the social worker because Agnes was not used to having her voice heard.

After all parties agreed to the community treatment plan, rights advice was requested from the Psychiatric Patient Advocate Office (in Ontario). Agnes needed help to understand that although her substitute decision-maker consented to the CTO for her, she still had the legal right to challenge the plan and the order before the Consent and Capacity Board. By understanding her rights in relation to the CTO, her rights related to making decisions about her treatment and her rights in relation to decisions of the substitute decision-maker, she took steps toward taking charge of more areas of her life.

Another aspect of acting in defence of the service user was to inform Agnes of her eligibility for resources. It is important that a social worker understand that resources exist in a historical and political context. In the 1960s a process of deinstitutionalization was initiated, the objectives of which were the dismantling and closure of large psychiatric institutions (Bennett, 1979), the discharge of patients into the community (Bachrach, 1981), and the decrease and prevention of new admissions. The underlying principle of deinstitutionalization was the belief that individuals have a right to live in the least restrictive environment and to receive services in the community. This philosophy assumes that the community is willing and able to provide the care previously provided by the institution (Bachrach, 1978, p. 574–575). The process of deinstitutionalization was not accompanied by adequate investment in community resources. Consequently, this led to a dramatic increase in homelessness, prisons becoming today's asylums (25–40 percent of people in prison have mental health problems), and a rise in substance abuse (Perez, Lefiman, & Estrada, 2003).

In the 1990s, the province of Ontario began a 10-year process of reforming the mental health system. The goal was to provide a continuum of services from health promotion and prevention to supportive community-based programs to hospital care, with priority given to case management, 24-hour crisis intervention, and housing. Other services included social supports and self-help initiatives, including those run by consumers/survivors and families as alternatives to the formal mental health system, (Ontario Ministry of Health, 1993). While more money has flowed into the community and new resources have been established, there is still a need for a comprehensive system of services to address the variety of needs of service users. Social workers operate in a context where there are many service users who remember the days of large institutions, the suffering they experienced in the name of treatment, and the experience of stigma associated with large mental institutions. There are service users who see CTOs as an extension of the institution, or as an institution without walls. Long waiting lists for resources compound the difficulties in providing care in the community.

Prior to admission, Agnes was living on her own but was experiencing difficulties in self-care and maintaining her living space. Another challenge for Agnes was coping with loneliness. Her adult son is married and has a young family. He and his wife both work full-time and live at the other end of the city. Helping Agnes find housing was a priority so that she could leave the hospital. Finding housing among the limited resources that would meet Agnes' needs and provide the support she needed was a challenge. The social worker assisted Agnes in identifying her priorities for housing by posing a series of questions. Is having her own room important? Is living near the bus stop important? The worker assisted Agnes in making a list of questions for prospective housing providers. She role-played with Agnes how to pose those questions in an interview and accompanied Agnes to visit the housing options and to necessary interviews.

Many social service organizations have service users on their board of directors to ensure that the voices, needs, and perspectives of service users are represented in the policies and procedures adopted by the board. Agnes was helped to gain acceptance on the board of an agency that provides housing to individuals with problems similar to her own. She was then able to advocate for the expansion of housing resources.

The last aspect of defence involves advocating for the service user with other members of an interdisciplinary team and teaching the service user to advocate for herself. This involves re-framing a service user's actions in a way that helps team members to understand the service user's perspective more clearly and to stop them from attributing service failure to service user deficits. Re-framing is a practice where one alters the understanding, definition, or interpretation of a problem (Spearman, 2005). Re-defining "is a consciousness-raising activity in which personal troubles are re-defined in political terms, exposing the relationship between objective material conditions and subjective personal experiences" (Mullaly, 2007, p. 313). While on a CTO, Agnes missed a psychiatric appointment due to a misunderstanding about who would transport her. Agnes was supposed to be driven to her appointment by her case manager. When the case manager did not arrive, Agnes assumed the meeting had been cancelled. The social worker needed to mediate the psychiatrist's reaction and help him to re-frame the event from one of non-compliance to one of understanding the structural barriers (i.e., poverty, absence of a sense of personal agency, pressures on the case worker who was supposed to pick her up) that contributed to her absence. While there may be times at which Agnes missed appointments because her mind is disorganized, this was not one of them. Nor was it an instance of Agnes not wanting to comply with treatment.

In this section, we have shown how a social worker operating from a structural perspective acted in "defence of a client" by forming a relationship of trust, helping the service user get advice about her rights in relation to the CTO, helping her access resources, and supporting her in being elected to a housing agency board of directors. When working with a multi-disciplinary team, a structural social worker also re-frames a service user's actions so that the team understands the structural barriers that have an impact on the individual's life.

Collectivization of Social Problems

This task refers to the work of "helping the client move beyond an individualistic understanding of their problem situation and solution" (Oliver, Chapter 2, p. 28). One way to help Agnes realize that there are others who share similar concerns would be to help her join a group such as the Client Empowerment Council. This council functions inside the mental health institution where Agnes has been hospitalized and is run by former service users. They meet monthly to discuss issues and advocate for improvements in care. There are also community groups for psychiatric survivors in general and groups for people with specific diagnoses (e.g., the Unsung Heroes—part of the Schizophrenia Society). They lobby political figures and provide community education to combat stigma against people with mental health difficulties. The challenge with a service user such as Agnes is that she does not identify herself as having a psychiatric problem. She believes that aliens are controlling her brain. Practising collectivization with Agnes will require the worker to assist Agnes to join with others who are at a similar stage in life, regardless of her mental health problems. Living on a fixed income and coping with loneliness are issues that Agnes has in common with other seniors. The worker was able to find a drop-in centre for seniors in the neighbourhood where Agnes went to live. The drop-in was welcoming and provided an opportunity for Agnes to socialize without a commitment to attend a regular group, which she felt would be too stressful. The seniors at the drop-in were also involved in community projects such as planting a community garden and inviting their MPP to a discussion on seniors' issues.

Unfortunately, when trying to integrate into the mainstream of our culture many service users experience stigma. The Kirby report, *Out of the Shadows at Last: Transforming Mental Health, Mental Illness and Addiction Services in Canada* (2006), found that the stories of discrimination recounted to them during their hearings were heart wrenching in revealing the attitudes and unjust treatment experienced daily by those living with mental illness. Many service users find their experiences of stigma to be much more difficult to deal with than their mental health issues (Kirby, 2006). CTOs in Ontario were marketed as "Brian's Law" following the murder of popular sportscaster by a person diagnosed with schizophrenia who was not taking prescribed medications. Using an act of violence as a rationale for this legislation arguably introduced an element of "guilt by association" for all service users subject to CTOs. Therefore, being on a CTO can be experienced as more stigmatizing than the diagnosis of mental illness. One service user had this to say about CTOs: "… the real issue was about will, whose will was stronger, and who's not getting their way with the decision about taking the medication" (O'Reilly et al., 2007, p. 519).

Social workers also have a responsibility to advocate for societal change so that discrimination disappears and services that will most help service users are available. This political action can take many forms—for example, this worker's agency has used a consumer survivor business to cater a holiday party. Service users have been organized to participate in a political demonstration at the provincial legislature against CTO laws that they feel are repressive. Finally, another worker has worked with service users to make a presentation during the development of the Local Health Integration Network by the Ontario Ministry of Health and Long-Term Care about their resource needs and to ensure that their voices will continue to be heard while the province restructures its system of service implementation and funding.

In this section, we have shown that the task of collectivization includes helping service users to find a group of individuals who have similar issues to help them realize that theirs is not an individual problem. In this case, the worker needed to respect Agnes' definition of her problems and found a group for seniors rather than one for people with a similar diagnosis.

Materialization of Social Problems

This task refers to the work of "grounding problems in access to resources" (Murray & Hick, Chapter 1, p. 14). Researchers have always found a strong correlation between poverty and mental illness. The lower a person's socio-economic status, the greater are his or her chances of suffering from mental distress (Hudson, 2005). Recent studies have shown that poverty, unemployment, and lack of affordable housing often precede a diagnosis of mental illness and psychiatric hospitalization, to the extent that they are considered to be causal factors (Hudson, 2005). Therefore, help acquiring access to decent housing, employment, adequate food, and so on is extremely important in the prevention of mental health problems, as well as in resolving them.

One of Agnes' housing situations post-discharge on a CTO was a supervised residence where she was required to share a room with three other women. This arrangement did not alleviate Agnes' loneliness, but instead was competitive and further contributed to her feelings of powerlessness. This housing broke down when Agnes refused to return there. She was once again taken to hospital against her will and another CTO was issued. Fortunately, the connections Agnes made while acting on the board of the social service agency helped in this situation. Another board member knew of a possible living situation for Agnes. The worker helped Agnes to see that this was not just a lucky chance, but was due to the hard work that she engaged in while on the board.

In many large urban areas, service users, with the help of government grants, are trying to start their own businesses, often offering catering or couriers, run for and by people with mental health problems. While this was not a resource that Agnes was interested in, social workers can help service users get jobs in these companies. They operate on a model of empowerment, peer advocacy, and peer support offering supportive workplaces for many people who have been told that they are permanently unemployable. These organizations are usually more flexible in the number of hours they require someone to work and more understanding when an employee needs time off due to emotional difficulties.

Client Empowerment

Increasing Power in the Worker–Client Relationship

This task refers to the work of reducing the power differential between the client and worker by "maintaining respect for the client's dignity and autonomy, validating strengths, articulating limits to the professional role, clear contracting, reducing distance, sharing the rationale behind interventions, encouraging self-help, and the use of groups and self-disclosure" (Lundy, 2004, p. 114). There are many ways to reduce the power differential between service users and social workers. One example of this in working with Agnes was inviting her to choose a regular meeting location that she was comfortable with, such as the coffee shop near where she lives. This lessened the need for her to go to the social worker's environment. Murray & Hick (Chapter 1) talk about the importance of reducing social distance between the worker and service user by using first names, talking in language they understand, and demystifying the social worker's role by clarifying and sharing the rationale behind interventions. This was accomplished by explaining to Agnes what would happen at the various hearings to institute the CTO, the role she could play at these hearings, and her rights in relation to them.

Contracting is a process in which the social worker and the service user negotiate back and forth what will be included in a service plan, and can be used in the construction of a CTO. In the context of a CTO, this means avoiding unnecessary jargon so that service users can clearly understand what is expected of them. It also means explaining the rationale for the provision of services spelled out in the CTO. One of the primary purposes of the CTO is to ensure that Agnes takes her medication. The worker helped Agnes to have her voice heard in relation to what form the medication would take (pills rather than an injection) and where she would receive the medication (in a community health centre where she had a relationship with the nurse practitioner).

Enhancing the Client's Power through Personal Change
This can be accomplished by "encouraging disruption of destructive thoughts, feelings, and behaviours" (Murray & Hick, Chapter 1). At times, Agnes feels a great deal of shame about her situation and self-blame. She feels that she was not a good mother because of her struggles with her mental state. As one social worker in a study by Moreau et al. put it,

> I don't see women in those kinds of situations as the problem. I think there is a difference between not defining them as the problem but also encouraging them to take some responsibility for the situation. So part of my work would be in helping to redefine the problem so that they stop

blaming themselves, but also that they don't then completely sidestep any responsibility they have for making things different. (Moreau et al., 1993, p. 103)

Mullaly has described a process of inferiorization where the "oppressor gets into the head of the oppressed" (2007, p. 276). Oppressed persons, according to Mullaly, participate in reinforcing their own oppression by psychologically or socially withdrawing, engaging in self-destructive behaviours that cause them to be rejected by others, becoming fatalistic (which can be interpreted as docility or apathy), and engaging in self-depreciation. It is important to recognize this process in Agnes. Social workers have become burnt out by working with service users who are hospitalized repeatedly because they do not understand this process.

A next step is to work with service users to decode what they may be expressing through forms of intermediary language such as metaphoric language, disembodied voices, self-harm, hearing voices, and so on (Tew, 2005). Once the social worker understands what is being expressed by self-destructive behaviour, another way to increase a service user's sense of autonomy and personal control is to create an action plan (also called advance directives) and a relapse plan. These become necessary if the service user feels that they are going to do something harmful and they want to have options to regain control of themselves and the situation. On one occasion as an in-patient, "the aliens" convinced Agnes that there was going to be a fire and that she would be hurt because she was trapped in the hospital. She dialled 911 and reported an impending fire. This caused quite a bit of chaos and upset in the hospital. At other times Agnes was able to realize that the aliens did not really exist, and it was in one of those moments that the worker helped Agnes to create an action plan where she lists the steps she will take to check out her suspicions about imminent harm. In this plan she listed the people she trusts to help her figure out what is and is not real. This is an example of a strategy where the social worker and Agnes worked together to identify external supports that will ensure safety, with the longer-term goal of assisting Agnes in retaining her ability to trust herself and build effective support systems.

One way to maximize her potential to change would be to assist Agnes to acknowledge and fulfill roles that she has other than that of service user. Agnes is a mother and grandmother. Her adult children have lived with her illness their entire lives and have a difficult time acknowledging the changes she has made. The social worker, with Agnes' permission, could begin to reach out to her family. There is much compelling evidence that engaging family members enhances positive outcomes for service users (Dixon et al., 2001). The social worker encouraged the family to join a support group for family members. With education and a lot of support, the family were able to be more supportive of Agnes. Agnes was invited to join the family for her grandson's birthday.

Conclusion

This is an exciting time to be a social work practitioner in the mental health field. The Kirby report has brought the concepts of anti-oppression and empowerment into the mainstream. In an era that focuses on inter-professional practice, social work has much to teach our colleagues in other health professions.

Agnes' journey continues to evolve. Hopefully this chapter has introduced you to the complexity of implementing structural social work in practice with mental health service users and given you ideas about how this might look in practice. We have included a brief history and an overview of mental health policy so that you can understand the context of services and resources available to service users. In addition, we have discussed skills and techniques that are similar for other individuals seeking help and those that are unique to individuals with mental health problems.

References

Bachrach, L.L. (1978). A conceptual approach to deinstitutionalization. *Hospital and Community Psychiatry, 29*, 573–578.

Bachrach, L.L. (1981). Continuity of care for chronic mental patients: A conceptual analysis. *American Journal of Psychiatry, 138*, 1449–1456.

Bennett, D. (1979). De-institutionalization in two cultures. *Milbank Memorial Fund Quarterly, 57*, 516–531.

Berger, P., & Luckmann, T. (1966). *The Social Construction of Reality: A Treatise in the Sociology of Knowledge*. Garden City, NY: Doubleday.

Campbell, J., Brophy, L., Healy, B., & O'Brien, A.M. (2006). International perspectives on the use of community treatment orders: Implications for mental health social workers. *British Journal of Social Work, 36*, 1101.

Dawson, J., Romans, S., Gibbs, A., & Ratter, N. (2003). Ambivalence about community treatment orders. *International Journal of Law and Psychiatry, 26*(3), 243–256.

Dixon, L., McFarlane, W.R., Lefley, H., Lucksted, A., Cohen, M., Falloon, I., Mueser, K., Miklowitz, D., Solomon, P., & Sondheimer, D. (2001). Evidence-based practices for services to families of people with psychiatric disabilities. *Psychiatric Services*, 52, 903–910.

Dreezer & Dreezer Inc. (2005). *Report on the legislated review of community treatment orders required under section 33.9 of the Mental Health Act*. Retrieved October 21, 2007, from http://www.health.gov.on.ca/english/public/pub/ministry_reports/dreezer/dreezer.html

Everett, B. (2000). *A fragile revolution: Consumers and psychiatric survivors confront the power of the mental health system*. Waterloo, ON: Wilfred Laurier Press.

Heinonen, T., & Metteri, A., (2005). *Social work in health and mental health: Issues, developments, and actions*. Toronto, ON: Canadian Scholars' Press Inc.

Hudson, C.G. (2005). Socioeconomic status and mental illness: Tests of the social causation and selection hypotheses. *American Journal of Orthopsychiatry*, 75(1), 3–18.

Hunt, A., daSilva, A., Lurie, S., & Goldbloom, D.S. (2007). Community treatment orders in Toronto: The emerging data. *Canadian Journal of Psychiatry*, 52, 647–656.

Kirby, J. (2006). *Out of the shadows at last: Transforming mental health, mental illness and addiction services in Canada*. Ottawa, ON: The Standing Senate Committee on Social Affairs, Science and Technology. Retrieved October 23, 2008, from http://www.parl.gc.ca/39/1/parlbus/commbus/senate/com-e/soci-e/rep-e/rep02may06part1-e.htm

Lundy, C. (2004). *Social work and social justice: A structural approach to practice*. Peterborough, ON: Broadview Press.

Mental Health Act, R.S.O. 1990, Chapter M7. Retrieved October 23, 2008, from http://www.e-laws.gov.on.ca/html/statutes/english/elaws_statutes_90m07_e.htm

Moreau, M.J., Frosst, S., Frayne, G., Hlywa, M., Leonard, L., & Rowell, M. (1993). *Empowerment II: Snapshots of the structural approach in action*. Ottawa, ON: Carleton University.

Moreau, M.J., & Leonard, L. (1989). *Empowerment through a structural approach to social work: A report from practice*. Ottawa, ON: Carleton University.

Mullaly, B. (2007). *The new structural social work* (3rd ed.). Toronto, ON: Oxford University Press.

O'Brien, A.M., & Farrell, S. (2005). Community treatment orders: Profile of a Canadian experience. *Canadian Journal of Psychiatry*, 50, 27–30.

Ontario Ministry of Health. (1993). *Putting people first: The reform of mental health services in Ontario*. Retrieved October 23, 2008, from www.ontario.cmha.ca/docs/policy/puttingpeoplefirst.pdf

O'Reilly, R. (2004). Why are community treatment orders controversial? *Canadian Journal of Psychiatry*, 49(9), 579–584.

O'Reilly, R.L., Keegan, D.L., Corring, D., Shrikhande, S., & Natarajan, D. (2007). A qualitative analysis of the use of community treatment orders in Saskatchewan. *International Journal of Law and Psychiatry*, 29(6), 516–524.

Perez, A., Lefiman, S., & Estrada, A. (2003). Reversing the criminalization of mental illness. *Crime and Delinquency*, 49(1), 62–78.

Reaume, G. (2002). Lunatic to patient to person: Nomenclature in psychiatric history and the influence of patient's activism in North America. *International Journal of Law and Psychiatry, 25*, 405–426.

Spearman, L. (2005). A developmental approach to social work practice in mental health: Building on strengths. In T. Heinonen & A. Metteri (Eds.), *Social work in health and mental health: Issues, developments, and actions* (pp. 45–64). Toronto, ON: Canadian Scholars' Press Inc.

Szasz, T. (1987). *Insanity: The idea and its consequences*. San Francisco: John Wiley & Sons.

Tew, J. (2005). *Social perspectives in mental health: Developing social models to understand and work with mental distress*. London, UK: Jessica Kingsley Publishers.

CHAPTER 8

"We Have a Voice":
Helping Immigrant Women Challenge Abuse[1]

BEN CARNIOL AND VIVIAN DEL VALLE

Introduction

Our perspective on structural social work is informed by progressive ideologies that help us understand how systemic structures enable one group of people to obtain power, benefits, and privilege at the expense of other people. As structural social workers, we work with others to transform oppressive structures into equitable processes based on economic, political, and social justice (Baines, 2007; Benjamin, 2007; Bishop, 2002; Campbell, 2003; Carniol, 2005a, 2005b, 2005c; George & Marlowe, 2005; Lundy, 2004; McIntosh, 1998; Moreau,1979; Mullaly, 2007; see also, in this volume, Murray & Hick, Chapter 1). Oppressive structures exist at multiple levels. They include laws, policies, practices, institutions, norms, values, ideologies, beliefs, interpretations, and narratives that create or aggravate injustices.

When we apply a structural analysis to new Canadians, we begin with a recognition of the consequences for First Nations peoples of the genocide, theft of land, and cultural oppression that were compounded by the coerced immigration of African slaves to the Americas. Partly because of this history, the unofficial Canadian agenda toward immigrants has been, and continues to be, their integration into unjust social relations. By unjust social relations, we mean the unjustifiable ways that "power over" is structured—based on class, cultural backgrounds, gender, sexual orientation, (dis)abilities, lightness or darkness of skin, facial features, age, and other systemic forms of domination.

While many immigrants face hardships, such as poverty wages, some female immigrants face additional challenges. Examples include abuse by male family members, fear, isolation, no information about social services, and employment in precarious jobs while being totally responsible for the household.

This chapter demonstrates how some immigrant Latinas[2] have been helped by a structural approach to social work. To protect confidentiality, we have changed the names and some of the facts about the situation we will be examining.

As we documented our practice example we divided it into six segments, each consisting of a description of practice, followed by our reflections about that practice. Flowing from these descriptions/reflections, we then identified the following six themes as corresponding to each of our practice segments:

1. finding voice;
2. finding oppression;
3. finding resiliency;
4. raising critical consciousness;
5. standing up for client rights; and
6. developing solidarity for emancipation.

Practice Example: Carolina
Events Leading to Counselling

Jorge and Laura came to Canada from Colombia 10 years ago, along with their three young daughters and Laura's mother, Carolina. Their troubles began soon after arriving in Canada. Jorge's income from construction work was too low to meet the family's expenses. Tension increased between Jorge and Laura. She obtained a job cleaning offices at night.

While Laura was at work, Jorge began to sexually and emotionally abuse his mother-in-law. He threatened Carolina that if she ever said anything to her daughter, he would harm the children. She was terrified and told no one. Laura noticed that her mother was losing weight and developing severe skin infections that continued despite prescribed medication. Whenever Laura asked her mother what was happening, Carolina answered that she missed Colombia. Meanwhile, the entire family continued going to church together every Sunday and the abuse continued.

One evening, after Laura had celebrated Carolina's 67th birthday, Jorge came home late, intoxicated, and demanded dinner. He complained that Laura was not behaving like a good wife any more, and that she had pushed him to having sex with her mother for several years. Shocked, Laura looked at her mother and got silence. Laura immediately called the police, who, after intense investigation, arrested Jorge that evening.

That night Carolina stopped speaking. Frantic, Laura searched for help. Her doctor referred them to a Spanish-speaking psychiatrist. Carolina spoke no English. She remained silent with the psychiatrist, who diagnosed her as clinically depressed and prescribed medications, which she refused to take. The psychiatrist then phoned the manager of a social agency who assigned the case to a Spanish-speaking clinical worker, a Latina Mestiza[3] who is co-author of this chapter. We will present what happened and our reflections in a first-person narrative.

Finding Voice

Practice

When Carolina entered my office, she sat down right away and started doing her knitting. Speaking Spanish, I welcomed her and introduced myself. A long silence started. I concentrated on her knitting. She knitted very quickly without looking at her hands. She wasn't looking at me either. She was looking at my small office and its colourful collection of Latin American paintings. I remained silent.

She fixed her eyes for few minutes on the big Aztec calendar on my wall. As the silence continued, I sensed that Carolina was starting to become more comfortable. After a while, she looked at me in the eyes for the first time. I smiled, paused, and then I said, "The colour of that wool is my favourite … what kind of wool is it?" She replied, "It's alpaca wool, the warmest wool in the world." I was astonished that Carolina had actually spoken! In between pauses, I gently continued a conversation about the wool and her knitting. Carolina agreed to see me on a weekly basis.

Reflection

This first meeting was crucial because Carolina would decide if she would speak to me at all. Although I was supposed to be doing an agency assessment, I did not. It was more important that I tune in to her as a person, showing a respectful attitude from which Carolina could feel safe with me. My silent support, my attentive yet relaxed body language, and my non-threatening questions about her knitting helped to achieve this purpose. My office, with its Latin American crafts, also helped Carolina to feel welcome. All of these factors contributed to the start of a therapeutic relationship. From my clinical experience with women and children who have been sexually abused, I know how important it is for the counsellor to take the time to create a safe space and to understand clients' own perceptions of the abuse, their responses, and the context.

Researcher Donna Baines (2007) has documented ways that many social agencies make it difficult or impossible for workers to have enough time to carry out accurate assessments of the social relations impacting on clients. Funding cuts and the political climate often result in workers processing clients in an assembly-line fashion, under the supervision of arbitrary managers. Fortunately, my workplace allowed me the time and autonomy to tune in to Carolina's needs. Due to my ideological perspective, I understand patriarchy as having created illegitimate male privilege by normalizing male power and control over females. This perspective helped me, as a woman, to seek an unspoken bond of solidarity with Carolina, just as I do with other women who have been abused by males acting on patriarchy. A structural version of clinical counselling was pivotal to my helping Carolina find her voice. Structural social work transforms the therapeutic relationship away from a conventional, vertical, top-down practice and toward power sharing "as much as possible between worker and service user and each is considered to have different but equivalent wisdom and expertise" (Mullaly, 2007, p. 317).

Finding Oppression

Practice

Carolina talked about how her mother, an Indigenous woman, had taught her to knit when she was a girl. She explained how in her Indigenous community it was common practice for young men to kidnap girls for a year or longer "to make them wives and mothers." Carolina told me she was kidnapped when she was 14 years old, and when her kidnapper brought her to visit her parents after she had been hidden from them for a year, her parents blamed her for returning pregnant and unmarried. Carolina said she had no choice but to marry her kidnapper, and that now she was proud to have been a "good wife of a man I never loved and good mother to my nine children who I adore."

Reflection

The way I do my agency's assessment reflects Latin American cultures as storytelling cultures. I listen carefully without interrupting the client's story, and right after each session I fill in the form with the answers to questions we covered during that session.

While these assessment sessions provided many examples of Carolina having been oppressed, I refrained from responding with my values and perspectives because it was critical to hear Carolina's perceptions about the abuse, her life, her values, and her needs. As structural workers, we use techniques developed by conventional practitioners, such as those developed by therapist Judith Herman, known for her work with trauma survivors. She has emphasized the importance of active listening and being disciplined "to make no assumptions about either the facts or the meaning of the trauma" to the people we work with (Herman, 1997, p. 179).

During our sessions, I made no assumptions about the meaning Carolina assigned to her own painful experiences. At the same time, based on structural analysis, I constructed a picture for myself that recognized Carolina as a survivor of patriarchy's subservient female roles, interwoven with cultural, colonial, and other dimensions of domination that she had probably internalized a long time ago (Lundy, 2004; Barnoff & Coleman, 2007).

Finding Resiliency

Practice

As Carolina and I developed a therapeutic relationship based on trust and respect, Carolina disclosed the following: "That man hurt me." Over the next few sessions, she talked about how Jorge had repeatedly raped her, and about how she felt when he raped her. She told me, "I had two very long, thick, white hair braids, which he pulled violently towards him every time he did sex that hurt me. So one day, I cut off all my hair, but it didn't help. He hit me hard, and it seemed it would never end. Later, Jorge accused me of becoming mentally sick, asking my daughter and grandchildren 'why did she cut her hair? She's crazy!' It broke my heart when they agreed with him. Later the psychiatrist also thought there was something wrong with me."

I responded, "Jorge did not have sex with you, he raped you. It's important to understand the difference. You never agreed to have sex with him, he used his power to threaten you and he forced you. That's called rape, and it's a crime."

Carolina and I had a discussion about rape being a crime, then I said, "Your family didn't know that you were being silenced and getting raped. They didn't know you were trying to protect yourself when you cut off your braids."

Carolina said, "Yes, but everybody thought I was crazy. Actually, I was a prisoner. I was dead inside. My body was gradually failing, but I was still breathing. I prayed to God that I wanted to die. This went on for eight years."

I wondered where she got the strength to survive. Over the next sessions she provided some answers. She talked about her great love for her children and grandchildren, how much she cared for and enjoyed Chispa, her dog, and about the importance of her spiritual and religious beliefs. "My great-grandmother had taught me to love nature—its rivers, animals, trees, and sky. During the years when Jorge was hurting me, I walked with Chispa to a nearby park. I sat under my favourite tree. It was the only place I was able to find some peace. That's where I prayed to God. I offered up my pain to Virgin Mary who suffered like me.[4] And in that park I felt I was part of a bigger universe. I knew I was not alone."

Reflection

Carolina obtained her resiliency partly from her loving relationships with her children and grandchildren. Furthermore, her daily experience in the park, engulfed by nature, gave her some spiritual respite. During her childhood, her great-grandmother had taught her an Indigenous perspective about her interconnections and interdependence with nature.

Her Christian beliefs were painfully paradoxical. On the one hand, they implicitly approved of her suffering:

> Through religious and cultural images, women often feel that it is their lot in life to suffer. They are defined by their family roles, and their primary obligation is to preserve the family. These characteristics of Latino society place a woman in the typical role of victim. (Florez-Ortiz in Mattson & Ruiz, 2005, p. 524)

More specifically, "Marianismo" refers to the way many Catholic Latina women look up to the Virgin Mary as a role model who was totally obedient in accepting her lot in life (Del Valle, 2008; Flake, 2005). Therefore, Carolina expected herself to graciously and quietly accept her own oppression. On the other hand, as Cole-Arnal (1998) noted, the Catholic Church also teaches that God especially loves people who experience oppression.

This dynamic of religious support for oppressive attitudes, while supporting the aspirations of the oppressed, is not restricted to the Catholic Church, but is also found in other religions. Similarly, within North America's mental health sector, its pathologizing labels are being challenged by some mental health workers:

> What we call "clinical depression" cannot be fully addressed separately from the poverty, sexism, racism, social alienation and other oppressive forces experienced by many people bearing this label. Temporary relief may be provided in the form of medications and verbal therapy, but the social problem and struggles in which many sufferers find themselves must also be analyzed and addressed through actions such as critical consciousness-raising.... (Baines, 2007a, pp. 5–6)

Raising Critical Consciousness

Practice

Carolina told me there had been a schoolyard fight between her 12-year-old granddaughter Maria and Andrew, an older student. The principal believed Maria was lying when she claimed Andrew had spit in her face. He suspended Maria from school for one week, telling her to write an apology to Andrew. Laura was furious at her daughter's behaviour.

When Carolina paused, I asked, "What's your opinion?" Carolina responded, "I believe Maria is telling the truth. I know her well. She doesn't lie. Anyway, her friend Jen told her that she didn't tell the principal that Andrew spat in Maria's face because Jen was too afraid of Andrew. But I have to support my daughter by not saying anything." Carolina planned to convince Maria to write an apology to Andrew.

I asked, "If you believe Maria is telling the truth, then why should she write an apology?" Carolina responded, "You and I know we can't win 'against the giants.' Maria will have to learn to take her place in life." I asked Carolina if she wanted tea because I needed to gather my thoughts and feelings and figure out how to best respond. After I prepared tea for both us, I asked, "How would you like to see your granddaughters treated by boys and by men?" Carolina answered, "My dream is to see them treated fairly, with love, with respect— but I know it's not possible." I interjected, "It is possible! Is it fair for Maria to apologize to Andrew?" Carolina answered, "No, but life isn't fair." I said, "Young girls have rights." Carolina laughed, "We don't have rights. I was kidnapped at 14, and I had to learn to live with it."

I praised Carolina for surviving that ordeal. Then I said, "Kidnapping is a crime. Today in Canada, your granddaughters can live a life without abuse. It's the law. Things have changed since you were a girl." Then I told her a short story about the women's movement: how women came together, shared their stories, found their strength as women, decided to organize, and pushed for equal rights and for new laws.

There was a long silence. Then I added, "Many women still suffer in silence, but today in Canada your granddaughters can live the dream you have for them—to be treated with fairness, love, and respect—it is possible!" Carolina's eyes were wide open with wonder, followed by the first tears in our sessions.

Then Carolina smiled and asked "So Maria doesn't have to apologize?" I said, "That's right, she doesn't have to. We'll need to start by supporting Maria." Carolina agreed. She signed a consent form to allow me to follow-up with the school.

I contacted the school principal, met with him, and he investigated further. Andrew confessed to him that he had spat on Maria because when she and Jen were talking and laughing, he thought they were laughing at him. It turned out, they were not. The principal stopped Maria's suspension, and instead he suspended Andrew, telling him to write an apology to Maria.

Reflection

Within a therapeutic process, structural social workers use critical analysis to raise critical consciousness (Baines, 2007; Carniol, 2005b; Hick & Murray, 2008; Lundy, 2004; Mullaly, 2007). We do more than support client strengths; we challenge client attitudes, feelings, and behaviours when clients express stereotypes or assert privileges that are harmful to themselves or to others. Earlier, I had challenged Carolina's words when she had said her son-in-law "had sex" with her. I had pointed out this was not sex, but abuse of male power, and it is called rape, which is a crime. In that example, I gave reasons for opposing language that masks abuse. Additional ways of respectfully challenging clients come from counselling practices that are client-focused, strength-based, and change-oriented. An example of such practice suggests that the counsellor "create and amplify, in the client's mind, a discrepancy between present behavior and broader goals … between where one is and where one wants to be" (Miller & Rollnick, 1991, pp. 56–57).

When I asked Carolina how she would like to see her granddaughters treated by boys and by men, I was inviting Carolina to express her goals for her granddaughters. Her answer created a discrepancy between her goals for equity (respect for her granddaughters) and what she planned to do (convince her granddaughter to apologize for something she had not done). When I asked Carolina, "If you believe Maria is telling the truth, then why should she write an apology?" I was amplifying this discrepancy. Carolina responded by devaluing her own her goals. As a structural clinician, I challenged her response by becoming an ally with her own goals for equity. We had sufficient rapport that I could oppose her internalized gender subservience.

When using techniques developed by non-structural professionals, we connect these techniques to critical analysis. Colleen Lundy (2004) wrote that what differentiates structural social work is the centrality of its "critical analysis of the social structures in society and attention to social justice and human rights" (p. 58). In our example, I widened the discrepancy in order to challenge illegitimate male privilege. I deepened this challenge by providing information about how the women's movement had struggled and achieved changes in some laws. My re-framing efforts were aimed at critical consciousness-raising. Then I was deliberately quiet to allow Carolina to process my input.

Standing up for Client Rights

Practice

Carolina told me that after Andrew was suspended from school, Maria seemed to have more confidence and to be happier. As Carolina talked with me about these results she said, "I can see that today, it's possible for women to be heard when they fight for their rights, and to have decisions in their favour. I never thought I was going to live to see this happen."

Carolina and I talked about the court date that was set for Jorge's trial. She said in a troubled voice, "I would like to see him in jail, but I'm still very afraid of him. Will he go to jail if I tell the court what he did to me?" I answered, "I don't know: the decision will be up to the judge." Carolina said, "So what's the point of me telling the court?"

I replied in a passionate voice, "If you say in court, the horrific abuse that he inflicted on you—your repulsion at his abuse, your feelings of being trapped and powerless, your constant fear for the safety of your grandchildren, how you lost your appetite, could not sleep, developed a painful skin condition—you would be breaking the silence you have kept deep inside you for eight years. You would be fighting for your rights in front of a judge!"

Carolina said, "I don't know if I can do that. I know he abused me really bad. I would like to tell the court, but it may be too much for me. I feel confused." There was a silence, then I said, "It's normal to be confused. Anyway, you don't have to decide now. The court day is a few months away. I have a suggestion: let's prepare ourselves as if you were going to testify, and later, when the day approaches, you can decide."

She asked, "How can I prepare myself?" I explained about the Victims' Witness Program that is offered by the court to explain its procedures to potential witnesses. She asked, "If I decide to testify, will you come with me to court?" I answered that yes, I would accompany her.

At our next counselling session, Carolina seemed filled with new energy as she declared, "I talked with Laura about me testifying and I'm deciding to face my fear head on! I can do it! And I want to do it!"

Reflection

Her granddaughter's vindication had a major impact on Carolina's understanding of what was possible. She was learning that females could stand up for their rights. Nevertheless, her fears of testifying were very real. Although Jorge had terrorized her into silence, over time Carolina had been able to describe the abuse to me. But finding a voice with a therapist where the client feels safe in resisting the structures of oppression is very different from the same client finding a voice in the public arena. Courts and other public forums can be extremely intimidating for survivors of abuse.

In our example, after Carolina asked, "What's the point of me telling the court?" I used re-framing skills (away from fear and resignation, toward hope based on realistic assessments). I explained that while her testifying would not guarantee a guilty verdict, her testimony could help the judge to better understand what had happened. In addition, I was passionate about what it could mean for Carolina to find her public voice in court.

We cannot hope to end inequity and social injustice merely by being professionally detached and impassive. Instead, we should be passionate about the need for social justice and work continuously to expand our intervention skills to include those that build resistance and enthusiasm for equity and social change. (Baines, 2007b, p. 192)

In our example, the therapeutic alliance between client and worker, guided by a structural approach, constituted a solid building block to help Carolina discover her public voice. Next, we follow Carolina's public voice in court and in a participatory education/support group with other abused Latinas.

Developing Solidarity for Emancipation
Practice
Laura and I accompanied Carolina to court. As Carolina testified, she periodically made eye contact with me because I had suggested that by her doing that, I could give her non-verbal emotional support. She faced ferocious cross-examination from Jorge's lawyer. The trial lasted two days, at the end of which the judge found Jorge guilty and sentenced him to prison. On the day he was sentenced, Carolina said, "This is the happiest day of my life. I feel heard and validated for the first time in my whole life!"

I invited Carolina to participate in a group for Latinas who had been abused. During the previous months, I had teamed up with a female, Spanish-speaking professional from another community agency: together we advocated for a Spanish-speaking group for abused Latinas, which we would co-facilitate. The managers from both of our agencies approved our request to start such a group on a weekly basis, 12 times, with two hours for each session. We made arrangements for free childcare, tickets for public transportation, and snacks. We chose topics with input from women during our intake process. Each week, there were usually 24 women and 10 children who attended. Aside from our common Spanish language we wanted to be culturally relevant, so we created a colourful, star-shaped "pi–ata."[5]

On each point of the pi–ata's star we wrote an example of oppression: colonialism, sexism, ageism, able-ism, classism, racism, and heterosexism. We summarized these as the various "isms." We also created a new "ism," and added it on the pi–ata: "immigrant-ism," to name one set of barriers that all of us, as immigrant women, had experienced in Canada. As group facilitators, we explained the meaning of words in a new vocabulary: structural inequalities, internalized oppression, internalized privilege, cognitive distortions resulting from normalizing oppression, social justice, women's rights, and personal and social change.

Group participants became highly interactive via role-playing and discussions that were often intensive. In sharing their personal stories and using their newly learned vocabulary, group members said:

"Now I realize there was sexism in my family, and that it came with patriarchy that was brought by the colonizers."

"Through counselling I learned he didn't have the right to abuse me, and that abuse is a crime."

"I felt guilty because sometimes I had orgasms when he raped me; now I understand that my body was responding, not me. I don't feel guilty any more."

"I'm not alone any more: other women like me also want to fight injustices."

"I had learned to take care of my family. I think it's a great new concept for me to start taking care of myself."

At the close of the group we had a potluck dinner. Carolina chose the message written on the top of our cake: WE HAVE A VOICE! Since then, her hair has grown back and her skin infections are gone. She is not taking any medication. I see her less frequently for counselling. She seems vibrant and satisfied. Meanwhile, we have started more groups for abused Latinas and, along with others, I continue to explore how to resist the abuse still experienced by Latinas.

Reflection

The judge's decision to send Jorge to prison was a life-changing event for Carolina. It was my assessment that Carolina would benefit from a group that included critical analysis:

> There is widespread agreement among many anti-oppressive writers and progressive social work writers that to become a member of a group process with other persons who are similarly oppressed is the most effective way for oppressed persons to develop political awareness of their situation. In such a group context, the members can self-define a more authentic identity than the one imposed on them by the dominant group,

develop the self-confidence to "come out" and assert their more authentic identity, and establish solidarity in order to take action against their oppression. (Mullaly, 2007, p. 304)

The pi–ata helped group members to articulate, often for the first time, how they had been abused not only by individual men, but also by a patriarchal-machista[6] system that is wrapped up with colonialism and other interlocking oppressions that had excluded women from many spheres within economic, social, and political life.

As a result, Carolina and other group members not only felt less isolated, but also developed bonds of solidarity as they brainstormed different ways of emancipating themselves from oppression. This new consciousness enabled some women to reject psychiatric labels, such as the label of "clinical depression" that had missed the cause of Carolina's silence. Self-blame among the group members seemed to be reduced, validating what structural social work writers have suggested happens when mistreatment is recognized as not only personal, but also systemic (Carniol, 2005a; Lundy, 2004; Mullaly, 2007).

Our social agency managers, being progressive, fully supported our advocacy to develop a group for Latinas. Also helpful, my agency supported worker self-care in addressing the vicarious trauma experienced by its workers who "absorb the sight, smell, sound, touch and feel of the stories told in detail" (Richardson, 2001, p. 7) by survivors of violence. Self-care is crucial in helping us to keep going in the face of our emancipatory efforts (Hick & Murray, 2008; Mullaly, 2007).

Conclusion

We recognize that all six of our practice themes are present simultaneously, to different degrees, within each of our six practice segments. Moreover, these six themes resonate with our experience in other practice situations. Neither linear nor sequential, these themes are also easily found in the literature on anti-oppression and structural social work. Therefore, we conclude that these six overlapping and interactive themes, and their associated practice skills, constitute some of today's core components of structural social work. We suggest they be applied and tested, then affirmed or changed by others as they reflect on their practice.

While we have good reason to celebrate the effectiveness of structural social work, we know that the structures of neo-liberal capitalism often block change or, alternatively, absorb change while escalating inequalities and exploitation, both locally and globally (Finn, 2008; Klein, 2008).

Nevertheless, we are encouraged by the resiliency of Carolina and other Indigenous people who are finding their public voice to express the cultural wisdom of their ancestors (Baskin, 2006; Freeman, 2007; Lavallée, 2008). A First Nations Anishnabek Elder, Waubauno Kwe, from Canada offers us a teaching from her community:

> We see the interdependence and inter-relatedness and inter-connected-ness of all things among human beings, animals, plants, elements, and the universe. (Riley in Carniol, 2005b, p. 68)

This ancient wisdom is a reminder that reality is more than the flawed and cracked structures of power manipulated by people who revere dysfunctional economic, social, political, and religious doctrines. Beyond their catastrophic legacies, our own perspective on change is shaped by a critical consciousness that is supported by progressive ideologies and allied with a universal, communal, and personal spirituality anchored to social justice. Respecting differences, we find that, as structural social workers, we are part of a larger human quest for equity, democratic accountability, and non-violent social transformation. Together, as we harness our passion, courage, and determination, we take on a daunting task: to dismantle the corrupt structures that exploit people, destroy environments, and imperil all life on this planet.

Endnotes

[1] The authors of this chapter are very appreciative of the support from the book's editors and for the suggestions by this chapter's reviewers.

[2] "Latina" refers to women from Latin America.

[3] "Mestiza" refers to a bi-racialized woman having Indigenous and European ancestors.

[4] In the Catholic religion, the Virgin Mary is believed to have given birth to Jesus, the son of God, and to have silently accepted her suffering at Jesus' crucifixion.

[5] The pi–ata, popular in certain Latin American countries, is a decorated container filled with candy and toys suspended from a height, and then broken by sticks swung by blindfolded children and adults at their celebrations.

[6] "Machista" is based on a stereotype that emphasizes hyper-masculinity associated with Latin American males, a legacy of the Conquest by the Spanish conquistadors.

References

Baines, D. (2007a). Anti-oppressive social work practice: Fighting for space, fighting for change. In D. Baines (Ed.), *Doing anti-oppressive practice: Building transformative politicized social work* (pp. 1–30). Halifax, NS: Fernwood Publishing.

Baines, D. (2007b). Extending a radical tradition: Building transformative, politicized social work. In D. Baines (Ed.), *Doing anti-oppressive practice: Building transformative politicized social work* (pp. 191–195). Halifax, NS: Fernwood Publishing.

Baines, D. (2007c). If you could change one thing: Restructuring, social workers and social justice practice. In D. Baines (Ed.), *Doing anti-oppressive practice: Building transformative politicized social work* (pp. 83–94). Halifax, NS: Fernwood Publishing.

Barnoff, L., & Coleman, B. (2007). Strategies for integrating anti-oppressive principles: Perspectives from feminist agencies. In D. Baines (Ed.), *Doing anti-oppressive practice: Building transformative politicized social work* (pp. 31–49). Halifax, NS: Fernwood Publishing.

Baskin, C. (2006). Aboriginal world views as challenges and possibilities in social work education. *Critical Social Work, 7*(2). Retrieved September 14, 2008, from www.criticalsocialwork.com

Benjamin, A. (2007). The importance of resistance, history and strategy. In D. Baines (Ed.), *Doing anti-oppressive practice: Building transformative politicized social work* (pp. 196–204). Halifax, NS: Fernwood Publishing.

Bishop, A. (2002). *Becoming an ally: Breaking the cycle of oppression in people* (2nd ed.). Halifax, NS: Fernwood Publishing.

Brown, C. (2007). Feminist therapy, violence, problem drinking and re-storying women's lives: Reconceptualizing anti-oppressive feminist therapy. In D. Baines (Ed.), *Doing anti-oppressive practice: Building transformative politicized social work* (pp. 136–138). Halifax, NS: Fernwood Publishing.

Campbell, C. (2003). *Anti-oppressive social work: Promoting equity and social justice.* Halifax, NS: Author. Retrieved September 15, 2008, from http://aosw.socialwork.dal.ca/index.html

Carniol, B. (2005a). Analysis of social location and change: Practice implications. In S. Hick, J. Fook, & R. Pozzuto (Eds.), *Social work: A critical turn* (pp. 153–165). Toronto, ON: Thompson Educational Publishing.

Carniol, B. (2005b). *Case critical: Social services and social justice in Canada* (5th ed.). Toronto, ON: Between the Lines.

Carniol, B. (2005c). Structural social work (Canada). In J.M. Herrick & P.H. Stuart (Eds.), *Encyclopedia of social welfare history in North America* (pp. 391–393). Thousand Oaks, CA: Sage Publications.

Cole-Arnal, O. (1998). *To set the captives free: Liberation theology in Canada.* Toronto, ON: Between the Lines.

Del Valle, V. (2008). *Resources that assist immigrant Latinas to overcome social barriers in leaving their abusive partners after settling in Canada.* Unpublished master's thesis, York University, Toronto, Ontario, Canada.

Flake, D.F. (2005). Individual, family and community risk markers for domestic violence in Peru. *Violence Against Women, 11,* 353–373.

Finn, E. (2008). Poverty amidst plenty: Why isn't inequality a key issue in the latest election? *CCPA Monitor.* Retrieved March 22, 2009, from www.policyalternatives.ca

Freeman, B. (2007). Indigenous pathways to anti-oppressive practice. In D. Baines (Ed.), *Doing anti-oppressive practice: Building transformative politicized social work* (pp. 95–110). Halifax, NS: Fernwood Publishing.

George, P., & Marlowe, S. (2005). Structural social work in action: Experiences from rural India. *Journal of Progressive Human Services, 16*(1), 5–24.

Herman, J. (1997). *Trauma and recovery: The aftermath of violence—from domestic violence to political terror.* New York: Basic Books.

Hick, S.F., & Murray, K. (2008). Structural social work. In M. Gray & S. Webb (Eds.), *Social Work Theories and Methods.* Thousand Oaks, CA: Sage.

Klein, N. (2008). *The shock doctrine: The rise of disaster capitalism.* Toronto, ON: Random House.

Lavallée, L. (2008). Balancing the medicine wheel through physical activity. *Journal of Aboriginal Health, 4*(1). Retrieved on March 25, 2009, from http://www.naho.ca/english/journal/jah04_01/09MedicineWheel_64-71.pdf

Lundy, C. (2004). *Social work and social justice: A structural approach to practice.* Peterborough, ON: Broadview Press.

Mattson, S., & Ruiz, E. (2005). Intimate partner violence in the Latino community and its effect on children. *Health Care for Women International, 26*(6), 523–529.

McIntosh, P. (1998). White privilege: Unpacking the invisible knapsack. In M. McGoldrick (Ed.), *Re-visioning family therapy: Race, culture and gender in clinical practice* (pp. 147–150). New York: Guilford Press.

Miller, W.R. & Rollnick, S. (1991). *Motivational interviewing: Preparing people to change addictive behavior.* New York: Guilford Press.

Moreau, M.J. (1979). A structural approach to social work practice. *Canadian Journal of Social Work Education, 5*(1), 78–94.

Mullaly, B. (2007). *The new structural social work* (3rd ed.). Toronto, ON: Oxford University Press.

Richardson, J. (2001). *Guidebook on vicarious trauma: Recommended solutions for anti-violence workers*. London, ON: Centre for Research on Violence Against Women and Children in London, Ontario for the Family Violence Prevention Unit, Health Canada.

Riley, B. (1994). Her Indigenous name: Waubauno Kwe. Teachings from the medicine wheel: Theories for practice. *WUNSKA Network*. Canadian Association of Schools of Social Work, Ottawa.

CHAPTER 9

Structural Social Work
from a (dis)Ability Perspective

JUDY E. MACDONALD AND GAILA FRIARS

> Shame will no longer structure our wardrobe or our discourse.
> (Linton, 1998, p. 4)

Social work has a long history of working with people with (dis)Abilities. This history includes working within institutions such as acute care hospitals, rehabilitation centres, or mental health facilities; for non-profit organizations providing services within the community; within the government, writing or enforcing social policies; and for disability organizations advocating for services. However, social work intervention with (dis)Abled persons has not always been in the best interest of the client. Gilson, Bricout, and Baskind (1998) found that social workers tended to reinforce common stereotypes about (dis)Abled persons, while failing to recognize their unique characteristics and needs. From a structural perspective, this chapter will challenge social workers to practise using rights-based interventions, including the dismantling of oppressive structures and barriers within society while promoting the inclusion of people with (dis)Abilities.

Historical Lens

People with (dis)Abilities face numerous oppressions throughout their lives. Historically, they have been hidden away in family attics, institutionalized in state-based and private asylums, physically, emotionally, and sexually abused, sterilized against their will, socially segregated, and politically silenced (Chadwick & Dias, 2000; Linton, 1998; MacDonald, 2005; Oliver, 1990, 1996; Wendell, 1996). They are judged against the structure of normalcy, denying the unique characteristics of their being (Goffman, 1963). One of the most blatant forms of oppression came with Hitler's T-4 eugenics program, which began by preventing procreation and escalated to the elimination of people with (dis)Abilities. Hitler wanted to purify the race and therefore deemed anyone with physical or mental abnormalities as a threat. Historians have estimated that 250,000 people with (dis)Abilities were murdered, originally by gassing and later by starvation (Chadwick & Dias, 2000). North America was not immune to atrocities committed toward people with (dis)Abilities. For example, until the mid 1940s people with (dis)Abilities were used as a source of entertainment in circus-like freak shows and paid very little, if at all, to be made objects of ridicule. Under the parameters of the "mental hygiene movement," sterilization was a common practice in many provinces of Canada, often performed under the pretence of an appendectomy (Stienstra & Wight-Felske, 2003). People with (dis)Abilities were segregated from society in numerous ways, through being hidden in family attics or basements, by attending special schools, and by using segregated transportation (Linton, 1998; MacDonald, 2005; Oliver, 1999).

Disability rights activists suggest that the modern-day extinction of people with (dis)Abilities is found in current medical practices. People with (dis)Abilities are having "do not resuscitate" orders placed on their charts without discussion or consent, and they are being denied access to transplants (Stienstra & Wight-Felske, 2003). Furthermore, prenatal genetic screening that detects an "abnormality" in the fetus often leads to a recommendation for termination (Stienstra & Wight-Felske, 2003).

Economic Costs

In 2001, over 3.4 million adults (aged 15 years and over) in Canada lived with a (dis)Ability, equalling 14.6 percent of the adult population (Human Resources and Social Development Canada [HRSDC], 2006). As one ages, the likelihood of living with a (dis)Ability increases: 40.5 percent of people aged 65 years and over are identified as having a (dis)Ability (HRSDC, 2006), while 4.6 percent of children aged five to 14 years live with a (dis)Ability (Statistics Canada, 2008). The household income of adults with (dis)Abilities was $20,000 lower than the household income of adults without (dis)Abilities (HRSDC, 2006). The DisAbled Women's Network of Ontario (2003) reported that women with (dis)Abilities in Canada are living well below the poverty line with an average income of $8,360. Women living with severe (dis)Abilities were the poorest of the poor.

(Dis)Ability touches us all, either through knowing someone with a (dis)Ability, personally identifying as a person with a (dis)Ability, or being "temporarily abled-bodied." The likelihood of spending at least some portion of your life with a (dis)Ability is statistically close to 100 percent (Zola, 1982). The oppression and silencing of people with (dis)Abilities has formed a meta-narrative within our cultural storyline.

Language and (dis)Ability

Language is powerful, a component of social organization that "largely reflects the interests and world views of dominant groups" (Mullaly, 1997, p. 117). Structural social workers need to promote the reassignment of terms toward the empowerment of marginalized groups—for example, by deconstructing terms such as mentally retarded, crippled, or mad and replacing them with people-first language. "People with disabilities" puts the person first while identifying disability as one characteristic, while "disabled persons" highlights the disability issues (Linton, 1998; MacDonald, 2005, 2008a, 2008b). Both terms will be used interchangeably throughout this chapter. Disability activists have reclaimed derogatory terms such as crip, gimp, and crazy. However, there is a danger of potentially reinforcing the traditional derogatory intent. In this chapter, disability is written as (dis)Ability: "(dis)" to respect the person's social and physical connection with disability, and "Ability" to highlight the creative and innovative ways of dealing with societal barriers (MacDonald, 2008b).

(Dis)Ability Models

Enns and Neufeldt (2003) identified five dominant models in (dis)Ability: medical, charity or philanthropic, sociological, economic, and socio-political. The medical model is centrally associated with health services where the person with the (dis)Ability can receive services in the form of diagnosis, treatment, and ultimately cure. The medicalization of (dis)Ability is based upon the "sick" role theory (Parsons, 1951), whereby the goal is to fix the (dis)Abled person. The charity or philanthropic model evokes sympathy from the general populace who view people with (dis)Abilities as unproductive welfare recipients of society. They are to be pitied; their (dis)Ability viewed as a tragic misfortune. People with (dis)Abilities can respond to these stereotypes with "shame, embarrassment and, sometimes, hatred" (Neufeldt & Enns, 2003, p. 7). The charity lens is believed to be the most dominant view of (dis)Ability throughout the world (MacDonald, 2008b). The sociological model views people with (dis)Abilities as deviants, defying or failing to meet societal norms. Societal roles and functions are examined with specific emphasis on the stereotypes and stigmas associated with having a (dis)Ability. The economic model examines the costs and benefits associated with people with (dis)Abilities in relation to job placements, schooling, housing, and services. The socio-political model is a (dis)Ability rights model that refuses to view (dis)Ability from an individual problem base. (Dis)Ability is seen within its social and political context; for example, the stairs-only entry to the bank is viewed as a community-access problem, not a personal problem of the wheelchair user. Personal ownership of societal barriers is refuted (MacDonald, 2005, 2008b).

A spiritual lens to (dis)Ability is associated with meaning, growth, and communion, extending "an invitation to respond to another's pain and suffering, and to be faithful in relationships" (Favaro, 2002, p. 216). The spiritual quest of finding meaning in one's struggle can bring a new level of insight about the human condition, where individuals, social workers, and communities rediscover people with (dis)Abilities (Vash, 1981).

A structural critique of (dis)Ability looks beyond individual pathology. The universalization of the body is the normative context from which all (dis)Abled bodies are judged such that "[d]isabilities are covered over, and made invisible, by the structures and assumptions of normalcy" (Titchkosky, 2001, p. 133) or "bodies deemed inferior become spectacles of otherness while the unmasked are sheltered in the neutral space of normalcy" (Thomson, 1997, p. 8). A structural critique shifts to a social recognition of oppression by identifying the barriers associated with inaccessibility, exclusion, and difference (Wendell, 2006). What restricts and isolates persons with (dis)Abilities needs to be deconstructed, taken apart, and exposed. (dis)Abilities are multiple, fluid, and evolving and, therefore, cannot be categorized into a single defining entity for the purpose of medicine or social organization.

Case Studies

Social workers have been working with people with (dis)Abilities on numerous fronts, from community development to establishing advocacy groups, community living centres, and, overall, a place for (dis)Abled persons within society. They also help families secure the services and resources necessary to combat barriers associated with accessibility and accommodation, and engage in individual work recognizing the person with the (dis)Ability as the expert on his or her own life and abilities. No matter what the context, be it hospital social work, community work, or policy development, structural social work from a (dis)Ability perspective recognizes the personal, social, political, and economic aspects of intervention (Moreau & Leonard, 1989; Mullaly, 1997, 2007). Furthermore, it is often the intersection of oppression that has a profound impact upon (dis)Abled persons because race, class, gender, and/or sexual orientation heighten their experiences of being (dis)Abled within an ablest world (Murray & Hick, Chapter 1). "Opposing the systemic inequalities that create so much despair and hardship in service users' lives" (Smith, 2007, p. 145) is a definitive role for social work.

The case studies in this chapter have been drawn from a compilation of practice and research experiences. Through each case, practice principles and learnings will be derived to guide structural social work practice from a (dis)Ability perspective. The chart following the case studies outlines specific structural skills that have been demonstrated through the cases, their related practice principles, and the dominant discourse that needs to be unsettled. Spiritual sensitivity skills and the use of self are believed to be skills that cut across all intervention and, therefore, are not specifically associated with one case.

Mohan

Mohan, an 80-year-old East Indian man, lived with his wife of 60 years. Together they had two sons, one a physician and one an engineer, both living in another part of the country. Over the last five years Mohan's wife had noticed his declining memory, confusion, and an inability to financially manage their affairs. His wife was finding household management and Mohan's care increasingly difficult as she struggled with her own health-care issues. The sons were concerned about their parents because they recognized that their father's cognitive functioning was compromised and feared the added-care responsibilities upon their mother. They had requested an in-home assessment from long-term care. A social services social worker came to their home to meet Mohan and his wife to assess their needs. The worker made a referral for a full geriatric assessment. The worker was conscious of the significance of cultural nuances, connections to the couple's sons, and their community ties. The social worker believed it was important to listen to Mohan and ascertain his understanding of the current situation. Elders are often ignored or simply left out of the assessment process, particularly if there are signs of dementia. However, it is important to take the time to be with the service user, listen to his or her perspective, and explore his or her feelings, "especially the issues behind the issues," because this will lead to heightened understandings (Jones & McCullough, 2008, p. 237).

The social worker needed to be aware of the social and political tensions that can exist between parents and their adult children when it comes to life decisions associated with elder care. Worried about their parents, the sons wanted them to give up their home and move into a seniors' apartment. Mohan and his wife did not want to leave the home they had worked hard to create, yet the couple's needs had to be addressed. The social worker acted like many professionals who are generally empathic and supportive of older persons' continued independence and self-reliance (Harbison et al., 2005). Personal and home-care services were initiated, enabling the couple to enjoy their home for a few more years.

Practice Principles

Treat all persons with (dis)Abilities with respect. Historically, (dis)Abled persons have been pushed aside, ignored, or outrightly rejected. As a structural social worker working from a (dis)Ability perspective, it is essential to validate the service user and to form a "working with" relationship. Furthermore, it is important to identify societal barriers, which, in this case, consisted of ageist assumptions.

Learnings

To meet the person with the (dis)Ability where he or she is, while consciously attending to respect, empathy, and genuineness.

Sophie

Sophie was a 35-year-old woman, post-stroke, severely aphasic (difficulty in producing and understanding speech), and otherwise physically able, but unable to communicate by verbal or written expression. She was estranged from the father of her six-year-old son, and had a male partner of one year. Sophie was very volatile, resulting in emotional and anger outbursts. Complicated health issues led to her hospitalization. A social worker was consulted to assist Sophie with application forms for disability benefits and custody issues related to her six-year-old child. Sophie experienced frustration and sheer exhaustion in a process found by many women to be demeaning. In a study of women in the helping professions who were able to communicate in written form and represent their needs when completing application forms, the women experienced disability insurance agents as "nasty, rude, dismissive, dehumanizing and judgmental," and the application process to be a "nightmare, exhaustive and devastating" (MacDonald, 2008b, p. 222).

Sophie would try to communicate through written notes. However, it soon became apparent that the social worker was not able to interpret the notes with the meaning that Sophie had intended. There was a disjunction between what Sophie was trying to communicate and what got relayed. A communication board was ineffective and computer technology was inaccessible (not available in hospital rooms).

Custody access was dependent upon Sophie's partner being available to assist with childcare. When their partnership broke off, it put her access to her child in jeopardy. Driedger and Owen (2008) noted that women with (dis)Abilities have an increased chance of becoming a single parent. Sophie had to find other adults to assist with her visitations or she would be denied access.

The social worker would read Sophie's verbal and non-verbal cues. For example, when Sophie was anxious or concerned about her child and the custody battle, she would bring out the custody papers and a picture of her son, point to the picture, and say "mine." Sophie's perception of time and location gave rise to particular difficulty. The social worker would have to repeat court dates, bring out a calendar, and physically point to the date, often repeatedly. Sophie would often react with angry outbursts. It was difficult to ascertain if these outbursts were associated with her frustration in the communication process or distress related to the topic being discussed. Because assumptions and stereotypes foster judgment against people with (dis)Abilities and their abilities to parent (Crawford, 2003), the social worker had a responsibility to inform Sophie of these potential biases, and to advocate on her behalf for a solution that would address both her needs and the needs of her child.

Verbal communication was relayed in single words. For example, when Sophie was having uncontrollable migraines she would grab her head and repeat "hurt." Often her single words did not relay a clear message because she had difficulty with word finding. Reading the expression in her eyes, paying close attention to her body language, and tuning into emotional distress were all clues the social worker used to understand the service user.

Practice Principles

Listen and observe in the broadest context, including paying attention to body language, emotional expressions, and responses to physical surroundings, in attempts to communicate with the service user. Modes of communication for people with (dis)Abilities can vary. In a fast-paced society, social workers need to take the time to listen to the service user. This may mean relying upon technology or expertise outside of the worker's comfort zone.

Learnings

Explore and identify various modes of communication and expression of the service user, using these creative methods to assist with your assessment and intervention.

Karen

Karen was a 40-year-old woman who was diagnosed with multiple sclerosis (MS) in her early 20s. She was in a relationship for four years. MS left her body debilitated, leaving her totally dependant in relation to activities of daily living—including personal care, getting up from a chair or bed, housekeeping, and so forth. She had no strength, and lifts were required to assist with transfers. Karen would often be hospitalized for weeks or months at a time. She wanted to maintain a sexual relationship with her partner. Hospital staff resisted providing a private space for the couple. A social worker was consulted and began advocating for Karen's rights. People with (dis)Abilities are often viewed as asexual. Kaufman, Silverberg, and Odette (2003) identified the number one myth in relation to people with (dis)Abilities as "people living with disabilities and chronic illnesses are not sexual" (p. 2). This myth is associated with the belief that people with (dis)Abilities are helpless, childlike, and have different wants and needs from our own:

> You may have sixty years' life experience, with the body, brain, temperament, and libido of an adult, but if you can't feed yourself, or need help wiping your ass, or getting in and out of the car, you are considered a child. Thus they deny our sexualities. (Kaufman, Silverberg, & Odette, 2003, p. 2)

Initially, the social worker met with high resistance from hospital staff when trying to arrange accommodations for the couple. After stressing how important this relationship was to Karen and its significance to her mental health and quality of life, arrangements were forthcoming, either in the form of private hospital space or weekend passes. Eventually, when the relationship deteriorated and ended, Karen grieved her loss of sexual expression, thus indicating the significance of this in her personal life.

Practice Principles

Validate the knowledge base of service users and respect their lived experience. Deconstruct normalcy and advocate for rights-based services.

Learnings

In advocating for service user's rights, promote self-knowledge pertaining to quality of life issues and self-identified needs.

Deidra

Deidra, a 17-year-old young woman, required a heart and lung transplant. She had spent many weeks in hospital as the doctors tried to control her symptoms. While Deidra lived inside a 17-year-old body, she had a heart of a 90-year-old and the cognitive/behavioural development of an eight-year-old. Deidra lived with her parents and three siblings in a small home about 20 kilometres outside of the city. Her father worked seasonal jobs, raking blueberries in the summer and logging trees during the winter months. Deidra's mother was not employed outside of the home. Both community and hospital social workers had been called to intervene numerous times. Some referrals had been related to securing medical resources such as expensive heart medication; others related to resources associated with hospitalizations or illness complications, such as transportation to and from hospital and tutoring services; and one referral was associated with neglect, when the physician claimed that Deidra's parents were not following the medical regime prescribed. Deidra lived in poverty and had both developmental and physical (dis)Abilities. All of the helping professionals involved with her care knew that her life hung on the prospect of her receiving a heart–lung transplant.

In the end, Deidra was deemed to be at too high a risk for a transplant. The social worker involved with the psychosocial assessment was frustrated. He had outlined the resources the family would need to have in place prior to and following a transplant, yet it was this very assessment that the transplant team used in declaring Deidra an unfit candidate. Transplant recipients follow a rigorous post-operative protocol and the team believed that Deidra did not have the family support, intellectual capability, or financial means to follow through with this protocol. Denial of Deidra's transplant was a violation of Canada's public health-care policy, under which equal access is provided to all without discrimination. It was Deidra's developmental (dis)Ability and her family's lack of money and education that in the end would cost Deidra her life. The social worker tried to influence the team's decision. He even presented the case to the hospital ethics committee. Transplant teams have to make life and death decisions because there are only a limited number of transplants and more potential recipients than organs. However, the social worker believed that poverty and (dis)Ability were the real reasons behind the team's decision. Rioux (2006) wrote, "Widely held prejudices against people with disabilities often result in discrimination in their access to the benefits of medical treatment" (p. 96).

Practice Principles

Re-define individual problems as societal issues and strategize around systemic change. Social workers, allies, and (dis)Abled persons need to work together to challenge the oppressive ablest structures within society. Given that we live in an ablest society, chances are that the struggles of people with (dis)Abilities are going to be based on societal oppression that is associated with a (dis)Ability identity.

Learnings

Work toward a social system that values and centralizes human need, and is inclusive of persons with (dis)Abilities. Help service users to understand the political context of their experience and that they are not the problem.

Nora

Nora was a 50-year-old Aboriginal woman who lived on a rural reserve in the Maritimes. She had MS and was a wheelchair user. In all, 31 percent of Aboriginal peoples live with a (dis)Ability compared to the national average of 15 percent of the population (Assembly of First Nations, 2004). Nora lived in a small bungalow with a wheelchair ramp extending to her front door. The reserve had limited resources and all public buildings were inaccessible. As a consequence, Nora could not attend community functions unless people were available to physically lift her chair over steps and, even then, she faced inaccessible building structures once inside. Personal care was provided from an informal network of family and friends. No public home-care access was available on the reserve.

Nora's experience is common among Aboriginal women living with (dis)Abilities. The Native Women's Association of Canada (NWAC) (2007) identified numerous barriers that Aboriginal women living with (dis)Abilities face on reserves, such as a lack of means to pay for services and/or assistance, limited or no vocational training, inaccessibility (e.g., wheelchair ramps, automatic door openers), a lack of respite care, and no Braille translation for their languages. Nora was dependent on the kindness of others for her well-being. She lived on a fixed limited income and resided on a reserve with few resources. Aboriginal peoples living with (dis)Abilities are more likely to be unemployed and live in poverty compared to abled-bodied persons (NWAC, 2007). Numerous structural barriers faced her as she tried to navigate through life as a woman with a (dis)Ability. This reserve was located in a rural area, thus creating transportation issues and inaccessibility to medical services. Reserves are often located on isolated land, barren of natural resources, where poverty is the major social concern. "Aboriginal women with disabilities are also negatively affected by conflicts over jurisdiction and the delivery of health services to Aboriginal peoples. The result is often that no agency will take responsibility to respond to their needs" (NWAC, 2007, p. 4). Their needs are "frequently neglected by the federal and provincial governments, health care services, non-Aboriginal disability organizations and sometimes Aboriginal leaders and communities" (p. 2).

Practice Principles
Adopt a rights-based intervention that puts the (dis)Abled person first, promoting their rights to services, health, and social participation.

Learnings
Be cognizant of one's own values, beliefs, and principles and how these inform one's impressions. Deconstruct the assumptions, biases, and myths associated with Aboriginal peoples, their culture, and living environments.

Structural Practices

In Table 9.1, structural practices have been pulled from the writings of respected authors on structural social work theory and practice, including Maurice Moreau (Moreau & Leonard, 1989) and Bob Mullaly (1997, 2007). Ben Carniol (2003) and Leni Dominelli (2002), who write on anti-oppressive social work intervention, were also used as references. Finally, (dis)Ability rights advocates and authors were also referenced, including Gary May and Martha Raske (2005), Peter Dunn, Roy Hanes, Susan Hardie, Donald Leslie, and Judy MacDonald (2008). The table highlights three areas:

- Learnings: The learnings highlight an extension of the structural practices identified in the first column, derived from a combination of insights gained through listening and working with (dis)Abled persons and structural social work education.
- Practice principles: Based on structural social work intervention, a disability rights perspective and learnings from the presented cases, practice principles are identified as a general guide to working with people with (dis)Abilities.
- Meta-narrative challenges: The final column, meta-narrative challenges, represents identification of the dominant discourse in services to persons with (dis)Abilities, taken from the literature, plus the experiences of practitioners and service users. Each column, moving from left to right, subsequently challenges and displaces the meta-narrative identified in this final column.

Current Issues Facing Social Workers

Social workers in the field speak about the difficulties in trying to serve the needs of people with (dis)Abilities. Having a solid knowledge base pertaining to the programs and policies that impact the (dis)Abled becomes essential to their work. Working within and against the system (Mullaly, 2007), social workers need to advocate for the rights of people with (dis)Abilities, including their right to health (Rioux, 2006). Social workers describe themselves as often in a position of fighting the "helpers" and gatekeepers of services for access to resources for (dis)Abled persons. For example, applying for and receiving disability benefits

TABLE 9.1: Structural approach to working with people with (dis)Abilities.

Structural practices	Learnings	Practice principles	Meta-narrative challenges
Empathy skills: understanding of service user's feelings and situation. Expand to social empathy.	To meet the person with a (dis)Ability where he/she is: show respect, empathy, and genuineness.	Treat all persons with (dis)Abilities with respect: regard helping as a privilege; individual, cultural, and societal analysis.	Pathologizing practice of labelling: e.g., dismissing the story, identity, or location of people with (dis)Abilities.
Empowerment and appropriate entitlement: enhancing service user's power within worker–user relationship and re-organization of rights to services (Moreau & Leonard, 1989).	To promote rights-based access to services promoting quality of life, self-identified needs of the person with (dis)Ability, and goals of self-sustaining independence.	Validate knowledge base of service user: show recognition of service users' struggles and recognize that they are the expert on their lived experience.	Helping professionals' (e.g., social work, therapeutic services, medicine) hierarchal position and role as expert.
Communication skills: identifying barriers to traditional modes of communication: listening, clarifying, and focusing on alternative communication styles (Carniol, 2003; Dunn et al., 2008).	Identify and accommodate the various modes of communication and expression of the service user brought into the assessment and intervention processes.	Listen in the broadest context to communicate with the service user: truly listen and be receptive to the service user, his or her experiences and knowledges to inform intervention.	Relating through traditional two-way written and verbal communication.
Advocacy skills: access to better services/resources. Defends social rights, social movements/community connections (Carniol, 2003).	For helping professionals to act upon these conscious and ethical beliefs: advocating for service users' rights/disrupting the hierarchal ordering (deserving vs. non-deserving) of social services, health care, and employment.	Deconstruct normalcy and advocate for rights-based services: locate experiences of persons with (dis)Abilities within socio-political, economic, and physical context (May & Raske, 2005; Moreau & Leonard, 1989).	Power of helping professionals to define normalcy and its impact on assessment and intervention.

Critique of social system: awareness and analysis of the limitations of our social order in its ability to meet the needs of persons with (dis)Abilities.	To develop a social system that values and centralizes human need and is inclusive of persons with (dis)Ability (Dunn et al., 2006, 2008; Mullaly, 2007).	Re-define individual problems as societal issues: "social problems are not amenable to individual, family or subcultural solutions" (Mullaly, 2007, p. 288).	Individual pathology viewed as the directive for intervention.
Analytic and strategy skills: views interventions in a broader social and organizational context (Dominelli, 2002).	Persons with (dis)Abilities face numerous oppressions: personal, communal, and societal.	Strategize around systemic change: education, health-care access, rights-based multi-modality, multi-disciplinary service delivery, and policy changes.	Person with (dis)Ability needing to be fixed.
Spiritual sensitivity skills: locates spiritual support for social and economic justice. Holistic ways of knowing and helping (Carniol, 2003).	Extend the obvious clinical interventions to connect with the human spirit; meet the service user where he or she is and offer hope.	Use of self: judicious use of self-disclosure and consciousness-raising (Cautionary note on minimizing experiences of persons with [dis]Ability).	Treatment principle of therapeutic distance.
Assessment skills: to identify (re. service user) (1) how oppressive structures are harmful and (2) immediate and long-term needs contributing to personal, structural, communal, and spiritual emancipation (Carniol, 2003).	To be cognizant of your own values, beliefs, and principles and how these inform your impressions.	Rights-based intervention: self-determination re. persons with (dis)Ability; respect for dignity; identification of socially constructed barriers.	Deficit-orientated intervention, with a rehabilitative focus (Linton, 1998; May & Raske, 2005; Wendell, 1996).

(including Workers Compensation, Canada Pension Disability, and private disability benefits) can often be a gruelling process that leaves the (dis)Abled person feeling pathologized, disbelieved, and outright unworthy (Hebert, personal communication, April 16, 2008; MacDonald, 2008a, 2008b).

A social worker in a tertiary rehabilitation centre has described feeling like a fraud because there is such a distinct lack of resources. There is so little available that some speculate that only 10 percent of the (dis)Abled can access the full range of services (Mazerolle, personal communication, April 25, 2008). Services are reserved for those persons who are most likely to become self-sufficient and the "health needs of people with disabilities are regularly limited to curing or improving their impairments, rather than improving their health" (Rioux, 2006, p. 96).

There are several issues that can impinge on the effectiveness of social workers' efforts. In medical social work, intensity and acuity are heightened—that is, people are sicker, in hospital for less time, with a higher turn-around time (Armstrong & Armstrong, 2003). Acute medical care is the focus, with little time given to long-term care and chronic health-care delivery. Service users may be medically discharged, no longer needing hospitalization but waiting for a long-term care bed, admittance to a rehabilitation centre, or for other services to be approved. In some jurisdictions, being medically discharged can trigger a daily fee for every remaining day in hospital. This payment method was originally devised to recover seniors' pensions while still in hospital to treat them financially as though they were already in a long-term care facility. From a social work perspective, this is a social justice issue in that the payment method strips seniors of their income and puts a fee for service on their health care. Social workers in some facilities have to inform service users and their families of this billing and have them sign a form, which can potentially have a negative effect on the therapeutic alliance.

Medicare and provincial income assistance, as well as private health-care plans, have a limited formulary, an approved list of medication benefits. For example, Medicare and most provincial assistance plans do not pay for prosthetics or some costly medications for the treatment of cancer, MS, and other chronic conditions. Often people with (dis)Abilities cannot meet their medical needs. Hospitals and rehabilitation centres may be reluctant to re-admit for therapeutic services and offer limited out-patient services. A rights-based model would focus on quality of life rather than basing services on those deemed the most deserving and/or judged fixable (Rioux, 2006).

Conclusion

(Dis)Ability is a major political issue, and asks questions about the unequal and discriminatory value placed on different people's worth to society. People with (dis)Abilities are often perceived as not able to contribute to society, becoming invisible when value is weighted on productivity and employability. Accordingly, the medical model would try to fix the person with a (dis)Ability. In contrast, structural social work identifies the systemic barriers and works toward a new definition of contribution. Social workers need to become familiar with (dis)Ability programs and policies, and develop a critical lens for existing services so that barriers creating inadequate service delivery can be identified. Both social workers and service users can work together in advocating for appropriate resources. We cannot have the number one tip for better health for (dis)Abled persons to be "don't be poor" (Raphael, 2006, p. 119). We must work to address the structural inequality of (dis)Abled persons having a much greater probability of living in poverty. People with (dis)Abilities have been shamed, hidden, and ignored (Chadwick & Dias, 2000; Linton, 1998). (Dis)Abled persons deserve to be listened to, shown respect, accommodated within their work and living spaces, and, most of all, valued for who they are.

References

Armstrong, P., & Armstrong, H. (2003). *Wasting away: The undermining of Canadian health care* (2nd ed.). Toronto, ON: Oxford University Press.

Assembly of First Nations. (2004). *Resolution 85, special chiefs assembly*. Retrieved June 8, 2008, from www.afn.ca/article.asp?id=210

Carniol, B. (2003). *Generalist skills in social work*. Unpublished work in progress, Ryerson School of Social Work, Toronto, Ontario, Canada.

Chadwick, P., & Dias, S. (2000). *Disability social history project*. Retrieved January 15, 2005, from www.disabilityhistory.org/projects_new.html

Crawford, N. (2003). Parenting with a disability: The last frontier. *Monitor on Psychology, 34*(1), 68. Retrieved June 10, 2008, from www.apa.org/monitor/may03/challenges.html

DisAbled Women's Network of Ontario. (2003). The economics of ability. Retrieved June 11, 2008, from dawn.thot.net/economics_of_ability.html

Dominelli, L. (2002). *Anti-oppressive social work theory and practice*. Basingstoke, UK: Palgrave Macmillan.

Driedger, D., & Owen, M. (Eds.). (2008). *Dissonant disabilities: Women with chronic illnesses explore their lives*. Toronto, ON: Canadian Scholars' Press Inc.

Dunn, P., Hanes, R., Hardie, S., Leslie, D., & MacDonald, J. (2008). Best practices in promoting disability inclusion within Canadian schools of social work. *Disability Studies Quarterly, 28*(1). Retrieved February 1, 2008, from www.dsq-sds.org

Dunn, P., Hanes, R., Hardie, S., & MacDonald, J. (2006). Creating disability inclusion within Canadian schools of social work. *Journal of Social Work in Disability and Rehabilitation, 5*(1), 1–19.

Enns, H., & Neufeldt, A. (Eds.). (2003). *In pursuit of equal participation: Canada and disability at home and abroad*. Concord, ON: Captus Press.

Favaro, P. (2002). Spirituality and people with disabilities. In M. Nash & B. Stewart (Eds.), *Spirituality and social care: Contributing to personal and community well-being* (pp. 215–225). London, UK: Jessica Kingsley Publishing.

Gilson, S.F., Bricout, J.C., & Baskind, F. R. (1998). Listening to the voices of individuals with disabilities. *Families in Society, 79*(2), 188–196.

Goffman, E. (1963). *Stigma: Notes on the management of spoiled identity*. New York: Simon and Schuster.

Harbison, J., Coughlan, S., Karabanow, J., & VanderPlaat, M. (2005). A clash of cultures: Rural values and service delivery to mistreated and neglected older people in eastern Canada. *Practice: Social Work in Action, 17*(4), 229–246.

Human Resources and Social Development Canada (HRSDC). (2006). *Advancing the inclusion of people with disabilities*. Retrieved May 15, 2008, from www.hrsdc.gc.ca/en/disability_issues/reports/fdr/2006/page08.shtml

Jones, J.W., & McCullough, L.B. (2008). The shifting sands of senility: Canceled consent. *Journal of Vascular Surgery, 47*(1), 237–238.

Kaufman, M., Silverberg, C., & Odette, F. (2003). *The ultimate guide to sex and disability: For all of us who live with disabilities, chronic pain and illness*. San Francisco: Cleis Press.

Linton, S. (1998). *Claiming disability: Knowledge and identity*. New York: New York University Press.

MacDonald, J. (2005). Physical challenges. In F. Turner (Ed.), *The Canadian Encyclopedia of Social Work* (pp. 281–283). Waterloo, ON: Wilfrid Laurier Press.

MacDonald, J. (2008a). Anti-oppressive practices with chronic pain sufferers. *Social Work in Health Care, 47*(2), 135–156.

MacDonald, J. (2008b). Untold stories: Women, in the helping professions, as sufferers of chronic pain (re)storying (dis)Abilities. (Doctoral dissertation, Memorial University of Newfoundland, 2006). Ottawa, ON: Library and Archives of Canada (microform AMICUS no. 33872393).

May, G., & Raske, M. (Eds.). (2005). *Ending disability discrimination: Strategies for social workers*. Boston, MA: Pearson Education.

Moreau, M.J., & Leonard, L. (1989). *Empowerment through a structural approach to social work: A report from practice*. Ottawa, ON: Carleton University.

Mullaly, B. (1997). *Structural social work: Ideology, theory, and practice* (2nd ed.). Toronto, ON: Oxford University Press.

Mullaly, B. (2007). *The new structural social work* (3rd ed.). Toronto, ON: Oxford University Press.

Native Women's Association of Canada (NWAC). (2007). Aboriginal women and communicable/chronic diseases and disabilities. Retrieved June 20, 2008, from www.nwachq.org/en/documents/NWAC_AboriginalWomenandCommChronicDis easesandDisabilities_June2007.pdf

Neufeldt, A., & Enns, H. (2003). Introduction: Canada and disability issues. In H. Enns & A. Neufeldt (Eds.), *In pursuit of equal participation: Canada and disability at home and abroad* (pp. 1–18). Concord, ON: Captus Press.

Oliver, M. (1990). *The politics of disablement: A sociological approach.* New York: St. Martin's Press.

Oliver, M. (1996). *Understanding disability: From theory to practice.* London, UK: MacMillan Press.

Oliver, M. (1999). *Disabled people and the inclusive society: Or the times they really are changing.* Public lecture on behalf of Strathclyde Centre for Disability Research and Glasgow City Council. Retrieved March 10, 2009, from http://www.leeds.ac.uk/ disability-studies/archiveuk/Oliver/SOCEX.pdf

Parsons, T. (1951). *The social system.* Glencoe, IL: Free Press.

Raphael, D. (2006). Social determinants of health: An overview of concepts & issues. In D. Raphael, T. Bryant, & M. Rioux (Eds.), *Staying alive: Critical perspectives on health, illness, and health care* (pp. 115–138). Toronto, ON: Canadian Scholars' Press Inc.

Raphael, D., Bryant, T., & Rioux, M. (2006). *Staying alive: Critical perspectives on health, illness, and health care.* Toronto, ON: Canadian Scholars' Press Inc.

Rioux, M. (2006). The right to health: Human rights approaches to health. In D. Raphael, T. Bryant, & M. Rioux (Eds.), *Staying alive: Critical perspectives on health, illness, and health care* (pp. 85–110). Toronto, ON: Canadian Scholars' Press Inc.

Smith, K. (2007). Social work, restructuring and everyday resistance: "Best practices" gone underground. In D. Baines (Ed.), *Doing anti-oppressive practice: Building transformative politicized social work* (pp. 145–159). Halifax, NS: Fernwood Publishing.

Statistics Canada. (2008, May 27). Participation and activity limitation survey: Education experiences of children with disabilities. *The Daily.* Retrieved June 4, 2008, from www.statcan.ca/Daily/English/080527/d080527a.htm

Stienstra, D., & Wight-Felske, A. (Eds.). (2003). *Making equality: History of advocacy and persons with disabilities in Canada.* Concord, ON: Captus Press.

Titchkosky, T. (2001). From the field—coming out disabled: The politics of understanding. *Disability Studies Quarterly, 21*(4), 131–139. Retrieved March 10, 2009, from www.dsq-sds.org

Thomson, R. (1997). *Extraordinary bodies: Figuring physical disability in American culture and literature.* New York: Columbia University Press.

Vash, C. (1981). *The psychology of disability.* New York: Springer Publishing Company.

Wendell, S. (1996). *The rejected body: Feminist philosophical reflections on disability.* New York: Routledge.

Wendell, S. (2006). Toward a feminist theory of disability. In L. Davis (Ed.), *The disability studies reader*, 2nd edition (p. 243 – 256). New York, N.Y.: Routledge.

Zola, I.K. (1982). *Missing pieces: A chronicle of living with a disability*. Philadelphia, PA: Temple University Press.

The Promise and Relevance of Structural Social Work and Practice with Queer People and Communities

MARION BROWN, BRENDA K. RICHARD, AND LEIGHANN WICHMAN

Introduction

Why is it relevant to include a chapter on working with lesbian, gay, bisexual, transgender, intersex, and questioning (hereafter referred to as queer) people in a book on structural social work practice? Why is it meaningful to draw a particular connection between the lives and issues of queer people and the theory and practice principles of structural social work?

Addressing these questions begins with understanding the prevailing ideologies regarding sexual orientation, which in Western society are rooted in heterosexism and homophobia. Analysis of heterosexism and homophobia is where any discussion of the lives and challenges of queer people must begin, because the challenges faced and coping strategies utilized by queer people do not result from individual pathology, deficiency, or weakness, but rather result from the historic and contemporary discrimination, prejudice, and violence levelled against queer people and communities through the exploitative societal constructs of heterosexism and homophobia. It is amid these constructs and within these contexts that social work with queer persons is practised. This chapter details how structural social work's demand for analysis of context and transformative action offers ideal ideological and practical congruence for working with queer people and communities.

This chapter presents four principles of structural social work that have been developed by the authors on the basis of the work of Mullaly (1997, 2002, 2007) and our own analyses and practices over the years, which have been informed by our politics, lived realities, and countless conversations with colleagues in the field. We offer examples of each of the four principles, drawing on the experiences of queer elders to contextualize the work of the Youth Project, a non-profit organization with the mission to "make Nova Scotia a safer, healthier, and happier place for lesbian, gay, bisexual and transgendered youth through support, education, resource expansion and community development" (Youth Project, n.d.).[1]

Congruence with structural social work practice calls us, the authors, to locate ourselves within this material. We write as three White women with ages spanning three decades, all with a personal history of involvement with the Youth Project and a deep commitment to the eradication of harassment, exclusion, discrimination, and violence on the basis of sexual orientation and gender identity. These are passions that we share and that drive our practice, research, and scholarship. Brenda Richard is a lesbian faculty member at Dalhousie University's School of Social Work who, in 1993, supervised the genesis of the Youth Project as a social work student's field placement. Leighann Wichman is a former youth consumer at the Youth Project and is now the agency's Executive Director. Marion Brown is a former board member and long-time ally of the Youth Project, and is also a faculty member at Dalhousie University's School of Social Work.

It is an impossible task to address all of the ways to work responsibly with all queer issues, given due respect for myriad personal and public circumstances and the multiple dimensions of possibility and peril that lie within the contexts of homophobia and heterosexism. At the same time, we consider it likely that some of the experiences and activities of the Youth Project and conceptual practices with elders can be transferred across practice sites and populations of queer people and communities. We close the chapter with practice suggestions for structural social work borne of our work with queer youth and elders.

Setting the Context

Homophobia has been widely defined as the irrational fear and hatred of people whose intimate relationships are with members of the same sex (Herek, 2000; Janoff, 2005; Mallon, 2008). The original intent of creating this definition was to remove focus from the queer person and emphasize the illogical reaction aimed toward him or her. Lived experience and further analysis of this term over the years, however, has led to the critique that the suffix "phobia" suggests a psychological condition, which absolves the homophobic person of social responsibility and obscures the legitimization of homophobia throughout social processes. Furthermore, use of the descriptor "irrational" to the targeted fear and hatred has been challenged on the basis that misinformation about, exclusion of, and violence toward queer persons has indeed been rationalized, with scientific evidence, biblical belief, and cultural customs offered as support. Finally, use of the term "homophobia" maintains an emphasis on individual thought, feeling, and behaviour, diverting attention from the systemic discrimination toward queer persons that the culture of homophobia perpetuates (Herek, 2000; Janoff, 2005; Mallon, 2008). Far from the isolated actions of a few individuals, homophobia has a clear political agenda and wields mighty social significance.

Heterosexism refers to the process and outcome of institutionalized homophobia: it legitimizes the exclusion of, oppression of, and prejudice toward queer persons through explicit social structures and systems as well as through implicit social practices and discourses (Elze, 2006). Heterosexism is the pervasive and inherent preferencing of heterosexual union, behaviour, and identity over all alternatives, and it grants social acceptance and sanction upon those who align with its expectations. Heterosexism lays the groundwork from which homophobia flourishes. For example, heterosexism is the unspoken assumption that the new social worker at one's agency is heterosexual unless and until proven otherwise; homophobia is the shock and disgust felt by colleagues on learning that she is lesbian.

Homophobia and heterosexism are social constructs, creations of human beings in social environments, grown from prevailing discourses and dominant value orientations, patterns of thought, feelings, and behaviours. These discourses have been repeated over generations and institutionalized through organizational policies in the areas of education, religion, medicine, law, and government legislation (Elze, 2006; Herek, 2000; Janoff, 2005; Mallon, 2008).

Structural Social Work and Practice with Queer People and Communities

Structural theory takes the human condition and contextualizes it according to social, political, and economic parameters. Attention and understanding begin at the individual level, while at the same time analysis and action attend to societal practices that require change. Structural theory is particularly relevant to social work with queer people and communities because of the societal contexts and constructs of heterosexism and homophobia: their construction in ideology and manifestations in societal structures. Structural theory responds directly to context and constructs. In application with queer people, structural theory hears the personal stories of struggle and pain through a filter that distills the role of "social institutions, social processes, social practices and social relationships" (Mullaly, 2007, p. 249). It erases the dichotomy between self and society, locating individual experience squarely within the social context. In this regard, structural theory merges analysis of social processes with political practice for social change (Mullaly, 2007).

As the above contextualization of social work practice with queer people illustrates, this is the approach required for responsive and responsible social work within queer communities. The personal challenges and obstacles for queer people result from the public, political realities evident in prevailing ideologies and in their concrete manifestations. Thus, the congruence between structural social work principles and queer politics fits hand in glove.

Principles into Practice

The authors have developed the following four principles of structural social work practice, based on our understanding of the work of Mullaly (1997, 2002, 2007) and augmented by our practice as social workers engaged with queer people and communities. Each principle is named and subsequently illustrated through the example of working with queer elders and/or youth.

Principle 1: Historical and Contemporary Contexts Shape Social Structures and Social Experiences

In Canada, critical antecedents have profoundly impacted the lives of queer elders and these must be held in our consciousness as we engage in our social work practice. Queer seniors grew up with the Great Depression, World War II, and the McCarthy era, navigating these times under the stigma, ridicule, and persistent public exclusion that accompanied them (Fullmer, 2006). Canadian legal, medical, educational, and religious institutions were designed to formally exclude anyone who declared him or herself to be gay or lesbian: in the absence of federal or provincial human rights acts, discrimination in housing, health care, and employment was rampant; the *Diagnostic and Statistical Manual* classified homosexuality as a psychiatric pathology; schools ensured that only content with a heterosexist orientation was available; and churches of all denominations sent clear messages that queer persons were unwelcome within their interpretations of the divine (Brotman, Ryan, & Meyer, 2006; Peterkin & Risdon, 2003).

Survival for queer persons has often depended upon locating oneself within a small number of friends or a group for refuge and support. Communities may have had one small private bar or club that afforded semi-public social-izing opportunities. Such gathering places gave respite from the pervasive social manifestations of the message that one was not only unwanted, but was criminal, mentally unwell, and inherently evil (Fullmer, 2006). Responses to this politically sanctioned climate included hostility and gay bashing from those with heterosexist privilege and sometimes an internalized self-hatred in those without. Many suicides baffled families and communities whose own homophobia prevented the decoding of these tragedies. The particular form of discrimination against queer persons often meant that the loss they feared most was that of family and those they held dearest to them (Brotman, Ryan, & Meyer, 2006; Messinger, 2006).

Today much has changed, yet the historical context framing the lives of queer elders remains a crucial component of many present challenges. Constant navigation of the invisibility of discrimination often remains today. For having been told one has no rights one may be less inclined to invoke them even now. Enforced invisibility also sealed the unworthiness quotient so that shame and lack of self-esteem may prevent many queer elders from seeking their rights as full and equal citizens in a country that still publicly debates their right to marry. Decades of struggle are only now being addressed. For example, it was not until 2003 that a study of gay and lesbian seniors' access to health care was funded federally, headed by faculty at the School of Social Work of McGill University (Brotman, Ryan, & Meyer, 2006). Structural social work maintains the centrality of such historical context and its contemporary impact.

Working with young adults, the practices of the Youth Project directly address the principle that historical and contemporary social structures shape social experiences. First, by its very existence, the Youth Project provides a concrete, community-based venue to offset the exclusion and marginalization experienced by queer people. Exclusion and marginalization are logical con-sequences resulting from the way society is structured to include and endorse people and perspectives that align with the dominant ideology regarding preferred sexual orientation and gender identity. Social structures have been developed and deployed by dominant, relatively small groups who have more power and resources than other groups. The structures of society therefore reflect their beliefs and values and this ideology is imposed on others. This imposition is an issue of social organization, not individual merit; thus, venues and methods for inclusion must be created and actively promoted. The Youth Project is a social structure that provides such venues and methods, directly addressing issues of exclusion and marginalization within society.

The system of governance at the Youth Project addresses the principle that social structures shape social experiences, in the form and function of the Youth Board. The Youth Board represents a structural level of governance that institutionalizes the commitment to an inverted hierarchy, where young people are responsible for and resourceful in contributing to the design and implementation of services to meet their needs. Youth Board membership requires that all participants are under the age of 26 years and represent the diversity of experiences and identities surrounding sexual orientation and gender identity. Although, as a registered organization, the only legally recognized entity governing the Youth Project is its board of directors, all of the organizational documentation, philosophy, and policies reflect the principles and priorities of the Youth Board. As a result, the Youth Board operates at an equal level with the board of directors as an organizational standard, regardless of legal recognition.

The Youth Project has identified schools as significant and influential social structures that reinforce and promote heterosexism through curriculum, policy, and social norms, thus rendering queer youth invisible, marginalized, or targets for social degradation. Given the broader social parameters of heterosexism and homophobia, and their expression as exclusion and, often, violence, queer youth are often less connected to the school environment and less likely to find safe spaces in which to converse, collaborate, and influence change (Peters, 2003). The Youth Project began an initiative to promote the development of Gay/Straight Alliances (GSAs) in schools. These student-led, staff-supported groups provide queer students with positive space within the dominant social structure, where celebration, affirmation, and validation are fostered. GSAs also provide opportunities for straight students to collaborate, show solidarity, and build support by acknowledging their heterosexist privileges. Some groups provide a safe social space, while others get involved with education. The Youth Project provides schools with information kits on GSAs, support resources, and an opportunity to network with other GSAs in Nova Scotia through a province-wide roundtable. The promotion of GSAs within schools allows those within the education system to create and influence social structures at all levels, and help contribute to the work of the Youth Project by providing the opportunity for one social structure to shape positive social experiences. Among these positive social experiences is an increase in the young person's sense of power when working with service providers.

Principle 2: Personal Troubles Must be Linked to Public, Political Issues through Consciousness-Raising in Collectives and Alliances

At the Youth Project, each young person's story is heard as uniquely experienced and deeply felt. Authentic stories can be shared, because staff and volunteers at the Youth Project explicitly recognize that social practices devalue, dismiss, harass, exclude, isolate, and victimize queer people. The Youth Project staff and volunteers present and embody an alternative vision: a place where experiences of hatred and domination are absent, and support, education, and social opportunities are offered. Through naming, deconstructing, and then reconstructing a "third place," experiences of isolation, shame, and loneliness are transformed into experiences of acceptance, celebration, and finding oneself among peers. Through discussion groups, films, and Pride events that are led by youth, we talk about the world outside and how it has come to be as it is, what keeps the systems of oppression in place, and how we cannot only be shaped by, but ourselves shape, the social world around us. We believe that individual agency is tapped by involvement with these political processes, and that together, social change occurs.

The staff and volunteers of the Youth Project recognize that in order to link personal troubles to public and political issues, access to collectives and alliances must be facilitated. The Youth Project's visibility is more readily apparent given its location in the province's capital of Halifax Regional Municipality. However, programming includes outreach to small communities across the province (a minimum of five days per week on the road) as well as consultation to schools and services throughout the province at any time. Currently, approximately 30 percent of the Youth Project's consumers live in rural settings, suggesting that the means taken to acknowledge regional disparity in access to services are indeed addressing this structural issue. Consciousness-raising is advanced by sharing stories of the rewarding lives that are possible through social change, connection, and awareness. An example of one such initiative is the Transmissions project undertaken by the transgender youth support group (aptly named Transformers). The Transmissions project uses the stories, advice, and personal reflections of transgender youth across the province to create a resource written for and by transgender youth. This province-wide project recognizes the forces of oppression that have marginalized and excluded transgender youth, while at the same time offering a venue for voices and expertise. It provides a concrete and effective instrument in which to participate and influence social change. The result of this project not only provides youth with a relevant and meaningful reflection of themselves, it also provides those living and working in oppressive social structures with a concrete method for consciousness-raising that centralizes first voice.[2]

Principle 3: Collaborative Conversations Propel Social Change

Developing responsive and inclusive programming on issues of sexual orientation and gender identity requires having collaborative conversations. Engaging in dialogue means that all parties are considered to be contributing meaningful knowledge, experiences, and worldviews to the conversation. This constitutes a dialogical relationship, a central means through which power in the therapeutic relationship is explored, deconstructed, and understood by all involved (Mullaly, 2007).

At the Youth Project, there are several layers of collaborative conversations always underway. Through the programs at the Youth Project, young people participate in opportunities to dialogue with each other, with staff and volunteers, and with guests who have been influential in social change in various settings and through collaborative tools such as music, film, politics, and literature. Through creative and interactive programs, youth have used their own experiences to create art, theatre, and educational workshops in order to facilitate learning about how to make change happen.

With representation from the many GSAs throughout the school system, the GSA roundtable seeks to strengthen GSAs by working collaboratively to understand social systems to develop and implement programs and activities on a systemic, rather than individual, GSA level. Within the roundtable, stronger and more active GSAs collaborate and share experiences with smaller and less active GSAs, which can connect and participate with a larger movement of awareness and social change. This collective also lends a powerful voice to students as they develop programs, resources, and events that span the diversity of schools, grades, and students. The base of the roundtable sits within the affirming structure and safety of the Youth Project and is supported and championed by the Youth Board. The GSA roundtable has connected schools and promoted a collaborative voice and partnerships beyond the individual school setting into the larger political and public realms. This practice of collaborative conversations, which develops collective consciousness, propels social change that is the foundation of structural social work.

In addition, the Youth Project participates in conversations held at the level of government policy, specifically through the provincial departments of Health, Education, and Community Services. The staff of the Youth Project bring the priorities and voices of queer young people to these levels of social structures, because we are invited to work within hierarchies and bureaucracies that are often not accessible to young people. From within, the staff of the Youth Project promote youth engagement in order to create collaborative opportunities. The staff of the Youth Project sit on several intergovernmental, multi-sectoral committees that focus specifically on youth issues. The Youth Project speaks the voices of queer youth and leads the progressive dialogue of sexual orientation and gender identity, and the strategies and practical applications necessary for social change.

Principle 4: Both Modern and Postmodern Developments Contribute to Social Change

Because structural social work responds to context and constructs, it must be continually updated. For example, the coming-out model of Troiden (1979) is finding less relevance among today's youth, who report feeling as constrained within a linear, label-focused model as they do by heterosexist assumptions and biases (Savin-Williams, 2006). Far from the experience of their elders, youth do not consider the articulation of a stage-based process, which predetermines a binary outcome of either homosexual or heterosexual, to be affirming or liberating. Rather, they are questioning the sexual orientation and gender categories themselves, content to align with variable and shifting identities, and otherwise reluctant to be confined to static, mutually exclusive conceptualizations of sexual orientation and gender (Savin-Williams, 2006). This first-voice experience follows the work of Butler (1999) and others (e.g., McPhail, 2004) who have critiqued that, while modernist critical social theory has led the way for increased rights and opportunities, many of the essentialist assumptions underlying identity categories have been left intact. Postmodern contributions allow for challenging the binaries of male/female and heterosexual/homosexual and suggest new norms in relation to gender and sexual orientation (McPhail, 2004).

As a result of these changing ideologies, the Youth Project continually re-examines the use of language, operational philosophies, resource collections, and programming in order to reflect the evolution of relevant discourses such as structural and post-structural/modern and postmodern. Mirroring the broader discourse, and based on a motion of the Youth Board, the Youth Project, which was known for 13 years as the Lesbian, Gay, and Bisexual Youth Project, elected to remove all identifying labels from its title. The new name reflects that the Youth Project is an organization that works with youth populations across sexual orientations and gender identities; the new name allows for movement within those identities and shifts identity focus away from static individual ideologies and into a more elastic continuum.

Clearly, there are tension points here. Queer elders, having lived through the pivotal moments prior to and including significant societal changes that have lessened discrimination and exclusion, may consider it a loss to no longer claim overt, public space for the gay, lesbian, and bisexual identification (Fullmer, 2006; Peterkin & Risdon, 2003). Opening language to less specific identities could be seen to undo the solidarity and history that has framed the analysis and action for work in this area. This decision can be seen to run counter to some of the politi-cized messaging and public solidarity that was considered crucial for gay rights in decades past; in other words, the modernist contributions to social change. At the same time, this name change can be seen as responding to shifting contexts, the contemporary needs of participant groups, and different political times. The Youth Project is moving forward with the change, and is committed to finding new ways to communicate identities that maintain comprehensive understanding yet openness to evolving ideologies, discourses, and understandings.

As a further example of the tensions inherent in structural social work's rec-ognition of modernist and postmodernist contributions to social change, ques-tions regarding plans for Pink Triangle Day at the Youth Project were recently met with confused stares and blank faces. The preferred title for February 14th is

Valentine's Day, with celebrations planned that are considered distinct and equal to the heterosexual romance, love, and desire that inundates popular media. This shift suggests that these young people do not feel a need to separate their experiences from those of the dominant heterosexual population. Instead, they are identifying and expressing themselves in accordance with similarity as opposed to difference, where the emphasis is on inclusive youth events and activities, rather than sexual orientation and gender-identity-based constructions. The modern gay liberation movement indeed set the stage for entitlement to equity; postmodernism opens the possibilities for fluidity and multiple identity locations over segregation. Work with queer people and communities illustrates this "both/and" principle of structural social work clearly, recognizing that if it had not been for the work of generations before, evolution of identities could not occur within the same social context young people are experiencing today.

Practical Suggestions for Future Work

The principles detailed above make it clear that structural social work practice demands analysis and action, and social workers are well positioned to effect change on both individual and institutional levels because heterosexism and homophobia permeate society. We offer the following suggestions for action, first regarding specific areas of focus and their differential actions for work with queer elders and youth, and, second, with a list of actions for all recipients of services.

Specific Areas of Focus and their Differential Effects for Queer Elders and Youth

The Role of History

Queer elders have lived through times of intense homophobic discrimination, social ridicule, public shame and humiliation, institutionalization, incarceration, purposeful exclusion and substantial fear of personal and familial loss, and, critically, the legitimization of these by societal structures. While there is certainly much residue of this oppressive history still in place today, it cannot be denied that queer youth are living in different times, and have not directly experienced the ways in which social structures and processes upheld these violations to queer persons. The self-concepts of queer elders may reflect this historical trauma and neglect. Queer youth have inherited the benefits of the milestones to which queer elders have contributed.

Institutional Response

Agencies communicate their orientation toward queer people by addressing the issues in policies, mandates, information packages, and visual representations, and equally by saying nothing. Either way, the person who is queer takes note. Here too, however, there are important distinctions between the youth and senior populations. Queer youth expect their identities, lifestyles, and choices to be legitimized and have a recognizable place within society. The members of the Youth Project express appreciation for ample visible representations of queer identities, lifestyles, issues, and needs, and consider these as validating—not threatening—to who they are. In contrast, these inclusions may be felt by seniors as increasing their vulnerability, especially given the justifiable need to be cautious about self-identification.

Meanings of Community

Practitioners must understand the complexity and personally held meanings of the concept of a queer community. Practitioners need to hear each person's definition of community and desire for affiliation or distance from it. Many seniors continue to exist within a variety of smaller, informal queer communities of support given the historically grounded and contemporarily experienced need to be safe from harm. In contrast, young people today are questioning the plausibility of a coherent, unified community of any sort, finding less meaning in having membership among a group when they feel distinct and unique in their expressions of self.

The Concept of Family

The concept of family can carry fears of loss of family connection for simply being oneself, and residual family tensions may be particularly strong within the traditional family structure. Elders may have a partner, friends, or previous partners who form the substantive chosen family that sustains them and whom they deem would best represent their interests. Young people are self-identifying at an earlier age as gender variant, gay, lesbian, or bisexual than in decades past, seeking to invoke their rights to full self-expression, given the cultural shifts that endorse this actualization.

Language

Practitioners should use the language and terminology regarding queer issues and identities that are used by the person seeking services. Among elders, there may be a reluctance to announce ownership of identity as a queer person given a justifiable lack of trust and the residue of harassment and discrimination. For example, an elder may use the term "friend" to serve euphemistically for "partner" until ease is established. Young people are expressing a different relationship with terminology, not content to be reduced or labelled according to one component of who they are. Although perhaps for different reasons, in work with both youth and seniors, understanding that the words we use carry personal and political meanings and messages must be an anchor in our structural social work practice.

Attention to Material Conditions

Structural social work always responds to the material conditions of people's lives. For queer elders, financial issues related to pensions and spousal benefits are hard-won rights, yet not universally granted. People who have lived with their lifetime friend who has now passed away might have explicit concerns regarding material conditions that are not known until sought.

For Work with All Queer Persons

Do your own work:

- Examine your own beliefs, attitudes, and knowledge about queer people, issues, and communities; learn the myths and stereotypes; educate yourself on cultural heterosexism and read about the diversity of queer people. Examine how you contribute to the oppression, marginalization, powerlessness, and exploitation of queer people.
- Eliminate heterosexist language from your spoken use, and from forms and assessments in your workplace.
- Know resources for and about queer people and issues, both local and beyond, and share them widely, not only within queer circles.
- Take the challenge to interrupt homophobic and heterosexualist behaviours and comments wherever you see them and at the same time educate regarding how the behaviour was oppressive.

- Be proactive in countering heterosexism: pose the same-sex scenario first, in using examples; bring in reading materials that have gender-variant examples.

In work with individuals:

- Validate the stories of stigma and victimization and connect them to their historical, structural, and political origins.
- Listen to the coping strategies, frustrations, and anger and draw from them to develop potential actions that impact social conditions.
- Recognize the fortitude required of queer people and communities to move forward, and draw people together to build the strengths of collective action.

In institutions:

- Take active steps to create your agency as one where queer people and heterosexual allies would like to work and/or come for service.
- Develop non-discriminatory and anti-harassment policies for the explicit protection of queer staff and clients.
- Hire, retain, and validate the contributions of queer people.

Conclusion

Structural social work upholds the tenet that experiences of marginalization are logical consequences that result from structural manifestations of unequal power and resources and dominant ideology. This analysis resonates particularly strongly within communities of queer people. This chapter has illustrated four principles of structural social work theory through drawing on the experiences of queer elders to contextualize the work of the Youth Project (www.youthproject.ns.ca). Moving forward, structural social work with queer communities continues to validate context, both historical and contemporary, knowing that social structures, social experiences, and personal struggles are linked to public, political issues. We continue to draw insight and strength from both solidarity movements and critiques of their essentialism, knowing that queer people and issues benefit from the analyses that both modern movements and postmodern consciousness provide. And we continue to collectivize and critically dialogue within and across identity groups, knowing that to do so can shift oppressive discourses and, inch by inch, transform oppressive structures.

Endnotes

[1] It would be ideal to compare and contrast two organizations, one working with queer youth and the other working with queer elders. The fact that a community agency offering support and services for queer elders does not exist in Nova Scotia is a reflection of the very issues under discussion in this paper.

[2] First voice is common parlance in social work; it refers to the person within whom the experience originates—the self speaking, rather than being spoken about.

References

Brotman, S., Ryan, B., & Meyer L. (2006). *The health and social service needs of gay and lesbian seniors. Final Report.* Montreal, QC: McGill School of Social Work.

Butler, J. (1999). *Gender trouble: Feminism and the subversion of identity.* New York: Routledge.

Elze, D.E. (2006). Oppression, prejudice, and discrimination. In D.F. Morrow & L. Messinger (Eds.), *Sexual orientation and gender expression in social work practice: Working with gay, lesbian, bisexual and transgender people* (pp. 43–80). New York: Columbia University Press.

Fullmer, E.M. (2006). Lesbian, gay, bisexual, and transgender aging. In D.F. Morrow & L. Messinger (Eds.), *Sexual orientation and gender expression in social work practice: Working with gay, lesbian, bisexual and transgender people* (pp. 284–307). New York: Columbia University Press.

Herek, G. (2000). The psychology of sexual prejudice. *Current Directions in Psychological Science, 9*(1), 19–22.

Janoff, D.V. (2005). *Pink blood: Homophobic violence in Canada.* Toronto, ON: University of Toronto Press.

Mallon, G. (2008). *Social work practice with lesbian, gay, bisexual, and transgender people* (2nd ed.). Philadelphia, PA: Haworth Press.

McPhail, B.A. (2004). Questioning gender and sexuality binaries: What queer theorists, transgendered individuals and sex researchers can teach social work. *Journal of Gay and Lesbian Social Services, 17*(1), 3–21.

Messinger, L. (2006). A historical perspective. In D.F. Morrow & L. Messinger (Eds.), *Sexual orientation and gender expression in social work practice: Working with gay, lesbian, bisexual and transgender people* (pp. 18–42). New York: Columbia University Press.

Mullaly, B. (1997). *Structural social work: Ideology, theory, and practice* (2nd ed.). Toronto, ON: Oxford University Press.

Mullaly, B. (2002). *Challenging oppression: A critical social work approach.* Toronto, ON: Oxford University Press.

Mullaly, B. (2007). *The new structural social work* (3rd ed.). Toronto, ON: Oxford University Press.

Peterkin, A., & Risdon, C. (2003). *Caring for lesbian and gay people: A clinical guide.* Toronto, ON: University of Toronto Press.

Peters, A. (2003). Isolation or inclusion: Creating safe spaces for lesbian and gay youth. *Families in Society, 84*(3), 331–337.

Savin-Williams, R.C. (2006). *The new gay teenager.* Boston, MA: Harvard University Press.

Troiden, R.R. (1979). Becoming homosexual: A model of gay identity acquisition. *Psychiatry, 42*(40), 362–373.

Youth Project (n.d.). *Mission statement.* Retrieved March 10, 2009, from www.youthproject.ns.ca

CHAPTER 11

Envisioning Structural Social Work Practice:

The Case of the Grassroots Youth Collaborative

KRISTIE WRIGHT, SHAHINA SAYANI, ANDREA ZAMMIT, AND PURNIMA GEORGE

Introduction[1]

In the last four years, the sector of youth work in the City of Toronto has experienced many changes. These changes have centred on the prioritization of youth as a sector, increased funding for youth-serving organizations, and the engagement of youth in decision-making and change processes. In this chapter, we share the work of the Grassroots Youth Collaborative (GYC) in influencing these changes and challenging dominant perspectives about youth, youth work, and funding processes in the City of Toronto.

The work of the GYC provides evidence of successful engagement within the dialectical nature of structural social work practice to achieve its twin goals (for discussion see Murray & Hick, Chapter 1). Through effective utilization of structural social work practice skills, the GYC has been able to mobilize youth and member agencies in order to enlighten stakeholders, funders, and governments to the realities of marginalized youth living in communities across Toronto. The work of the GYC provides a novel insight into work with funders, which has culminated in an innovative and germane model of funding for the youth sector. The accomplishments of the GYC have resulted in a renewed hope for solidarity and strength among the members of the GYC, even within the current context marked by competition and clamour for resources. This chapter provides a story of hope and a direction for moving structural social work practice forward in the current context.

The chapter is informed by the personal involvement of the three of the four authors within the work of the GYC. Two of these three authors were founding members who held important positions within the GYC for a period of over two years and who constituted an integral part of the change process.

The fourth author is an academic and has known about the work of the first three authors in the youth sector for seven years. Since this is an account of the work of a larger group, for the purpose of accuracy the authors consulted members of the GYC prior to writing this chapter.

The Context

The 1990s were an era most notably remembered by those working in the social service sector as the Common Sense Revolution. Driven by deficit reduction, the neo-conservative agenda of Premier Mike Harris' conservative provincial government supported massive cuts to social services (Aronson & Sammon, 2000; Baines, 1996; City of Toronto, 2003; Lightman & Baines, 1996; Little, 2001; Razack, 2002), leading to a breakdown of Ontario's social safety net. Progressive social work practice that focused on social change was abandoned (Aronson & Sammon, 2000; Baines, 2004). It was replaced by a residual and market-driven model of welfare characterized by managerialism (Ife, 1997), deprofessionalization, corporatization (Levitt, Beckerman, & Johnson, 1999), deskilling (Baines, 2004), and the bureaucratization of social services (Moffatt, 1999), all of which diminished the role of the welfare state. In accordance with rules set forth by the Canada Revenue Agency, limitations were imposed on the amount of advocacy-related work charitable organizations could perform (Warner, 2005).

This trend adversely affected grassroots community-based organizations, ethno-specific organizations, and organizations serving people with multiple needs (Abramovitz, 2006; Barnoff, George, & Coleman, 2006; Bischoff & Reisch, 2000; Cox, 2001). These agencies were dealing with organizational constraints such as a lack of core funding and short-term, project-based funding with complex reporting requirements (Abramovitz, 2005; Aronson & Sammon, 2000; Birkenmaier, McGartland Rubio, & Berg-Weger, 2002; Dominelli, 2002; George, Coleman, & Barnoff, 2007; Hyde, 2004; Razack, 2002).

The youth sector was not an exception. Services for marginalized youth ceased to be recognized as a priority area for governments or funding organizations (McNamara, 2007). Youth-serving agencies in general experienced a cut in funding for extracurricular programs that provided critical supports, guidance, and alternatives for young people. Observation from the field showed that the situation was particularly grave for new and smaller youth-led grassroots agencies and programs that were emerging out of a dislike of programming provided by mainstream organizations. The new groups not only struggled to gain credibility in the eyes of funders; they also lacked the sustainable resources required to effectively support youth programming. Small grassroots agencies lacked the necessary space and had minimal access to funds to run programs. Their lack of access to resources prevented the development of any capital cost projects to increase space and infrastructure. Their struggle for survival was so intense that it did not provide them the time to network and support one another. The struggle to stay active was compounded by the very fact that groups were forced to compete with one another for what minimal funds could be accessed. Above all, there was a lack of respect for the credibility of racialized young front-line practitioners doing effective grassroots youth organizing in marginalized communities (Warner, 2005).

This trend of funding resulted in the failure to prevent youth violence. During the latter months of 2004 and later throughout 2005, Toronto witnessed an increasing prevalence of gun violence affecting youth from marginalized communities (Diebel, 2005). There was a realization among funders that the neglect of services provided specifically for the youth sector, coupled with the residual effects of the Common Sense Revolution, contributed to the worsening situation. There was recognition of an urgent need for corrective action through the channelling of funds to the sector.

Based on this realization, adult-led groups were formed to address youth issues. The strategy of adults solely addressing youth issues was unacceptable to certain progressive individuals, referred hereinafter as allies, who were working with government and non-government funders. The allies were familiar with the work of a few youth-led grassroots agencies, and valued the contributions these agencies made to front-line work with racialized and marginalized youth. They wanted these agencies to inform the strategic planning and decision-making processes of the government and non-government funders. Hence, the allies advised these agencies to come together as a united front to project themselves as legitimate and credible to various stakeholder groups. Accordingly, an alliance was formed between six grassroots agencies serving ethno-racial youth from marginalized communities across the city. During the initial stages the allies supported the work of the alliance in many ways, including providing space for meetings, sharing information related to funding processes and sources, and facilitating contacts and connections in funding agencies.

Establishment of the Grassroots Youth Collaborative

The initial task of the alliance was to decide on a name and to develop a mission statement and terms of reference. Choosing a name proved to be a lengthy yet strategic process. Members felt it was important that the terms "network" or "coalition" not be used to describe the group due to the traditional connotations behind these types of bodies. Members decided that "collaborative" would be the term used to describe their work. Individuals felt it was important for "youth" and "grassroots" to be used in the title. Hence the name Grassroots Youth Collaborative was chosen.

Developing a mission statement for the GYC was another lengthy process. After much deliberation, the GYC developed the following mission statement:

> The [GYC] was formed in May 2004 to advocate for policies that empower young people to have a voice and contribute to their communities. We are a collective of culturally and racially diverse youth-led organizations that work in underserved, lower-income, at-risk communities where violence, especially youth violence, is regularly in the media spotlight. The programs delivered by our members reach out and engage young people who are typically missed by more mainstream youth programming. (Fortier, 2006)

While creating the terms of reference, the members deliberated and decided on six criteria for admitting agencies to become members of the GYC. First, an agency must be a not-for-profit organization or group and be based in the City of Toronto. Second, the agency should primarily serve youth and be youth driven, meaning that youth between the ages of 13 and 29 years should be fully represented in all areas of the agency and account for over 50 percent of all their volunteers and staff. Third, youth should also be significantly represented within the board of directors. Fourth, agencies should have an annual operating budget below $300,000 before becoming a GYC member, and have an organizational structure that operated at arms' length from a lead or sponsoring agency. Fifth, the agency should be community-based. Regional or national groups were excluded from becoming members. Last but not least, the agency had to be committed to anti-oppression and anti-racism practices and policies. Members also decided that any prospective member agency had to be formally approved by the GYC membership.

To coordinate the work, the members elected a Chair to serve on a volunteer basis and act as the GYC's coordinator. Decision-making would occur by consensus. Whenever no consensus could be reached, the decision of the majority would hold. The members of the GYC also developed objectives for directing the work of the GYC. Their first priority was to establish the legitimacy of youth-led, grassroots organizations that were doing front-line work with young people. Second, the GYC was keen on bringing awareness to the issues and challenges of marginalization and oppression experienced by young people of colour. Third, they wanted to address the myriad challenges related to a lack of core and consistent funding experienced by member agencies and other youth-led groups. Lastly, they wanted to build solidarity and increase the capacity of member agencies through the sharing of information and resources and the provision of mutual support. Combined, all of these objectives had the larger transformative agenda of strategically supporting the larger youth-serving sector and youth-organizing activities happening in Toronto.

Major Activities

In order to accomplish the above-mentioned objectives, the GYC developed a strategic plan of action. For the purposes of clarity, the strategic activities of the GYC are described in this chapter in isolation of its integrated parts. In reality, work on these activities most often went on simultaneously at different levels. The impact of the work done on each activity had a cumulative effect on the overall work of the GYC.

As a newly formed collaborative, GYC members had to find ways in which they could effectively communicate their mission and their values to other groups. They knew that they would have to build legitimacy with funders and stakeholders so that their mission and work would be respected and fully understood. At this formative time, an ally from a funding agency provided the GYC with information about upcoming funding opportunities. The ally also promised to offer support around grant writing. The GYC strategically decided on using research for launching work on its progressive agenda because research is a legitimate tool with which to achieve credibility. With the support of the ally, the GYC secured its first grant from an Ontario regional office of a federal funder. The project funding was for research on best practices in youth engagement with a focus on the members of the GYC. The research was to be conducted through a literature review, interviews with key stakeholders, and focus groups with front-line practitioners. The purpose of this research was to educate stakeholders by capturing the perspectives of youth-led organizations on issues of critical importance around youth organizing and front-line work. Through this research, the GYC also wanted to create opportunities for knowledge sharing, networking, and creating dialogue among youth-led, grassroots organizations. Specifically, they aimed to engage in dialogue around successful practices and policy issues surrounding youth engagement in Toronto. Against the conventional practice of using quantitative research methodology, the GYC strategically decided to use qualitative research methodology. The data would be collected through focus groups because these would provide opportunities to participants for networking, dialogue, and strategizing. Young community members with experience in research were hired to conduct the research. As anticipated, the focus groups provided an excellent opportunity for the otherwise marginalized grassroots youth-led agencies to voice their challenges, experiences, and most effective practices. In order to educate and create awareness among funders, the GYC decided to compile the findings into a report and strategically disseminate the findings at a public event.

A large number of funders and representatives of various levels of government were invited to the dissemination event. In order to provide easy access for youth, the event was held at a youth-friendly venue. The GYC and its member agencies used the event as an opportunity to familiarize funders, government, and community agencies with its mandate. A report on the findings of the research entitled *Youth on Youth: Grassroots Youth Collaborative on Youth Led Organizing in the City of Toronto* (Warner, 2005) was released, and the findings were presented to the public. Significant outcomes of the research included identification of the challenges, successful experiences, and best practices of youth-led agencies. Key research findings demonstrated the effectiveness of youth-led programming and the ability of young people to reach and engage their peers. The report cited the importance of arts and popular culture as a pedagogical tool and medium for youth engagement. It also made significant contributions to challenging the social construction of marginalized youth as "at-risk" youth. The report made recommendations around programming and the funding needs of agencies to the various stakeholders present at the event. The event was a significant milestone for the GYC. The report made timely contributions to the heightening public recognition and realities of youth marginalization and alienation in the City of Toronto. The report is still quoted by many funders and organizations across Toronto today.

Following the dissemination event, the work of the GYC became ever more critical in the context of increasing violence and the targeting of racialized youth in Toronto. The year 2005 later became labelled the "Year of the Gun." During this period, four neighbourhoods were identified as "high-risk" in the city. The GYC did not find it acceptable that these neighbourhoods were overly stigmatized by the media due to the perceived increase in violent crimes and homicides in the city. The GYC decided to resist the increased targeting and criminalization of racialized youth by organizing a public forum.

The purpose of the forum was to educate, create awareness, and allow opportunities for dialogue between different stakeholder groups regarding the situation. A large number of community members, agencies working in the youth sector, funders, policy makers, and representatives from government attended the forum. At this event, GYC member agencies provided their critical perspective on the violence, and its impact on the youth they worked with and their communities. These presentations created opportunities for dialogue between various stakeholders. The GYC also used this opportunity to screen a documentary prepared by one of the member agencies. In contrast to the negative media publicity, the documentary portrayed the inherent strengths and capacities of two of the four neighbourhoods that were labelled as "high risk" communities by the city. The GYC also challenged the label of "at risk" given to marginalized youth on the basis that "at risk" was not a human trait, but rather a socially constructed environment in which some youth live. From there on in, the GYC placed a disclaimer about the term "at-risk youth" in every funding proposal to define the term as youth who have not had equitable access to opportunities. In combination, these events enabled the GYC to establish its credibility amongst funders, government bodies, and the sector at large. The funders began listening and paying attention to the recommendations made by the GYC and its member agencies.

The work of the GYC continued to expand to address the issues of multi-barriered and newcomer youth with a focus on women. In order to alleviate the pressure and growing demands on the Chair, who was working on a voluntary basis, a decision was made to apply for funding in order to hire a full-time coordinator. Since it was not possible to obtain funding for networking and advocacy-based activities, the GYC decided to apply for project funding. Among members, there was recognition that funding could change the structure of the GYC and would create added responsibilities related to program outcomes.

The GYC was successful in receiving a grant to hire a coordinator who could organize workshops, conferences, and a series of forums on youth-engagement strategies. Through these activities the GYC hoped to be a credible and strong voice in influencing policies concerning culturally sensitive and relevant programs for youth. The goal was to develop a model of youth collaboration and advocacy that could be replicated elsewhere. Many workshops and mini-forums were held to address issues of concern to multi-barriered and newcomer youth. A resource guide was developed as a practical tool to be used by GYC member agencies, youth-serving organizations, funding bodies, planning councils, and governments to improve service coordination for newcomer young women and multi-barriered youth across Toronto. In addition to organizing conferences and forums, the new coordinator offered supports to member agencies. The types of supports included, but were not limited to, grant writing, training on budgeting, policy development, and various forms of assistance during times of staff transition.

Subsequently, through an ally from a funding agency, a department of the federal government approached the GYC to organize a forum addressing youth violence. The government department wanted the GYC to work with mainstream youth groups on this project and to increase its membership. Instead, the GYC used this opportunity to connect with many grassroots youth-led groups that it had not previously partnered with. The GYC also decided to use this funding opportunity to shift the focus of youth violence from individuals to systemic issues affecting youth. The two-day forum, called "From the Roots Up," was organized with the aim of bringing racialized youth together from marginalized communities all over the city of Toronto to discuss issues of systemic violence. All of the arrangements for the forum were done by tapping into the existing skills and talents of community youth, and using available resources from member agencies. Three youth from the community were hired to work with the coordinator to make arrangements for the forum. Instead of hiring outside contractors, groups of youth from member agencies were hired to take care of various aspects of the forum. For instance, one of the youth groups from a neighbourhood identified as "high risk" was appointed to record the proceedings of the forum, and another youth group was hired to edit and prepare a documentary on the forum. The venue for the forum was selected based on its easy accessibility for community youth. As part of their outreach strategy, GYC member agencies attracted youth from their communities to attend the forum.

The forum took place with over 250 youth participants. Youth were bused in from all areas of the city. The GYC paid transit fares to youth for attending the forum and hired another group of youth to prepare meals for the attendees. The youth participated in workshops and shared their experiences related to increased police targeting, racial profiling, and the impact of these experiences on them. They also deliberated on strategies for building healthier and safer communities.

The GYC believed that it was extremely important that the recommendations made by youth at the forum be followed up with action. To accomplish this, members developed a follow-up report entitled *From the Roots Up! A Youth-Led Report on Building Safe and Healthy Communities* (Fortier, 2006). The report made a series of important recommendations to funders, policy makers, and government. It suggested a better coordination of funding streams for youth-led initiatives among all levels of government, and advocated for multi-year core funding and streamlined reporting processes. The report also recommended a structural shift away from funding mainstream programs and organizations to funding grassroots, youth-led community initiatives. The funding shift would be a means of recognizing and supporting youth who were already doing this front-line work. Instead of focusing on youth criminalization, the report challenged funders to focus on social programs that valued youth empowerment and channelled youth talent through the cultural arts. The most significant recommendation put forth in the report centred on supporting youth-led programming at the grassroots level in order to build healthier communities. As a strategy to promote youth engagement, the report recommended the coordination of tri-level funding and/or a subsidy program to open up buildings, provide affordable space for youth-led initiatives, and develop and expand current programming. The findings of the report were disseminated to diverse stakeholder groups on different occasions.

The report was disseminated at Metro Hall to high-level decision-makers from all three levels of government. The GYC used its credibility and leveraged its contacts to bring together these officials. On a later date at an accessible community cultural centre, the report and a documentary prepared by youth who had attended the forum were presented to youth, community members, community organizations, and funders. The latter event was intentionally organized on the anniversary of a youth's death. The youth was from a GYC member agency, and had been lost to gun violence. The organizers used this event to verbalize the heinous and devastating impacts of the deaths of young people in Toronto's communities. Through speeches from the members of the GYC, effort was made to shift the focus away from the symptoms of violence to the root causes of violence in marginalized communities. GYC members also advocated for action against poverty, the multi-dimensional root cause of the problem. To be proactive, one of the member agencies announced a scholarship fund it had started in memory of two youth lost to gun violence. The purpose of the scholarship was to increase marginalized youth access to educational opportunities.

Following distribution of the report and documentary, the GYC was approached by a municipal department to take part in applying for a diversion project that was labelled as a Gang Exiting Program. The GYC challenged the construction of marginalized youth as gang members and refused to participate in the proposal for funding. The member agencies decided to remain in solidarity and not one of them applied for the project funding. The resistance proved successful and the municipal department could not launch the Gang Exiting Program without the partnership of GYC member organizations.

At around the same time, the GYC was also consulted for a research study conducted by an arts network in Toronto. The purpose of this research was to receive input on changes that community-based organizations wanted to see with regards to arts-based funding in the youth sector. As a participant, the GYC played a critical role in shaping the research findings. Since the initial draft of the report did not fully reflect youth perspectives and the GYC's input, the GYC coordinator provided revisions that were incorporated in the final version of the report. This report was then later utilized as a critical tool to support the development of a new and unique arts-funding program for youth.

The new funding initiative marked a shift away from conventional forms of funding, as it brought 10 different funding bodies together for funding the youth arts sector. The funding program was to support projects that demonstrated both the engagement of excluded youth and the creation of opportunities to bring forward their personal, social, and cultural issues through artistic forms. The funding model took a grant preparation approach that provided youth with technical supports, workshops, and resources in the areas of grant writing, financial management, and much more. In order to increase trustworthiness to the process of funding, the initiative created a volunteer Grant Review Committee that included young artists from diverse neighbourhoods in Toronto who came together to assess funding applications. In this manner, the initiative was transformative in the much-needed area of funding and capacity building for the youth sector.

It is interesting and important to note that solidarity and capacity building were woven intricately within all activities of the GYC. GYC member agencies networked, provided organizational development supports, shared various resources, and provided support to each other during periods of crisis. Member agencies often acted as trustees for smaller, non-incorporated projects or groups and administered funds for them. The GYC also provided support to newer and smaller groups in the areas of grant writing, board development, financial management, and human resource management. GYC members shared their resources while planning and organizing events. Resource sharing also took the form of sharing "inside" information on upcoming grant opportunities, sharing the contact information of key stakeholders, participating in joint training sessions, and sharing office spaces to save on leasing expenses. Against the normal trend of secrecy and competition between agencies for funding, GYC members transparently discussed funding opportunities and supported each other's applications through sharing funding contacts, providing references for one another, engaging in trustee relationships, and offering technical support. Another unique way that support was shared between member agencies was during times of crisis. Throughout the last few years, multiple member agencies have dealt with issues of violence in the lives of their youth participants. Staff members from different member agencies have relied on one another during times of crisis to deal with difficult losses and jeopardizing incidences that have had a great impact on the daily operations of their agencies. GYC member agencies have been able to share knowledge around organizational policies such as a Police No-Entry Policy. Together, they have learned how to manage challenges arising from a peer model of work where youth and staff members often lived in the same community.

Impact of Work and Current Challenges

The narrative of the work of the GYC highlights its accomplishment of the objectives outlined at its inception. The GYC has gained credibility with various stakeholders, including funders, policy makers, and different departments within all
three levels of the government. The GYC is continually consulted by the stakeholders on critical issues pertaining to the youth sector in Toronto. Through its
various activities, the GYC has successfully been able to influence funding patterns
in the youth sector. The GYC has created and sustained solidarity among its member agencies, and is a great example for other sectors and organizing bodies.

Over the years, the GYC has grown to its current size of 11 organizations. As an
independent entity, the GYC has been able to secure funding for two contracted
full-time staff positions. With the arrival of funds and a growth in membership,
the GYC is currently at a crossroads and is faced with new challenges. The first
challenge begs the question that given the flow of funding and the potential to
receive additional funding, should the GYC adopt the role of an intermediary
funding agency for other community-based youth groups and agencies? Second,
how should the GYC balance the different needs of smaller and more-developed
member agencies? Last, based on the different needs of member agencies, how
should the GYC maintain its original vision of transformative change?

Discussion

The account of the GYC's work presented in this chapter has focused on four
major areas closely related to the objectives outlined at its inception: educating and awareness building, resisting conventional perspectives and practices,
creating solidarity, and influencing funding patterns. As a collaborative, the
GYC has played an important role in educating stakeholders about the challenges faced by racialized youth and the detrimental impacts of targeting and
criminalization on youth and their communities. As the voice of its member
agencies, the GYC has provided the perspectives of front-line practitioners
regarding the challenges facing their sector. The GYC has played a critical role
in drawing stakeholders' attention from violence to its root causes of poverty
and resource deprivation in racialized communities.

In its work, the GYC has fearlessly challenged the existing misconstruc-
tion of youth and the underlying assumptions of funding programs. It has
resisted the labelling of racialized youth as "at risk" in public forums and grant

proposals. To challenge the existing stereotypes of deficit and pathology (i.e., high risk) associated with neighbourhoods inhabited by poor and racialized members, the GYC has prepared and screened a documentary projecting strengths of two of the four neighbourhoods identified as high risk by the city. The GYC has effectively challenged the underlying assumption of youth as gang members through its refusal of funding for gang exiting programs. Last but not least, against the conventional practice of adults planning programs for youth, the GYC has practised and advocated for a youth-led model for programming and organizational governance.

Through all of its activities, the GYC has focused on building solidarity among youth-serving agencies and among youth living in marginalized communities. The GYC has brought member agencies and youth together to share resources and information, provided mutual supports, and built a stronger voice of resistance against the challenges facing them. One of the most important contributions of the GYC rests in its influence over funding patterns, as was demonstrated in being consulted in the development of an experimental youth arts funding program in 2006. The formation of this innovative funding program is a transformative response to funding challenges experienced by youth-serving agencies.

The work of the GYC clearly highlights the GYC's adherence to the tenets of structural social work practice both in the establishment, governance, and day-to-day operations of the GYC, as well as in its practices with youth. The mission statement, objectives, and terms of reference of the GYC demonstrate a firm commitment to upholding the values of equity, fairness, and justice (George, 2003). The GYC's resistance to marginalization and the criminalization of racialized youth is founded in the critical theoretical underpinnings of structural social work theory. The GYC's firm belief in the inherent capacities of these youth to change their life circumstances is reflective of the non-pathological perspective of service users held by structural social work practice (Mullaly, 2002).

This perspective has informed all of the GYC's work to be extremely intentional and strategic. Every activity of the GYC has been directed toward accomplishing the larger agenda of social systemic change. The work of the GYC is dialectical in nature, wherein the GYC has established a strong connection between the individual experiences of victimization and targeting with the deeper structural issues of inequity and deprivation of material resources experienced by racialized communities (George & Marlowe, 2005). The GYC has used this understanding to inform its dialectical approach to practice. For instance, a GYC member agency's initiative of creating a scholarship for education was a response at the personal level to support youth to overcome barriers to higher education and employment. Along with this, the GYC has advocated for government attention to address poverty, the root cause of violence that has so negatively affected marginalized communities. The GYC's work with racialized youth from diverse ethnic communities, its work with newcomer youth, and its advocacy work around the youth-led model of youth organizing and service provision is also evidence of the GYC's deep understanding of how multiple forms of oppression, including racism, classism, ageism, and immigration status, intersect in the lives of youth from marginalized communities. The work of the GYC demonstrates a challenge to the existing socially constructed racist view of racialized and impoverished youth as "at risk" or "gang members."

The work of the GYC also demonstrates effective utilization of a number of structural social work skills (Moreau, 1990; Moreau et al., 1993; Murray & Hick, Chapter 1 in this volume). It is important to note that even though the work has entailed the use of more than one skill at a time, for the purposes of this discussion the authors have focused on one skill at a time. One of the most important and core skills of structural social work practice utilized by the GYC is the skill of converting personal troubles of victimization into the political issues of targeting and a lack of social infrastructure. The GYC has used this skill to successfully launch its attack on the oppression of racialized and marginalized youth in Toronto.

Using skills of collectivization through grassroots mobilization and organizing public events and forums, the GYC has developed a collective consciousness with youth about their issues. These events have transformed powerless youth and member agencies into social change agents who educate stakeholders and challenge dominant discourses and practices. Strategically, the GYC has also used these events as opportunities to highlight the strengths and capacities of so-called "at-risk" youth.

The GYC has focused on enhancing the power of member agencies and youth through collectivization and the creation of opportunities for networking. The GYC has enhanced members' power by providing access to resources (e.g., sharing information about grants and policies, sharing common spaces) and by engaging in capacity-building opportunities (e.g., grant-writing skills, financial management). The GYC has redistributed the material resources it obtained as funding for events and forums to youth and member agencies by hiring their services. Every activity undertaken has used the existing resources and potential within the community and member agencies. Above all, the GYC's recommendation for a youth-led model of practice was rooted in enhancing the power and encouraging the self-determination of young people.

A noteworthy lesson from the GYC's work is the use of research as a tool for transformation. The narrative provides a detailed account of the manner in which the GYC used the strategy of research as a legitimate tool to promote a political mission of galvanizing communities, establishing the GYC's credibility, and pushing for a transformative agenda. Through research, the GYC successfully brought the voices of youth and youth-serving agencies from the margins to the centre stage of action.

Above all, the most significant contribution of this case study to structural social work practice lies in the demonstration of strategic relationship building by GYC members with particular allies from funding agencies. The authors use the word "strategic" to qualify these relationships because they were intentional, goal directed, and outcome centred. Rather than applying the modernist understanding of perceiving all funders as "oppressive," GYC members used their discretion in building strategic relationship with selective, progressive individuals (allies) from funding agencies. Relationships with such individuals have proved to be extremely useful to the GYC for its inception, survival, consolidation, and growth. This case study demonstrates the tremendous potential of building critical bridges with influential insiders within institutions. However, it is important to note that these strategic relationships with a few allies did not change the GYC's overall perspective about funders and funding practices. As seen in this case study, GYC members have not hesitated to challenge funders on their use of stigmatizing labels to describe youth, their neighbourhoods, and their programs. The GYC has not succumbed to the temptation of financial security, and hence stability, and has even refused funding for programs that do not fit with the GYC's critical perspective. On the contrary, the GYC has effectively used its credibility to influence funders in shaping the development of an unconventional youth-funding initiative. This strategy fits well with the current thinking on structural social work, which incorporates postmodern thinking (Hick & Pozzuto, 2005; Lundy, 2004; Mullaly, 2007) and challenges simplistic and dichotomous constructions of power (Carniol, 2005).

Conclusion

The work of the GYC provides an excellent example of structural social work in practice. The account of major activities provides useful insights into practices that address the twin challenges of supporting individuals and communities in dealing with marginalization and simultaneously resisting dominant societal structures that perpetuate oppression and marginalization. The GYC's work with funding agencies contributes to the existing body of knowledge on structural social work, and provides a new direction for moving the practice forward in current times.

Endnote

[1] The authors wish to acknowledge the contribution of GYC member agencies for providing and verifying information in relation to the work of the GYC.

References

Abramovitz, M. (2005). The largely untold story of welfare reform and the human services. *Social Work, 50*(2), 175–186.

Abramovitz, M. (2006). Social work and social reform: An arena of struggle. *Social Work, 43*(6), 512–526.

Aronson, J., & Sammon, S. (2000). Practice amid social service cuts and restructuring: Working with the contradictions of 'small victories'. *Canadian Social Work Review, 17*(2), 167–187.

Baines, D. (1996). Rebel without a claim: Women's changing bases to claim on the state. *Canadian Social Work Review, 13*(2), 187–203.

Baines, D. (2004). Losing the "eyes in the back of our heads": Social service skills, lean caring, and violence. *Journal of Sociology & Social Welfare, 31*(3), 31–50.

Barnoff, L., George, P., & Coleman, B. (2006). Operating in survival mode: Challenges to implementing anti-oppressive practice in feminist social service agencies in Toronto. *Canadian Social Work Review, 23*(1/2), 41–58.

Birkenmaier, J., McGartland Rubio, D., & Berg-Weger, M. (2002). Human service nonprofit agencies: Studying the impact of the policy changes. *Journal of Social Work, 2*(2), 133–147.

Bischoff, U.M., & Reisch, M.S. (2000). The impact of welfare reform on community-based non-profit organizations: Implications for policy, practice and education. *Journal of Community Practice, 8*(4), 69–91.

Carniol, B. (2005). Analysis of social location and change: Practice implications. In S. Hick, J. Fook, & R. Pozzuto (Eds.), *Social Work: A Critical Turn* (pp. 153–165). Toronto, ON: Thompson Educational Publishing.

City of Toronto. (2003). *Cracks in the foundation: Community agency survey 2003: A study of Toronto's community-based human services sector.* Toronto, ON: City of Toronto.

Cox, E.O. (2001). Community practice issues in the 21st century: Questions and challenges for empowerment-oriented practitioners. *Journal of Community Practice, 9*(1), 37–55.

Diebel, L. (2005, November 20). Enough: Everybody's losing somebody somewhere. *The Toronto Star,* pp. A1, A8.

Dominelli, L. (2002). *Anti-oppressive social work theory and practice.* Basingstoke, UK: Palgrave Macmillan.

Fortier, C. (2006). *From the roots up! A report back from the youth-led forum on building safe and healthy communities.* Toronto, ON: Grassroots Youth Collaborative.

George, P. (2003). *Going beyond the superficial: Capturing structural social work practice.* Research Report for the Faculty of Community Services. Toronto, ON: Ryerson University.

George, P., Coleman, B., & Barnoff, L. (2007). Finding hope in a hostile context: Stories of creative resistance in progressive social work agencies. *Canadian Social Work, 9*(1), 66–83.

George, P., & Marlowe, S. (2005). Structural social work in action: Experiences from rural India. *Journal of Progressive Human Services, 16*(1), 5–24.

Hick, S., & Pozzuto, R. (2005). Introduction: Towards 'becoming' a critical social worker. In S. Hick, J. Fook, & R. Pozzuto (Eds.), *Social work: A critical turn* (pp. ix–xviii). Toronto, ON: Thompson Educational Publishing.

Hyde, C.A. (2004). Multicultural development in human service agencies: Challenges and solutions. *Social Work, 49*(1), 7–16.

Ife, J. (1997). *Rethinking social work: Towards critical practice.* Melbourne, Australia: Longman.

Levitt, L., Beckerman, A.H., & Johnson, P. (1999). Defending social and health services under threat: Questions and strategies. *Journal of Social Work Research, 13*(1), 59–67.

Lightman, E., & Baines, D. (1996). White men in blue suits: Women's policy in conservative Ontario. *Canadian Review of Social Policy, 38,* 145–152.

Little, M. (2001). A litmus test for democracy: The impact of Ontario welfare changes on single mothers. *Studies in Political Economy, 66,* 9–36.

Lundy, C. (2004). *Social work and social justice: A structural approach to practice.* Peterborough, ON: Broadview Press.

McNamara, R. (2007, November 7). The youth program that worked. *Eye Weekly,* pp. 1, 20–21.

Moffatt, K. (1999). Surveillance and government of the welfare recipient. In A.

Chambon, L. Epstein, & A. Irving (Eds.), *Reading Foucault for social work* (pp. 219–245). New York: Columbia University Press.

Moreau, M.J. (1990). Empowerment through advocacy and consciousness-raising: Implications of a structural approach to social work. *Journal of Sociology & Social Welfare, 17*(2), 53–67.

Moreau, M.J., Frosst, S., Frayne, G., Hlywa, M., Leonard, L., & Rowell, M. (1993). *Empowerment II: Snapshots of the structural approach in action.* Ottawa, ON: Carleton University.

Mullaly, B. (2002). *Challenging oppression: A critical social work approach.* Toronto, ON: Oxford University Press.

Mullaly, B. (2007). *The new structural social work* (3rd ed.). Toronto, ON: Oxford University Press.

Razack, N. (2002). *Transforming the field: Critical antiracist and anti-oppressive perspectives for the human services practicum.* Halifax, NS: Fernwood Publishing.

Warner, R. (2005). *Youth on youth: Grassroots Youth Collaborative on youth-led organizing in the City of Toronto.* Toronto, ON: Grassroots Youth Collaborative.

CHAPTER 12

The Association of Black Social Workers (ABSW):
A Model of Empowerment Practice

WANDA THOMAS BERNARD AND VERONICA MARSMAN

Introduction

Mullaly (1997) asserted that "The guiding principle for structural social work practice is that everything we do must in some way contribute to the goal of social transformation" (p. 164). Yet most practitioners know how daunting that prospect can be, especially for those who practise from the margins. The Association of Black Social Workers (ABSW) in Nova Scotia has been in existence since 1979, and has practised structural social work since its inception. Using a case-study approach, this chapter will describe and discuss ABSW's use of structural social work theory within an Africentric framework in practice with a focus on successful examples. From this theoretical base, we will examine some of the work ABSW has engaged in, such as providing counselling and educational services to individuals, families, and communities; consulting; providing training for and advising community organizations; conducting research; and advocating for communities. The case study offers a critical appraisal of the challenges that ABSW has faced, including its successes and community involvement.

Structural and Africentric Social Work: A Positive Alliance

We agree with Murray and Hick (Chapter 1) that structural social work is a transformative and radical approach to practice. Key strengths of this approach include the emphasis on multiple oppressions and the potential to unify critical perspectives. Structural theory is rooted in an analysis of how best to address power imbalances and the realities of multiple forms of oppression. In practice, this means viewing an individual's problems in a broader structural context of social, political, and economic realities that frame everyone's lives. The great promise of structural social work is the linking of personal problems to broader structural issues, and the challenging work of breaking down power imbalances and barriers between workers and clients. We concur, however, with Murray and Hick that structural social work only marginally addresses the experiences of First Nations peoples, and add that the same can be said for the experiences of African peoples. Africentric theory picks up where structural social work ends in terms of linking individual concerns to structural contexts, and specifically addresses the African reality. It begins with a centring of the individual from a holistic perspective and links the individual's concerns to the structural realities that frame those concerns. A theory of change, liberation, and affirmation, Africentric theory challenges dominant paradigms and provides a framework for addressing the needs of African people and communities.

ABSW's work is timely, given the emergence of the significance of worldviews in the delivery of culturally relevant and culturally specific health and human services that has gained prominence over the past 20 years (Este & Bernard, 2003). The Africentric worldview centres the experiences of African people. It assigns them meaning and validates and legitimizes the experiences and contributions from disenfranchised people who have been, or, as some might argue, are still banished to the margins of scholarly work. It is also holistic and takes into account the structural realities for people of African descent regardless of their location in the diaspora, such as the glass ceiling, failing educational institutions, and lack of access to things that many take for granted. The central tenet of Africentric theory is the reassessment of social phenomena from an African-centred orientation (Asante, 1988; Collins, 1990; Schiele, 1996). It is a newly conceptualized theoretical framework that allows for the possibility for social theorists to see African people as subjects; therefore, as active participants with the capability to shape their own experiences. It is a theory of affirmation, "conceived to generate new knowledge and to pursue the path of liberation" (Bekerie, 1994, p. 133).

There are four major tenets that underpin Africentric theory (Schiele, 1996):

1. the interconnection of all things;
2. the spiritual nature of human beings;
3. collective identity; and
4. the affective dimension.

Building on these tenets, Este and Bernard (2003) identified the following practice principles: emphasizes an African worldview that includes harmony, collectivity, and non-materialistic qualities of people; holds a holistic conception of people; connects people culturally, historically, spiritually, and with community; views the experiences of African people as key movers of their own liberation; is rooted in the African value system; fosters and develops a collective consciousness; and analyzes context and systemic realities. ABSW began its work from an African-centred perspective and has continued to embrace that worldview.

The main connection we make between structural theory and Africentric theory is the responsibility to address issues from a holistic perspective, including an analysis of both individual and structural issues. Awareness and analysis of the larger, macro-level reasons for social problems facilitates a more in-depth analysis of the structural reasons for social problems, which in turn can lead to social action to address them.

Africentric Theory: From Research to Practice

From 1995 to 1996, members of ABSW engaged in a transformative research project that used dialogue as the chief instrument in the development of a theoretical framework, which sought to empower marginalized individuals by creating opportunities to dialogue about their practice in a safe space. Within this framework there is room for both the definition and analysis of experiences. Called "Africentric Perspectives in Social Work: Nova Scotian Experiences," data for the study were collected in two phases. In phase 1, researchers compiled a list using purposive sampling of 90 African social and human services workers located throughout Nova Scotia. A questionnaire was designed to enable participants to reflect on their practice and those components of their training that best prepared them for practice. The questionnaire was mailed with a self-addressed, stamped envelope. Fifty questionnaires were returned (a 56 percent return rate). The data were analyzed to identify predominant themes, which were then used to guide focus group discussions in phase 2. A thematic analysis was used to analyze the focus group data.

Findings of this study suggest that African Nova Scotian social workers and human services workers hold an Africentric worldview. Although the workers did not always use the language of Africentric theory, the discussion and descriptions of their practice were consistent with the theoretical and philosophical underpinnings of Africentric theory. Their perspectives on the significance of race, racism, life experiences, and collective consciousness suggest a clear understanding and analysis of the oppression and marginalization of themselves as workers and of their clients. There is recognition of the cultural alienation and disconnection from community that many clients struggle with (Bernard, Benton, & Baptiste, 1999).

ABSW was concerned about the limited effectiveness of traditional programs and services in dealing with social and economic issues that confront people of African descent (Este & Bernard, 2003). Like similar organizations in the United States and Britain, ABSW was formed to address racism and systemic barriers that social workers witnessed in their communities. It embraced Africentric social theory as a guide for practice, even though, as suggested above, this was more intuitive in the early years of its existence.

Why Form an Association of Black Social Workers?

ABSW was formed out of necessity. The first group in Canada was established by a small group of social workers in Montreal in 1977, following their attendance at a conference organized by the American group, the National Association of Black Social Workers (NABSW). This nucleus kept up its momentum for two years with modest support from NABSW; however, the social workers were not able to sustain the group beyond 1979 (Jacobs, 2006). At about the same time, a social work intern with Nova Scotia roots moved back to that province, and helped to form the Nova Scotia ABSW group in 1979.

The Nova Scotia ABSW, a non-profit, volunteer group of Black social workers and human service workers, was formed by four women who were concerned with transforming a system that was not responsive to the problems and concerns of African Nova Scotians, a fact supported by the literature (Pachai, 1990; Saunders, 1994). Bernard and Hamilton-Hinch (2006) asserted that these four women were all community minded, socially conscious political advocates who realized that their collective forces were needed to address the concerns they witnessed in their community. Their experiences, coupled with recurring concerns and criticisms from community members, helped them to both readily identify social injustices that were having detrimental effects on their communities and to address, through solution-driven dialogue, those issues that had somehow been moved to the periphery of social agencies. They were especially concerned about African Nova Scotian children and youth in the care of the state, most of whom were in White foster homes in rural communities. These four women had a vision to transform the capacity of social services by introducing multi-lateral mechanisms that would enable social agencies to become responsive to the plight of Black families and communities.

As ABSW approaches its 30th anniversary, this is an opportunity to reflect on its successes and challenges. Today, ABSW has over 30 active members and approximately 80 corresponding members from across the country. Membership consists of social workers, human service workers, and social work students. The Nova Scotia chapter is the only one in Canada, and is affiliated with the NABSW. An action-oriented group, ABSW serves as a source of support for its members, who are all working in the field, and who give their time as volunteers to assist the group in fulfilling its mission. In addition, ABSW members work with individuals, families, and communities, and network with other agencies and organizations to effect change. The group also organizes workshops and training events for the social work community (this work is discussed later in the chapter).

The original goals of ABSW were as follows:

> To provide a structure and forum through which Black social workers and human service workers could exchange ideas, offer services and develop programs in the interest of the Black community and the community at large.
>
> To work in cooperation with, or to support, develop or sponsor community welfare projects and programs which would serve the interest of the Black community and the community at large.
>
> To examine, develop and support social work and community based programs of direct service or assistance to individuals in the Black community. (ABSW, 1985)

Thirty years later, these same goals continue to guide the work of ABSW as it sets priorities for major initiatives in its work with families and the community. ABSW's community work might best be discussed under the following key areas: work with children and families, and community education. We discuss this work, and reflect on the successes and challenges in each of these areas.

Work with Children and Families

ABSW's first project in 1979 was a summer program for Black and Bi-racial youth in care. The ABSW Summer Program for Black and Bi-racial Youth in Care was designed for those youth who were living in White foster and adoptive homes, based on the founders' concerns about these children's well-being. The program offered workshops and activities to help the youth understand and deal with issues of racism. They also focused on identity confusion, and introduced the youth to the rich culture and history of African people. The majority of these children were living in isolated rural White communities, with no contact with their birth families or the wider Black community. The child welfare agencies indicated that they could not find Black foster and adoption homes for these children (ABSW, 1979). The experience of racism and cultural alienation was an everyday occurrence for most of these children at home, at school, and in the neighbourhood. The ABSW summer program was a welcome intervention because it linked the youth with each other, and with other Black youths from Black communities. The ABSW summer program provided workshops for youth on basic topics such as hair and skin care. There were also lessons in African Nova Scotian and world history, and sessions on building self-esteem and positive racial identity. In addition, ABSW provided seminars on dealing with racism and handling conflict.

We agree with Bernard and Thomas Bernard's (2002) assertion that an unanticipated outcome of the program was the fact that it reunited siblings. Youth who were separated when they went into foster care, and who did not know that they had biological siblings, were suddenly in contact with them. Additionally, links with other community youth developed into ongoing friendships. This linking of Black and Bi-racial youth to their birth communities afforded them opportunities to build extended family and kin relationships that remain important for them to this day.

One of ABSW's founders (personal communication with Althea Tolliver, July 15, 2005) recalls some memorable experiences from the summer youth program, which ran for three years:

> I remember one young woman who met her birth sister.... They were both amazed at the family resemblance. The sisters were so happy to have each other it gave them the courage to look for their birth mother.

Just thinking about the communities where these Black foster children were being raised filled me with anger and rage. They were so isolated and it must have been very lonely for them. The only saving grace was that many of the homes had several Black children, like farming, so the kids had each other, and those bonds were so strong.

The ABSW Position Statement on the Placement of Black and Bi-Racial Children

Perhaps considered a bold move in 1989 for a relatively small and powerless group, ABSW created a position statement about the placement of Black and Bi-racial children in White foster and adoptive homes. This community advocacy was necessary if ABSW hoped to meet its objective of social change and transformation. ABSW found support for its position in the work of the NABSW in the United States, which had a similar policy. ABSW stated that "the Black child should grow in a safe, secure environment with parents who are able to transmit to that child a positive sense of culture, identity and well being" (ABSW, 1989, p. 2), and further:

> The Association of Black Social Workers oppose [sic] the child welfare practices of trans-racial adoption and the foster placement of Black children in White homes. The Association of Black Social Workers adheres to the position that Black children be placed in Black homes where they belong physically, psychologically and culturally in order that they receive a total sense of themselves and are free to develop to their fullest potential. In the adoption/fostering of a child of minority racial or minority ethnic heritage, in reviewing adoptive/foster placement, the court shall consider preference, and in determining appropriate adoption/foster home, the court shall give preferences, in the absence of good cause to the contrary to (a) a relative or relatives of the child, or if that would be detrimental to the child or a relative is not available, to (b) a family with the same racial or ethnic heritage as the child or if that is not feasible, to (c) a family of different racial or ethnic heritage from the child that is knowledgeable and appreciative of the child's racial or ethnic heritage and has ongoing contact with others of the child's ethnic or racial background. (ABSW, 1989, p. 1)

This statement was instrumental in positioning ABSW to have active involvement in the development of the revised *Children and Family Services Act* in 1991, and the inclusion of a policy around the provision of culturally specific services for children and families as part of the *Act*. ABSW also assisted with cultural sensitivity and anti-racism training for staff of various child welfare agencies in the province as part of the implementation of the new *Act*, and continues to provide this service.

The position statement and subsequent changes to the Nova Scotia *Children and Family Services Act* has made an important contribution to the provision of child welfare services in the province. Child welfare workers and agencies now have the legislative responsibility to take racial and cultural issues into consideration when providing child welfare services, from the first point of entry in the system to service provision. The ABSW position statement was issued almost 20 years ago, and while it may be seen as successful in many regards, there are also lingering concerns, which will be discussed later in the chapter. ABSW's efforts did not stop at the establishment of the new policy; another structural barrier was the implementation of the policy, and the need to recruit and retain Black foster and adoptive homes. ABSW also lobbied for the hiring of Black social workers to do this recruitment. In addition, ABSW helped to promote fostering and recruit families in the African Nova Scotian community. This became a challenging job due to the history of distrust and discomfort between child welfare agencies and Black communities.

Recruitment of Black Foster and Adoptive Homes

ABSW established a recruitment campaign to help agencies find suitable homes for Black and Bi-racial children in care. A poster was prepared for use in the campaign and sent to strategic locations. In addition, ABSW members visited local churches and Black organizations to create awareness of the need for Black families to provide culturally specific foster and adoption options for these children. This work was further developed by a student member of ABSW as part of her field placement. The student organized a series of "kitchen-table talks" to recruit and train Black foster families to help fulfill the need for more culturally specific homes.

This initiative also assisted in the hiring of Black social workers in various agencies in Nova Scotia to actively recruit, train, and support Black foster and adoptive families. While this has been successful in urban centres, there are still major gaps in the recruitment of both Black workers and adoption and foster families in rural communities.

Success and Challenges

ABSW's work with children and families was obviously successful on a number of levels. Most significant were the unanticipated positive outcomes—the linking of birth families and the building of relationships through the summer program for youth in care—that have had a long-term effect on the individuals involved in the summer program; however, these positive outcomes were not without challenges. The children and youth referred to the summer program had been with their foster families for many years, and most had strong family bonds with their foster parents, foster siblings, and community friends. Their emerging racialized identity and new sense of racial pride often left them confused, frustrated, and angry. There were few opportunities to express and address their emotions. We facilitated and witnessed their collective consciousness-raising, and their individual and collective empowerment, yet there was a vulnerability because of the structural conditions they lived with. ABSW was pleased to see policy changes, but was concerned about instituting the policy without adequate training of those responsible for its implementation.

Another challenge was that ABSW did not have core funding to run the program. The reliance on summer grants and agency referrals severely limited the scope of the program. ABSW was also concerned about the policy that allowed trans-racial placements without adequate training or supports for the parents. ABSW recognized the need to address the larger structural problems if real change was to be realized. Structurally, ABSW was forced to demand changes in a child welfare system that was unwelcoming and culturally insensitive to the specific needs of Black families. Working from the ground up, ABSW has helped to bridge and repair relationships between social service agencies and the African Nova Scotian communities. Despite these challenges, ABSW's work with children and families is ongoing, and it continues to engage in community education and capacity building. Members who work within the system find additional burdens and responsibilities within their agencies. For Black workers fighting for change within the system, the personal is very political every day. ABSW continually seeks ways to work with and to challenge those realities, one of which is through community education.

Community Education

Community education has been a significant component of ABSW's work over the past 30 years. This has included support groups, workshops, and training programs, all developed by members of ABSW. Some of the successes and challenges with community education are discussed here.

Noting an absence in the literature of data from adoptees in the discourse about trans-racial adoption, a graduate student who was also an ABSW member conducted a research study on the experiences of Black and Bi-racial adults who were raised in White foster or adoption homes and who had no contact with their birth family or the cultural community (Johnson, 1991). The participants of this study later formed a support group so they could continue the dialogue and support each other on their journey to racial consciousness. Although these adult adoptees had survived trans-racial adoption, without connection to their culture, it was not without pain and an incredible sense of loss. The support group facilitated by ABSW helped them to find themselves, and they helped the organization understand the need to change policy in this area to include issues of race, culture, and religion in the assessment and provision of services.

ABSW would suggest that this program was very successful for the group of people who participated, and their experiences led to significant policy changes; however, the program was not able to continue due to lack of supports and funding. ABSW was so reliant on student and volunteer services that as people's interests and availability shifted, so did its programming emphasis.

A second support group was started a few years later by another social work graduate student as a part of her research. Marsman (1993) was conducting a study on the development of identity in Bi-racial children and, using participatory action research, developed a group called SEARCH (Support, Education, and Appreciation of Race, Culture, and Heritage) with White parents of Black and Bi-racial children. As Marsman began her research, she quickly realized that the parents she was interviewing were also searching for answers, support, and assistance to help them raise their children in this race-conscious society. Marsman worked with ABSW to develop the SEARCH group, which provided support, education, training, and counselling services for these White parents (adoptive, birth, and foster parents) and mixed-race couples who were raising Black and Bi-racial children.

As Roker (2006) stated:

> The SEARCH group enabled the parents to come together in a safe forum, to address how best to meet the needs of their children. The group also provided opportunities for the youth to come together to address issues that were important to them. Many of the youth were dealing with issues of racism that they had not been able to discuss with their parents. Additionally, the parents developed a heightened awareness and analysis of their role in effectively parenting their children to deal with the racism that they experienced. They also gained practical skills such as managing hair and skin care, how to access community resources, and the power of establishing networks in the community. (p. 37)

SEARCH was successful in implementing numerous community-level programs that were aimed at introducing African-Canadian culture to youth who had been disconnected from their heritage. The group eventually took off on its own, even getting to the stage where its members organized a local conference to reach the wider public. As the children aged, however, and the parents involved no longer had the same needs, the group dissipated. The success of the group depended largely on the volunteer efforts of those who were directly affected. It had no institutional support, and ABSW had moved on to other projects and was unable to continue to provide support and direction to the group. Nevertheless, ABSW continues to receive referrals to provide services such as those offered by SEARCH. Perhaps it is time for a program of this nature to become a core program in the provision of child welfare services.

Anti-Racism and Cultural Sensitivity Training for Social Workers

Early in its development, ABSW recognized that changes in service delivery to African Nova Scotian clients were more likely to happen if it expanded its work to include both social work students and workers. To help facilitate this, ABSW created an interactive, experiential anti-racism workshop (Thomas Bernard & Thomas, 1991), based on Jane Elliott's "Blue Eyes, Brown Eyes" exercise, which it initially piloted with undergraduate students at the local school of social work. The workshop established a process that allows participants to simultaneously experience oppression and critically reflect on their own experiences of power and privilege. This was a challenging workshop, often with mixed reviews, delivered by two ABSW members in two parts with a focus on awareness, analysis, and action. Many participants were angered by the exercise that put them in the role of "oppressor"; however, those same participants typically said it was this exercise that had the greatest impact on their learning (Roker, 2006). Although ABSW presented this workshop to over 50 agencies and organizations throughout Nova Scotia and other parts of Canada during the 1990s, it was discontinued after careful reflection on the best use of ABSW's limited resources. ABSW members realized that, although there were many long-term benefits for participants, as reflected in the external evaluation by Chaytor in 1995, it was difficult and challenging work for its members, and there were few supports and resources for those who were victims of racism. Following this experience, ABSW developed an educational program called *Strategies for Dealing with Racism in the Workplace* for its members and other African Nova Scotian Human Services workers, to help them develop skills for dealing with racism.

Africentric Training Program

More recently, ABSW developed and delivered an eight-month training program for adoption and foster care workers in Halifax called "The Africentric Training Initiative." Despite their efforts to address earlier concerns regarding the placement of Black children, legislative changes, and active recruitment of Black homes, there was still much work to be done. ABSW continued to receive complaints that African Nova Scotian children were being placed in White foster and adoption homes, and that many of those placements were taking place because of ties to White birth families or foster families that were difficult or near impossible to break. The Africentric Training Program was designed to provide more in-depth training for the workers who were placing children in foster care and adoption families. The specific goal was to develop an awareness of the lived realities of African Nova Scotians and Africans in the diaspora, to introduce skills needed in the use of Africentric assessments for custody and placement cases involving African Nova Scotian (Black) and Bi-racial children, and to evaluate the assessment tool developed by Bernard and Roker (Roker, 2006, p. 39).

The training took place with one session a month over an eight-month period, providing an opportunity for workers to develop rich understandings of the communities, Africentric theory, and the lived experiences of Black and Bi-racial youth in trans-racial care. During the same time frame, a similar program was offered to foster care and adoptive parents on the specific needs of the African Nova Scotian and Bi-racial children in their care. The training offered interactive workshops on hair and skin care, and seminars on Black history, racism, and identity. Seen as a pilot project in Halifax, the training initiative was evaluated and recommendations were made for its ongoing use in the provincial community services department.

The most significant component of the training program was the use of the cultural assessment tool that was developed by Bernard and Roker (Roker, 2006) based on their experiences of completing cultural parental and place-ment assessments; working with Black and Bi-racial children and youth in care, as well as trans-racially adopted youth and Bi-racial families; and their involvement with ABSW. The tool was designed for use in the assessment of potential foster homes for Black and Bi-racial children, in cases of custody and access involving parents of Bi-racial children, and in cases of cross-cultural or trans-racial placement of Black and Bi-racial children. The tool focuses on the culturally specific needs of Black and Bi-racial children (both short- and long-term), with particular attention to whether the home in question is appropri-ate to meet those needs. It allows the children's needs to be examined within a child development context and from an Africentric perspective, which here denotes a worldview that allows African peoples and those of African descent to be seen as critical agents of their own experience.

The tool also allows for parental assessment using the "Triple A Paradigm for Cultural Competence: Awareness, Analysis and Action," which was developed by Wanda Thomas Bernard and Candace Bernard (Bernard and Bernard, 2001) to redress the lack of standardized assessment procedures and training for foster parents in the province of Nova Scotia. The first part of the assessment focuses on parents' awareness of the culturally specific needs of African and Bi-racial children. Social workers are prompted to discover how the parents define racism, their understanding of how children form racial identity, and how racism affects identity formation. This section also includes an evaluation of parents' awareness of the need to develop coping strategies and methods to deal with racism.

The analysis section evaluates parents' ability to develop a critical perspective on the ways in which systemic racism affects Black and Bi-racial children in Canadian society. The social worker assesses parents' capacity for critical self-reflection and for helping the child develop an analysis of the effects of racism. Factors to consider include what strategies are employed to deal with issues of race and identity formation in relation to having a dual heritage, and whether parents are aware of their own limitations within the family and the supports they need.

The action section includes an assessment of the strategies developed by parents to deal with racial barriers. Social workers are trained to recognize and evaluate what actions parents have taken, and if they have created a home environment that allows for the positive and meaningful exploration of the child's heritage. Other factors to consider are the parents' ability to network with the school and community to provide culturally specific supports for the child and what community supports exist in the neighbourhood, school, extended family, friends, or wider community.

Moreover, each of the six items from Freeman and McRoy's (1986) environmental scan are included as part of the action assessment. Specific issues for social workers to address include what opportunities the children are given to discuss racism and cultural issues; what steps have been taken to address racism and foster positive racial identity; how the family addresses racism or acts of discrimination and prejudice; and what strategies the family uses to address racism, prejudice, and discrimination. Important considerations should include whether children interact with both Black and White peers, if the neighbourhood and school reflect racial diversity, and if the school's curriculum and activities reflect the student body and the children's heritage. Other indicators of cultural sensitivity include whether the family participates in cultural events, how they feel about attending events in the Black community, and if the child has positive Black role models. In custody cases, it is also important to determine if there is contact with the non-custodial parent and family.

Recommendations are based on an analysis of the strengths and limitations that emerge from the three-fold paradigm evaluation. Recommendations to make the home more culturally appropriate might include encouraging the use of community-based, culturally specific resources, joining support groups for White parents and those parenting Black and Bi-racial children, participating in Black community events, visiting local or regional Black or African Heritage Cultural Centres, inviting Black children and community members to family events, and attending a Black church. In addition to these suggestions, the agency may also provide assistance to families in developing strategies to deal with racism and locating and utilizing community resources.

Since completing the pilot training, ABSW has offered training to 50 adoption workers throughout the province, and has discussed the training tool at various conferences. The tool is being used by social workers in adoption, but there is a level of discomfort among White social workers who are reluctant to push White adoptive and foster parents on issues of race and racism. Perhaps they are not so comfortable with those topics themselves, and have not integrated the reasons to address such cultural issues into their frame of reference. Furthermore, questions about adoption often come after a child has been with a family in a culturally different foster home for a number of years. To be truly effective, social workers need to do these assessments for foster and adoption homes, and active recruitment of Black foster and adoption homes needs to be more of a priority. These are institutional changes that are needed to make the placement of Black and Bi-racial children a more culturally sensitive practice. There seems to be a disconnection between the vision of the program and some practitioners who are experiencing difficulties in implementing the change. Reasons for this disconnection should be addressed, perhaps through dialogue between ABSW and service providers, or further research.

Reflections on Community Education

ABSW's community work has had two core foci: the African Nova Scotian community and the professional social work community, and each is consistent with the organization's goals. The community education initiatives have raised the profile of ABSW and Black social workers, and helped to break down barriers between the community and social agencies. The services and programs offered have been well received; however, a concern has been the lack of consistency, with programs being offered only on a project basis with no secure funding. This has meant an over-reliance on the time, resources, interests, and commitment of volunteers, and a lack of continuity when people move on to other things, which could leave community members feeling abandoned. The programs have all been rooted in a structural and Africentric perspective, and as such have facilitated empowerment and challenged oppressive conditions. ABSW advocates for culturally appropriate practice as the norm that all clients are entitled to, yet because of the structural realities of the organization's very existence, it cannot ensure this reality for many clients.

It can be said that some of the greatest accomplishments have been the structural and policy changes that ABSW has helped to facilitate in the social work professional community. ABSW's involvement with the school of social work and the provincial department of community services has led to long-term policy and structural changes. These changes have emerged partly from its community educational activities, which have had a significant impact on the community as noted in the evaluation completed by Chaytor in 1995. The very existence of ABSW, its work with allies, and its vision of "what is possible" has kept members involved and engaged as they fight for change in policies and practices.

Conclusion

ABSW's work is grounded in an Africentric perspective in that every action taken is centred on the experience of African people, and is considered from a lens that has a core operating principle of "How will this benefit the community?". This is very closely aligned to structural social work practice, which has a goal of social transformation. ABSW has had a long and distinguished practice with individuals, families, and community groups. In addition, through research and community advocacy, ABSW has helped to influence and change policy that informs social work education and practice. As previously noted, there have been many accomplishments in its work with children and families, and community education.

Despite these successes, ABSW is currently at a crossroads. The vision of the founding members to transform the capacity of social services has not been fully realized, and the group cannot expect to meet its ambitious goals as a volunteer body. It is clear that project-based funding has not led to the desired long-term structural changes, and the group will therefore have to determine the best way to move forward. ABSW must, and should, build on its positive connection with the African Nova Scotian community. Utilizing structural and Africentric models of practice would help ABSW to maintain its autonomy, its grassroots focus, and its capacity to facilitate empowerment and transformation.

ABSW has worked tirelessly for the past 30 years and has many accomplishments to be proud of. Working at both the community level and with senior managers and decision-makers, and using structural and Africentric perspectives, ABSW has helped to bring about some changes at both individual and systemic levels. This has not been without its challenges and struggles, however; the most serious of which has been the lack of sustainable funding for its programs and services. Nevertheless, the very existence of the group serves as a model of empowerment for its members and others as they challenge oppressive conditions and structures. Imagine the impact ABSW could have if it had an office with core staff to continue the fight for change.

References

Association of Black Social Workers. (1979). Unpublished minutes. Halifax, Nova Scotia, Canada.

Association of Black Social Workers. (1985). Unpublished minutes. Halifax, Nova Scotia, Canada.

Association of Black Social Workers. (1989). Unpublished position statement. Halifax, Nova Scotia, Canada.

Asante, M.K. (1988). *Afrocentricity*. Trenton, NJ: Africa World Press.

Bekerie, A. (1994). The four corners of a circle: Afrocentricity as a model of synthesis. *Journal of Black Studies, 25*(2), 131–149.

Bernard, W.T., Benton, W., & Baptiste, R. (1999). *Africentric perspectives in social work.* Unpublished project report. Halifax, Nova Scotia, Canada.

Bernard, W.T., & Hamilton-Hinch, B. (2006). Four journeys, one vision: ABSW comes to Halifax. In W. Thomas Bernard (Ed.), *Fighting for change: Black social workers in Nova Scotia* (pp. 18–26). Halifax, NS: Nimbus Publishing.

Bernard, W.T., & Thomas, G. (1991). Social services sensitivity training program. *Canadian Social Work Review, 8*(2), 237–245.

Bernard, C., & Bernard, W.T. (2001). *Triple A paradigm for cultural competence: Awareness, analysis, and action: An Africentric assessment tool for African and bi-racial children.* Unpublished training tool. Halifax, Nova Scotia, Canada.

Bernard, C., & Bernard, W.T. (2002). Learning from the past/visions for the future: The Black community and child welfare in Nova Scotia. In B. Wharf (Ed.), *Community work approaches to child welfare* (pp. 116–130). Toronto, ON: Broadview Press.

Chaytor, K. (1995). *Experiencing the difference: An evaluation of the racism awareness workshop offered by the Association of Black Social Workers.* Unpublished research report, Maritime School of Social Work, Dalhousie University, Halifax, Nova Scotia, Canada.

Collins, P.H. (1990). *Black feminist thought: Knowledge, consciousness and the politics of empowerment.* New York: Routledge.

Este, D., & Bernard, W.T. (2003). Social work practice with African Canadians: An examination of the African Nova Scotian community. In A. Al-Krenawi & J. Graham (Eds.), *Multicultural social work in Canada: Working with diverse ethno-racial communities* (pp. 306–337). Toronto, ON: Oxford University Press.

Freeman, E., & McRoy, R. (1986). Racial identity issues among mixed race children. *Social Work in Education, 8,* 167–174.

Jacobs, D. (2006). The National Association of Black Social Workers comes to Montreal. In W. Thomas Bernard, (Ed.), *Fighting For change: Black social workers in Nova Scotia* (pp. 12–17). Halifax, NS: Nimbus Publishing.

Johnson, B. (1991). Black perspectives on foster care: A project exploring the experience of foster care placement on Black children placed in White foster homes. Unpublished master's thesis, Dalhousie University, Halifax, Nova Scotia, Canada.

Marsman, V. (1993). The identity of the Bi-racial child. Unpublished master's thesis, Dalhousie University, Halifax, Nova Scotia, Canada.

Mullaly, B. (1997). *Structural social work: Ideology, theory, and practice* (2nd ed.). Toronto, ON: Oxford University Press.

Pachai, B. (1990). *Beneath the clouds of the promised land* (Vol. 1). Halifax, NS: Black Educators Association of Nova Scotia.

Roker, C.B. (2006). The Association of Black Social Workers in Halifax: A brief history. In W. Thomas Bernard (Ed.), *Fighting for change: Black social workers in Nova Scotia* (pp. 27–45). Halifax, NS: Nimbus Publishing.

Saunders, C. (1994). *Share and care: The story of the Nova Scotia home for colored children.* Halifax, NS: Nimbus Publishing.

Schiele, J. (1996). Afrocentricity: An emerging paradigm in social work practice. *Social Work 14*(3), 284–294.

PART 3

Future Directions

Practices and Skills for Building Social and Ecological Resiliency with Individuals and Communities

MISHKA LYSACK

Only days earlier, I had sat on the high bluffs of a cliff on the Cabot Trail in Cape Breton, watching a pod of whales breeching the surface of the Atlantic, listening intently to their breathing. On that occasion, I felt myself transported to another realm saturated with mystery and peace, suspended in the web of life. Later, on a warm summer day in Nova Scotia, I stood on the edge of the Sydney tar ponds. As I gazed across the black expanse, I noted that the ponds do not look like water at all, but like a thick plastic tarp. Around the tar ponds I was especially struck by the absence of any life. There were no birds flying over the pond, no insects hovering, not even any wind; a virtual silence brooded over the ponds. There was only death, not life, emanating from this toxic chemical stew, flowing like the river Styx out to the ocean.

Shrouded in sadness and loss, I turned and walked across Frederick Street to a small, working-class home metres from the tar ponds. Signs beckoned us to go into the backyard, where I was greeted with dolls and manikins, signs affixed, representing the politicians who had failed in their promises, and caricatures of children and families suffering from the chemical poison spreading through their basements and land. It was a dark carnival of political burlesque, encircled with the tragic air of a wake that no-one had attended. Looking around at the vista of figures, I felt a shiver of eeriness. As I walked around the pathetic community of dolls and figures, I could feel my sadness becoming infused with despair and anger in reaction to the injustice visited upon the people living here. My *grief* regarding the ecological degradation of life in tar ponds and my *anger over the injustice and suffering* experienced by the residents of Frederick Street were not two separate experiences, but two closely intertwined dimensions of the same response. Then and there, I decided to become re-involved with the environmental movement. The sense of ecstasy with the whales and the sense of loss and anger at the tar ponds combined to open up new portals for me, reconfiguring how I saw my profession as a social worker relative to ecological action. There was no turning back. Not now.

Justice, Sustainability, and Social Work

Since I was young, this sense of the essential unity between *social justice* and *environmental sustainability* has always been with me, the threads woven effortlessly into a seamless whole of education, organizing, and protest. As I entered social work, I was surprised to discover that this field was devoid of any substantial discussion of environmental issues or engagement with ecological problems. My surprise deepened into confusion and concern as I realized that even those approaches in social work that are intentionally focused on social justice—such as structural models—were all but completely absent from the realm of environmental discourse and action. Despite the public's growing awareness of environmental issues, such a vacuum of interest is still the case at social work conferences and in mainstream journals, where environmental discussion is rare.

Other educators and scholars (Berger & Kelly, 1993; Besthorn, 2003; Besthorn & Saleebey, 2003; Coates, 2003a, 2003b; Hoff & McNutt, 1994; Keefe, 2003; Lysack, in press; Mary, 2008; Muldoon, 2006; Park, 1996) have reached the same conclusions regarding the absence of social work engagement with environmental issues, be it the areas of policy, theory, or practice. In *Ecology and Social Work*, Coates (2003a) concluded that despite the fact that social work could "take a significant role in addressing the negative consequences on individual and social well-being of our culture's environmental devastation ... the profession has not seriously considered the environmental crisis, nor has it considered the tasks and demands of a new vision" (p. 3; see also pp. 39, 58). Such a conspicuous lack of engagement with environmental concerns coincides with the omission in mental health generally, including psychology (Kidner, 1994; Roszak, Gomes, & Kanner, 1995) and family therapy (Lysack, 2007).

Unlike psychology's more individualistic orientation, social work has had a history of interest in locating the individual within a larger context, as evidenced by the prominence of the person-in-environment model. This attention to the "environment" could have provided the incipient resources for developing an ecological sensibility by conceptualizing humankind as one species among others on Earth. However, Coates (2003a) concludes, "Attention to environment has almost exclusively been directed to the social environment and its relationship to personal troubles. Attention to human relationships with the larger, natural environment has not entered the mainstream of social work thought and practice" (p. 44). Given the "mounting evidence of the negative effects brought about by market-dominated industrialism, pollution, loss of habitat and extinctions" (p. 45), this lack of response in social work to threatening ecological problems is all the more disturbing.

The structural approach to social work, both in its initial formulation by Maurice Moreau (Moreau & Leonard, 1989) and in its subsequent developments as a model for social work thought and practice (Carniol, 1992; Mullaly, 1997, 2002), has critiqued mainstream social work's focus on working with the de-contextualized individual. As an alternative, structural social work has proposed linking the personal problems and suffering of a person with larger public issues and with structural realities on a social level (Lecomte, 1990). Feminist approaches to social work, in their analysis of patriarchy and the oppression of women, have continued to develop the lens of *gender* as part of social work's practices of empowerment, while anti-oppressive models of social work have further explored the particularities of *race* and *economic class* and their roles in the political oppression and economic exploitation of individuals and communities. Subsequently, critical (Leonard, 1994) and radical social work approaches (Fook, 1993, 2002) refined the notion of the *contextual self*, operationalizing this perspective into forms of social work practice.

Through its acuity for sensing inequities in power relationships and its facility in highlighting the impact of oppression and exploitation on people's lives, the structural approach has made an invaluable contribution to the field of social work by reconfiguring its professional self-understanding and realigning its orientation to practice. Instead of understanding individuals as de-contextualized persons separated from the contexts of their lives, structural social work brings the effects of oppressive relationships, exploitative social structures, and disqualifying discourses into the foreground of practice and theory. However, while structural social work has appropriately challenged the notion of a *de-contextualized person*, it has nonetheless fallen prey to the anthropocentric orientation of contemporary society in its embrace of a *de-contextualized society*, supposedly detached from the biosphere of the Earth. There are few explicit references to environmental injustice or to the natural realm as a site for exploitation in the canon of structural or critical social work literature. For instance, Mullaly (1997) refers to the need for environmental planning that would include the "prohibition of activities resulting in pollution, urban planning, and development of new communities" (p. 38), but did not elaborate further regarding the implications for either social work practice or theory. For Coates (2003a), structural social work regrettably confined itself "to the 'social' environment and did not challenge the exploitation inherent in the industrial-growth imperative of modernity and its attitudes toward non-human nature" (p. 45).

The limitations of structural social work lie in both its *theoretical* orientation as well as with respect to its actualization in *practice*. Despite its vectoring toward such techniques as consciousness-raising and practices of empowerment, structural social work excels in developing practices that challenge the oppression of individuals and communities, but is largely neglectful in its responsibility to challenge the exploitation of species other than the human species. "The target of empowerment is people, and the target for anti-oppressive activity is people. Nature continues to be exploited" (Coates, 2003a, p. 54). A tragic irony emerges as Coates, a social work educator himself, examines the theoretical foundations for structural social work being remiss in engaging in environmental activism. Coates noted that "These approaches do not challenge the view that nature is simply instrumental to human needs, nor do they question the fundamental exploitation inherent in growth-oriented industrialism, which also exploits the physical environment as it exploits people" (p. 54).

Given the severity of current environmental problems—the decline of the environment as a whole (McKibben, 2006), the alarming increase in species extinctions and the decline in the Earth's biodiversity (Wilson, 1984), and global warming (Monbiot, 2006)—this lack of attention to the environment is more than a simple oversight. Coates (2003a) is direct and uncompromisingly clear about the failure of the field of social work as a whole, including structural social work approaches, to engage in any meaningful manner with ecological threats to life on Earth. "The almost exclusively anthropocentric focus of social work interventions throughout the twentieth century and the profession's near absence from environmental discourse reflect a general set of beliefs and values that ignore and indirectly support ecological degradation" (p. 45). By failing to respond to the pressing environmental problems that we as a species face, social work is effectively absent at this critical turning point of our planet, thereby denying the important contributions of our contextual ideas and actions to the struggle for environmental justice. As such, through our absence, we risk being complicit in the ongoing devastation of the biosphere and the planet itself.

The question emerges: what would be the features of a social work practice with an environmental orientation and sensibility? The next section describes the particular skills in three major areas that would exemplify a social work practice with an enhanced ecological orientation and sensitivity: (1) orienting skills, (2) practice skills, and (3) use-of-self skills.

Orienting Skills
Re-Discovering Our Embeddedness in the Web of Life

In Macy's (1995) inquiry into a psychology of the environment, he advocated cultivating an understanding and "appreciation that we do, in fact, have a relationship with the Earth itself, and the degree to which that relationship has become inimitable to the sustaining of human lives and those of countless other species" (p. 287). Contemporary industrial/consumer society has inculcated an anthropocentric worldview in our awareness that obscures the biological reality of our dependence on the planet for our survival. If our practices as social workers are to develop an ecological sensibility, these practices need to be grounded on the counter-perspective of a biocentric worldview, where we are one species among many in a network of ecological systems within a larger cosmological exchange of energy, matter, and life. This perspective is reflected in the theoretical framework for the 12-part "Ecological Credo for Social Workers" developed by Berger and Kelly (1993, pp. 524–525), which outlines guiding principles for an ecological re-orientation of social theory and practice.

Activist and teacher Joanna Macy (Macy & Brown, 1998) highlighted the importance of a *shift in perceptions of reality*, both cognitively and spiritually, as a foundation for despair/empowerment work with individuals and communities (pp. 21–24). This re-orientation of perception emerges from multiple sources, including (1) the movement from environmental despair to the ecological self; (2) breakthroughs in systems thinking, and similar ecological and scientific thought; and (3) resources in the wisdom writings and spiritual voices in the religious traditions (see also Berry, 1999, pp. 176–195).

Inquiry into Politics and Economics from an Environmental Perspective

An ecologically informed practice would also entail an *analysis of structural causes* through a critique of societal dynamics, underlying cultural agreements, and interlocking economic forces that undergird the industrial/consumer society and the extractive, non-renewing economy that are complicit in the degradation of the natural world (Macy & Brown, 1998, pp. 19–21). Our political and economic institutions, and the parallel cultural discourses that incite the pursuit of material wealth beyond the carrying capacity of the Earth, are expressions of attitudes toward our planet and the species that inhabit it, and have "a compelling life of their own" that inhibits the emergence of environmentally sustainable institutions and forms of collective life (Mack, 1995, p. 287; see also Merchant, 2005).

For social workers, this perceptual skill involves moving from understanding our work within a de-contextualized society to re-contextualizing our practice within a larger ecological realm, reconfiguring our contextual/structural analysis from an anthropocentric to a more *biocentric/ecocentric* worldview. Macy & Brown (1998) insisted that this skill of recontextualizing our lives in a larger environmental realm dovetails with practice skills of creating *alternative societal and economic institutions*, and facilitating the emergence of forms of capacity and resilience on a community level, such as renewable forms of energy, permaculture, and organic farming, sustainable practices of forestry and fishing, and local "deep economies" (McKibben, 2007).

A Map for Despair/Empowerment Work

In his exploration of the linkages between social work and ecology, Coates (2003a, 2003b) emphasized the importance of social workers developing the skills to enable individuals and communities to enter into their experience of environmental despair and powerlessness in order to find personal healing and restoration. Such a healing pilgrimage is crucial because it facilitates persons to be no longer incapacitated by their grief, but to be empowered to take purposeful action both personally and collectively. By using a series of educational activities as community practice, Macy (Macy & Brown, 1998) developed a multi-faceted group process for persons to transform their environmental despair into a sense of an ecological self, identifying their lives as being co-extensive with other forms of life on Earth through widening circles. With this new perspective, any activities that threaten the planet are now perceived as actions inflicted against our own ecological self, health, and well-being. From an eco-psychological perspective, the suffering of the Earth is perceived as speaking through the distress and sensitivity of individuals who are concerned about the plight of the biosphere on Earth (Conn, 1995), constituting a call to engagement and action. Thomashow (1996) wrote: "By acknowledging these feelings, people summon deep collective energies, create communities of empowerment, become able to discuss their feelings, work together to form reservoirs of strength and vision, and take responsibility for transforming their fear and suffering into commitment and action" (p. 149).

In her approach to despair/empowerment group work, Macy (Macy & Brown, 1998; see also Macy, 2006) developed a thematic sequence of learning activities that form a pathway for persons to discover forms of healing and restoration. In Macy's form of community practice, these seven clusters of exercises incrementally build on one another, spiralling into a larger organic whole, progressively deepening the transformative experience of participants. The dimensions include the following:

1. affirmation: re-discovering gratitude as a foundation for action;
2. despair work: owning and honouring our pain for the Earth;
3. the shift: seeing interconnections of the planet with new eyes with compassion;
4. deep time: reconnecting with past and future generations;
5. the council of all beings: rejoining and cultivating empathy for the natural world;
6. going forth: learnings and actions that we bring back into our lives and communities; and
7. meditations for "coming back to life" and grounding ourselves mindfully in our practice.

These interlocking dimensions constitute a practice "map" or a psychological and social cartography for despair/empowerment work with individuals or communities with an enhanced ecological sensibility. This sequence of interweaving different dimensions of knowing is also an icon of the geography of the territories of life that are involved with the healing of ecological grief, the emergence of an ecological self, and the development of an environmental sensibility and a sense of committed environmental citizenship.

Practice Skills

Sensitivity to Physical Space in Enhancing Ecological Practice

In their clinical work of creating a conversational domain for clients, Griffith and Griffith (1994) were attentive to the ways in which they created a physical and biological context for clients to share and reflect upon their personal stories. Being aware of how a posture of mobilization (flight or fight) interferes with the counselling process, they were intentional in their use of language and physical position in order to evoke a climate of alert tranquility or attentive listening. By physiological tracking and mirroring of clients' body language and responsively selecting their bodily posture, practitioners can actively structure a setting for healing conversations that contribute to the emergence of a dialogic space between themselves and their clients that is implicitly ecological in its orientation.

It is not simply the physical dimensions of the interpersonal relationship that can evoke the healing qualities of an ecologically informed practice. Research has suggested that patients who are recovering from physical or mental illness have improved recovery rates when they have access to green spaces or gardens, such as windows that are open to gardens and natural landscapes (Suzuki & McConnell, 1999). It comes as no surprise that helping professionals often use images of plants, nature, or natural landscapes to decorate the offices in which they work with individuals and families. Drawing on this research, we can be attentive to utilizing natural images or objects in our work environment to enhance our own sense—and that of our clients—of being connected to the natural realm.

Using Nature Metaphors to Evoke Language of Healing

In my practice, I have noticed that many of the metaphors for healing in the language that emerges in clinical work are rooted in nature or natural processes. Our language regarding "healing patterns," "being grounded," or "being rooted" is drawn from a biologically grounded discourse related to an ecological world-view of interdependence and connection. Anthropologist Abram (1996) explored how the development of our language and our perception of the world emerges through our responsive and dialogic interaction with the natural environment, shaping our perceptions and inscribing our language with categories and semiotic material from the natural realm. As social workers, we can orient the way in which we use language in an ecological direction in order to promote a conversational space that is evocative of healing.

When I ask clients to provide an image that encapsulates a healing direction for their lives and relationships, the images are frequently nature metaphors or images drawn from childhood memories of comforting places in nature. This use of nature metaphors is also characteristic of work with persons who have suffered various forms of trauma, because the availability of these memories of *healing places* is crucial in order for individuals to anchor themselves against intrusive memories or flashbacks that they may suffer. As a preventative measure, clients identify a location or an object that is representative of this healing place, so that they may use this place or object as a psychological tool in order to stabilize and re-ground themselves in the present moment when flashbacks occur.

Understanding Problems in a Larger Ecological Context

Many approaches in the helping professions conceptualize problems as symptoms of a personal inner deficiency or as signs of an intrinsic weakness of the individual, separated from the larger social or environmental realm. By way of response, social workers have developed ways of enabling persons to re-contextualize their difficulties in the larger social and cultural milieu by heightening particularities of personhood such as gender, race, and class. Similarly, practitioners with an environmental sensibility reconceptualize society as being within a larger ecological context, working with clients to re-vision their suffering "not only as an expression of their unique personal history or circumstances, but also as an expression of the Earth's pain" (Conn, 1995, p. 168). In her account of her therapeutic work, Sarah Conn described how in listening and engaging with clients she tries "to tack back and forth between the personal level and the level of larger cultural, political, and more often now, ecological systems" (p. 168). Conn warns helping professionals against imposing this perspective on clients as an agenda in clinical practice, insisting that the timing and sensitivity to responsively and sensitively co-develop these perspectives with clients are crucial elements of a practice.

Understanding problems in the larger environmental context is also central to the emergence of a more ecologically orientated assessment, where a reconfigured format for the social worker and client to assess the influence of the problem in the client's life and relationships would include identifying and tracing the impact of environmental hazards on the client's physical and emotional health. Given the increasing rate of ecological decline and the rise of toxins in the environment, Soine (1987) wrote that what is not "debatable, however, is the fact that social workers will encounter the consequences of environmental contamination in their work with clients, whatever the field of practice" (p. 44).

A worldview where linkages are perceived between *personal* relationships (where control and disrespectful behaviours are accepted), and the *political and ecological* relationships (where similar attitudes of control and exploitation are pervasive and influential) is foundational for practice with an environmental sensibility. O'Connor (1995), an eco-social worker, insisted that as we examine all of our personal issues from a global ecological perspective, we can "see that the patterns of control, denial, and projection that sabotage intimate relationships are the very patterns that endanger the world. To change these patterns is to change not just our social lives but our relationship to the planet" (p. 151). Conn (1995) utilized a similar approach in her practice, where she was not only curious about the connections between abuse in relationships and the society at large, but also the abuse that "occurs in a still-larger context by looking at the abuse at all levels that we are confronting as a species: between men and women, between adults and children, between humans and animals, and between humans and the Earth" (p. 168).

Using Questions and Conversation to Enhance Ecological Reflexivity

Eco-social workers (O'Connor, 1995), family therapists (Casey, 2000, 2002), and eco-psychologists (Conn, 1995, 1997, 1998; Roszak et al., 1995) have all recognized the potential of effective therapeutic conversation and reflexive questions to assist clients to develop new perspectives on their lives in an ecological context. For Conn (1995), "asking questions is an essential part of the healing process" (p. 166) in her eco-psychology practice. In attending to the suffering of her clients in the larger context of our collective ecological interconnectedness, questioning is "often used in psychotherapy to enhance certain kinds of awareness, [and] is a way to point to these aspects of their experience" (p. 166).

Casey (2000) also explored the heuristic of how questions in healing conversations can contribute to clients being able to evoke new ways of perceiving and acting with more environmental sensitivity in the world. Drawing on a diversity of approaches in therapy, Casey (2002) developed particular categories of questions that have the intention of opening space and enhancing awareness embedded in their linguistic formulation (pp. 141–143; see also Casey 2000, p. 182):

- Questions that diminish our sense of species dominance and enhance a biocentric perspective: "If we were to see ourselves as a species among many species, how might we plan our cities differently?"
- Questions that deepen empathy for other species: "If other species had a voice, what might they be asking of us in the ways that we live our personal and social lives?"
- Questions that challenge our attraction to a growth/consumer-oriented society: "If you were less attracted to this stressful and driven lifestyle, how might your life be different?" "If you were able to access ways of disentangling yourself from the things that stress you out, what do you think they would be?" "As you separate yourself from the demands of our consumer society, what might you find yourself doing instead with your time and energy?"
- Questions that invite greater environmental responsibility: "If I were to tell you about factories that have reduced their waste stream, how much energy and interest would you have to explore these possibilities?"
- Questions that challenge the constraints to making environmental changes: "Given that some companies are now finding ways to care for the environment as well as growing their business, what prevents you and your company from becoming a leader in these developments?" "In continuing to dispose of your waste in a manner that harms the environment and threatens our health, what are you doing that goes against your better judgment?" "If someone on your street were to take the lead in organizing a car pool, what is preventing that person from being you?"
- Questions that trace the time trends of growing environmental problems: "Let's imagine that in one decade the Earth's environment is on the brink because of pollution and environmental destruction. As we look back

from that point in the future, what do you think that we would be wishing that we had done differently now in the present?"

- Questions that challenge the rigid mindsets and attitude of powerlessness in the face of major environmental problems: "What contributions might you be making, as our society wakes up to our present crisis resulting from our misuse and exploitation of the environment?"

The intentionality of the practitioner who uses these questions is crucial, as the questions need to be used in the context of a respectful relationship, where the questions do not determine a client's awareness, but rather provide scaffolding for a person to develop their own knowledge and perspective on their concerns. Rather than utilizing statements in conversation that tend to *set forth* realities, questions are a means of *inviting forth* new realities, leaving the responsibility and control of the final shape of the perspectives in the hands of clients themselves.

Holding Actions in Defence of Life on the Planet

In Macy's (Macy & Brown, 1998, pp. 17–24) vision of moving from an industrial growth-dominated society to a sustainable earth culture in the "Great Turning," Macy highlighted different interlocking areas of activity. One such area involves *holding actions of resistance in defence of life* on Earth (pp. 17–18), a focus shared with other feminist eco-activists such as Kaza (1993, 2000) and Shiva (2000, 2005). Holding or protective actions include political, legal, and legislative initiatives, symbolic actions (vigils), awareness-building activities for the public (press conferences, educational events), habitat preservation, and forms of direct action/protest to prevent or minimize the destruction of the biosphere (animal and plant life) or ecosphere (rivers, wetlands, oceans, air). In this spirit, Mack (1995) proposed that helping professionals concerned about the environment "will need to become professionally and personally committed and involved outside their offices and laboratories" (p. 287). Similarly, Coates (2003a, 2003b) encouraged social workers to join existing environmental groups not only in order to contribute to these protective holding activities, but also to cultivate their ecological sensibilities by learning these practice skills from environmental activists and those involved with conservation work and habitat restoration.

Use-of-Self Skills

Linking the Personal and the Ecological

Just as social workers are familiar with the feminist idea "the personal is political," similarly, social workers also need to endorse the axiom "the personal is ecological" (Park, 1996). In developing an eco-social practice, practitioners should examine their own lifestyle and relationships to diminish their personal and collective ecological footprint (Wackernagel & Rees, 1996). There are many ways of accomplishing this goal, such as the Nature Challenge (www.davidsuzuki.org), where a person or organization can make changes in different life areas, including:

- eating habits (eating organically, locally, and low on the food chain);
- transportation (flying less or not at all, using public transport, carpooling or biking, using fuel-efficient cars);
- energy use at home and work (purchasing electricity from sustainable energy sources, purchasing energy-efficient appliances and lighting); and
- reducing our ecological footprint (composting, recycling, reducing, and refusing plastic bags and other items).

Sustaining Personal Integrity in Healing Practices

In her account of 40 years of community activism, Macy (2000) explored how burnout, or succumbing to anger or environmental despair, is an ongoing danger for those involved in any environmental action. Maintaining radical hope, commitment, humility, and compassion is a challenge that requires both personal and collective disciplines of cultivating mindfulness and compassion through meditative practices and sustaining networks of supportive relationships. For Macy, the metaphor of the Shambhala warrior (pp. 158–166), who cultivates the two "weapons" of *compassion* and the *insight* of the *interconnectedness of all reality*, encapsulates her self-understanding of her identity as an activist and teacher, a metaphor that I have personally found helpful in strengthening my own ecological identity.

In my practice and public educational work, I have encountered individuals of all ages suffering from forms of ecological despair and grief (Lysack, in press; Macy, 1995; McKibben, 2006; Windle, 1995), who are seeking personal healing and restoration as a foundation for a reinvigorated sense of commitment to take action on behalf of the Earth. It is crucial to embed one's own personal and anxiety regarding the future of our planet in a supportive matrix of ongoing personal disciplines of meditation, nurturing reading, spiritual rituals, sustaining friendships, and intentional educational and political activity (Kaza, 1993, 2000).

Re-Inhabiting our Bio-Regions and Bodies

The combination of our technological prowess, globalized economy, and our built urban environment has separated us from the ecological bio-regions in which we reside, and has surrounded us in a virtual world of our own making, maintained by illusions of control, self-sufficiency, and environmental entitlement. In contrast, bio-regionalism encourages us to *re-inhabit* the land and the environmental web of plant and animal life that makes up the ecological niche in which we are located, and to cultivate a sensitivity to the geological and biological history, climate, and biodiversity that constitutes our bio-region. Skilful means of cultivating this lived experience as a dimension of our re-inhabiting place could include frequenting a location in nature that we find healing, gardening, restoring a local habitat for endangered plant and animal species, and learning about the bio-region in which we live.

A closely related use-of-self skill would include body practices and disciplines that enable us to re-connect with our own physicality, thereby befriending our own bodies. Activities such as walking, yoga, tai chi, eating food mindfully, and other body-based activities constitute powerful counter-practices in a culture that incites us to disengage from our awareness of our bodies and the natural environment.

Cultivating a Deep and Critical Reflexivity of Culture/Economy

As social workers, we have a history of developing and enhancing our critical reflexivity relative to the power relationships in society and the forces of social injustice in cultural discourse and prevailing social structures. Given the hegemony of the growth imperative and species-ism in contemporary consumer/industrial society and the globalized economy, social workers need to refine a sensitivity to the environmental injustices embedded in the incitement to consume and acquire, and the accompanying attitudes of species entitlement implicit in our media and collective life. The development of environmental reflexivity would entail the analysis and deconstruction of the dominant anthropocentric perspectives and worldviews inherent in industrial society, while developing counter-discourses of biocentric thinking and perspectives that reposition us as a species to live in a mutually enhancing relationship with the Earth.

Deep Practice:
Transforming Society, Transforming Ourselves

> For the campaign against climate change is an odd one. Unlike almost all the public protests which have preceded it, it is a campaign not for abundance but for austerity. It is a campaign not for more freedom but for less. Strangest of all, it is a campaign not just against other people, but also against ourselves. (Monbiot, 2006, p. 215)

For social work, the task is to build on the contextual and social justice perspective that we have developed for working with *social–social relationships* (Deudney & Matthew, 1999; see also Woodbridge, 2005), and to extend and expand this approach so that it encompasses the larger environmental context of *social–nature relationships* in which we are embedded as a species. As such, the campaign for sustainability and for our environmental survival is focused on challenging and transforming social structures, our social and ecological practices, and our cultural discourses.

The focus of our new work as guardians of the environment also necessarily entails a transformation of human consciousness that has led to our present ecological crisis. Our current environmental crisis has a history, rooted in how we have evolved as a human community in our eco-social practices and our thinking. In other words, there are cultural and social antecedents that have inevitably led us to the planetary emergency that we now face. As McKibben (2006) noted, the paradox of sustainable ecological change that confounds us is that the difficulty "is almost certainly more psychological than intellectual—less that we can't figure out major alterations in our way of life than that we simply don't want to" (p. 163). Both McKibben and Monbiot (2006) have perceptively observed that the challenge of the work of healing and social transformation that is required of us is to confront the forces deep inside of us that are internalizations of outer anti-environmental social forces: our drive for control, our appetite to accumulate endless material wealth, and our need to be at the centre of the universe rather than contenting ourselves with sharing the planet with the community of life on Earth.

Wilson (1984) underlined how the critical questions that we face as a human species ultimately coalesce around ethics, or what we value most as a human community. In this light, Wilson posed a key question: "Is it possible that humanity will love life enough to save it?" (p. 145). It is we ourselves who need to answer this question, both for ourselves and for all life on Earth. It needs to be answered soon, before the question is overshadowed by a desperate search for the mere survival of human culture as global warming and ecological decline accelerate (Wright, 2004). Moreover, we need to engage with this question if we are to enter the plenitude of life that awaits us: a cosmic humility, a radical hope, an elegant simplicity of lifestyle, a richness of relationships, a weaving of environmental and social justice, and the joy of reclaiming our vocation as guardians of life on Earth.

References

Abram, D. (1996). *The spell of the sensuous: Perception and language in a more-than-human world*. New York: Random House.

Berger, R., & Kelly, J. (1993). Social work in the ecological crisis. *Social Work, 38*(5), 521–526.

Berry, T. (1999). *The great work: Our way into the future*. New York: Bell Tower.

Besthorn, F. (2003). Radical ecologisms: Insights for educating social workers in ecological activism and social justice. *Critical Social Work, 4*(1). Retrieved March 19, 2007 from http://www.criticalsocialwork.com

Besthorn, F., & Saleebey, D. (2003). Nature, genetics and the biophilia connection: Exploring linkages with social work values and practices. *Advances in Social* Work, 4(1), 1–18.

Carniol, B. (1992). Structural social work: Maurice Moreau's challenge to social work practice. *Journal of Progressive Human Services, 3*(1), 1–20.

Casey, D. (2000). Therapy on an exhausted planet. *Australian and New Zealand Journal of Family Therapy, 21*(4), 177–183.

Casey, D. (2002). Therapy and ecology: Viewing the natural world through systemic lenses. *Australian and New Zealand Journal of Family Therapy, 23*(3), 138–144.

Coates, J. (2003a). *Ecology and social work*. Halifax, NS: Fernwood Publishing.

Coates, J. (2003b). Exploring the roots of the environmental crisis: Opportunity for social transformation. *Critical Social Work, 4*(1). Retrieved March 19, 2007, http://www.criticalsocialwork.com

Conn, S. (1995). When the earth hurts, who responds? In T. Roszak, M. Gomes, & T. Kanner (Eds.), *Ecopsychology: Restoring the earth, healing the mind* (pp. 156–171). San Francisco: Sierra Club Books.

Conn, S. (1997). What aileth thee? Ecopsychological principles and practices for activists. Retrieved November 1, 2006, from http://ecopsychology.athabascau.ca/0197/intro.htm

Conn, S. (1998). Living in the earth: Ecopsychology, health and psychotherapy. *Humanistic Psychologist, 26*(1–3), 179–198.

Deudney, D., & Matthew, R. (Eds.). (1999). *Contested grounds: Security and conflict in the new environmental politics.* Albany, NY: SUNY Press.

Fook, J. (1993). *Radical casework: A theory of practice.* St. Leonards, Australia: Allyn & Unwin.

Fook, J. (2002). *Social work: Critical theory and practice.* London, UK: Sage Publications.

Griffith, J., & Griffith, M. (1994). *The body speaks: Therapeutic dialogues for mind–body problems.* New York: Basic Books.

Hoff, M., & McNutt, J. (1994). *The global environmental crisis: Implications for social welfare and social work.* Brookefield, VT: Avebury.

Kaza, S. (1993). Buddhism, feminism, and the environmental crisis: Acting with compassion. In C. Adams (Ed.), *Ecofeminism and the sacred* (pp. 50–69). Seattle, WA: Continuum Press.

Kaza, S. (2000). To save all beings: Buddhist environmental activism. In C. Queen (Ed.), *Engaged Buddhism in the west* (pp. 159–183). Boston, MA: Wisdom Publications.

Keefe, T. (2003). The bio-psycho-social-spiritual origins of environmental justice. *Critical Social Work, 4*(1). Retrieved March 19, 2007, from www.criticalsocialwork.com

Kidner, D. (1994). Why psychology is mute about the environmental crisis. *Environmental Ethics, 16,* 359–376.

Lecomte, R. (1990). Connecting private troubles and public issues in social work education. In B. Wharf (Ed.), *Social work and social change in Canada* (pp. 31–51). Toronto, ON: McClelland & Stewart.

Leonard, P. (1994). Knowledge/power and postmodernism: Implications for the practice of a critical social work education. *Canadian Social Work Review, 11*(1), 11–26.

Lysack, M. (2007). Family therapy, the ecological self, and global warming. *Context, 91,* 9–11.

Lysack, M. (2009, in press). From environmental despair to the ecological self: Mindfulness and community action. In S. Hick (Ed.), *Mindfulness and Social Work.* Chicago, IL: Lyceum Books.

Mack, J. (1995). The politics of species arrogance. In T. Roszak, M. Gomes, & T. Kanner (Eds.), *Ecopsychology: Restoring the earth, healing the mind* (pp. 279–287). San Francisco: Sierra Club Books.

Macy, J. (1995). Working through environmental despair. In T. Roszak, M. Gomes, & T. Kanner (Eds.), *Ecopsychology: Restoring the earth, healing the mind* (pp. 240–259). San Francisco: Sierra Club Books.

Macy, J. (2000). *Widening circles: A memoir.* Gabriola Island, BC: New Society Publishers.

Macy, J. (2006). *The work that reconnects* [Training two-DVD set]. Berkeley, CA: Joanna Macy Intensives.

Macy, J., & Brown, M.Y. (1998). *Coming back to life: Practices to reconnect our lives, our world.* Gabriola Island, BC: New Society Publishers.

Mary, N. (2008). *Social work in a sustainable world.* Chicago, IL: Lyceum Books.

McKibben, B. (2006). *The end of nature* (2nd ed.). New York: Random House.

McKibben, B. (2007). *Deep economy: The wealth of communities and the durable future.* New York: Times Books, Henry Holt and Company.

Merchant, C. (2005). *Radical ecology.* New York: Routledge.

Monbiot, G. (2006). *Heat: How to stop the planet from burning.* Toronto, ON: Doubleday.

Moreau, M.J., & Leonard, L. (1989). *Empowerment through a structural approach to social work: A report from practice.* Ottawa, ON: Carleton University.

Muldoon, A. (2006). Environmental efforts: The next challenge for social work. *Critical Social Work, 7*(2). Retrieved March 19, 2007, from http://www.criticalsocialwork.com

Mullaly, B. (1997). *Structural social work: Ideology, theory, and practice.* Toronto, ON: Oxford University Press.

Mullaly, B. (2002). *Challenging oppression: A critical social work approach.* Toronto, ON: Oxford University Press.

O'Connor, T. (1995). Therapy for a dying planet. In T. Roszak, M. Gomes, & T. Kanner, (Eds.), *Ecopsychology: Restoring the earth, healing the mind* (pp. 149–155). San Francisco: Sierra Club Books.

Park, K. (1996). The personal is ecological: Environmentalism of social work. *Social Work, 41*(3), 320–323.

Roszak, T., Gomes, M., & Kanner, T. (Eds.). (1995). *Ecopsychology: Restoring the earth, healing the mind.* San Francisco: Sierra Club Books.

Shiva, V. (2000). *Stolen harvest.* Cambridge, MA: South End Press.

Shiva, V. (2005). *Earth democracy: Justice, sustainability, and peace.* Cambridge, MA: South End Press.

Soine, L. (1987). Expanding the environment in social work: The case for including environmental hazards content. *Journal of Social Work Education, 23*(2), 40–46.

Suzuki, D., & McConnell, A. (1999). *The sacred balance.* Vancouver, BC: Douglas and McIntyre.

Thomashow, M. (1996). *Ecological identity: Becoming a reflective environmentalist.* Cambridge, MA: MIT Press.

Wackernagel, M., & Rees, W. (1996). *Our ecological footprint: Reducing human impact on the earth.* Gabriola Island, BC: New Society Publishers.

Wilson, E.O. (1984). *Biophilia.* Cambridge, MA: Harvard University Press.

Windle, P. (1995). The ecology of grief. In T. Roszak, M. Gomes, & T. Kanner (Eds.), *Ecopsychology: Restoring the earth, healing the mind* (pp. 136–145). San Francisco: Sierra Club Books.

Woodbridge, R. (2005). *The next world war: Tribes, cities, nations, and ecological decline.* Toronto, ON: University of Toronto Press.

Wright, R. (2004). *A short history of progress.* Toronto, ON: House of Anansi.

CHAPTER 14

Concluding Thoughts and Future Directions

HEATHER I. PETERS, TRACY LONDON, TAMMY CORNER, AND STEVEN F. HICK

By describing the diverse ways of utilizing structural social work theory in practice, the examples in this book counter the criticism that structural social work theory is more abstract than practical. The chapters display a wide variety of concrete skills and approaches that practitioners can take. Here we seek to highlight the book's key themes, drawing attention to the common ground. Finally, we reflect on some of the challenges facing structural social work in the future, and potential directions for the continued development of the theory and its use in practice.

Setting the Stage: Highlights of the Opening Chapters

The opening chapters set the stage for the book by developing an understanding of structural social work as a theory, as a set of principles and skills for practice, and in the context of a model of theory–practice integration. Structural social work as both theory and practice has moved beyond a conventional approach focused on individual change to a structural approach, which seeks to understand individual issues in the larger context of political, economic, and social structures. It goes beyond simply recognizing that oppressive relations exist, thereby relieving some of the pathologizing aspects of practice, and becomes a practice that seeks to change structures while simultaneously helping people. In Chapter 1 Murray and Hick argue that key features of structural social work include this feature, as well as those of understanding that there are multiple sites of oppression, incorporating the agency–structure dialectic, and seeing the transformation of society as the solution to social issues. Murray and Hick also describe the development of structural social work theory and discuss critiques and current debates in the field, such as the role of postmodernism, the challenges of a focus on multiple oppressions, and the blurred boundaries between structural social work theory and others such as radical, critical, and anti-oppressive theories and approaches.

In Chapter 2 Olivier returns to the original writings on structural theory by Moreau et al. (1993) and Moreau and Leonard (1989), identifying Moreau's principles of structural practice and highlighting key practice tools for each principle. Olivier brings together Moreau's description of structural practice skills with current-day approaches to structural practice found in various works such as those of Carniol (2005), Fook (1993), Lundy (2004), and Mullaly (2007). Chapter 2 highlights the two complementary, and challenging, goals of structural social work practice as described by Mullaly (2007): (1) to alleviate the problematic effects of oppression, and (2) to transform society in a way that eliminates the causes of social problems. Olivier describes the ways in which he continuously examines his own practice for evidence that he is on the right path.

In spite of the well-developed theoretical framework of structural social work and the long list of structural practice skills, as evidenced in Chapters 1 and 2, Chapter 3 points out that the integration of theory into practice has had a long and rocky road in social work. This pertains to theories in general, as well as to structural social work theory in particular. In Chapter 3, Peters notes that the literature has traditionally focused on a discussion of the gap between structural social work theory and practice. In her analysis of the literature on this topic, Peters has developed a model for theory–practice integration. The model outlines the various spaces between theory and practice, thus leading to a more integrated understanding of the barriers between the two. More importantly, it also sets the stage for an exploration of how to use these spaces between theory and practice as catalysts for their integration. The model is used to highlight the chapters and the ways in which practitioners are successfully utilizing structural theory into their practice, offering a bridge rather than a gap between theory and practice.

Themes from Practitioners' Experiences

There are many lessons that can be learned from practitioners' experiences in Part 2 of the book. Four key themes are highlighted here.

Structural Social Work Theory
Can Be Integrated Effectively into Practice

One theme from Part 2 of the book is that structural social work theory is being, and can be, used effectively in social work practice. This contradicts the criticism that the theory is idealistic and unrealistic, and therefore not an adequate practice theory. Starting from the position of "How do you use structural theory in practice?" rather than "What are the barriers to its use in practice?" allows the discussion of theory–practice integration to move in a very different direction than it usually does in the literature. Every chapter in this book is evidence of a practitioner bringing structural social work theory to practice. As a collective voice, the practitioners in this book are a microcosm of social work activists worldwide; we are woven together as a community through the depth of our belief that justice and equality matter. These practitioners impart their honest accounts of their personal and professional challenges and achievements in turning structural social work principles into effective action within multiple fields of practice: children's rights; women's rights; lesbian, gay, bisexual, transgender, two-spirited, queer, and intersex (LGBTTQI) rights; (dis)ability rights; youth rights; Black rights; immigrant and refugees' rights; and mental health clients' rights. There is no hierarchy of meaningfulness of one practitioner's work over another's. Instead, there is a common purpose for structural change regardless of the field of practice or focus of the intervention.

The success of these practitioners brings us hope. Hope first of all that just as they have developed ways of bringing structural social work practice to life, so, too, can other social workers draw on these successes and add to them in their own structural practices. There is further hope: we are not just individual social workers working in isolated settings longing for social transformation. The successes in this book remind us that we are a part of a larger social movement where each of our individual efforts holds a collective potential to challenge oppressive structures. The slow pace of social change can itself be oppressive, but the accomplishments of other structural practitioners remind us that, together, change is possible and worth working toward.

Micro, Mezzo, and Macro Levels are
Integrated in Structural Social Work Practice

A second theme from Part 2 is that structural social work practice occurs in and across all three levels of practice: micro, mezzo, and macro. Conventional social work, with its history of specialized practice fields, has ingrained in us the often unspoken and hidden separation of these three levels of practice. However, the focus of structural social work theory is that personal problems are social issues that may be faced by individuals and families, but are inextricably linked to the social structures that cause and exacerbate the problems. When personal issues (micro level) have oppressive social structures (macro level) at their root, then a separation of micro, mezzo, and macro in social work practice all but guarantees that we will never solve or prevent such problems. It is only in working across all three levels that we can begin to understand and address the structural causes of oppression faced by individuals and groups. The writers in Part 2 demonstrate over and over again that their work, no matter how traditionally micro in appearance, also contains elements of connecting the personal to the political, collectivization, community development, consciousness-raising, and advocacy for policy change.

Two chapters that exemplify individual direct social work practice activities (micro level) that incorporate all three levels of practice are Chapter 4's focus on child sexual abuse, as discussed by Feehan, Boettcher, and Quinn, as well as Carniol and Del Valle's discussion of work with individual women who have experienced abuse in Chapter 8. Likewise, work at the macro or mezzo levels (such as the administrative and community development work of Burrill and Peters described in Chapter 6) is also tied to micro-level work. Managing an organization, advocating at political levels, and encouraging staff community development activities necessitates consciousness-raising with staff. Staff thereby understand how their own problems are political, and become better able and willing to work with clients' issues at both personal and political levels. In Chapter 10, we see how the political and community development work of an organization for LGBTTQI is tied to an admonishment to us as social workers to work on our own issues first before we will be able to be effective allies in this field. Brown, Richard, and Wichman also indicate that there needs to be a balance between working on our own issues, assisting individuals on a personal level, and working at community and political levels.

The intricate and complex webs that connect micro, mezzo, and macro levels of practice are clearly demonstrated throughout the various chapters in Part 2. Effective structural social work needs to happen at and across all levels simultaneously. More importantly, as social workers we need to understand the interactions between the levels and the importance of working across the levels in our practice, even when authorities tell us we have been hired for only one particular level of work. This is not an impossible task; it is not only do-able, but every chapter in Part 2 is an example of how it is being done.

Structural Social Workers Combine and Invent New Practices

A frequent call of practitioners is for a clear set of structural social work practice skills that can easily be transported into practice. The chapters in this book provide guidance on this issue. In her edited collection *Doing Anti-Oppressive Practice*, Donna Baines (2007, p. 174) found that social justice oriented practitioners draw upon a variety of skills depending on the setting and issue. Further to that, in this book we have found that structural social workers are creative in combining mainstream practice methods within a structural framework. For example, Carniol and Del Valle discuss how the therapeutic relationship is central to work with individuals and list many traditional qualities that social workers should bring to their engagement with clients. They also outline how they work toward encouraging a critical consciousness within the client when engaged in the therapeutic relationship. This mingling of structural social work with other approaches, particularly drawing on other skill sets, is paramount. This does not mean that we can incorporate mainstream ideas into structural social work willy-nilly; it involves using existing skills without losing the structural focus. This approach is consistent with Moreau's early discussions of structural social work (Moreau & Leonard, 1989; Moreau et al., 1993). It might also mean that additional theory is required to examine the tensions and congruencies of various approaches.

Identification of Spaces and Activities that Promote Structural Practice

Another theme from this book is the identification of many ways in which structural social work practice is, and can be, supported and encouraged, and the spaces where this is likely to occur. First of all, the theory itself moves us from a place of focus on individuals to a focus on societal structures. Goals of social transformation and collectivization encourage workers to go beyond conventional approaches to social issues and suggest that social change is not only necessary, it is possible. If we are not told that we can and should have social change as a goal, then we are less likely to even think that it is an option. New organizations have been developed to support LGBTTQI youth, women, Black social workers, and others because people believed that these could make a difference.

Second, these organizations in turn offer a supportive environment that encourages structural workers to continue with and expand on their structural analyses and responses to social issues. Such organizations turn down funding for programs that are contrary to structural perspectives and instead work with funders to create alternative programs (Chapter 11); they allow workers to take the extra time needed to build a rapport with clients (Chapter 8); they insist that the people they are serving be involved in decision-making for the organization (Chapter 9); they bring like-minded people together to support each other (Chapter 11); and they develop agency policies that encourage structural analyses throughout organizations (Chapters 6 and 12).

Third, practitioners themselves also have a role to play in supporting and further developing structural social work practice. Several chapters point out that in order for us to work in an empowering way and from an anti-oppressive perspective, we must have addressed, or be addressing, issues of power and oppression in our own lives. We must also be able to shift from the traditional role of expert to the role of being an ally.

Fourth, in operating within an empowerment model, clients also have a role to play in making choices about what works for them. Feehan et al. (Chapter 4) and Carniol and Del Valle (Chapter 8) give examples of respectful and empowering work with clients that challenges them to understand structural connections to their issues. The positive response of clients to our structural work lets us know that our work is making a difference and is worth continuing.

Last is the important role of education in creating safe spaces for structural practice. Support for structural practices and analyses also come from one's colleagues and peers. Where such support does not yet exist, structural social workers work to develop it. All of the chapters give examples of how structural workers build the support they need by taking the time to educate their colleagues (Chapter 7), peers (Chapter 10), funders (Chapter 11), social work students (Chapter 12), and supervisors (Chapter 6), as well as clients and the public about structural analyses and ways of working (Chapters 5 and 6). Educational institutions also have an important role to play in educating future social workers about structural theory and practice, and in creating and supporting the development of safe places for structural social workers to work (Chapters 9 and 12).

The more of these supports that exist in any given context, the more likely it is that workers will feel comfortable and safe in working from a structural perspective. As more social workers are educated to understand the importance of structural and anti-oppressive ways of practising, the more people there are to support the development of these safe spaces for structural practice. In Chapter 3, Peters organizes these spaces into a conceptual framework in order to better understand what they are and how they work together. The goal is to see all of the supports listed above as catalysts that assist us in the integration of theory and practice; in this way we start to focus on the bridge between theory and practice, rather than the gap.

Into the Future

Since we have no crystal ball that allows us to see into the future, we can only surmise about the future challenges and directions of structural social work theory and practice. But there are some important possibilities that are open to us.

First of all, in Chapter 13 Lysack points out that social justice and environmental care and sustainability have a natural alliance. He goes further to state that environmental issues must be encompassed by structural social work for the theory, and our practice, to be complete. After all, the focus of structural social work is the person in their social, political, and economic environment; it is time that our physical environment is also acknowledged in that equation. There is much work to be done to bring these two together.

Second, while we have been diligently bringing structural analyses and approaches to our social work practice, with a goal of transforming society into a place of social justice, our national association, which had been backing us up in this work, silently walked away. The recent changes to the Canadian Association of Social Workers' Code of Ethics essentially erased references to our professional and ethical responsibilities to put clients first and to address issues of structural injustices at the root of social issues (Mullaly, 2007). Without a focus on our ethical responsibility to work for social justice, we risk simply supporting the status quo: that of injustice. It is our duty as social workers to ensure that our national organization returns to a place of supporting the goal of social justice.

Third, it is time for structural social workers to build alliances across disciplines and fields of practice. Although we sometimes think we are alone in this work, we are not. One of the editors of this book has just finished working with two nurses to stage a conference about harm reduction. Conference attendees included social workers, nurses, drug and alcohol counsellors, physicians, mental health workers, child protection workers, workers from homeless shelters, students, and others. While structural social work theory and the harm-reduction approach are not interchangeable, they are compatible. They have some similar goals, such as client-directed practice, client empowerment, and the belief that we need to change policies and societal attitudes to better address social issues. The practitioners in this book describe times when their colleagues from within and outside of social work were important supports for their structural work. We work with professionals across disciplines. When our goals are compatible we need to build alliances and support each other in our shared work toward social change.

Conclusion

In thinking holistically about the personal narratives of the contributors, this book is more than just an expression of how individual practitioners work to bridge structural theory within their social work practice. This book is a testament to our solidarity as a community to work toward social change. We share a common structural theoretical foundation, as outlined by Murray and Hick (Chapter 1) and Olivier (Chapter 2). Grounded in our shared values and ethics, we are tied to each other through our collective mission to remedy structural injustices. The practitioners in this book demonstrate that our choice to undertake structural social work is more than just intellectual, professional, or vocational; it is a way of life. Far from being a theoretical exercise, structural social work practice engages our fundamental relationships with others, and even our relationship with our own core being. And it is happening. It is not just a theoretical proposition; it is not romantic idealism. We are engaged in structural social work practice and the chapters in this book are a testament to the fact that it is working. We are making a difference in the lives of clients and in our own lives, and we are making changes in societal structures. Our work is echoed in the words of Steve Earle (2004):

> The revolution starts now
> When you rise above your fear
> And tear the walls around you down
> The revolution starts here
> Where you work and where you play
> Where you lay your money down
> What you do and what you say
> The revolution starts now

References

Baines, D. (2007). *Doing anti-oppressive practice: Building transformative politicized social work*. Halifax, NS: Fernwood Publishing.

Carniol, B. (2005). *Case critical: Social services and social justice in Canada* (5th ed.). Toronto, ON: Between the Lines.

Earle, S. (2004). The revolution starts now. On *The revolution starts now* [CD]. New York: Artemis Records.

Fook, J. (1993). *Radical casework: A theory of practice*. St. Leonards, Australia: Allen & Unwin.

Lundy, C. (2004). *Social work and social justice: A structural approach to practice*. Peterborough, ON: Broadview Press.

Moreau, M.J., Frosst, S., Frayne, G., Hlyma, M., Leonard, L., & Rowell, M. (1993). *Empowerment II: Snapshots of the structural approach in action*. Ottawa, ON: Carleton University Press.

Moreau, M.J., & Leonard, L. (1989). *Empowerment through a structural approach to social work: A report from practice*. Ottawa, ON: Carleton University.

Mullaly, B. (2007). *The new structural social work* (3rd ed.). Toronto, ON: Oxford University Press.

Editors and Contributors

Editors

STEVEN F. HICK, BA, BSW, MA, DCD, PhD: Steven is an associate professor at the School of Social Work, Carleton University, Ottawa, Ontario, Canada. He is a writer, teacher, human rights advocate, and researcher. He teaches in the areas of mindfulness, advanced direct practice theory, human rights practice, social worker formation, and community development. He has a private practice offering mindfulness interventions and social worker training in interpersonal mindfulness within a structural social work framework. He is co-founder of War Child Canada, an organization that educates Canadian youth about war and helps children in war zones. He is widely published in peer-reviewed journals and his recent book publications include *Mindfulness and Social Work* (2009), *Mindfulness and the Therapeutic Relationship* (2008), *Social Work in Canada* (2nd ed., 2005), *Social Work: A Critical Turn* (2005), *Social Welfare in Canada: Understanding Income Security* (2nd ed., 2007), *Community Practice in the Internet Age* (2003), *Advocacy, Activism and the Internet* (2002), *Children's Rights and the Internet* (2001), and *Human Rights and the Internet* (2000).

HEATHER I. PETERS, BA, BSW, MSW, PhD (candidate): Heather worked for six years as the executive director of a youth centre for "at-risk" youth in the central interior of British Columbia and spent several years in other community-based work, such as child abuse prevention and a communications position with an Aboriginal treaty process. At the youth centre she developed and managed new programs to meet the needs of local youth and worked with a local network of youth service providers to address issues at community and societal levels. Heather has also sought to connect local issues with community and societal structures in her volunteer positions with community-based HIV/AIDS and youth suicide-prevention organizations. Heather began work with the University of Northern British Columbia in 2001 and is an associate professor in the School of Social Work, where her research and teaching continue to focus on structural social work theory and its use in practice. She has published articles on research that explore access to social and health services by marginalized populations, including an examination of the role of policy structures in facilitating or impeding such access.

TAMMY CORNER, SSW, BSW, MSW: Tammy has worked in social services for 20 years. She has been involved at the community level working with developmentally (dis)abled adults and children, as a social assistance caseworker, with street-involved youth, and as a research assistant with the Canadian Union of Public Employees. Tammy has also

238

travelled to Guatemala, Mexico, and New Zealand, where she connected with individuals, communities, and organizations working with Indigenous peoples on social justice issues. For the past seven years, Tammy has been engaged in community development with Pinecrest-Queensway Community Health Centre, and is currently working as a health promoter. Her community development work has largely included developing programs and services that respond to the needs of culturally diverse individuals, families, and neighbourhoods in urban affordable-housing communities. Most recently, Tammy volunteered with a committee to start a local farmers' market. Tammy uses structural analysis to guide her work and maintains close connections with Carleton University's School of Social Work as a one way of linking theory and practice.

TRACY LONDON, JD, MSW, BA, PhD (candidate): Tracy's career as an environmental and human rights activist for corporate responsibility spans working with a major American corporate whistleblower to lobbying some of Canada's most powerful corporate and media executives. Tracy is an advisor to the Business and Human Rights Program with Amnesty International Canada (English Speaking), and producer of a documentary under development on the African-American women of the civil rights movement during Freedom Summer '64. She is a doctoral student at the University of British Columbia School of Social Work and Family Studies, examining activist strategies to realize corporate accountability for international human rights and environmental norms. She holds a JD and MSW from the University of Toronto, and a BA in Child and Youth Care from the University of Victoria.

Contributors

MAUREEN BOETTCHER, MSW: Maureen is currently the field education coordinator and a part-time faculty member at York University School of Social Work in Toronto, Canada. Maureen began practising social work in child protection services in 1983. Upon graduating with her MSW with a specialization in clinical practice from the University of Calgary in 1988, Maureen joined a team of social work professionals providing treatment services to sexually abused children and their families. As part of the team, Maureen engaged in individual and group counselling with individuals and families, many of whom lived in isolated northern communities in Alberta, the Northwest Territories, and Nunavut, where the impact of sexual abuse was community-wide. As part of her practice in the area of sexual abuse, Maureen designed and delivered numerous workshops and training sessions. In 1999, Maureen moved from practising to teaching social work, specializing in practice courses and field work where social work theory intersects with practice, and where the onus is on bringing theory alive through relationship building and skill development.

MARION BROWN, MSW, PhD (candidate): Marion is an assistant professor at the School of Social Work, Dalhousie University. Marion's current research focuses on constructions of girlhood and use of violence, and a climate survey on the experiences of lesbian, gay, bisexual, transgender, two-spirited, and intersex students, faculty, and staff, as well as heterosexual allies, at Dalhousie University.

ANNE BURRILL, BSW, MSW (candidate): Anne worked for seven years as the executive director of a women's centre in the central interior of British Columbia, where she was responsible for program development, staff supervision, and organizational strategic planning. She is currently working in a social planning and community development position with the City of Williams Lake. She has studied structural social work theory in both her BSW and MSW programs, and enjoys her work in community and administrative positions as opportunities to promote social change in social justice traditions at organizational and societal levels.

BEN CARNIOL, MSW, LLB: Ben is a social activist. He is also professor emeritus at Ryerson University, where he coordinates the delivery of social work education to off-campus Aboriginal students in partnership with the First Nations Technical Institute. He is author of numerous publications, including *Case Critical: Social Services and Social Justice in Canada* (5th ed., 2005), published by Between the Lines.

VIVIAN DEL VALLE, MSW, RSW: Vivian immigrated to Canada in 1995. She is a Latina, originally from Mexico. She works as a clinical counsellor at Toronto's COSTI Immigrant Services in the Family and Mental Health Division, where she is part of the COSTI Trauma and Abuse Program with Toronto's Latin American community. Vivian provides treatment services to Latinas and children who have been sexually abused. She also leads groups for Spanish-speaking service users at the Centre for Addiction and Mental Health (CAMH).

RICHARD J. FEEHAN, MSW, RSW, PhD (student): Richard has been a practising front-line social worker since graduating with his BSW in 1980. He has worked in a variety of settings, including Alberta Children's Services, Guelph and Wellington Children's Aid, the Edmonton Social Planning Council, Catholic Social Services of Edmonton, and private practice. His 12 years in private practice involved work with over 1,100 families in which sexual abuse occurred, over 100 community presentations about child sexual abuse, and work in dozens of communities in the Northwest Territories, Nunavut, and northern Alberta First Nations. Presently he is an instructor at the University of Calgary Faculty of Social Work.

GAILA FRIARS, MSW, RSW: Gaila is a social worker who provided clinical services to service users and families in a hospital setting until she retired from River Valley Health in Oromocto, New Brunswick, in 2007. She graduated with an MSW from Carleton University in 1986. As well as hospital social work, Gaila has participated in a seven-year research project on the military community under the auspices of the Muriel McQueen Fergusson Centre for Family Violence Research. Gaila has taught as a sessional lecturer at both St. Thomas University and the University of New Brunswick. She is the recipient of a Leadership Award from the Atlantic Centre of Excellence for Women's Health, the Raoul Léger Memorial Award from the New Brunswick Association of Social Workers, and the 2008 New Brunswick recipient of the Canadian Association of Social Workers' Distinguished Service Award. She has a particular interest in the study of violence against women and women's health issues.

PURNIMA GEORGE, PhD: Purnima is an associate professor with the Ryerson School of Social Work. She has a passion for community practice and social advocacy. Before her immigration to Canada in 2000, she was teaching and leading community projects with slum and pavement dwellers in Maharashtra, India. Her doctoral research was on studying the process of transformative change accomplished by a non-profit organization of Dalits in India. Over the years, Purnima has continued her connection with India through research and international placements for students. Building on this work, she is currently planning a formal partnership with the University of Mumbai College of Social Work and a number of other initiatives such as student exchanges, intensive courses, curricular enrichment of BSW, MSW, and PhD programs, and a program of research between both schools. Her work in Toronto is centred on studying the organizational practices of progressive/anti-oppressive organizations. Besides a number of research studies in this area, she is currently working with two other colleagues from the school on an SSHRC-funded project. Purnima has also been engaged with the South Asian diasporic community in Toronto and has initiated research that explores the issue of domestic violence within the South Asian community in Toronto.

DAWN HEMINGWAY, MSW, RSW: Dawn is an associate professor and chair in the Social Work Program at the University of Northern British Columbia. Her teaching and research interests include Northern/remote quality of life, aging, and women's health— all informed by empowerment processes such as community-driven policy, service development, and research. Dawn is an organizer and spokesperson for the Active Voice community coalition and Women North Network, as well as a board member on the Community Planning Council, the Stand Up for the North committee, and for the Prince George Sexual Assault Centre. She is president of the British Columbia Psychogeriatric Association and a co-director of the British Columbia Network for Aging Research. Dawn has received a number of awards in recognition of her work, including the Northern British Columbia Today's Woman Leader in Knowledge Advancement and Forging our Future with Education Awards, and the Bridget Moran Advancement of Social Work in Northern Communities Award.

CLARIE JOHNSON, RSW: Clarie has a degree in social work from the University of Northern British Columbia and is a registered social worker with the Board of Registration for Social Workers in British Columbia. She is the children's program coordinator and counsellor at the Prince George Sexual Assault Centre, where she has been employed for the past 13 years. Clarie has extensive experience in trauma effects after sexual violence and the impact on child development. As a counsellor, Clarie utilizes art and play therapy techniques as a mode for children to express their feelings, thoughts, and perceptions, and to work through their experiences of trauma and loss. She is very actively involved in the areas of anti-violence and women's issues locally and provincially. Clarie has chaired organization committees for events such as the Take Back the Night march and the first Take Back the Highway march to bring awareness to the missing and/or murdered women along Highway 16 West in northern British Columbia.

MISHKA LYSACK, PhD, RSW: Mishka is an assistant professor in the Faculty of Social Work and an adjunct assistant professor in the Department of Psychiatry in the Faculty of Medicine at the University of Calgary, where he teaches social work theory and practice, environmental issues, and family therapy. In February 2008, he initiated and organized the first teach-in on global warming and climate change at the University of Calgary, and is involved with a number of projects of public education and advocacy regarding global warming and other environmental issues. Mishka's current teaching, writing, and research interests include (1) healing ecological despair and grief; (2) enhancing ecological literacy and environmental citizenship; (3) creating political and institutional leadership regarding global warming and other environmental issues; (4) environmental social action and social work practice; and (5) ethics, spirituality, and the environment.

JUDY E. MACDONALD, MSW, RSW, PhD: Judy is an associate professor at the School of Social Work, Dalhousie University. She identifies as a woman with a (dis)ability, teaching and conducting research from this specific location. Judy's doctoral dissertation was titled "Untold Stories: Women, in the Helping Professions, as Sufferers of Chronic Pain (Re)Storying (Dis)Ability." Over the past few years she has been chair of the persons with disabilities caucus/interest group of the Canadian Association of Schools of Social Work (now the Canadian Association for Social Work Education). This group conducted a survey of schools of social work in Canada pertaining to (dis)ability curricula and schools' access and accommodations for students, staff, and faculty with (dis)abilities. Judy teaches a course at both the undergraduate and graduate level on (dis)ability policy and practice. In 2006, she received grant funding to adapt her graduate online (dis)ability course to an accessible format. Judy's work in promoting (dis)ability inclusion continues both within and outside the academy.

VERONICA MARSMAN, MSW, RSW: Veronica is president of the Canadian Association of Social Workers and member at large for the North American region of the International Federation of Social Workers. Veronica holds an MSW from Dalhousie University, is a registered social worker with the Nova Scotia Association of Social Workers, and is an active member of the Association of Black Social Workers. Veronica was employed with the Department of Community Services in Nova Scotia for over 24 years in a number of social work positions. Since August 2006, Veronica has been working at the Emergency Management Office as the senior project manager in the Business Continuity Management Office. As senior project manager, Veronica is responsible for leading a staff team to assist in the development of business continuity plans to ensure that critical government services will function in the event of an emergency. Veronica is also a sessional instructor with the Dalhousie School of Social Work and serves on the school's advisory committee. In addition, she is an active community volunteer with involvement in her church as treasurer and assistant Sunday school superintendent.

KATE M. MURRAY, MSW, PhD (candidate): Kate is a doctoral student in the School of Social Work at the University of British Columbia. Her research interests centre around the development and practice of social consciousness and activism. Kate has undertaken outreach, research, education, and communications activities in a range of community, professional, political, and academic settings. Her experience includes coordination of neighbourhood and community-based initiatives, and research in the fields of health care, eviction and homelessness, social services, evaluation, and governance. Kate has developed materials for social welfare and social policy education, and has undertaken an in-depth critique of municipal participation policy and the inclusion of residents with low incomes in policy making.

ANN-MARIE O'BRIEN, MSW: Ann-Marie completed an MSW at Wilfrid Laurier University in 1985. Her area of practice and research is mental health. Ann-Marie has authored papers published in the *Canadian Journal of Psychiatry* (2005) and the *British Journal of Social Work* (2006). She co-authored the *Report of the Ontario Association of Social Workers (OASW) Mental Health Survey* (2007) and contributed to the development of the OASW role statement for social workers in mental health (2007). She is an adjunct professor at the Carleton University School of Social Work. Ann-Marie is the professional practice leader for social work at the Royal Ottawa Mental Health Centre. She oversees the practice of 50 hospital and community-based social workers.

CLAUDE OLIVIER, PhD: Claude is an associate professor with the School of Social Work at King's University College, London, Ontario. As a social worker, he has over 10 years of experience with community-based AIDS organizations. This experience has provided much opportunity to put structural and anti-oppressive social work theory into practice. Before arriving at King's, Claude taught in the social work program at St. Thomas University, Fredericton, New Brunswick. His primary teaching interests are community organization, anti-oppressive social work practice, and group work. His research interests include population health, HIV/AIDS, and group work. Claude continues to maintain strong research and practice ties with HIV/AIDS communities.

KATHALEEN S. QUINN, MSW, RSW: Kathaleen has been a practising social worker since 1977, having obtained a diploma in social work from McEwan College, a BSW from the University of Calgary, and an MSW from Wilfrid Laurier University. Her clinical experience includes work at the Glenrose School Hospital, the University of Alberta Hospital, and in private practice, as well in the Neonatal Intensive Care Unit of the Royal Alexandra Hospital. She has brought a strong feminist perspective to her clinical work and is highly regarded for her clinical expertise and her mentorship of social workers in training. In addition to her clinical work, Kathaleen has been an instructor at the McEwan College Social Work program for over 18 years and returned to full-time teaching in the fall of 2007.

BRENDA K. RICHARD, PhD: Brenda is an associate professor at the School of Social Work, Dalhousie University. Brenda has a longstanding involvement related to gay, lesbian, transgendered, and queer issues, both in the community and in the teaching of social work practice that is intended to be transformative. She is a founding member of the Canadian Association of Schools of Social Work (now the Canadian Association for Social Work Education) caucus on gay and lesbian rights.

BRENDA ROLAND, BSW: Brenda specializes in childhood sexual abuse and sexual violence as a trauma counsellor; she works with women and men from all socio-economic backgrounds. As a structural social worker, Brenda believes in helping people to become aware of how our capitalistic society affects people's ability to be healthy and happy. She initiates conscious awareness and communication around issues and social determinants of life in Northern, rural, remote and culturally marginalized communities. Brenda has been involved in developing and implementing training events, presentations, workshops, seminars, and focus groups that are flexible and respectful in response to the inherent value systems of individual communities. Brenda has extensive experience in community development support in the area of violence against women and children; she has been involved in research on Take Back the Night events and the Women North Network.

SHAHINA SAYANI, BSc, BA: Shahina is the program manager for ArtReach Toronto, a funding program that supports arts initiatives and engages youth who have experienced exclusion. As part of this work, Shahina manages the collaborative efforts of multiple stakeholders and supports grant-making work by coordinating capacity-building initiatives that facilitate sustainable youth leadership in the arts. Shahina is the former executive director of the For Youth Initiative (FYI), a youth-led organization that works to increase youth capacity, encourage civic engagement, build life skills, and foster community development. She continues to support FYI as coordinator of their mentorship program. She served as a founding member of the Grassroots Youth Collaborative (GYC), a collective of key organizations and groups led by young people in Toronto. Shahina was awarded the Vital People Grant Award from the Toronto Community Foundation in 2004, and was co-author of a report entitled *Thinking about Tomorrow's Space Today: Youth Recreational Programming in the Former City of York* (2005). She is currently serving as advisor to the development of community-based research initiatives that will investigate methods to support a social infrastructure that facilitates sustainable youth leadership in communities. Her volunteer experiences include activities with Out of the Cold, the Canadian Cancer Society's Relay for Life, and Ernestine's Women's Shelter. She developed and is co-chair of the FYI Scholarship Program, a volunteer-driven initiative created in memory of two Toronto youth lost to gun violence in 2005.

KAREN SCHWARTZ, PhD: Karen received her PhD in Social Work from Columbia University in 1996. She has taught at Carleton University since 1999. Her areas of practice and research are in field education, mental health, and social work pedagogy. A focus of Karen's work in field education has been to explore how students integrate structural social work theory into practice during their field practicum and how to support students in this process. Karen has been involved in fostering numerous community–university partnerships. This has included fostering an ongoing relationship with the Somali Family Service Centre to encourage and support members of their community in admission to and success in the school of social work. Currently she is teaching a research course where students carry out research in community agencies.

WANDA THOMAS BERNARD, BA, MSW, PhD, RSW, CM: Wanda has a BA from Mount Saint Vincent University, an MSW from Dalhousie University, and a PhD from the University of Sheffield in England. She is a professor and director of the School of Social Work at Dalhousie University. Her teaching and research interests are in the area of discrimination, racism, oppression, and empowerment. One of Wanda's current research interests includes a project funded by the Canadian Institutes of Health Research that is examining the impact of racism and violence, including the violence of racism, on the health and well-being of Black men, their families, and communities, in Halifax, Calgary, and Toronto. Wanda is a community advocate who roots her research, teaching, and practice in current community struggles. She is a founding member of the Association of Black Social Workers, a past president, and currently serves as vice president. She is considered a national leader in her work on training for workplace diversity, and in 2005 was awarded the Order of Canada for her work on race and racism.

LEIGHANN WICHMAN, MEd (candidate): Leighann is currently working on a master's of education at Acadia University. She is coordinator of the Lesbian, Gay and Bisexual Youth Project in Halifax. Through her work with the Youth Project she has conducted professional development sessions, developed resources, and provided consultation to educators, health-care workers, parents, government employees, and community leaders. Leighann's work and passion are focused on the schooling rights and needs of lesbian, gay, bisexual, and transgender youth.

KRISTIE WRIGHT, BSW, MSW: Kristie currently works with the For Youth Initiative (FYI), a by-youth for-youth, non-profit organization located in the priority neighbourhood of Weston Mount-Dennis in Toronto's West End. Kristie has worked with youth—and lived—in this community for over five years. Starting as a placement student at FYI, Kristie has transitioned into many roles at the organization and currently holds the position of director of community engagement. Kristie's research experience includes co-authoring a participatory action research study that investigated what would constitute inclusive, engaging, and empowering programming for young, ethno-specific women living in the former City of York (2004) and co-authoring a report entitled *Thinking about Tomorrow's Space Today: Youth Recreational Programming in the Former City of York* (2005). Her major research paper, completed in 2005 for her MSW, investigated the *code of silence over violence* that exists in many of Toronto's low-income communities. More recently, Kristie has been volunteering her time as a member of the Youth Challenge Fund grant advisory committee and as a member of the North York Community House board of directors. Kristie enjoys working within Toronto's youth sector and is passionate about completing research that can be used as an advocacy tool to improve the lives of all young people across the City of Toronto.

ANDREA ZAMMIT, BSW, MSW: Andrea Zammit is working for Yorktown Child and Family Services as a youth outreach worker in the priority neighbourhood of Weston Mount-Dennis in Toronto's West End, and has been working with youth in this community since 2002. In the past, she has held a number of paid and un-paid positions with the For Youth Initiative (FYI), including the role of program director. She completed her BSW at Ryerson University in 2004 and her MSW at York University in 2005. Andrea completed her major research paper on using hip hop culture as a tool to educate and engage urban youth in schools and community organizations. Recently, Andrea resigned from her two-year term as the chair of the board of directors of the Grassroots Youth Collaborative (GYC). Andrea had a hand in starting the GYC, which is a collective of youth-led/driven organizations located across the Greater Toronto Area that have come together to network and support capacity building with one another and to advocate for an increase in the long-term sustainability of their organizations. She volunteered as acting coordinator of the GYC for 18 months until funding was granted to hire a coordinator. Andrea has recently joined the board of directors for the Somali Youth Association of Toronto, a youth-led organization in Jamestown. Andrea is excited to now be working in the Toronto Community Housing Corporation to continue to explore the needs of the youth.